MW00995244

Dear Dr. Silverman,
You mean it has a name?

—Christiane Lange Caratzas (website respondent)

Linda Silverman has written a graceful and much needed book that highlights different kinds of spatial intelligence. She has focused on the type of visual thinking women use and in so doing has turned the searchlight on a relatively unexamined area. This book will help change the way you think about "seeing."

—Leonard Shlain, M.D., author of the best-selling book, *The Alphabet vs. the Goddess,* and *Art & Physics*

Whoever you are—parent, educator, or just plain person–read this book! In its pages you will find new ways of understanding and supporting some of humanity's most useful minds. Linda Silverman provides a map to a complex and magnificent mental world where you or someone you care about may have felt lost.

—Stephanie Tolan, co-author of the award-winning book, *Guiding the Gifted Child,* and author of numerous books for young adults

Linda Silverman provides us with a holistic–visual–spatial perspective of the complexities of brilliant, but academically challenged, minds. She offers an understanding of their upside-down world. More importantly, she tells us how their struggles can be overcome!

—Ronald D. Davis, author of *The Gift of Dyslexia*

Linda Silverman has been a pioneer in the field of visual-spatial learners. Much of what I know about this special population originated from my early contacts with Linda. This book casts much needed light on a subject very much unexplored in print. I am thrilled to endorse this book and hope it sells millions of copies.

—Jeffrey Freed, author of *Right-Brained Children in a Left-Brained World*

I've been waiting for this book for years, and it is everything I hoped for and more. It is wise, warm, funny, practical, intensely personal, and truly inspirational. It belongs on the shelf of every parent whose child does not seem to fit in the mainstream, and of every teacher who wants to reach those students who have clear potential but just can't seem to "get it" when it comes to tests, and of all adolescents and adults who have struggled with those problems themselves and may still be struggling. I've shared Linda's paper on visual-spatial learners with students, friends and colleagues, and their reactions have always been electrifying: "Yes, yes—that's it exactly!" "I've been dealing with this stuff forever but I always thought my child was the only one!" "My God— she's stolen my diary!" I have no doubt that reading *Upside-Down Brilliance* will change their lives.

—Richard M. Felder, Ph.D, co-author of *Elementary Principles of Chemical Processes;* Hoechst Celanese Professor Emeritus, North Carolina State University

Parents, teachers and friends of visual-spatial learners will delight in this book. It is filled with illuminating insights, down-to-earth wisdom, and practical suggestions.

—Wendy C. Roedell, Ph.D., co-author of *Gifted Young Children* and *Early Violence Prevention;* Assistant Superintendent, Puget Sound Educational Service District

Linda Kreger Silverman

Upside-Down Brilliance

The Visual-Spatial Learner

DeLeon Publishing
Denver, Colorado

Cover design by Kim Jones.

Cartoon illustrations by Buck Jones, www.buckjonesillustrator.com.

Published by:
DeLeon Publishing, Inc.
P.O. Box 461027
Denver, CO 80246
www.deleonpub.com

Full-Sized Forms Available for download online!

To download full-sized 8.5 x 11 inch reproducible forms used in this book, please visit http://www.deleonpub.com/authors.html or http://www.visualspatial.org. They are in PDF format. You will need to have Adobe® Acrobat Reader installed on your computer in order to view the forms. Please visit Adobe's website at http://www.adobe.com to download this program.

ISBN 1-932186-00-X   (pbk)

04 05 06 07 08   09 8 7 6 5 4 3

Dedication

To my mother,
Bernice Gerstman Kreger,
artist, humanitarian, comedian, and the inspiration for this book.

Contents

Tables

Figures

Preface

After a 20-year period of gestation, it is a great joy to announce the birth of this book. *Upside-Down Brilliance* is lighthearted, filled with good humor—as you can see in Buck Jones' cartoons. Paradoxically, it will be released near the first anniversary of the terrorist attacks on the World Trade Center. Please bear with me as I reflect on the meaning of this tragedy in these next few pages.

"Turn on the TV." "There are no words." "Life will never be the same." These echoes remain in my memory. I was stranded in Los Angeles when it happened, and a few days later, I was able to get on one of the first flights leaving the L.A. airport (LAX). No stores were open. You couldn't buy a Starbucks' coffee. The typical hustle and bustle of LAX was replaced by an eerie stillness. Even the cell phones were silent.

Instead of working on their laptops, reading books, and talking on cell phones, people waiting to board the flight were present with each other. They asked about each other's experiences and losses. Everyone seemed kinder. No one was in a hurry. The busyness that permeates our lives was suspended. I had brought work to do on the plane, but there was no energy to accomplish it. I learned a lot about the people sitting near me in the boarding area, and the woman who sat next to me on the plane. I wasn't alone in this. People looked straight into each other's eyes. There were no strangers.

I had hoped that we would continue to treat each other in a caring manner, but soon we fell back into our old habits. Now, the bustle is back, the cell phones have taken over the boarding areas, and all eye contact is gone. We have become strangers again. I believe that we learned something about what is really important in those days that followed September 11th. I felt a shift in my own awareness, and I'm sad that I haven't been able to hang onto it. I can only hope that having experienced it once, it is still available to me and to all of us. I pray that we don't have to have another tragedy to access it again.

It took 11 days before I could resume work. Linda Greene, our webmaster, urged me to write some words of assurance to the parents we worked with at the Gifted Development Center. I sat down at the computer, and the column, "What Can We Say to the Children?" poured out of me. That same night, I wrote a powerful new Preface to this book. I felt that the information in *Upside-Down Brilliance* was critical to creating peace in the world. Now, a year later, it seems too heavy to put at the beginning of a fun book. But I would like to share with you a few fragments of that Preface as food for thought.

On September 11th, 2001, life as we knew it changed forever. The world became smaller, and our connectedness became apparent. We were all witnesses, we all suffered. If we had heard the news on the radio or from a family member, it would not have had the same impact. The way many people shared the event with each other was simply to say, "Turn on the TV." For days afterward, I heard, "There are no words; there are no words."

We watched the footage of the first plane crashing into the World Trade Center in stunned disbelief. As we tried to understand what had happened, we witnessed the next plane crash into the second tower *as it was happening.* We were there—a part of it all. These are images we will never forget. They are indelibly emblazoned on our psyches.

Upside-Down Brilliance is about the power of images. It's about visual-spatial learners, who think in images instead of words. It's about cherishing our mental camera—the right hemisphere. It's about how the world is changing. It's about how we need to educate learners differently in an image-oriented technological era. It's about seeing "the big picture," so that we can understand our interdependence and learn how to inhabit our planet peaceably.

In *The Alphabet versus the Goddess,* Leonard Shlain (1998) states that imagery is the "single most significant cultural influence" in modern times, altering the path of our development:

> The printing press disseminates written words. Television projects images. As television sets continue to proliferate around the world, they are redirecting the course of human evolution. The fusing of photography and electromagnetism is proving to be of the same magnitude as the discovery of agriculture, writing, and print. ...Television's popularity increased the power of images. (p. 409)

Leonard maintains that the image of the atomic bomb saved us from destruction.

> The first modern image to achieve universal recognition was the atomic bomb's mushroom explosion. ...It was the climactic end result of thousands of years of left-brain dominance. The world stared slack-jawed and wide-eyed at the awesome power of hunter/killer values carried to their farthest extreme. For all their virtues, abstract science, linear words, and sequential equations had led the world to the brink of extinction.

> ...If a *written* description of the atomic explosion's aftermath were all that had been available, the bomb would surely have been used. But the *image* of the bomb's destructive power was universally disseminated and that picture (worth many thousands of words) saved the world. (p. 410)

A more uplifting image allowed us to grasp the beauty and fragility of our planet:

> The first photograph of Earth taken from space flashed around the world in 1968, celebrating the interconnectedness of life. Like a Chinese ideograph, NASA's photograph of our blue marble conveyed multiple values simultaneously, values more intuitive than rational. …[It] began to instill in everyone who saw it an understanding that the Earth must be honored, protected, and loved. …[It] provided people with "the big picture." …The inviting, mute image of the home planet floating in dark space did more to change the consciousness of its residents than the miles of type concerning the subject generated by the world's writers. (p. 410)

More people witnessed September 11th than any other historic event. It served as an undeniable reminder of our interconnectedness. What touches one of us, touches us all. Annemarie Roeper (1989) urges us to let interdependence guide our daily actions:

> Interdependence is an unalterable fact of life for everything on this earth as well as in the universe. …All of our actions affect others who affect others and, in the end, affect us again. Ecology of behavior is a reality—a reality which seems self-evident and which we may be aware of; yet, it is not incorporated in our emotions, thoughts, activities and way of life. We have not really incorporated the concept that the world and everything in it, animate and inanimate, completely depend on each other. Nothing happens or exists that does not have an impact on anything else. It is thus a matter of survival to think in terms of global responsibility. (pp. 1, 7)

If interdependence is a fact of life, how is it possible for us to delude ourselves into thinking we can develop a weapon of destruction that won't, eventually, be used against us? Leonard Shlain's response would be that the delusion is maintained in our insular left hemisphere. Our holographic right hemisphere sees the big picture, and grasps the complexity of interdependence. Leonard believes that we are entering a new era of imagery that will bring balance to the world. As we activate our gentler, quieter right hemispheres, I believe that we will, indeed, see an evolution in consciousness.

Having said all this, I can re-experience the joy of discovery that conceived this book. I've dedicated *Upside-Down Brilliance* to all who think in images, rather than in words. More and more image-thinkers are being born throughout the world. In past generations, they were often crippled in our schools, and marginalized in society. But this millennium belongs to those who are gifted in imagery. It is their genius that created the technological era, and they are the ones who will thrive in the 21st century workforce. The left-hemispheric curriculum of reading, handwriting, and calculating, which dominated schools for centuries, is obsolete. Instead of worshipping the printing press, schools will need to prepare students for the computer-based, visually-oriented careers awaiting them.

And now the fun begins. If you find you aren't enjoying yourself, please skip to another section. Some parts were written for parents, some for teachers, some for psychologists, some for researchers, and some for visual-spatial adults. Find the part that was written for you.

The visual-spatial learner in a coconut shell

I've named those who think in images "visual-spatial learners" (VSLs). My colleague, Betty Maxwell, and I have been fascinated by visual-spatial learners for two decades. Betty summarized our thinking this way:

> There appear to be two major ways of learning: auditory-sequential (more left-hemispheric) and visual-spatial (more right-hemispheric). Auditory-sequential learners are good listeners, learn well in a step-by-step process, tend to be rapid processors of information, and are generally able to express themselves verbally. They are often able to compartmentalize their reasoning from their emotions.

> In contrast, visual-spatial learners are excellent observers, comprehend holistically—may have sudden "Aha!" understanding that leaps over steps—appear to think in images, may need translation time to put their ideas into words, and sometimes have word retrieval problems. Their thinking and emotions are very intertwined.

Betty solidified five years of the collective thoughts of our Visual-Spatial Learner Study Group in "*The Visual-Spatial Learner in School*" (Appendix A). After a brief description of the concept, she lists 32 positive characteristics of VSLs, organized in 8 clusters, and the school problems that may be associated with each characteristic. Anyone interested in children will find it eye-opening.

But this book is not just about children. If you want to discover to what extent you might be visual-spatial, please take the quiz on the next page. If this learning style describes you, someone you love, or some of your students, please read on.

The voice of this book is not my own; it is a choir of individuals who have experienced this way of being firsthand. I'm bringing their voices together for the first time, in hopes that my orchestration will allow you to hear them, see them, and experience them in a new way. Please listen with an open heart. They were kind enough to share their stories because they desperately need to be understood. Please hear their song.

Are You a Visual-Spatial Learner?

Please complete the following quiz to find out more about your learning style.

		Yes	No
1.	Do you think mainly in pictures instead of in words?		
2.	Do you know things without being able to explain how or why?		
3.	Do you solve problems in unusual ways?		
4.	Do you have a vivid imagination?		
5.	Do you remember what you see and forget what you hear?		
6.	Are you terrible at spelling?		
7.	Can you visualize objects from different perspectives?		
8.	Are you organizationally impaired?		
9.	Do you often lose track of time?		
10.	Would you rather read a map than follow verbal directions?		
11.	Do you remember how to get to places you visited only once?		
12.	Is your handwriting slow and difficult for others to read?		
13.	Can you feel what others are feeling?		
14.	Are you musically, artistically, or mechanically inclined?		
15.	Do you know more than others think you know?		
16.	Do you hate speaking in front of a group?		
17.	Did you feel smarter as you got older?		
18.	Are you addicted to your computer?		

If you answered *yes* to **10** of the above questions, you are very likely to be a visual-spatial learner.

This book was written for you!

(Hint: Start with the last chapter.)

Acknowledgments

The birth of an idea requires the collaboration of many insightful, caring friends. Betty Maxwell has been my midwife; she has worked closely with me in developing the Visual-Spatial Learner (VSL) construct and assisting VSL families. Betty contributed Appendices A and B and many of the teaching techniques in Chapter 13. Her critique of earlier drafts was invaluable. Linda Greene, our webmaster, has been a steadfast supporter, urging me to write this book. Linda assisted every step of the way, placing the VSL information on the website, monitoring the responses, developing the Internet Discussion Group, designing the graphics, and formatting the Quiz, Tables and Appendices. Linda Leviton, Director of our West Cost office, shared countless insights with me over the years from her own experiences as a visual-spatial learner.

I am grateful to all who participated in our Visual-Spatial Learner Study Group over the years, helping to refine the concept and create the *Visual-Spatial Identifier.* Steve Haas labored tirelessly validating the instrument. He offered excellent suggestions in previous drafts of the manuscript. Thanks to Jennifer Donald for her help with the proofreading. Alex Golon has been my cheerleader, organizing me, collecting additional resources, proofreading the final draft, determining where we needed Buck Jones' marvelous cartoons and marketing the book. Damion DeLeon, the consummate visual-spatial thinker, had the vision and determination to create a publishing house to bring this book to you. And I've been blessed with enormous emotional support from my husband, Hilton, as well as my family, friends and colleagues.

But this book could never have been written if so many visual-spatial learners hadn't shared their experiences with me. Thanks to all of you from the bottom of my heart.

Introduction

This book is for parents and teachers, for visual-spatial learners of all ages, for people who live with artists, musicians, inventors, and computer junkies, and for anybody who wants to know how intelligence on this planet is evolving. It really is evolving. A guy from Down Under, James Flynn, discovered that intelligence is increasing all over the planet at a dramatic rate. And the greatest gains have been in spatial-visualization and verbal problem solving, not in areas related to school-based learning. The Flynn Effect suggests that more and more children are being born all over the world with unusual visual-spatial strengths, often combined with higher verbal abstract reasoning. Researchers claim that these IQ gains do not appear to be matched by higher achievement (as measured by what, I wonder? Better reading scores?). Yet, the incredible technological advances and scientific break-throughs in the last 50 years, the staging and costuming of plays such as "The Lion King," and the vivid visual displays at the Olympics, are undeniably the result of advanced visual-spatial reasoning. How is it possible that we've failed to realize the importance of visual-spatial abilities? Why haven't we attempted to locate and nurture visual-spatial brilliance in children?

So my job is to enlighten you about visual-spatial learners. Why me? Because I listen to parents and take them seriously. That's where the information for this book originated. As a parent myself, I believe that parents really know their children. And I've been a teacher. (When I was 3, I said I would be a mommy and a teacher when I grew up, and that's exactly what I did.) I know what it's like to have 36 children with 36 different sets of needs in one classroom. And I'm female, which allows me to put a new spin on this subject. But *Upside-Down Brilliance* is not a self-portrait. I'm not a visual-spatial learner. And I'm not introverted (the personality type of many VSLs). I just happened to discover a fascinating profile of strengths and weaknesses 20 years ago, which I labeled, "the visual-spatial learner."

Let me tell you just how non-visual-spatial I really am. Last summer I went into a grocery store in Gravenhurst, Ontario, and saw a box that contained what looked like the perfect chair for me to use to work on this book while I was visiting my husband's family. My husband, Hilton, had created a makeshift desk for me at the cottage by placing a loose closet door on top of a dresser, securing it with a cinder block. I needed a chair that would adjust to sufficient height for me to reach the top of the dresser. I noticed that the box with the chair had been opened and taped shut, so I thought it would be a simple matter for Customer

Service to reopen it for me. I asked the woman at Customer Service to please bring a pair of scissors and follow me. When we reached the box, I told her that I wanted to see if the chair would rise to the proper height for me. She looked at me, looked at the box, looked at me again, completely puzzled, and said, "But, Ma'am, this chair is unassembled." It took me until I went to sleep that night to realize the utter stupidity of my question. Did I really think she could open a flat box and out would pop a three-dimensional chair that I could sit on and adjust the height? (Well, actually, yes!)

As you can see, I had to look at this phenomenon from the outside in. In many ways, that's a plus, because I can act as a translator to the rest of the world for those of you who think in pictures. I guess another good thing about it is that I don't bring to this endeavor the residual wounds of the visual-spatial learner, so I'm not antagonistic toward auditory-sequential teachers. I really want people like me to understand people like you. The down side is that, as an outsider, I may have over-simplified, overgeneralized, or just missed the boat on some points. Hopefully, with your feedback, I'll correct that in the next book.

Voices of VSLs

I knew that the visual-spatial learner concept was helping our clients enormously. Nevertheless, I was stunned by the feedback we received when we put a short description of the learning style on our website (**www.gifteddevelopment.com**) and asked people to tell me their stories. Here is a sample of the website responses:

> I'm *so* thankful for discovering your site this morning, and I thought it would be because it might give me insights for my eldest child. Instead, I'm sitting here weeping because you gave me insights to my younger son and I'd almost lost hope.

> I saw my son's entire story being played out before my eyes when I examined your profile of the "Visual-Spatial Learner." This concept allowed me a new, more positive perspective on S's struggles. I felt that perhaps someone might understand, after all.

> I was delighted to discover your web page on visual-spatial learners... reading your description of visual-spatial learners was like a light bulb going off, yes, yes, yes, this is my kid!

After reading your link on Visual-Spatial Learning I realized you're explaining my son exactly. Thank you for the relief you have given me. You have no idea what a burden you have helped to lift.

I've just nearly been knocked off my chair, reading your website. Not only does everyone in my household fit the "gifted" profile, but several of my children fit the characteristics of the visual-spatial learner perfectly. ...I have never, ever seen my eldest son described so perfectly.... I was just flabbergasted to read about the visual-spatial learner profile!!

The list of characteristics you have posted fit G to a T! I could not believe what I read—it was as if I was reading a composite of G himself. Even your list of weaknesses fit G. I can't tell you how relieved I am to discover what it is about G that makes him so unique.

I...could not believe my eyes. This perfectly described my daughter! ...I found Ms. Silverman's web-site and discovered a description of myself that has answered a fundamental question of my life. There was a description of myself and the answer to why I have always felt like an "alien." I cried from the sheer relief and profundity!

You mean it has a name?

It appears that the visual-spatial learning style is clearly recognizable, but up until now it has been nameless.

My husband...truly never knew that his learning style had a name to it.

I am definitely an auditory-sequential learner, as is my six-year-old son. My two-year-old definitely learns in a different manner, but until I came across this information, I couldn't quite put a finger on it.

I really didn't know what kind of learner P was, only that she was much different and we would need to find what makes her tick in order for her to succeed.

My son, who is now 10, seems to learn in this manner, although I've never had a name for it.

I've always felt that I learned things differently. It's nice to be able to put a name to it. Thanks.

Dear Dr. Silverman,

You mean it has a name?

A closely related book, *In the Mind's Eye*, by Thomas West, underscores these comments, adding the concern that until now this pattern of strengths and weaknesses has been viewed and labeled negatively, rather than positively:

> To make our definitional problem still more difficult, we are not always talking about "disabilities." We are just as interested, or perhaps even more interested, in the special talents and abilities that may (or may not) come, directly or indirectly, from the same early developmental processes or from the form of the giftedness itself.

> What we are talking about, then, is significant variation in both abilities and disabilities, notably mixed strengths and weaknesses manifested in a constellation of traits. *As yet, however, there does not seem to be a properly neutral and fully descriptive term covering all of these considerations.* Nearly all terms that have been in and out of fashion during the past ninety years or so, from "word-blindness" to "minimal brain damage," refer almost exclusively to the negative, to some deficiency or abnormality. (West, 1991, p. 80, emphasis added)

The visual-spatial learner appears to be the sought-after neutral term. It does not imply disability. Many highly gifted children and adults exhibit this learning style with no accompanying deficits. On the other hand, many individuals with weaknesses in reading, spelling, handwriting, calculation, attention, memory, organization, sequencing, or word retrieval, exhibit gifts in the visual-spatial domain that tend to be overlooked in school. Education often focuses on their weaknesses rather than their strengths. And how we are treated in school leaves a lifelong imprint on our self-esteem. The story at the end of this Introduction describes this pain.

I recently had a most extraordinary opportunity. Tom West and I were invited to speak at a conference on visual-spatial learners at Green

College, Oxford University. The symposium was sponsored by the Arts Dyslexia Trust in London. The Trust's founder, Sue Parkinson, had read some of my papers on VSLs and sent me an email:

> The list you give of these people's "Learning Characteristics" is the best and most accurate one I have ever come across during some 35 years of teaching and working with dyslexic artists and designers of all ages from 8 to 88.

The symposium included a remarkable display of the family lines of English Nobel-prize winners in physics. Artists and dyslexics abound in these families, and most have visual-spatial talents of one sort or another. The Arts Dyslexia Trust views the correspondence of artistic talent, scientific brilliance, and dyslexia in particular family lines as simply different aspects of visual-spatial thinking. Seeing the world differently, through the lens of the right hemisphere, can lead to both positive aspects (e.g., creativity in physics and in art) and negative aspects (e.g., difficulties with reading, writing and spelling). Until now, we have focused heavily on the negative manifestations, not realizing that hidden within these apparent deficits lay the seeds of brilliance.

But *Upside-Down Brilliance* is not specifically about dyslexia, learning disabilities, attention deficits, or the autistic spectrum, although bright individuals with these issues will relate strongly to the content. There are excellent books on these topics, such as Ron Davis' *The Gift of Dyslexia*, Tom West's *In the Mind's Eye: Visual Thinkers, Gifted People with Learning Difficulties, Computer Images and the Ironies of Creativity*, Jeff Freed and Laurie Parson's *Right-Brained Children in a Left-Brained World: Unlocking the Potential of Your ADD Child*, and Temple Grandin's *Thinking in Pictures and Other Reports from my Life with Autism*. These books encompass, to some extent, the visual-spatial characteristics discussed in these chapters.

Nor is this book about eminent men. Most of the books I've read about spatial abilities describe famous spatial geniuses—almost all male. (In fact, if media coverage is any indication, the word "genius" seems to be reserved exclusively for males.) It's important to know that some of our most brilliant physicists, mathematicians, inventors, statesmen, and artists were spatially gifted and did poorly at school. I've purposely not gone there because this information is readily available elsewhere (e.g., Tom West's *In the Mind's Eye*). But, in addition, women are conspicuously absent in this picture. Spatially gifted women must feel invisible, or defective in their femininity, because there are so few women role models in this literature base.

Can women be visual-spatial too?

Before I read the postings to the web, I wondered if the majority of visual-spatial learners were male. It's common knowledge that males are better than females in spatial tasks. The following statement appeared in an international directory of spatial tests: "When a test does not show a sex difference in favour of males, there is a suspicion that it is not a true spatial test" (Eliot & Smith, 1983, p. 449). But I have received so many emails from female VSLs, or describing visual-spatial daughters, that I am convinced that up until now we haven't conceptualized this phenomenon so that it included females, and that we haven't had the right tools to measure visual-spatial abilities in a gender-fair way.

Recently, a foxy young guy, Albert "Skip" Rizzo, developed some spatial tasks in virtual reality that women and men do equally well. Skip says that his results suggest that regardless of how women have performed on two-dimensional paper and pencil measures, they may do as well as men on "real-life" spatial tasks. When the women tried the paper and pencil tests after a brief period of training on the three-dimensional, interactive virtual reality tests, they did almost as well as men. Skip's findings challenge the age-old belief that women are just plain inferior to men in spatial perception.

Listen to how these women relate to the VSL construct!

My stars! I read your comparison of ASL and VSL, and I fit your Visual-Spatial Learner description to a tee!!!
I, for one, am glad to finally have a handle for my odd way of perception. I was afraid I was just a looney! ;-)

My daughter could be the visual-spatial poster child! My favorite example was the time we were...in the World of Science store. There was a block type pyramid puzzle (brain teaser) in pieces on the counter. My 10 year old glanced at the packaged pyramid that was for sale and then, immediately put the 4-5 piece puzzle together. She turns to me and says, "Why would anybody want to buy this?" The sales clerk nearly dislocated his jaw after watching her. I couldn't even get 2 of the pieces together, no matter how hard I tried.

My daughter [age 3] ...does a 100+ piece puzzle independently. She also loves to make animals with the Tangram set (surprise). Recently she has been asking me for a chess set....

I have four children all identified g/t, boys 12, 11, and 7 and a girl 9. My daughter is the visual-spatial learner. She seems to work twice as hard to get half as far, so the fact that she has excellent grades like her brothers is amazing to us.

C is 3.5 years old.... The definition of visual-spatial learner on the GDC web page fits her to a t.   Couldn't be a better fit.

The list of favorite activities of visual-spatial learners describes me perfectly. I have stacks of puzzle books and mystery stories, love to play Scrabble™ and Boggle™ (even by myself) and at one time, I played so much Tetris™ and Minesweeper™ that I developed tendonitis—and even then had a hard time quitting. When my kids were little I would buy them Lego™ sets and then sit down to build the models with them only to find that, after awhile, I was doing it by myself. Construx™ are even better—more geometric, pattern oriented, less structured. And my career choice—data processing analyst.

I went into the field of Robotics and did some design and some programming. Story for you, about Tetris™. I was expecting our first child, and was hooked on Tetris™. I had morning sickness and would play Tetris™ to keep my mind off the nausea and most of the time it worked. I would be so engrossed in the game that hours would fly by.

When hobbies were mentioned in this article, I found that I pretty much hit every one right on the nose. I LOVE to play Tetris™ (and find myself playing for hours on end), always was a puzzle freak, had all the Rubix™ cubes, snake, pyramid, etc. Also, I figure out how to use/program/etc. appliances, computers, etc., but I have no idea what the instruction booklet is talking about.

In *The Alphabet Versus the Goddess*, Leonard Shlain proposes that the right hemisphere, the home of imagery, is essentially our feminine side, and that it has long been under the domination of our overly developed "masculine" left hemisphere.

Associating images with the feminine would seem to fly in the face of numerous scientific studies that demonstrate that males are better at mentally manipulating three-dimensional objects than their female counterparts. Also, numerous other studies reveal that young females are more facile with words, spoken and written, than are their male peers. Despite these studies attributing different image and word skills, ...many cultural...and historical examples... solidly connect the feminine principle to images and the masculine one to words. (p. 5)

If the right hemisphere is the natural abode of the feminine in both men and women, and visual-spatial ability resides in the right hemisphere, wouldn't we expect to see stronger expressions of visual-spatial ability in women? Is it possible that those manifestations have always been there, but have gone unrecognized? Does traditional "women's work" entail more visual-spatial skills than we are aware of— creating meals, making clothing, decorating homes, attending to children's needs, and managing the complex social and emotional life of one's family and community? These are questions that deserve further exploration.

Perhaps spatially gifted females are a hidden group of visual-spatial learners. Maybe they pass as "normal" because of their verbal abilities. The whole relationship between visual-spatial abilities and gender is still foggy in my mind, even though *The Alphabet Versus the Goddess* shed some light on this mystery. In any event, I will welcome your input on this perplexing topic, and seek to correct my ignorance in the next book.

Upside-Down Brilliance

So why do I call this way of thinking "*Upside-Down Brilliance*"? Because right-hemispheric giftedness turns all our preconceived notions of "smart" upside down. Visual-spatial learners usually don't conform to the typical notions we have about bright people. We rarely think of them as gifted children. Yet, in adult life, it is visual-spatial reasoning that leads to true genius: scientific and technological breakthroughs, innovative forms of art, inventions, new perspectives in every field, and visionary leadership. And the way VSLs learn is upside-down: easy material often is hard for them and the hard subjects are easy. One woman wrote:

> When I was in college (majoring in math, of course) I took a 1-credit course in Fortran (this was thirty years ago before there was such a thing as Computer Science). Friends had warned me that it was an extremely difficult course, but I was amazed at how easy it was for me— especially when people all around me were pulling their hair out trying to understand it. At the time, I was struggling with agonizing over what to do with a math degree and this opened up a whole new world for me. I often say that I majored in math because I could look at the pictures and understand what was going on instead of having to read all about it.

Traditionally, we think of gifted children as academically successful, straight-A students, who excel in the three r's: readin', 'ritin', and 'rithmetic. These children have the good sense to bloom early. This is a left-hemispheric view of high intelligence. Individuals with greater right-hemispheric abilities are usually seen as oddballs, ill-supported within the educational system—often left to their own devices to figure out how to cope with learning things differently. If they survive in school long enough to get to geometry, physics, and higher-level mathematics, they may discover their strengths much later in their school career. Even then, they may not believe they are smart—especially if they still haven't memorized their multiplication tables! They definitely bloom late.

How do we define brilliance?

This book is about brilliance—illumination—of the artist, the composer, the creative spirit, the visionary, the healer, the technological genius, whose special way of looking at the world enlightens us. Many of these people suffer from deficits. Don't ask them to balance your check-book. But you aren't going to learn how to fix them here. Quite the contrary. I hope you will gain an appreciation of what is *right* about them and learn how to adapt to these atypical thinkers, instead of forcing them to adapt to the system—a system that was developed by and for people who think and learn in an entirely different way.

I hang out with the most brilliant children on the planet. Most of my professional career has been spent studying giftedness in all of its facets. Yes, the dreaded "g" word. It's admirable to be a superb athlete, a recording star, a great actor or actress, but it's not OK to be intelligent. I've met dozens of children who were beaten up for being smart, and hundreds more who were emotionally tormented. Why does society abuse its brightest children? One of the reasons the gifted are so unpopular is that the concept sounds "elitist." But Continental Airlines has it right: They don't give you an IQ test to see who sits in their elite class; they just take your money. Elitism is, and always has been, a socio-economic issue, not an intellectual one.

The number of definitions of the "g" word is downright silly. Its counterpart, retardation, undergoes periodic name changes, but its definition is pretty consistent. On the other side of the coin, countless efforts have been made to broaden the definition of giftedness to include the kinds of abilities that have been overlooked. The broadest perspective is that "everyone is gifted," which robs the term of any meaning whatsoever. Can you imagine a principal saying to a parent, "Well, Mrs. Davis, your child is no different from the others; **all** our students are retarded!"??

Every child is a gift. However, there are children with special needs at both ends of the spectrum who learn differently from 95 percent of the population, and need accommodations. So how do we determine which kids need special provisions? Ah, what a journey that question took us on in the 20th century! We began with the top 1%, then gradually broadened the group to 2%, 3%, 5%, 7%, 10%, 15%, 20%, 25%, 33%, and beyond, but no matter how many children were included, people were still unhappy. We tried different ways of looking at the phenomenon—recognizing various talents and intelligences—but these perspectives made the programs unwieldy, and people still weren't happy. You can't be all things to all people.

I think the biggest problem was that we never quite got the distinction between academic success and high intelligence. When gifted-ness is defined as academic achievement, we not only miss individuals with unusual abilities, we also miss brilliant children with astronomical IQ scores. They just don't fit the mold. Talent development models and multiple intelligence theories are noble attempts to be more inclusive, and they have increased awareness of the multitude of human abilities. But they have also led to a great deal of confusion, sometimes diluting special programs to the point where they are of little value to the children who need them most. This book does not leave out those individuals who traditionally have been identified as gifted; it simply adds a group that has been missing in the picture: those with right-hemispheric brilliance.

Visual-spatials and auditory-sequentials

There are two basic learning styles outlined in this book: *auditory-sequential* and *visual-spatial*. Some of my highly gifted, complex friends find this dichotomy too simplistic. Maybe it is. I certainly don't mean to imply that people are completely one or the other. I see each pair of the characteristics (listed in Chapter 6 and Appendix C) as a continuum, and I believe we are all a mixture of both sides. After all, we all have two hemispheres, and both hemispheres work together on the majority of higher level thought processes. But there are some people who fit an incredible number of items on the visual-spatial side. For example, my friend, Alan Roedell, fit 23 of the visual-spatial characteristics and only 4 of the auditory-sequential ones. Most of these people have felt like outsiders in society, and particularly in school. I've written this book for folks like Alan, for parents of VSLs, and to help teachers learn to identify such children and work more effectively with them.

Auditory-sequential learners are often model students. They listen well. They understand what they hear. They follow directions. They learn to read on schedule, they turn in their homework on time, and you can read their handwriting. They learn in a step-by-step fashion, progressing from simple to complex concepts. Reading, writing, spelling, and calculating are mastered at the right grade levels. Education as we know it is about the development of these auditory-sequential skills and it is well-suited for auditory-sequential learners. That's why I haven't provided any guidance on how to educate these more typical learners. We do this job well.

But the student body is changing all over the world, and a new way of knowing is emerging. The school curriculum was appropriate for the Age of Literacy. However, the 21st century is the Age of Information, and an entirely different set of skills is necessary for adult success. Reading, handwriting, spelling, and speed of calculation are not sufficient to gain employment in today's world. Creativity, facility with computers, visualization skills, and the ability to see and solve problems from many different perspectives are becoming more important. These visual-spatial skills have been peripheral in education. By the middle of the 21st century, I predict that they will be central. The skills we have prized for thousands of years will be relatively useless when every child has a computer. Handwriting will be an art form, not a method of note taking or communication. And who is going to care how fast you can spit out 7 x 6 = 42?

More and more children are being born with visual-spatial strengths, and some of them have auditory-sequential weaknesses. Dyslexia (difficulty with reading), and its partner, dysgraphia (difficulty with handwriting), are both on the rise. Instead of putting all our energies into correcting these deficiencies, we need to be paying more attention to what dyslexic, dysgraphic children do well. They have abilities critically needed in today's society.

More teachers need to be able to spot visual-spatial learners, so that their special talents can be developed. To this end, we have constructed a simple 15-item questionnaire that teachers can use to identify the VSLs in their classrooms. Parents can use this measure as well. We also have a self-report version for young people. Validation studies we conducted with middle-schoolers suggest that approximately **one-third** of the school population are probably visual-spatial learners! (See Chapter 14 for more information on the new *Visual-Spatial Identifier.*) Their numbers are growing and we simply can't afford to ignore them any longer.

Educators are becoming more responsive

School is hell. She loves music, art and ballet, hates all the rest.

Subjects he loves: Science, Art, Music, Gym, Reading, *parts of Math*.
Subjects he hates: Grammar/phonics, math facts, writing sentences...
writing period!

Now that I've learned a bit about visual-spatial learners... so much makes
sense. Everything fits. He almost perfectly fits the described characteristics... unfortunately, unless I *do* test and *prove* this... the school will not
accommodate. My only hope is that I can convince his teachers!

VSLs are at risk in most schools. Carol Gohm, Lloyd Humphreys, and Grace Yao studied over 1,000 spatially gifted high school seniors (578 boys and 511 girls—*hey, nearly as many girls as boys!*) and found them to be "disenchanted with education" (1998, p. 528). In their article, "Underachievement Among Spatially Gifted Students," the researchers reported that this group received less college guidance from school counselors, were less likely to go to college, and had lower career aspirations than equally intelligent students who excelled in mathematics.

> Spatial visualization, in addition to mathematical and verbal skills, is an important ability for becoming an engineer, physical scientist, or artist... Although industry and the military appreciate the predictive importance of spatial ability, the same may not be true in the academic environment. (p. 516)

> There is dependable evidence that the talents of spatially gifted students are needed by our society at the professional level of education and in professional occupations. (p. 530)

But school does not have to be a disastrous experience for VSLs. Many teachers already incorporate overhead projectors, computers, demonstrations, hands-on experiences, construction projects, and other methods that reach this population. They simply need to be encouraged to do more of it. Educators—even college professors—are becoming more responsive to different learning styles. (For example, see **www.ncsu.edu/effective_teaching**.)

In answer to the question on our website, "What was school like?" a 45-year-old dyslexic woman who recently returned to college wrote:

> When I was young, HELL! Now, sort of hell. There is a huge difference from the time I went to school as a child and now. Teachers back then taught on a single dimensional level. Now they seem to integrate different ways to introduce new material which includes the visual learners. It certainly helps!

Some teachers have begun to notice this learning style and are describing it to parents.

In preschool and kindergarten her teachers felt she was very bright, was actually thinking not just doing, was very creative, and the term "visual-spatial" was used, although at the time it didn't mean anything to us. …Her father and I are both graphic designers, so it seemed natural to us that she would be visual, as we assumed that's how we most likely taught her.

He seems to be a visual-spatial learner. His teacher brought this to our attention and I have been trying to learn as much about it as I can. It's beginning to make some sense now as to why he seems to be looking off into space when thinking. Especially when working with numbers. I'm always amazed at how he can figure his math problems out without concentrating on what's on the paper.

School will become more user-friendly for visual-spatial students as computers play a greater role in instruction. Computers were invented by VSLs for VSLs. They can magically transform the certainty of failure into the joy of success, as this man's poignant story illustrates.

I was reading a post on a bulletin board that was advising a lady to let her daughter use a word processor to write and to not worry about how words are spelled. Because if the child is thinking too much about spelling she would not be able to hold her train of thought. This prompted a flashback to my youth...

Whoa! Major flashback. I am in one of those one-person desks made out of metal with the wooden top and seat—some still have the hole in the top right corner for holding ink bottles. It is hot, there is no air conditioning in this small Central Texas school. The windows are open and the chirping birds outside are interrupted by the chalk squeaks on the blackboard as the teacher spells out the writing assignment. "One page before the bell." I know the topic, but it doesn't really matter, I know I won't do well. My pencil has only been sharpened a couple of times but the eraser is all but gone and the metal end has been squeezed together to force what little eraser is left, to bulge past the metal edge. I am concentrating hard—very hard. I start the first sentence, but I know I can't spell some of the words, even some simple ones. I reword the sentence and try again several times but know some words are still wrong. By now I have erased some places to the point the paper is about to be torn by the metal on the pencil. I peel the metal edge back on my pencil with my teeth to expose more eraser. If I am careful it may last through the class...

I reword the sentence over and over in my mind; somehow I have to make this work. I bite the knuckle on my right hand hard, sometimes the pain will make the confusion go away... The teeth marks will last for days. I concentrate even harder as I do. I grip the pencil harder and harder till cramps fill my hand. Still I continue on...

The ringing bell does not bring the normal relief I feel when class is over. My hand is aching, I have completed almost half a page...

I try to read over the sloppy writing quickly to look for mistakes...I know what I wanted to say, I knew the subject, probably better than the teacher, but I now realize this paper makes no sense, even to me.

Head down, I turn in my paper, glancing up only to see the teacher frown in disgust at the look of the messy page. I want to scream and do, only it is a silent scream of anguish and despair...

Were it not for word processors with spell-checkers I would never have been able to author the story above. Dyslexics, partly because of their intelligence, have found amazing ways of hiding their handicaps. You probably never guessed I was dyslexic. How could you, I didn't even know. Even with these new technologies, stories like the one above, that flash through my mind in a few seconds, can take hours to write. However, hours are so much better than never.

Thanks

I've peppered the text (I hope I didn't overseason the stew) with lots of excerpts from the website responses we have received. I'm deeply grateful to the hundreds of families of gifted visual-spatial learners who have contributed to this book in developmental questionnaires, in letters, on the phone, and in emails. You are the heroes of this story. Readers will remember your experiences far longer than my analysis of your experiences. You verify that the VSL idea is real, and you also have told us in your own words how you learn best. Each of you who sent me your stories has co-created this book with me. Thank you for teaching us.

And you, Dear Reader, are cordially invited to participate in this collaboration. Tell us your stories. Try any idea from the book, and give us feedback on how it worked. Add your own techniques. Take the concept and run with it. I give the visual-spatial learner concept to you to play with and develop. Thanks to all of you for caring about these maverick intellects. Happy reading!

Linda

How It All Began

Basically the list of characteristics of a visual-spatial learner describes me. Trying to learn things the way most people do is like trying to drive a car backwards—you can do it, you can learn to do it OK, but it's not the real thing. If you know something about computers, a better analogy would be to say that learning the typical way is like having software emulate hardware—you can get basically the same results, it just takes ten times as long and doesn't work as well in general.

I'd like to tell you a story. (Your right hemisphere is saying, "Oh goodie, I love stories!") I'd like to share with you how the visual-spatial learner concept came into being. I could say that it was conceived from the union of several lines of inquiry: assessment of gifted children; the study of gifted children with learning disabilities, such as dyslexia and attention deficits (AD/HD); brain research; research in audiology; and personality studies. But mostly, it was the result of my listening to thousands of parents describing their delightful, imaginative, quirky kids.

I was not the first person on the planet to discover visual-spatial abilities. However, contrary to how we assume that science progresses, I did not build on all the good work that had been done by others. Maybe it was synchronicity. In any event, I feel blessed to be able to share this way of knowing with you. I happened upon the idea while assessing gifted children. I was teaching at the University of Denver (DU), became a licensed psychologist in February, 1979, and, with Jana Waters, began the Gifted Child Testing Service (which later became the Gifted Development Center) in June of 1979. Throughout the next few years, I came across some rather puzzling characteristics in children and some surprising test results and tried to make sense of them.

First, we had some children who took the top off the test, scoring way beyond the norms in the manual. The way they did it was by solving very difficult visual-spatial, visual memory and mathematical reasoning problems, all of which require excellent abilities to visualize. The story begins in 1981.

Our first visual-spatial learner

One particular boy stands out in my mind as the catalyst in the development of this concept. I'll call him "Craig." Craig was 4 years old when he was tested. His mother reported that Craig would stand on the sidelines of his preschool class watching all the other children until the activity was almost over. He was also extremely cautious in his neighborhood, afraid to cross the street by himself. When Jana tested him, he froze and said, "I don't know" to nearly every question. But Jana was a master at getting children to reveal what they knew, and she didn't accept his "I don't knows." "What would the answer be if you did know?" "Why don't you take a guess?" "What does your dinosaur friend think it might be?" Eventually, Craig "guessed" himself into an IQ score beyond the norms in the manual! If he had had another examiner who believed his "I don't knows," his IQ probably would have been closer to 90 than 190. Craig had astonishing visual-spatial abilities. He was shown pictures of stacks of blocks that contained hidden blocks and he was able to count them all with no difficulty. This task was at the 10-year level of the test—more than twice his age.

What went on in the mind of this little boy? He was brilliant; yet, he stood on the sidelines in his class every day, and said, "I don't know" to test questions that he actually *did* know the answers to. 'Twas a puzzlement. This is when the concept of the **visual-spatial learner** struck me.

- ❧ What if Craig thought in pictures?
- ❧ What if the images didn't occur right away?

- ☙ What if he panicked inside when he was asked a question because the muse hadn't visited him yet and his mind was blank?
- ☙ What if he didn't think in steps at all and had no way of getting to an answer until a picture suddenly formed in his mind?
- ☙ And what if he had absolutely no way of knowing when that would happen?

That would be pretty scary. It would explain why he didn't know the answers immediately, why he stood on the sidelines at preschool and was cautious at home. If I was right, Craig's knowing was sort of like an on-and-off switch. Either he knew or he didn't know. If he didn't know, he didn't know how to get from not knowing to knowing. The light bulb came on all by itself without his control.

Since Craig was so shy, I felt that there was a connection between the visual-spatial learner concept and introversion. Introverts are very cautious, watch before they participate, and take a little longer to speak because they think through what they are going to say before they say it (unlike us extraverts, who think out loud). Introverts hold back what they know for fear of being humiliated if they happen to be wrong. They also have a strong need to be in control because they are easily overstimulated. I suppose you don't have to be an introvert to be visual-spatial, but I think most of the visual-spatial children I've seen over the years had some degree of introversion. Later on, in Chapter 10, we'll talk more about introversion and extraversion.

The plight of being non-sequential

In the beginning, I was focused on the amazing visual-spatial abilities of highly gifted children, who also have highly developed sequential abilities. (Sequencing is essentially learning in a step-by-step fashion.) Then I discovered that not only were the highest scorers on the IQ tests visual-spatial, so were many of the *lowest* scoring children who came for testing. These were children who fit most of the criteria on our checklist for giftedness (see Chapter 4), who seemed extremely bright when you talked with them, but bombed in school and often fell short of the gifted range when assessed. In analyzing the test protocols, I found that these children had difficulty with most of the sequential tasks.

Non-sequential children have a very hard time adjusting to school. The school curriculum is sequential, the textbooks are sequential, the workbooks are sequential, the teaching methods are sequential, and most teachers learn sequentially. Children are graded on their mastery of sequential subjects: reading, writing, spelling, and arithmetic. Sequential children feel smart, and non-sequential children feel dumb.

They dread long division, spelling, showing their work, step-by-step instruction when they don't know where it's leading, handwriting, rote memorization, drill and repetition.

Anne writes:

I was at Montessori [preschool] and we had a large puzzle of the U.S. I carefully took each state and traced around it on a sheet of butcher paper where it would go in the puzzle. This resulted in a map of the U.S. The sad part of the story is that my teacher loved the map and kept it—as an example of what her students could do. I wish she'd been able to sit down and talk with my parents about what my ability to do that meant. As it is, I feel like an enormous failure because of the bad spelling and bad penmanship and sloppy calculating and the weaknesses in algebra.... everything in a normal school setting depends on these things.

Some of the non-sequential children who came to our Center had behavior problems. They were sensitive to criticism and often reacted without thinking. For example, if the school bully started teasing little Zach, Zach was likely to take a poke at the bully and end up bloodied. A child with more sequencing ability would have quickly thought about the consequences of punching the bully, and would have come up with other strategies for dealing with the situation: running away, ignoring him, finding other children to help, calling the teacher, plotting a scheme to foil him, etc. Then he would have selected one of these alternatives to avoid being hurt. This planning ability is largely sequential. By comparison, Zach—a spatial child who has sequential deficits—lives in the moment and doesn't take the future into consideration. He may lack the ability to see the consequences of his behavior. When angered, Zach doesn't run through a mental list of alternatives. At that moment, he becomes his anger and simply reacts.

If you have a Zach, it must be maddening that he gets into trouble, can't plan ahead, can't delay gratification, and is so hopelessly disorganized. But I'd like you to take a second look. Instead of focusing on what he can't do, pay closer attention to what he **can** do.

- Is he capable of losing himself completely in the joy of the moment?
- Can he take any object and turn it into something else in his wonderful imagination?
- Is he ingenious in his ability to invent games?
- Does he have a contagious sense of humor?
- Does he study a ladybug with total absorption?

These beautiful qualities are so often overlooked in our quest to create "successful" children. These are the gifts of the right hemisphere. Seekers spend half their lives trying to learn how to live in the present. Zach hangs out there all the time, while we busily try to get him to learn from the past and worry about the future, so he can be more like the rest of us who live in our left hemispheres. Bet he's happier than we are... at least until we convince him that he's defective because he's not like us.

Time for VSLs to be recognized

I guess the early 1980s must have been the time for the visual-spatial concept to emerge in the collective consciousness of the planet. In 1983, John Dixon published his wonderful book, *The Spatial Child*, and Howard Gardner's popular book, *Frames of Mind*, came out, with "Spatial Intelligence" as one of his seven intelligences. Howard writes, "It has now been established beyond reasonable doubt that the left hemisphere is dominant for language in most normal right-handed persons, while the right hemisphere is dominant (though not to the same extent) for visual-spatial functions" (p. 51). The concept was obviously visible to others, and supportable. My own perspective varied from these authors in some ways, but we were all noting something important. Since that time, "spatial intelligence," "spatial learners," and "visual-spatial learners" have all been bandied about in education with no clear picture about how to identify and work effectively with this group of students.

My first paper on "The Visual-Spatial Learner" actually pre-dated these other works. I wrote it in 1982 for parents of the visual-spatial children we assessed, their teachers, and my students at DU. It focused on the differences between spatial and sequential learning, the early childhood characteristics of VSLs, and recommendations for spatial learners with sequential difficulties at school and at home. The paper generated a great deal of enthusiasm in the community, but for years I couldn't get it published. All I had were clinical observations, which were very meaningful to parents (and described many of the parents as well). Alas, no "objective data," no publication.

The richest source of information for me was the parents' description of their children in the developmental questionnaires. At first our questionnaires were only 2 pages long, but as they got longer (they are now 8 pages), they provided more comprehensive portraits. The children came to life. I began to notice the pattern that I eventually labeled "the visual-spatial learner" in these wonderful descriptions. Here is a classic example:

Information from the Parent Questionnaire of "D" [age 5]:

Why would you like to have your child tested?

> Assess him for learning disabilities. To understand his learning style. To select an appropriate curriculum.

Please describe your child's favorite activities and interests:

> Building with Legos™
> Drawing
> Imaginary Play

What activities during the school day does your child enjoy the most?

> Math & Drawing

What activities during the school day does your child enjoy the least?

> Phonics, Memory Games

Please describe your child as you see him or her (personality, attitudes, development of friendships, etc.)

> One of D's favorite activities is building with K'nex™ and Legos™. He'll spend hours building complex 3-dimensional structures and spaceships.
>
> D is highly creative and imaginative. He dictates wonderful stories with excellent...descriptions. These often go on for pages.
>
> He is keenly observant and often asks us questions like, "Do you remember the spots on the bird's chest we saw at the zoo?" a month or more after the event.
>
> He loves to re-enact movies—especially Star Wars. One Saturday evening, about age 4, D scurried about making costume changes and designating different pieces of furniture as various spacecraft as he lived the part of Skywalker while we watched Star Wars.
>
> We took D to the Riverdance show when he was 4½ as he had been watching the video and acting it out, complete with bows, for about 6 months.
>
> Seems advanced mathematically. He often listens in on his brother's math lessons—counts by 5's & 10's, understands place value.
>
> D has been making up and telling really awful jokes since about age 3. He'll have us read pages and pages of "bad" jokes if he can get us to.

From reading these snippets, it's clear that D is gifted in many ways: mathematically, artistically, creatively. He has a vivid imagination. He loves to construct (one of the best signs of visual-spatial ability). He has keen powers of observation, excellent visual memory, inventiveness, a sense of humor, and he is a wonderful storyteller. He can act and dance, and he loves to re-enact scenes he has seen in Star Wars and Riverdance. Altogether, a delightful little boy!

Nevertheless, notice his least favorite activities at school: "phonics" and "memory games." Compared to his strengths, these less favored activities seem irrelevant. But are they? The first reason that his parents expressed for bringing him to us was to "assess him for learning disabilities." D will be perceived as a struggling student rather than as a gifted one, unless he masters reading (phonetically) at the same time as his age peers. His poor auditory memory may interfere with spelling, following directions, and possibly attention or handwriting or both. The joyous five year old described above could easily become a sulky underachiever, unless we understand his learning style and try to teach him in the way he learns best.

I tried to capture all of this fertile anecdotal information in "The Visual-Spatial Learner" paper; but at that time journals had little regard for clinical observations. They wanted crunched numbers, and I had no numbers to crunch. I'm not in the numbers game. Regardless, in the last 20 years, whenever I've presented on VSLs, the response has been overwhelming. With or without numbers to verify its existence (left hemispheres believe that if you can't count it and run a statistical test on it, it's not real), the information consistently hits home.

However, for those of you who are enthralled with numbers, I have some brand spankin' new, mighty impressive statistics to report from our recent research. After a decade of work, we finally have a valid instrument for locating visual-spatial children (see Chapter 14). Our initial studies with 750 4th through 6th graders, Caucasian and Hispanic, in two school districts—urban and rural, suggest that around one-third of the student body are VSLs. Wow! That's much more than I would have guessed. This means that an enormous number of children in our schools are headed for underachievement unless we start paying attention to how they think and learn.

How do visual-spatial learners think?

He thinks in three dimensions, and his first "art" project, at about nine months, was a mountain made of tiny pieces of masking tape piled on the coffee table. I carried tape with me all of the time and he piled it on anything he could. (Mirrors were a favorite.)

I have a four-and-a-half year old who thinks in three dimensions.

I...store information differently. Everything learned goes into its own three-dimensional space. Strange enough, it is a carbon copy of the room I was standing in when I first encountered the information. For example, whenever I think about anything that is even slightly related to chemistry, I will find myself standing in front of a display case from grade school. That was where I first encountered the atom. Does everyone store information this way? I would like to know if I am more aware of a normal process of the mind or if this is a characteristic of being extremely visual-spatial.

At the start of each engagement, I would "see" a cloud representing the problem to be solved. As the engagement progressed, the cloud would gain substance and texture—become something I could shape and sculpt. In my mind, I would build a scaffold within the cloud and frame in the shape of the solution, chiseling in details as my analysis progressed. By the time I had completed a consulting engagement, I had completed a 3-dimensional solid sculpture in my mind. Five years later, I can still "see" some of my "sculptures" when I think of the...projects they represent.

Sue Parkinson, founder of the Arts Dyslexia Trust in London, explained the heart of the distinction between visual-spatial and auditory-sequential learners in an email she wrote to me in 1997:

It is the 3-dimensional aspect of the world perceived visually which we believe is the main difference and cause of possible conflict between visual thinkers and linear thinkers.

Three years later she elaborated this idea:

The ability to visualise three-dimensionally is what is often referred to as "visual-spatial" and/or a "right-hemispheric" function. It starts from direct perception of things as they are, not as they might be described in a line of text or in a mathematical equation. Words and/or figures are always that much further away from our real experience. They are a constructed, artificial framework that we put our directly perceived experience into, much as we put documents into a filing cabinet—so that we can find them or make cross references easily....

Asking the talented three-dimensional thinker to concentrate on a two-dimensional path is like asking them to put a full orchestral symphony into a one line melody—not easy! Hence all the "dyslexic" difficulties at school. It is equally difficult (I believe) for people who are predominantly 2D thinkers to turn one-line melodies into fully instrumented symphonies!

Not being able to think 3-dimensionally myself, I have to confess that, at first, I didn't understand what 3-D thinking was all about. I finally got it when I read a letter I received from the mother of a VSL child. She wrote to me after she heard my presentation on visual-spatial learners. I never mentioned 3-D thinking in that speech. Her letter contains one of the clearest descriptions I have ever seen of how a VSL thinks.

My son, Kendall, is the absolute visual-spatial learner and, probably to a lesser degree, so am I. To me, the essence of visual-spatial is the three-dimensionality. Everything, every name, every fact, every piece of information is processed as a 3-D object. Every one of these 3-D objects has a place or placement. I was pondering this idea when, with delightful serendipity, my son reaffirmed my belief. Kendall (who is not known for his spelling) heard the word "fear" misspelled. He was telling me about it and I asked him, "How do you spell 'fear'?"

"F-E-A-R" he quickly said.

"How did you know that?"

"Oh, I just took it off of the shelf in my brain."

"A shelf?"

"Yeah. Actually, there are three, one for spelling words, one for objects, and one for anything else. It's a shelf/cabinet kind of thing."

Representing "Tuesday," Kendall sees a large number 2 that rockets around and comes to a stop immediately in front of his face. He puts the numbers of his addition and subtraction problems "in jail" to keep the columns straight. Borrowing and carrying require the extra numbers to go on a roller coaster ride to the next column. He can draw or describe the roller coaster in terrific detail. The number and appearance of the cars change depending on the numeral being carried.

As a pre-schooler, he was watching an automated puppet show. While all of the other children were answering the puppets and dancing to their music, Kendall was sneaking around the back of the gypsy-cart stage. When I asked him if he got to see the puppeteer, he rolled his eyes and, not too patiently, explained, "Uh, Mom, it's a machine." As we stand in checkout lines he visually examines all of the electronic equipment (cash register, scanner, automatic conveyer belt) and proceeds to tell the cashier how it works.

At age one, he had landmarks all over town and relied on them to make sense of his world. Coming out of anesthesia at eighteen months old, he hopped off of the table and hit the ground running. He navigated the maze of hospital corridors, without one wrong turn, to the exit. Kendall could circumnavigate any child-safety device ever made. It is my belief that part of the reason Kendall has always been such a climber (30-ft. tree at three years old) is that he needs to get the "lay of the land." Perspective, relation and placement are vital to his sense of peace and understanding. It is also my belief that this is why he sometimes has a difficult time with transitions, change of plans, or unexpected outcomes. He has a vivid picture of his plans. Changing that picture is difficult. He has to tear down one picture and reconstruct another, sometimes less appealing, one. At best this is a lot of brainwork. At worst, he has bonded with the picture and tearing it down is unbearable.

Wouldn't it be wonderful to teach children to organize information in their minds in the way Kendall taught himself? Like having them mentally construct a jail to hold their numbers in place so that they line up properly when added or subtracted? And putting the numbers that need to be carried on a roller coaster ride from column to column? These are children who are capable of seeing from different perspectives, and they grasp concepts based on an understanding of their relationship to each other. For them, there is actually a physical relationship that they see in their mind's eye. Kendall's Mom writes, "Perspective, relation and placement are vital to his sense of peace and understanding." Suppose we asked VSLs to observe situations from different perspectives. Wouldn't that enhance their comprehension and memory?

"To me, the essence of visual-spatial is the three-dimensionality. Everything, every name, every fact, every piece of information is processed as a 3-D object." This is nearly inconceivable to those of us (like me) who lack this mental capacity. To perceive dimensionality is a true gift—essential to art, engineering, and invention in adult life. But when letters and numbers are perceived three-dimensionally instead of two-dimensionally, reading (a two-dimensional process) is compromised.

So are spelling, written calculation, and handwriting. Three-dimensional numbers and letters exist in dynamic rather than static space. They can roll around, turn upside down, and trade places with each other. They don't stay put the way two-dimensional figures do. Describing her experience using Ron Davis' (*The Gift of Dyslexia*) learning strategies in her special education class, Jodi Ringle writes:

> It wasn't long before they knew that most of them in my room saw the letters move. They never before realized that the letters weren't supposed to be three-dimensional. One of my students said that the letter 'o' looked like a doughnut... (Ringle, Miller, & Anderson, 2000, p. 10)

There are also clues in that letter for parenting VSL children. "He has a vivid picture of his plans. Changing that picture is difficult." The ability to vividly picture something in one's mind is the first step to creating it in reality. For VSLs, every mental picture is a reality in the making, and each time we ask them to change course, to do what we want them to do instead of what they see in their minds, we are interfering with their creative process. Of course, we have no choice in parenting and teaching them, but at least we can understand their frustration, and we can honor their thinking process by explaining why we need them to rearrange their mental picture. We can ask them respectfully to create a new picture that takes our needs into account. We could say something like:

> I know you wanted to finish your Lego™ tower this morning, and that you were really looking forward to seeing if it comes out like you picture it. But if we don't leave now, you'll be late for school, and your whole day will be off to a bad start. Can you imagine what that would feel like? I'll be upset with you and your teacher will be worried about you, and your friends will be wondering why you aren't there to play with them. You can finish the tower when you come home from school. I'll make sure no one disturbs it.

Compassion produces cooperation to a much greater extent than anger at their resistance.

The ability to perceive three-dimensionally is apparently a strength of the right hemisphere, as we shall see in the next chapter.

> Just as the left hemisphere evolved language,...perhaps areas in *the right hemisphere evolved ways of representing abstractly the two- and three-dimensional relationships of the external world grasped through vision, touch, and movement.* ...The ability to visualize a complex route or to find a path through a maze seems to depend on the right hemisphere. Although it is usually characterized as more spatial than the left, it is probably more accurately described as

more *manipulospatial, that is, possessing the ability to manipulate spatial patterns and relationships.* (Springer & Deutsch, 1998, pp. 306-307, emphasis added)

Residual feelings

If you are a visual-spatial learner, the chances are that school was a painful experience for you. Home life may have been as well. Reading about all the ways that VSLs could be taught or parented more effectively may bring up unresolved feelings from your childhood: "I wish someone had understood me like this when I was younger." If you are holding onto that pain, it may be holding you back from fulfilling your enormous potential in the world. It may help heal the wounds to know that the important functions of the right hemisphere were only discovered in the last few decades (see Chapter 2), and that this information is just now being translated into educational practice. With that realization, perhaps you can find it in your heart to forgive and to help a new generation to appreciate their unique learning style.

If you find that this is how you learn, hopefully this book will enable you to achieve a new level of self-awareness and acceptance. If this is how your child learns, or how some of your students learn, this book will enhance your understanding of the visual-spatial learning style, and guide you in living and working with these children joyously.

> I wonder what my life would be like had my education given as much attention to the development of my visual-spatial abilities as to my verbal abilities. (Lohman, 1994, p. 263)

Since coming upon your site yesterday I have been thinking of the impact and import of this way of thinking and its not being recognized... I never heard of such a way of thinking described. I think this way. I thought everybody did.... The fog and storms I suffered since a child have parted and I am able to see "myself" for the first time.

The Power of the Right Hemisphere

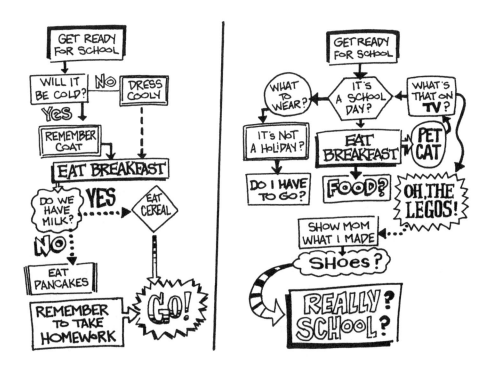

There are just gaps in my understanding that a lot of people don't understand. Like because I know something "advanced," I'm supposed to know something "simple," but I don't. If people could see it in terms of how I'm really structured, it would make sense, but most people see it in terms of how *they* are structured, and then say that I don't make sense or am being difficult or something. And I'm not intentionally difficult, but I don't pick up things in the same order as other people do.

Visual-spatial learners do, indeed, pick up information in a different order from most other people. Auditory-sequential learners learn in a step-by-step fashion, beginning with simple concepts as a foundation for understanding more advanced ideas. This is the basis for the scope and sequence in school. I call VSLs "upside-down" learners because they can handle complexity easily, yet they struggle with easy tasks. I first noticed this in testing a child who failed most of the items at age 8, but managed to pass all the items at age 9! We tested another who could not repeat 5 unrelated numbers but was able to repeat 6 of them. A third could not repeat simple sentences, but accurately recounted a long, complex paragraph. These children seemed to come alive with more difficult questions.

How could they pass the hard items and miss the easy ones? That flies in the face of everything we know about testing (and learning in general). We begin the test where they pass everything, on the assumption that they would have passed all the easier items, and stop the test where they fail everything, assuming that they would have failed all the harder items. But these children break all the rules. They do the same thing in school. VSLs miss the easy, sequential stuff and ace the harder, more complicated material. They often get smarter as they get older, as this woman recounts:

> When I was 4 - 5 years old, everybody in the family was thinking I would be an architect, because my main play was making structures from matchboxes and cigarette cartons. In my first year at elementary school, I could not learn how to write and read. I remember that my teacher was insisting on me being held on the first grade. But my mother did not agree with him, saying that I am different at home. Second and third grades were almost the same; I was labeled as a lazy kid. First, I ignored it, and did not care, then I felt so inferior. I hated school.

> At the end of the third year my uncle bought me "Red Kid," which was a cartoon book. It was so interesting that by looking at pictures and mainly guessing, I started reading. They started buying me all kinds of cartoon books. After the third year, I started reading and writing like some button was pushed in my brain. At fifth grade I was no longer the lazy kid. I graduated an honor student at high school. I was the only student who graduated from architectural school at the end of the fourth year. I had the highest degree at the master of Architecture examination, and was accepted to the best Architectural School as a master student in Istanbul-Turkey.

How, then, does one account for these late-blooming, upside-down learners?

Our right and left hemispheres

The next phase of my journey toward understanding VSLs takes place in Chicago. It is November of 1982. I'm speaking at the Illinois Gifted Education Conference in Chicago. Jerre Levy, a brain researcher from the University of Chicago, is speaking at the same time, so I don't get to hear her. But my friend, Lee Baska, a school psychologist in the Chicago Public Schools, tapes Jerre's session. I'm staying with Lee and Joyce VanTassel-Baska, and Lee is so excited about Jerre's presentation that he can hardly wait for me to hear it. I listen to the tape completely mesmerized. Lightbulbs go on! It's a profound, life-changing moment. Learning the functions of the two hemispheres, I grasp the connection between these maverick thinkers and the way the right hemisphere operates. I envision all kinds of powerful implications (see Chapter 15). In this crystallizing experience, the visual-spatial learner becomes vastly important to me.

Jerre explained how the brain functions more efficiently with harder tasks than with easier ones:

> When tasks are so easy that they fail to challenge mental capacities, communication between the two hemispheres declines and one hemisphere dominates processing with little participation from the other. Under these conditions, the attentional level is low and cognitive performance is poor. In contrast, in response to challenging tasks, the left and right hemispheres become tightly integrated into a unified brain system, which increases attentional resources and cognitive power. The right hemisphere is especially important in regulating attentional functions of both sides of the brain. Unless the right hemisphere is activated and engaged, attention is low and learning is poor.

While Jerre described this process for people in general, I could see that it was particularly true for VSLs (especially those with attention deficits)! For visual-spatial learners to grasp information, the right hemisphere clearly needs to get into the act. If the task is too simple, the right hemisphere checks out. If the right hemisphere stops attending, no learning can take place. As tasks become challenging, the right hemisphere becomes more alert, the two hemispheres communicate better, and the whole brain operates more efficiently. Voila! Hard tasks become easier than easy tasks!

I was blessed to learn about Jerre's research when I was in the beginning stages of creating the VSL construct. I had no idea what a giant she was in the field until much later. "Much of the early work that led to this reanalysis of hemispheric differences was conducted by Jerre Levy and her colleagues" (Springer & Deutsch, 1998, p. 49). Through Jerre's tape and research articles, I began to realize why so little had been known about the right hemisphere.

For thousands of years, the left hemisphere was considered the "dominant" or "major" hemisphere. It was assigned all of the important mental functions, with none of any significance allocated to the "subordinate" or "minor" right hemisphere. The left hemisphere was considered the seat of thinking and planning, and the right hemisphere was thought to be little more than a relay station. The prevalent view was that thinking and language were synonymous, and since language appeared to be localized in the left hemisphere, thought was assumed to occur only in the "dominant" left hemisphere. When I was working on my Ph.D. in learning disabilities from 1969-1972, I was taught that thought was simply subvocal speech. (Even then, I didn't believe that thought was just talking to yourself. What about imagery?)

> The most likely reason for the slow recognition of the importance of the right hemisphere, however, is that disabilities caused by lesions in the right hemisphere were not so easy to analyze and fit into the traditional ideas about brain function. Most damage to the right hemisphere did not abolish any obvious human abilities in an all-or-none fashion; instead, it disturbed behavior in fairly subtle ways. (Springer & Deutsch, 1998, p. 19)

Seen in the context of thousands of years, awareness of the importance of the right hemisphere is in its infancy. "Our current conception that both sides of the brain are fully human organs of thought, each with special processes and abilities, was born in 1961 at a seminal conference in Baltimore" (Levy, 2000, p. 113). In the 1970's, Roger Sperry, Jerre Levy, and their colleagues confirmed and elaborated the functions of the right hemisphere through a series of famous split-brain studies (see Chapter 15).

> A converging body of evidence...points to the conclusion that the *left hemisphere* is vastly superior and dominant to the right in linguistic processing, that it *thinks logically, deductively, analytically, and sequentially,* that its superiority derives from fundamental differences in the way it processes, decodes, encodes, and arranges information. *The right hemisphere is superior and dominant to the left in visuospatial construction, in recording the literal properties of the physical world, in visualizing the relationships of objects in space, and probably, in reaching accurate conclusions in the absence of logical justification.* (Levy, 1980, p. 253, emphasis added)

The two hemispheres think differently. Individuals who have enhanced right hemispheric development perceive and organize information in a different manner from those who have greater left-hemispheric development.

Two different realities

Tom West refers to the left and right hemispheres as "two modes of consciousness, each fundamentally different from the other—one that we know a little about, the other that we know almost nothing about" (1991, p. 26). Left-hemispheric reasoning is sequential; right hemispheric awareness is visual-spatial. The left analyzes (breaks the whole into parts) and the right synthesizes (puts the parts together to create a whole). Logical, deductive proof that follows an orderly sequence from hypothesis to conclusion is the realm of the left hemisphere. The right hemisphere sees and knows. The left hemisphere talks to us. The right hemisphere does not have speech; it communicates in images. While the right hemisphere perceives and experiences, the left hemisphere is continuously engaged in the process of explaining (rationalizing) that experience—a constant commentator. The right hemisphere reaches "accurate conclusions in the absence of logical justification." It is non-logical, non-sequential, nonverbal, and non-analytic. Without words, there are no explanations, nor is there any need for them. The right hemisphere records the concrete properties of the physical world and apprehends the whole. This is where art is born.

> Every painter knows that "black" is never black. It is an infinite variety of blue-blacks/green-blacks/violet-blacks, etc., and it varies according to what colour it is next to, so that what matters is the balance of colour in the picture as a whole. You cannot understand a picture by taking a two-dimensional path through it! There is no predetermined beginning or end to the journey your eye follows. No picture says "you must start looking at me here!" And the "end" is when you can appreciate the balance of colours and tones and textures and lines as an entirety—and that may take hours—years, sometimes.

> That is what is meant by "wholistic" vision. (I refuse to say "holistic" because to me that implies something with holes in it, a net perhaps, and that is the exact opposite of what "wholistic" means.) Every spot of paint, every tiny variation of colour alters the balance of the whole picture. It is probably a minute difference in measurement of colour intensity here or there that makes the difference between a masterpiece and a good average student painting. (Sue Parkinson, September 10, 2000)

Art provides an excellent metaphor for grasping the differences in the way auditory-sequential (left-hemispheric) and visual-spatial (right-hemispheric) learners process information. Art is conceived from images, not from words. Once an image is formed, it becomes the blue-print that the artist uses to create a product. An image does not need to be rehearsed, repeated, drilled, practiced, reviewed, or memorized, to be remembered; it is permanent. In many respects, VSLs are artists. They learn concepts by picturing them in their minds. Once the picture is formed, it becomes a permanent part of their knowledge base. Drill and repetition do not make a clearer image or make the image last longer. So these typical instructional methods, which work well with auditory-sequential learners, fail with VSLs.

In a well-designed piece of art, all of the strokes work together to create the whole, which cannot be analyzed into parts. It is easier for VSLs to grasp the whole and the relationship of the parts to the whole than it is for them to dissect the whole into elements. Seeing the forest, rather than the individual trees, they are "big picture" thinkers.

> I have recently been involved in organizing a group...and in working with the board I continually refer to "the big picture." For me, that's what it is. I can close my eyes and visualize exactly how I see this organization looking and working 2, 5 and 10 years from now. It's a little frustrating that it takes others months to learn and "see" what you see. Nonetheless, one of the board members jokingly told me that he was going to buy me a big picture frame to put the "big picture" in!

Is verbal the opposite of spatial?

Although visual-spatial abilities have been indelibly linked to the right hemisphere, the connection between auditory-sequential strengths and the left hemisphere appears less obvious. It is commonly believed that the right hemisphere is spatial and the left hemisphere is verbal. This sounds sensible because the left hemisphere has the words. But it is not the essential distinction.

> Split-brain studies, [conducted by Jerre Levy and her colleagues, revealed that] *right hemisphere specializations...* are nonlinguistic functions that seem to *involve complex visual and spatial processes....* As research into the specialized functions of the two hemispheres continued, the pattern of results suggested a new way to conceptualize hemispheric differences. *Instead of a breakdown based on the type of tasks (for example, verbal or spatial) best performed by each hemisphere, a dichotomy based on different ways of dealing with information emerged.*

> According to this analysis, the left hemisphere is specialized for language functions, but these specializations are a consequence of *the left hemisphere's superior analytic skills,* of which language is but one manifestation. Similarly, *the right hemisphere's superior visuospatial performance is* assumed to be *derived from its synthetic, holistic manner of dealing with information.* (Springer & Deutsch, 1998, pp. 45-49, emphasis added)

The left hemisphere analyzes sound patterns (the sequential arrangement of phonemes), which enables it to understand and produce speech. The right hemisphere cannot process phonemes; it only understands whole words—complete units of meaning that can be visualized. The right hemisphere may not be able to speak, but it is vitally important in our understanding and use of language. It helps us decipher the meaning of verbal communication. It decodes intonation, the emphasis placed on different words, facial expressions, gestures, body language, and all of the subtle nuances that are essential to comprehension. You can hear all the words and still not understand the meaning unless you pick up on all of these nonverbal aspects of communication. As Robert Ornstein puts it, the left hemisphere processes the text (the actual words), while the right hemisphere processes *context* (the frame of reference).

> *Context* is defined as a "weaving together." It is this joining information about who we are, what we can do, what our surroundings are, who is with us and what they can do and understand that determines our comprehension of where we are in the world, and in life. The individual words we speak, important though they are, are but the bare text that signs the details of life. Much of the recent research on language and the two sides of the brain provides surprising and important evidence that the two sides handle two very different portions of the world. (Ornstein, 1997, pp. 98-99)

> Many psychologists and linguists have until recently considered the text of speech as the only component of communication. But this myopic focus on the text ignores the essential context, which gives language its full meaning....

> All that we know isn't always available to speech; we need to draw or gesture to communicate fully. We produce facial expressions, differing tones of voice, accents, and changes of inflection to convey meaning. We also use speech indirectly, sarcastically, or in jokes....

> Recent work has dramatically changed the way we view the brain's handling of language.... The finding that has caused the most revision to the view that the right hemisphere is a mere appendage, or just a space processor, shows that *the right hemisphere is deeply involved in complex language.... We often don't say what we literally mean. (pp. 100-101, emphasis added)*

Suppose you say to a child, "Do you hear me?" The literal meaning of the question is: "Can you hear the words I am saying?" But I'll bet you didn't mean: "Am I within earshot?" Instead, you are probably saying: "You had better do what I said right now or you're going to be in trouble!" Your tone of voice, how loudly you speak, your hands on your hips, your facial expression, the situational context, and the child's experience of what happened all the other times you said those particular words in that particular way, are all clues to your real meaning.

Research with patients who have right hemispheric injuries shows that the left hemisphere can only comprehend the literal meaning of the words ("Yes, I can hear you.") It takes the right hemisphere's involvement in order to understand the meaning behind the words, to put the words in the context of the situation, and to read all the nonverbal signals as to what you are really trying to convey to the listener. The listener should get the message: "Uh oh, I'm in trouble. I'd better do what she said right away."

Another right hemispheric linguistic function is the ability to hold multiple meanings of words simultaneously, which is essential for understanding humor and the gist of most complex sentences. Robert Ornstein writes, "The right hemisphere has an ability to hold lots of different meanings of a word available for use while, by contrast, the left hemisphere quickly selects a single meaning" (1997, p. 108). If I tell you that I was unable to work on my book this morning because my sister's cat ate my mouse, you have to be able to keep two different meanings of "mouse" in your head at the same time to understand the absurdity of my statement. (The cat didn't actually "eat" the mouse, but I believe that she's hidden it somewhere, so I had to go out and buy another one!)

So, the opposite of spatial cannot be verbal. Both hemispheres are needed for the comprehension and communication of language. Gifted visual-spatial learners do not lack linguistic competence. Quite the contrary. They often have early language development and excel on the verbal portions of IQ tests (see Chapter 8.) Sue Parkinson, whom I quoted several times, is an excellent example. Although Sue is a dyslexic, visual-spatial artist, she also demonstrates giftedness in her ability to communicate her ideas verbally.

David Lohman, a researcher who studies intelligence, wrote a thought-provoking article entitled, "Spatially Gifted, Verbally Inconvenienced." David seeks to set the record straight and correct the modern myth that you're *either* verbal or spatial:

> The problem is erroneously labeled a discrepancy between verbal and spatial abilities, which it is not. The key is not verbal ability, but *fluency in retrieving words, particularly on the basis of their sound patterns,* or fluidity in assembling novel utterances. On the spatial side, it is the ability to generate and manipulate...whole patterns, usually of a fairly concrete sort, but in a fluid and flexible way. (Lohman, 1994, p. 252, emphasis added)

Verbal fluency—rapid word retrieval—is left-hemispheric territory. As David points out, the ability to retrieve words is based on understanding their *sound patterns*. Sound patterns enter the brain through the *auditory* channel. Phonemes are non-meaningful sound bites. The left hemisphere is able to arrange these sound bites *sequentially* into words that it comprehends and can reproduce. Phonemes are abstract units that cannot be visualized—you can't picture them. Therefore, the right hemisphere is of little value in phonemic awareness (essential for learning phonics).

And the left hemisphere arranges the words *sequentially* into sentences. Syntax—the way in which words are sequenced to form phrases, clauses, or sentences—determines the meaning of a string of words. The following two sentences have altogether different meanings:

"The dog chased the boy."
"The boy chased the dog."

Same words, different order. Both the right and left hemisphere can understand the meaning of these two sentences, because both sentences can be visualized. But the right hemisphere by itself cannot distinguish the difference between the following two sentences:

"The boy chased the dog."
"The boy was chased by the dog."

Syntax and grammar are the province of the left hemisphere. Rules of grammar are not easy to visualize. Diagramming is an attempt to bring the right hemisphere into the act, but grammar is essentially a left-hemispheric game. It is a function of the left hemisphere's linearity and time sense. The right hemisphere is also incapable of distinguishing the differences between these sentences:

"The boy chased the dog."
"The boy chases the dog."

A slight difference in one letter conveys the time frame in which the event occurred. The right hemisphere does not grasp time. Everything it visualizes is happening (for the right hemisphere, anyway) right now.

> Actually, I thought everyone thought in pictures. As a small child, I could remember how to get to and from places quite easily... When someone verbally tells me directions for travel or describes something I've got a vivid mental picture of where I'm supposed to be or what it is. I can get so into the mental picture of the moment that all other surroundings get washed out...

> Just last week in my English class I was demoralized because the instructor called on me to ascertain if a verb in a sentence was regular or irregular. I had to bite my lip to keep from crying in the classroom! Have you ever tried to conjure up a picture of an irregular verb? It actually feels like a short circuit is occurring in the brain... I couldn't get a mental image to form in my mind's eye. So it has been all of my life—"No image, no understand."

So, if the opposite of spatial isn't verbal, what is it? Jerre Levy says that the left hemisphere thinks sequentially and the right hemisphere thinks spatially. Robert Ornstein holds that the left hemisphere has a sequential perception of the world and the right hemisphere perceives the world in a simultaneous (all-at-once) way. Brain research seems to suggest that the opposite of spatial is actually "sequential," rather than "verbal."

We use terms such as "visuospatial," "spatial visualization" and "visual-spatial" to describe the inextricable connection between *visual* and *spatial*. We apprehend spatial information visually. Although I don't know of any other writers who are connecting *auditory* with *sequential*, it makes sense to me that the opposite of *visual* is *auditory*. We apprehend most sequential information, such as speech sounds, auditorally. Therefore, I call the person with right hemispheric strengths a visual-spatial learner, and the person with left-hemispheric strengths an *auditory-sequential learner.* While no evidence currently exists that links hemispheric arousal to specific cognitive patterns or learning styles, I am willing to bet that future research will confirm this connection. Most people show at least a slight advantage of one hemisphere over the other, and an inclination for one learning style over the other, just as they show preference for one hand over the other.

Eye movement patterns

How can you tell if someone favors the left hemisphere or the right hemisphere? Eye movement patterns appear to be fairly good indicators of hemispheric arousal. "Animal studies," Jerre says, "show that when a region of the frontal lobe is electrically stimulated, the eyes deviate in the opposite direction (e.g., stimulation of the right cortex produces left-ward eye deviation)." When you ask people questions that make them think, and their eyes move consistently to the right, they have greater activation of the left hemisphere; if their eyes move consistently to the left, they have greater activation of the right hemisphere. (I don't use the slang terms "left-brained" and "right-brained" because it sounds like we're describing halfwits.)

All cognitive tasks activate both sides of the brain, but one side may be more activated than the other depending on the task. Katherine Kocel, David Galin and Robert Ornstein found that people's eyes turn to the left or right depending on the question that you ask. If you ask, "How many rooms are there in your house?" they will shift to the left; if you ask, "How do you spell *Mississippi?*" they will shift to the right. Try it with your family or your class and see what results you get. If their eyes shift to the left regardless of what type of question you are asking, chances are they are visual-spatial.

> An individual's eye-movement pattern is very stable. Once you find out what a child's way of thinking is, you use his or her strengths to educate both sides of the brain. If you approach through the weaknesses, you are going to be blocked. If you approach through the strengths, then you are educating both sides of the brain, particularly if you can get a child emotionally engaged. ...If a teacher engages the emotions of the child—if a child becomes excited and interested—that necessarily integrates the brain into a highly functional organ. (Levy, 1982)

Engaging the right hemisphere

It is important to become aware of the intelligence of the right hemisphere, despite its lack of speech. Traditionally, we have considered talking synonymous with thinking. Children who are "preverbal," and adults who are unable to speak due to left-hemispheric strokes, may understand everything they hear. They may have excellent receptive language abilities. However, their intellect is severely underestimated by their inability to talk. Intelligence is often judged on the basis of communication skills. This can be seen in the double meaning of "dumb" (e.g., "dumb animals")–*devoid of the power of speech* or *markedly lacking in intelligence.*

We also equate intelligence with *speed* of verbal production (verbal fluency). Improvisational geniuses, like Jonathan Winters and Robin Williams, *think fast* on their feet. Individuals who are just learning a second language take a longer time to make sense of the sound patterns they hear and to reproduce these patterns in speech. People who are slow processors, or who take longer to express themselves, are perceived as "slow" learners. In many people's minds, *fast* equals smart, and *slow* equals stupid. Some visual-spatial learners are dysfluent (stutter), which again gets misinterpreted as signifying less intelligence. (It's interesting that individuals who are dysfluent do not stutter when they sing, and patients with left-hemispheric strokes, who cannot speak, can often sing lyrics perfectly. Singing appears to be under the control of the right hemisphere.) No matter how bright they are, those VSLs who lack verbal fluency or speed of processing are perceived as stupid, and these perceptions deeply affect their self-concept. We place a high premium on fast talking!

It is also important to know the types of information handled by each hemisphere. While the left hemisphere can deal well with non-meaningful bits of information, the right hemisphere can only deal with meaningful material. The right side of the brain is superior at recognizing faces, interpreting facial expressions, understanding maps and doing puzzles. It is critically important in activating attention and in the integration and experience of emotion. Jerre noted that patients with damage to the right hemisphere "have great difficulty understanding and drawing maps, they cannot do block designs, they can't understand humor in stories, they are underactivated, and they have inappropriate emotional reactions."

The right hemisphere also has difficulty visualizing absence, implied by "no" and "not." The second sentence is easier to visualize than the first:

"The shirt is not dirty."
"The shirt is clean."

To test this hypothesis, ask yourself, "How would I draw a picture of the first sentence"? This is a good test of how accessible any concept is to a visual-spatial learner.

In order to engage the right hemisphere, we need to make sure information is *meaningful*. It needs to be relevant to the listeners' experience and interests and able to fit in with what they already know. Help them to create a *visual image* (as the woman said earlier, "no image, no understand"). Engage them *emotionally* (love works wonders). Use *humor* liberally. The right half of the brain gets the jokes, because it can hold multiple meanings simultaneously.

Jerre suggests that the more challenging the task, the more efficiently the brain functions:

> The brain functions at its peak when it is appropriately challenged. Challenge engages both sides of the brain, evokes intimate communication between hemispheres, and increases attentional resources. The way to educate the whole brain is to challenge it, don't make it easy. When the brain is relaxed it goes to sleep! A little bit of tension improves learning.

Challenging verbal or analytic tasks engage the high functional abilities of the right hemisphere. Learning abstract concepts and underlying principles apparently pulls the two halves of the brain together. When the task is hard, the whole brain wakes up, and when it is too easy, the brain falls asleep and the person may be seen as "spacing out." No learning can take place when the brain is underactivated. The profoundly gifted rarely have hard enough tasks to fully engage their brains. Listen to this exchange between a cellist and her brilliant son:

> *Rebecca (Lewis's Mom):* "You often play better when you're deliberately trying to do a huge number of things well."
>
> *Lewis:* "Yes, and when I do that, I have even more extra attention."
>
> *Rebecca:* "Do you mean that the harder the job you give yourself on the cello, the more empty space you have in your head that could be filled with even more difficult stuff?"
>
> *Lewis:* "Yes, I think so. My brain likes to try to do too much because that gives me more brain."
>
> *Rebecca:* "You're saying that your brain needs huge amounts of stuff piled onto it, and that creates even more extra brain than you had before."
>
> *Lewis:* "Yes, Mommy, that's it exactly."
>
> I had seen into his mind. I had been inside it. It was like a cave that kept getting bigger and bigger. Every time I thought that we were at the last cavern, another one opened.

I thrive on complexity—I always have.... But I had not yet come to understand my own lost and buried learning style.... At the next opportunity I began treating myself as I had so successfully dealt with Lewis. I gave myself "too much" to do while practicing.

The results exceeded my wildest expectations. The more things I tried to do well, simultaneously, the more I could do, and the easier it was. My playing got better and better. (Hein, in preparation)

Jerre chastised the educational system for concentrating all its attention on the weaker functions in an attempt to equalize abilities. "This makes no sense. Children learn best when approached through their strengths. If you try to get adults to do a task by using their special talents, they are more successful." We need to appreciate how much diversity there is in the human brain and to develop educational methods responsive to that diversity.

Complementarity

Despite its initially camouflaged role, the right hemisphere does play a vital part in human behavior. It is now clear that both hemispheres contribute to complex mental activity while differing to an extent in their function and organization. The idea that each hemisphere is specialized for different functions is known as complementary specialization. (Springer & Deutsch, 1998, p. 19)

Spatial (right-hemispheric) and sequential (left-hemispheric) preference are two different mental organizations that affect perceptions and lead to different worldviews. One readily synthesizes, allowing the individual to see the whole, and the other analyzes, dissecting the whole into parts that can be compared, contrasted, and placed in a hierarchical order. Information deemed central to one worldview appears less relevant from the other perspective. Although you can gain more facility with one or the other mode through learning, it is unlikely that a person inclined toward a sequential view can learn to perceive the world in exactly the same way as an individual born with higher spatial perception or vice versa. I am not an artist. I am incapable of seeing perspective the way an artist does. We rely on our preferred mode of information gathering and practice it almost exclusively unless something interferes with it.

If you had two stations that could receive the same television program, where Channel 1 receives it perfectly 100 percent of the time and Channel 2, 83 percent of the time, you'd always tune in to Channel 1. We use the best of what we have. But if Channel 1's system went down, you'd just switch to Channel 2 with the remote. Similarly for the body: The left and right hands aren't completely

different, of course, in writing ability, but a right-hander would
never use the left if she didn't have to. (Ornstein, 1997, p. 15)

As we moved through the 20th century, we became aware of the
damage done whenever left-handed children had been forced to become
right-handed, and in many countries, left-handedness has become acceptable. Now that we are in the 21st century, we are beginning to understand
the damage we do when we try to make children with enhanced right-
hemispheric development more like the rest of us. Instead of trying to
remake one or the other style of learning, we need to accept these inherent
differences in perception and appreciate their complementarity.

It is becoming increasingly clear that most activities involve both
hemispheres to one degree or another. ...there is evidence for two
very different but complementary modes of thought, each generally
associated with one of the hemispheres of the brain....

Research into the possible connection between creativity and the
functions of the two hemispheres has shown that some creative
individuals have the ability to balance, and alternate between, the
right and left hemispheres (and the corresponding dissimilar modes
of thought). ...the alternation between two modes of consciousness
is rather clearly shown in descriptions of the creative process by
Albert Einstein and others. A similar alternation has also been
documented in studies of gifted children. (West, 1991, pp. 14-15)

Jerre Levy and Tom West agree that creativity requires both
hemispheres, not just the right hemisphere. All learning involves both
hemispheres. So this book is not another treatise on how to teach an
isolated right brain. In the following chapters, you will find many
practical suggestions for parenting and teaching children whose right
hemispheres appear to be better developed than their left hemispheres.
These methods strengthen the functions of the right half without weak-
ening those of the left. They support the integration of both halves of the
brain, and will assist all children in learning more efficiently.

Obviously, the two hemispheres need input from each other and the
ability to collaborate in order for us to do most mental functions. We
need to apply this same rule of complementarity in the world at large.
Leonard Shlain suggests that humanity has had an unhealthy domination of left-hemispheric values for the last 5,000 years, which has left in
its wake the subjugation of the feminine to the masculine. But he sees
us moving toward greater appreciation of right-hemispheric values,
greater collaboration between our right and left hemispheres,
egalitarianism, and celebration of the wonderful diversity in the world.

I am convinced we are entering a new Golden Age—one in which the right-hemispheric values of tolerance, caring, and respect for nature will begin to ameliorate the conditions that have prevailed for the too-long period during which left-hemispheric values were dominant. Images, of any kind, are the balm bringing about this worldwide healing. It will take more time for change to permeate and alter world cultures but there can be no doubt that the wondrous permutations of photography and electromagnetism are transforming the world both physically and psychically. The shift to right-hemispheric values through the perception of images can be expected to increase the sum total awareness of beauty. (Shlain, 1998, p. 432)

The world needs both right-hemispheric and left-hemispheric intelligence in a continuous interchange of information—a beautiful dance.

Notes:

The Hidden Culprit in Underachievement

You mean to tell me that you can do this complex math problem, but you can't tell me what day follows Tuesday?

T's grade 3 teacher thought she had focusing problems and was not progressing.... She often did not understand the teacher's explanations and would seek out further guidance. The teacher often responded by accusing T of not paying attention the first time. T became afraid to ask for more assistance and started trying to figure out things on her own. When she was told she wasn't following instructions, her self-confidence became very low... "I am stupid, and I can't do anything." ...She was failing spelling tests week after week. Although we studied and she did perfect at home, T succeeded in failing every test she was ever given.

We took her to a psychologist where she tested out as a visual-spatial learner. T scored at a grade-6 level in reading and science, grade-4 level for math and most other things, but a late grade-2 level for all auditory parts of the test. ...I was told that the auditory part of the test brought down her score considerably.

There was something else I noticed about the way visual-spatial learners performed on assessments, besides the fact that they did better on the harder items, and failed the easy ones. An interesting pattern of strengths and weaknesses jumped off the test protocols and demanded that I pay attention. These upside-down learners performed exquisitely on puzzles, mazes, copying designs with colored blocks, copying abstract designs from memory, and imagining how a folded and cut piece of paper would look unfolded. But they couldn't name the days of the week, repeat a series of numbers, repeat a sentence, spell easy words, tell the names of the characters in a little story they had just heard, or follow a three-step direction.

IQ tests are categorized according to cognitive functions (e.g., memory, verbal reasoning, perceptual organization, etc.), not according to modality strengths (e.g., vision, hearing, touch). This is when the Ph.D. in learning disabilities that I earned with the late Leo Buscaglia[1] at the University of Southern California came in handy. In my special ed. program, I learned a lot about identifying children's modality strengths and weak-nesses. As I examined the profiles of underachieving VSLs, I was struck by the immense discrepancies between their performance on visual and auditory items. Highly gifted VSLs were successful at both visual and auditory tasks; they were just extremely advanced on the visual-spatial items. For them, visual-spatial learning was a preferred style rather than a necessary mode of learning. But what was causing the underachievers to miss so many auditory items?

The impact of early ear infections

Now a new hypothesis began to form. Did the VSLs who were struggling with auditory-sequential tasks have hearing problems? I scoured the parent questionnaires and found no hints. Nothing under medical history. No learning disabilities. So I started probing during the follow-up conferences. Did little Stephanie have a hearing problem? "No." Was there a history of hearing problems in the family? "No." Did she ever have tubes placed in her ears? "Yes." "Aha! Tubes! They must be the culprit! I'll bet they're damaging the left hemisphere." **Wrong!** I started asking all the parents if their child had had tubes. Some had, some hadn't. Then I noticed that some children who had had tubes did better on the auditory items than those who hadn't. That turned out to be a blind alley.

Then I thought about why doctors insert tubes: to open the ear canal when children have had chronic ear infections. So I began asking about ear infections. **Bingo!** As I asked more and more about ear

---

[1]Leo Buscaglia wrote many books, including *Love*. He had a newspaper column and was a popular presenter. When I was at USC, I also took Leo's "Love" class. Actually, I can't credit Leo for making me a better diagnostician, but he did help me become a more passionate presenter and a better human being. A master at the art of public speaking, Leo would remain after a lecture to give a bear hug to as many as 6,000 people. His greatest legacy was the message that the most important gift any human being can give another is love.

infections, the pieces of the picture started to fall into place. Why hadn't the parents listed "ear infections" under the child's health history? They didn't think it was important. "All children have ear infections, don't they?"

Ear infections (*recurrent otitis media with middle ear effusion*) turned up in more places than I anticipated. Children who appeared smart at home but underachieved in school, and children who fit most of our descriptors of giftedness but did not test in that range, were more likely to have had a high incidence of ear infections in the first three years of life.

> When my daughter was 18 months old, I grew concerned about her lack of progress in speech. We visited the pediatrician for a hearing test; as I suspected, she had chronic otitis, which effectively created a hearing impairment (later corrected through PE tubes). As I was discussing the hearing/speech problem and special interventions with the pediatrician, I suddenly noticed that she had disassembled his otoscope and made jewelry out of the tubes and fittings. "Well," said Dr. Gold, "there certainly isn't a cognitive problem here!"

It is now 1985. I get a call from a reporter from a new newspaper— *USA Today*. Psychologists are often contacted by the media about various topics, and I had put "GIFTEDNESS" in big block letters at the top of the list of topics I would be interested in addressing. But the media never called about that until recently. Second on my list was "adolescence" because I was teaching Adolescent Development at the University of Denver, and we had taken about 16 teenagers into our home over the years.

The reporter from *USA Today* was my first encounter with the national press. She wanted to know Madonna's impact on teen-age values. I had no idea who Madonna was, but I knew that parents had the greatest impact on their children's values. So I jabbered away— "Did you know that 97% of teenagers have the same values as their parents?"—while I wrote a note to my teenage daughter: "Who is Madonna?" (I'm born with the ability to talk without thinking. I'd make a good politician...) Miriam pantomimed well enough to show me that Madonna was a sexy rock star. This didn't change my opinion, so I continued my monologue, and then, *without taking a breath*, I suddenly switched topics on her: "But what you **really** should write about is gifted children..." and I rattled off, as fast as I could, everything I could think of about the gifted that I thought might interest her before she had a chance to hang up. It worked! (Next time you get a call from the media, try this technique. Just remember not to breathe...) The angle that caught her attention was that I had found a high incidence of ear infections in underachievers. She ended up writing a front page story about this discovery.

As a result, an inspiring woman entered my life. Marion Downs, one of the leading audiologists in the country (considered, strangely enough, the "godfather" of infant auditory screening), happened to read the article on a plane on her way back to Colorado from Nebraska, and she called my office. I learned more in the afternoon I spent with Marion than I can tell you. I asked her why my little study of the effects of tubes proved futile.

"Did you ask at what age the tubes were inserted?" *No.* I learned that in order to make a real difference, tympanostomy tubes had to be in place before the age of three—during the critical learning period.

"Did you ask the age of onset of the ear infections?" *No.* The earlier the ear infections begin, the more damage they can do to auditory processing abilities. And the earlier the intervention, the more effective the results. Auditory skills are extremely important in cognitive development. Children with hearing impairments who are recognized and treated before 6 months of age have higher IQ scores than those who are discovered later.

"Did you ask how many infections had occurred before the age of three?" *No.* Children who have had 9 or more bouts of otitis media before three years of age are more likely to have difficulties paying attention, understanding directions, hearing the teacher's voice in an open classroom, comprehending, and spelling.

"Did you ask whether the right, the left or both ears were involved?" *No.* Recurrent infections in the right ear lead to more school problems. "Literate people use the right ear more for listening to words. This means their left hemispheres are more active" (Ornstein, 1997, p. 40). But the biggest problem is when both ears are involved.

"Did you ask if the child had a high pain tolerance?" *No.* Otitis media can occur with no observable symptoms. That means that a child can have ear infections without anyone finding out, particularly if he or she has a high pain tolerance and doesn't complain. I learned from Marion that recurrent otitis media actually results in a conductive hearing loss, which looks like it goes away when the ear infections clear up, but actually has long term after effects.

I asked Marion why gifted children with otitis develop language on schedule, but often fall apart later on when it comes to handwriting. She laughed, and said, "My dear, think of all the practice we get with speaking versus the amount of practice we get with writing." I still couldn't get the connection between language and writing. So Marion had me do the following exercise:

Put your fingers in your ears as hard as you can and then listen to what someone is saying.

(Try it!)

This exercise lets you experience what the world sounds like to a child who has had frequent ear infections. Notice how everything sounded muffled as if you were listening in a tunnel? What range of sound were you unable to hear? Could you tell that it was the *higher frequencies* that got lost in the bargain? High frequencies are processed in the left hemisphere. When those frequencies are blocked during the critical learning period of the first three years of life, the left hemisphere receives less stimulation and less development.

> The right hemisphere seems to "get" the low frequency sounds, and the left hemisphere also seems to become more highly specialized for handling the high auditory frequencies. (Ornstein, 1997, pp. 153-154)

These higher frequencies are responsible for *sequencing* as well as other language functions. What is the most sequential task we can ask children to do? Writing! First they have to figure out what direction the letters go, then they have to link those letters together in a particular sequence to spell words. Then they have to link those words together in a particular order to make sentences. Then they have to link those sentences together in a particular order to make paragraphs. Then they have to link those paragraphs together to make reports, stories and essays. No wonder my underachieving VSLs hated to write!

> Why is the hemisphere that controls speech also the one that usually controls a person's dominant hand? Is it a coincidence, or is there a profound relationship that should tell us something about what is

involved in both speech and manipulative skills? Doreen Kimura and her colleagues have obtained evidence that the left hemisphere may be essential for certain types of hand movement.... [It] is specialized for motor control of both oral and manual musculature...

It is possible that the evolutionary advantages offered by the development of a hand skilled at manipulation also happened to be a most useful foundation on which to build a communication system, one that at first was gestural and utilized the right hand but later came to utilize the vocal musculature. As a result, *the left hemisphere came to possess a virtual monopoly on control of the motor systems involved in linguistic expression, whether by speech or writing.* (Springer & Deutsch, 1998, pp. 304-305, emphasis added)

And the right hand—the writing hand for most individuals—is controlled by the left hemisphere, which is weaker than the right hemisphere for non-sequential, visual-spatial children.

Ever since the first Sumerian had pressed a pointed stick into wet clay five thousand years ago, one dominant hand, controlled exclusively by the dominant hemisphere, had dictated the mechanics of writing. It made no difference whether the implement used was a stylus, a chisel, a brush, a quill, a crayon, a pen, or a pencil, the...left lobe of the brains of both men and women directed the muscles of the...right hand to write. (Shlain, 1998, p. 391)

So children who had had a lot of ear infections in their first three years suffered a conductive hearing loss, which blocked out the higher frequencies responsible for left-hemispheric auditory sequencing and the fine-motor sequencing required in handwriting. It finally made sense to me why otitis kids are at higher risk for underachievement.

I asked Marion if the residual impact of otitis media could be prevented. To my surprise, she answered "Absolutely!" She recommends getting down on eye-level with a toddler, touching her arm and gaining eye contact, and then **talking louder** to her, not only during the time of the ear infection, but up to 3 months after each ear infection, because the fluid can stay in the middle ear that long. In some cases, she recommends placing hearing aids on toddlers so that they hear the full range of auditory stimulation during this critical learning period.

Why aren't doctors more concerned about ear infections?

If otitis media is really this important, why aren't pediatricians giving this information to parents of toddlers? Marion explained that the medical community is not convinced of its importance. That was even more surprising, so I went to the medical journals and read studies on otitis media, and read Marion's work on this topic. Sure enough, Marion was right. On the whole, the medical community does not believe that ear infections have any long-term impact on language or cognitive development. But nearly all of the medical studies have been conducted on children of average or low average ability.

Marion gave me a study to read by the Boston Otitis Media Group. This study was interesting for many reasons. It compared children in two socio-economic groups: those from families that could afford to pay for regular pediatric care with those who received public health care. It used siblings as the control group, because the medical field assumes (correctly) that brothers and sisters are close in intelligence. (Too bad this isn't common knowledge among educators and psychologists.) Siblings who had had bouts of otitis for over 130 days of their first three years were compared on several measures with siblings who had had less than 30 days of otitis in their first three years. No differences were found in the lower socio-economic group on any of the measures. By way of contrast, differences as great as **20 IQ points** were found in the higher socio-economic group between children with a high incidence of otitis media and their healthier siblings. The researchers explained their results in terms of differences in health care in families at different socio-economic levels.

I looked at their data and came up with an entirely different conclusion. I noticed that the IQ scores in the lower socio-economic group ranged from 95—116, while the higher socio-economic group in this study happened to range from 115—130. They were two different IQ ranges. In the average range, no differences were revealed between children who suffered a conductive hearing loss for at least 12% of their young lives and their more fortunate siblings who had dealt with ear infections for less than 3% of their lives. As IQ increased, the impact of otitis media became much more evident. Why?

A year later I finally got the answer from interviewing Elizabeth Hagen [co-author of the *Cognitive Abilities Test* (CogAT) and the fourth edition of the *Stanford-Binet Intelligence Scale*]. Elizabeth is a long-time researcher of intelligence. She explained that because there are so many items that place an average child in the average range of intelligence, he can miss all the auditory items without it affecting his IQ score. *It takes fewer items to score in the gifted range; so, if a gifted child misses all the auditory items, her score will be knocked down to the average range.* We found this to be true.

One study we conducted showed that in most cases children who had had more ear infections than their brothers and sisters had considerably lower IQ scores than their highly gifted siblings. In one family, the difference was **67 IQ points!** The sister, who had no ear infections, achieved an IQ score of 185, whereas her brother, who suffered 4 to 6 ear infections a year from 6 months to 8 years of age (32-48 bouts of otitis), had an IQ score of 118. We know from other evidence that otitis kids are actually as smart as their siblings, but they can't demonstrate it on an IQ test. They get abysmally low scores on the verbal sections of IQ tests, because their auditory-sequential skills have been compromised by their ear infection history. Unfortunately, medical researchers remain unaware of how recurrent ear infections can severely depress IQ scores, because they never study gifted children with otitis.

> This is where your research hits home. I had a hard time getting the professionals to take me seriously when I suspected a speech issue when he was 1½. I could see how advanced he was in his ability to understand the world around him, though his speech was delayed. I was told not to worry. They told me that I was comparing him to his brother who was orally advanced. I pressed on, trying to understand why my younger son's speech was delayed. I fought and was finally able to get him in speech therapy at age 4. Turns out that his speech was distorted because his hearing was distorted. He had many ear infections until age 6. They found that even when he did not have an infection he had fluid in his ears that didn't belong and was disregarded by his doctor.

After my delightful encounter with Marion Downs, we began asking extremely detailed questions about ear infections on our parent questionnaire. We've probably collected more data on otitis media in gifted populations than anyone cares to know. But it helped us discover that repeated ear infections, in many cases, not only depress IQ scores, but can seriously interfere with school performance as well.

I think my 8-year-old son fits your visual-spatial profile. His spatial skills are strong; he seems to have an internal compass in his head. He was unable to hear for the first two years of his life.

Are VSLs born or made?

Do all visual-spatial learners have a history of otitis media? No, most of our VSLs had no ear infections at all. Instead, they had at least one strongly visual-spatial parent. For the most part, visual-spatial abilities are inherited. But children with chronic ear infections often become visual-spatial learners or at least their visual-spatial strengths are enhanced.

If your ears were blocked so that it was difficult to understand what you heard, what would you use as your main mode of gathering information? Your eyes! Did you notice how important your eyes became when you put your fingers in your ears? And the reliance on vision builds the right-hemispheric visual-spatial circuits. Otitis kids are usually visual learners. The combination of a strongly visual-spatial parent and a history of 9 or more ear infections in the first few years of life, beginning at 6 months or younger, is a certain recipe for a visual-spatial learning style.

The whole auditory system is perplexing. Parents sometimes seem dubious when I tell them that their children have central auditory processing problems. Instead, they think that their children are "selectively deaf." "She can't hear me when I'm in the same room with her calling her for supper, but when we're three rooms away and talking about candy, she can hear every word we're saying!" I've heard stories like this so many times that I've come up with my own theory about VSLs' "selective" hearing. I think these children lack what I call *peripheral audition,* which is sort of like peripheral vision. They can only hear (attend to) one stimulus at a time. If they are watching television, or reading a book, or talking on the telephone, or engrossed at the computer, or playing outside with friends, or concentrating on some deep thought, they cannot hear (process) competing auditory information. But when they are completely concentrating on one auditory stimulus, they can hear it quite clearly—sometimes too clearly. Acute hearing may actually interfere with the development of listening skills. Some children hear so much that they have difficulty attending to what is important.

Here's a story about the problems associated with auditory processing difficulties (hearing the background noises) in a visual-spatial learner...

My 6½ year old daughter, K, came out with this one this morning: "Oh, mummy. I would have played that piece perfectly but the noise you made putting on your socks distracted me and I lost my place."

What about music?

The other issue that confuses parents about this learning style is when children with high spatial abilities are musically inclined. Wouldn't that indicate that they are auditory learners? I had observed that many of my most mathematically gifted students were also musicians. I had heard that when they started the High School for Mathematics and Science in Durham, North Carolina, they found that they had to hire nearly as many music teachers as math teachers. I knew that higher level mathematical talent was dependent on a solid foundation of visual-spatial abilities. And I learned from my colleague, John Feldhusen, that Mozart **saw** an entire movement of a symphony all at once in his head and then had to laboriously write down all the notes one at a time. But isn't music auditory?

Marion said that the right ear receives the higher frequencies and sends them to the left hemisphere, and the left ear receives the lower frequencies and sends them to the right hemisphere. The high frequencies control verbal and sequential abilities. The low frequencies control "intonation, rhythm, and emotion." "That's music!" I squealed. I finally understood the connection between visual-spatial abilities and music.

> Because the right hemisphere seems to be specialized for hearing low tones, this very early ability may well lead to the later right-hemispheric dominance in a variety of nonlanguage sounds. ...The left-ear (right hemisphere) advantage for low musical notes occurs much earlier than right-ear advantage for speech. Also, children understand and produce the emotional intonations of language, conveyed by tones, before they understand the content of the speech. The right hemisphere's role continues throughout life. In one study, adults were faster and more accurate judging low frequency sounds presented to the right hemisphere and high-frequency sounds presented to the left hemisphere.... The right hemisphere's ability to deal with the low tones may make it also more likely to be responsive to the speaker's tone of voice, basic accent, and the stress the speaker gives to different words, which are all nonlinguistic aspects of linguistic communication. (Ornstein, 1997, p. 154)

Brain research suggests that "the right hemisphere is in some way critically involved in music.... The ability to sing is frequently unaffected in patients suffering from severe speech disturbances" (Springer & Deutsch, 1998, p. 18). Jerre Levy reports that timbre (tone) and musical chords are processed by the right hemisphere, but that the left hemisphere plays an important role in apprehension of rhythm.

A is musical and rhythmic: he moves in rhythm with the action on the [computer] screen; e.g., if it is a racing game, his body weaves from left to right along with the car on the screen.

I am looking for any information on an ability that I seem to find myself having. This ability is one that allows me to "see" a "live 3D" mathematical formula when listening to music.

What are the signs of central auditory processing disorder (CAPD)?

If you have a child who had many ear infections in early childhood, be on the lookout for auditory processing weaknesses and visual-spatial strengths.

- ✂ Was your child a late talker compared to your other children?
- ✂ Does she understand what you are saying when she cannot see your face?
- ✂ Does she fail to hear her name called when playing or concentrating?
- ✂ Does she mishear and misunderstand you?
- ✂ Does she seem not to listen?
- ✂ Does she space out a lot?
- ✂ Does she have persistent difficulties pronouncing certain letters or words?
- ✂ Does she cover her ears in noisy situations?
- ✂ Does she turn the television set on loudly?
- ✂ Does she have difficulty remembering multi-step auditory directions?

If so, these are signs of auditory processing difficulties. Your child should have a complete audiological evaluation, including a central auditory processing battery. If you have a student in your class who seems spacey, ask the parents about the child's ear infection history.

- ✂ Does he ask to have directions repeated?
- ✂ Does he watch the other children to find out what he is supposed to do?
- ✂ Does he seem particularly distracted in an open classroom setting or when the other students are noisy?

    ⚘ Does he have a loud voice?

    ⚘ Does his voice sound flat with little vocal intonation?

    ⚘ Does he misunderstand what you are saying?

    ⚘ Does he mispronounce sounds or words?

    ⚘ Does he daydream after ten minutes of instruction?

If you see these symptoms, refer the student to the special education team and request an audiological exam. (See Table 11.2 in Chapter 11 for a more complete list of symptoms of central auditory processing disorder.)

Activities to enhance auditory processing

For many years, I thought that if children had a central auditory processing disorder, the only thing you could do was teach them to compensate using their visual strengths. (I don't know why I thought this. With my special education background, I should have known better.) We sent dozens of children who had pronounced auditory-sequential weaknesses and slight visual weaknesses for vision therapy to enhance the visual system; we felt that we had to optimize their strongest modality in order to help them compensate.

Then Betty Maxwell and I came across the Tomatis Ear Technique, developed by Alfred Tomatis in France, and that seemed to be promising. While assessment techniques vary in different centers, the main goal is to determine which auditory frequencies are missing in the central nervous system. One way is to monitor the intonation of the person's voice. Individuals who are missing certain auditory frequencies tend to talk in a monotone. Remember when you put your fingers in your ears how the high frequencies were blocked out? Well, the Tomatis Technique is designed to reprogram the central nervous system to register the high frequencies.

If you're a music lover, this technique might be hard on you aesthetically, because you listen to mostly Mozart with all the low frequencies filtered out. And while you're listening to the music, you're doing some kind of nonverbal activity, like a puzzle or drawing. They report that the technique is also helpful with attention deficits, depression and phobias. *The Listening Program*, a sound stimulation auditory therapy partially based on the Tomatis Technique, consists of eight CDs with gradually increasing levels of difficulty. This home-based intervention can be used to supplement the therapy, under the guidance of a specialist.

We also send children to Joan Burleigh, an audiologist/researcher at Colorado State University in Fort Collins, Colorado. Joan helped develop the Central Auditory Processing Battery with her mentor, Jack Willeford.

She fits many children and adults with ear filters specially calibrated to block out the background noise that is most distracting for them. Parents report that these filters make a world of difference in their children's lives. Joan's work is described in Temple Grandin's book, *Thinking in Pictures* (pp. 68-70).

However, it was Cody who helped me to see that auditory processing weaknesses could be corrected through practice. Cody came for assessment from Las Vegas when he was 5½, in Kindergarten. He had extremely high scores in abstract reasoning, but scores bordering on the disabled range in Digit Span, a test of auditory short-term memory for non-meaningful number sequences. So we sent Cody to an audiologist for the Central Auditory Processing Battery. As we had anticipated, the test documented that he had central auditory processing disorder.

These auditory issues depressed his IQ score, so Cody's Mom decided to bring him back again the following year. We re-administered the test, and were baffled to find that instead of being near the disabled range, Cody was now in the *gifted* range in auditory short-term memory! How could that happen in a year's time? So we sent him back for another Central Auditory Processing Battery, and, sure enough, his auditory processing problems had disappeared.

We asked Cody's Mom, "What did you do to help his auditory processing since we saw you last?" She replied that *every day she gave Cody instructions and had him repeat them to her.* Sometimes she did this twice a day. She made sure she had eye contact with him first. Magic! I retested Cody myself six months later on the old *Stanford-Binet,* because it looked like we still had an underestimate (not because of auditory processing issues, but because the ceiling of the first test was too low). Not only did he achieve an astronomical IQ score, his greatest strength was in auditory short-term memory!

That convinced me that auditory issues could be remediated, so I put together a list of activities to assist parents and teachers in developing auditory-sequential memory. I started with a game that my parents used to play with us as kids on car trips. Do you remember, "I'm Going on a Picnic"? I've heard different variations, like "I'm Going to the Grocery Store," and "I'm Going to Mars."

I'm Going on a Picnic

The first person says, "I'm going on a picnic, and I'm going to bring an _____" (e.g., apple, armadillo, albatross, etc.—anything that begins with "a"). The second person repeats what the first person says and adds something that begins with the letter "b" (e.g., "I'm going on a picnic, and I'm going to bring an apple and a banana"). The next person repeats what the first and second person have said, and adds something that begins with the letter "c." The game continues until no one can remember all of the previous items. The alphabet provides a memory clue. When the children can remember all 26 words, vary the game by removing the alphabetical order, using various categories of words or any nouns. This is a good game for a classroom, since it can be played with any number of players. It is also great for families to play in the car. Invent similar games.

Silly Steps

Each day each member of the family gets to give one of the others a set of silly directions to follow. Begin with two-step directions, such as, "Go get a spoon from the kitchen and bring it back to me on your head." Gradually increase the number of directions, elaboration of the directions, and complexity, such as "Bring me the ruler in the back of the third drawer of my desk, come back into the kitchen, and turn around three times." When your child succeeds, he or she gets to ask you to follow a silly set of directions.

Repeating Instructions

When giving your child or a student in your class directions, have him or her look at you and repeat what you just said. Do this on a daily basis (as Cody's Mom did!).

Cumulative Verse Songs

Sing songs that involve repeating previous verses, such as "Old MacDonald Had a Farm," "The Twelve Days of Christmas," "There Was an Old Lady Who Swallowed a Fly," "The Green Grass Grows All Around," etc. (What other songs like this do you know?)

Going on a Lion Hunt (or Bear Hunt)

The leader chants each line, which is then repeated (R) by the group while walking in place and alternately slapping knees in cadence. There are movements that accompany each section. "Let's go on a lion hunt." (R). "OK!" (R) "Here we go!" (R) (Start walking action.) "Oh look!" (R) "There's a gate." (R) "Can't go around it." (R) "Can't go under it." (R) "Have to go through it." (R) (Opening gate with creaking motion.) This sequence continues with each obstacle in their path. Next, the group encounters a bridge, a field, then some mud, then a river, then a cave. Then they see two eyes, a nose, and fur, and shout, "IT'S A LION!" They walk very fast, pretending they are running, and then retrace their steps as quickly as they can, making the sounds that accompany each part and end with "Whew! We made it!" They have to remember the entire sequence in reverse order. There is a book available describing the activity as a bear hunt. New obstacles can be added as the children become proficient at it. (This came from a Girl Scout manual!)

Reversed Sentences

Take turns saying sentences in reverse, starting with three or four words, gradually lengthening the sentences.

Hand Motions

Start with a simple set of hand motions, such as 2 claps, 2 finger snaps, 2 knee slaps. Have your child repeat these motions. Then have him or her make up a set for you to repeat. Gradually increase the number and complexity of the hand motions.

See and Say; Simon; Bop-It; Computer Sequencing Games

There are a number of toys available that require a child to repeat a series of sounds, lights, numbers, directions, etc. Some games of this nature are available on the computer.

Accommodations for children with central auditory processing disorder (CAPD)

Children who have a history of otitis media learn best if they are taught as if they were deaf or hard of hearing. Here are some ideas:

Accommodations for CAPD

- Speak concisely. Pause between main ideas to allow the child to process.
- Use gestures to aid understanding.
- Limit the number of directions presented.
- Write directions on the board, on overheads, or on paper.
- Let the child observe others before attempting new tasks.
- Provide models of the end product desired.
- Use as many visual aids and hands-on experiences as possible.
- Touch the child's shoulder to get attention when he does not hear you.
- Place the child near you and away from distracting noise.
- Provide a quiet place for the child to work.
- Industrial strength earphones may be needed when the child is working on assignments.
- Allow another student to take notes for him during lectures.
- Pair him with a student who has excellent audition who can give him information he misses.

I'm a completely visual-spatial learner. ... For years and years I've struggled to achieve my full potential in school... I cannot perform on tests due to...the fact that there is a huge discrepancy in my visual-spatial skills and a specific area of my auditory-sequential intelligence.

...Often I have been labeled as a moron because I don't pick up auditory instructions or details that the average idiot is capable of doing with ease. I often need simple directions repeated to me and I always have to try extra hard to concentrate and input instructions. I learn very well from watching people in action. I can only learn on the tennis court from watching, not listening ... (ranked top 7 in the Northeastern part of the US in my respective age group in tennis).

I am 44 years old and until today I did not understand what was wrong with me. All my life I have been trying to find that out—what a relief to know nothing is wrong...

My girlfriend is a child psych. and told me I was spatial and had auditory problems but I didn't understand the concept of that till today. I knew I learned visually but...this explains a whole lot. I feel like I came home today reading your articles....

My three children are also...spatial and I want to thank you for making this known, as now I can help them understand and they don't have to wait till they are 44 to understand themselves.

Are All Visual-Spatial Learners Brilliant?

In my research (in its infancy) I find "visual-spatial and gifted" or "visual-spatial and A.D.D." Is there visual-spatial and "regular" and are there different learning methods for each?

From the beginning, I considered VSL another (less popular) form of giftedness. It didn't occur to me that "regular" kids could also be VSLs until nearly a decade later. In March, 1989, the VSL concept made its official debut in an article entitled, "Spatial Learners" in my mini-journal, *Understanding Our Gifted*. And, at long last, "The Visual-Spatial Learner," written in 1982, found a home in the inaugural issue of *Preventing School Failure*. Then, "Invisible Gifts, Invisible Handicaps," on spatially gifted children with auditory-sequential learning disabilities appeared in the September issue of *Roeper Review*. Finally, the VSL concept was published. Not long after, I began to be asked to do presentations on VSLs. This is when I discovered that the visual-spatial learning style is not limited to the gifted.

The first time I was invited to present on visual-spatial learners, by Mary Toll, the gifted coordinator in West Palm Beach, Florida, the suggestion was planted that this way of thinking had a much broader audience. The principal at the school where I gave the presentation told me that she thought most African-American students learned this way. This surprised me because African-American children are generally highly verbal. But, eventually I came to understand the "wholistic" framework of most ethnic cultures and realized the wisdom of her words.

Two years later, in 1991, I was invited to speak to the Rockwood School District in St. Louis, Missouri. During lunch, Steven Barr, the state director of curriculum, asked me if I would be willing to make a videotape on visual-spatial learners in their new telecommunications studio. The video was to be televised by satellite to all the school districts in the state. The hitch was that I was not allowed to use the "g" word. Steve felt that the topic was important for all teachers to learn about, in all subject areas, at all grade levels—from Kindergarten through 12th grade. I was nervous about stepping outside the field I knew about and I said I had to think about it awhile. For most of my career, I had focused my energies on the gifted and I didn't know if my observations were applicable beyond giftedland.

Scared about how I would be received, I agreed to do the videotape. The filming turned out to be the most exciting experience I had ever had! What a ham! The little studio audience of regular classroom teachers and principals was very enthusiastic and my fears disappeared. It was a thrill to learn that the VSL teaching techniques were useful for the entire spectrum of students.

Three groups, however, embraced the construct most vigorously: advocates for dyslexia, advocates for AD/HD and advocates for the gifted. While the ideas apply to a substantial number of students in the regular classroom, they are particularly relevant for twice exceptional children and highly gifted children.

Visual-spatial learners with dyslexia

At least one-sixth of the children we test at the Center are "twice exceptional"—that is, both gifted and learning disabled. And many of these children are visual-spatial. Giftedness is hard to recognize in learning disabled children and learning disabilities are more difficult to diagnose. Gifts mask disabilities, and disabilities depress IQ scores. Children who are twice exceptional may not score in the gifted range on IQ tests and achievement measures. Their strengths and weaknesses cancel each other out, making them appear "average" to someone who hasn't studied both exceptionalities. (There is more to come on this topic in Chapters 8 and 9.) Only very advanced children with extreme disabilities are recognized, such as highly intelligent children who cannot master reading, writing, calculation or memorization. This is where Ron Davis, author of *The Gift of Dyslexia*, enters the story. (See Chapter 13 for a description of Ron's methods.)

Betty Maxwell, the Associate Director of the Gifted Development Center, had come across Ron's work several years before his book came out, in an issue of *Brain/Mind Bulletin* and became very excited about it. Ron's insights fit with other knowledge she had acquired about intuition and she was eager to share Ron's work with me. Some time later, one of our clients went out to Burlingame, California, to enroll in the Davis Dyslexia Correction Program. She returned with detailed stories of the methods he used and the progress her daughter had made in reading. She shared with Ron some of our articles on VSLs. Ron immediately saw the connection between our work on visual-spatial abilities and his on dyslexia. Later on, he printed sections of "Strategies for Gifted Visual-Spatial Learners" in his *Dyslexic Reader Newsletter,* and then placed it on his website. Through Ron, we came to know some of the nicest folks we've ever encountered: gifted dyslexics.

Recently, I met three teachers from Illinois who had come to a symposium to hear me speak about VSLs. They had been using Ron Davis' techniques in their reading program with remarkable success.

I am uncertain as to what percentage of dyslexics are visual-spatial, but Sue Parkinson of the Arts Dyslexia Trust in London, and Jodi Ringle, a special education teacher from Illinois, both seem to be convinced that the shoe fits.

> I spent the summer of 1999 researching reading techniques. I downloaded and read through 133 pages of current research and "best teaching practices" for students with reading difficulties. It was a "been there, done that" experience. I must admit I was pleased that everything I had been doing was considered "best practices" by the "experts." I was also upset that the "experts" didn't seem to be aware of or care to address the needs of children like my student, because for children like him, these "best practices" don't work. In seven short years, in one small rural district I was aware of four such children who were obviously bright, but were extremely low in reading ability. How many others were there in our world? In this modern age of brain research, was there nothing else out there to help them? I needed some answers.

> They finally came in July 1999. I found the book *The Gift of Dyslexia* by Ronald D. Davis....

> [As a result of the Davis program] I had two students go back to the regular classroom and only need support help, and another one will go back this fall. Two students showed dramatic improvement in their speech and language skills, one of whom was dismissed from speech services in a single school year. All of my students had significant gains, some had up to two years' growth and the one boy who'd had no gains in over a year had almost a year's gain....

> There is a different style of teaching that I have not been trained in, yet these types of children must have this style. Sadly, there are very few people who even know we need to teach this way.... That is my goal for the near future. I would like training...in how to teach in the visual-spatial way these students require. (Ringle, Miller, & Anderson, 2000, pp. 7, 16)

Visual-spatial learners with AD/HD

As "visual-spatial learner" became a buzzword around Colorado, therapists in Denver became familiar with the idea, and began to notice this learning style in other clients who were not as advanced. In 1992, Betty and I put together a study group of individuals from different fields who were interested in the visual-spatial learner. We hoped that a multi-disciplinary team would help us see different parts of the elephant, refine the concept, and develop a tool for identifying VSLs throughout the IQ range. And they did. The process was fascinating. (See Chapter 14 for more details.)

At various points, we had input from a mathematics mentor, a psychologist specializing in children with attention deficit disorder, a well-known tutor, an artist, two reading specialists, two coordinators of gifted programs, an occupational therapist, a behavioral optometrist, a neuropsychiatrist, two social psychologists, an audiologist, a kinesiologist, a psychiatrist employing the Tomatis method, a researcher in gifted education, several parents, and a businessman. It took 5 years to get all these people to agree on the wording of the instrument. (And then it had to be turned into "kid-talk" by a dedicated group of gifted fifth graders!) But it was worth it. It enabled us to step outside the gifted box and see the broader implications of the concept.

One particular meeting stands out in my mind. Jeff Freed, the tutor, turned to George Dorry, the AD/HD specialist, and asked if he had ever seen a child with AD/HD who was a sequential learner. George said, "Come to think of it, no." Jeff had seen such a powerful connection between AD/HD and right-hemispheric, visual-spatial thinking that he subsequently wrote the book, *Right-Brained Children in a Left-Brained World: Unlocking the Potential of Your ADD Child.*

Does this mean all individuals with AD/HD are visual-spatial? I'm not sure, but I do think that they tend to be non-sequential. So what's the difference between "non-sequential" and "visual-spatial"? This is what our group concluded: "Non-sequential" is considered a weakness, while "visual-spatial" is a strength. Not all non-sequential learners are blessed with visual-spatial strengths. And not all VSLs are non-sequential. The highly gifted often prefer the visual-spatial mode of learning, but their sequential reasoning is excellent as well. (More on this in Chapter 5.)

Children who lack sequencing abilities, who show little visual-spatial strength, and who do not exhibit many of the characteristics of giftedness in Table 4.1 below, are better termed "non-sequential learners." However, they would definitely profit from the techniques outlined in this book. Visual-spatial methods work well with all children and adults who are visual learners—individuals who think in pictures. Children with hearing impairments, with central auditory processing disorder, or who have suffered recurrent ear infections in the first years of life, undoubtedly would benefit from these techniques. Other groups likely to have a high incidence of VSLs are dyslexics, underachievers, children with AD/HD, learning disabled children, children with Asperger's Syndrome, left-handed children, and children from different ethnic groups—particularly Asian, Latin American, Native American, Islanders and other indigenous people. And, if the principal at the school in Florida is right, and I believe she is, African-American children as well. Black children are "wholistic" thinkers. The ideas in this book are particularly useful for individuals within these groups who are blessed with exceptional right-hemispheric gifts.

Gifted visual-spatial learners

Visual-spatial ability is another way of being smart; it is just less often recognized than the left-hemispheric, sequential skills that lead to academic success. Individuals who demonstrate **exceptional** *visual-spatial strengths, imagistic thinking, complexity of thought, humor, empathy, musical talent, artistic expression,* or *creative imagination,* are, indeed, gifted. They may not always score in the highest ranges on IQ tests, because these measures are geared more for sequential learners. Most IQ tests emphasize verbal abilities, with few items that assess visual-spatial abilities. And these items are usually timed, so the examinee has to be fast as well as adept. The strengths of the visual-spatial learner are harder to assess (How do you measure if someone has superior visual imagery??), but these individuals are still gifted. At the very least, they should be assessed on untimed nonverbal tests in addition to verbal tests. (See Chapter 8.)

So if the tests don't capture visual-spatial abilities, how can we tell if a VSL is gifted? I actually trust the characteristics of giftedness (in Table 4.1) more than the test scores. We've studied the prevalence of these characteristics since 1979 with more than 4,000 children. We found that if children fit three-fourths of them, they test in the superior range 84% of the time. Another 11% show some sparks of giftedness, combined with weaknesses that pull down their test scores. The list is equally capable of identifying visual-spatial and auditory-sequential learners, girls and boys, rich kids and poor kids, and children of various ethnic groups. If three-fourths of these characteristics fit your child, it would be a good idea to get an assessment to verify your child's gifted-ness. If these characteristics fit you when you were a child, guess what? (If you're curious, we also have a list of characteristics of gifted adults on our website: **www.gifteddevelopment.com.**)

Table 4.1

Characteristics of Giftedness

Parents are excellent identifiers of giftedness in their children: 84% of the children whose parents say that they fit ¾ of the following characteristics score at least 120 IQ (the superior range). Over 95% show giftedness in at least one area, but are asynchronous (uneven) in their development, and their weaknesses depress their IQ scores.

Compared to other children your child's age, how many of these descriptors fit your child?

- ✎ Reasons well (good thinker)
- ✎ Learns rapidly
- ✎ Has extensive vocabulary
- ✎ Has an excellent memory
- ✎ Has a long attention span (if interested)
- ✎ Sensitive (feelings hurt easily)
- ✎ Shows compassion
- ✎ Perfectionistic
- ✎ Intense
- ✎ Morally sensitive
- ✎ Has strong curiosity
- ✎ Perseverant in their interests
- ✎ Has high degree of energy
- ✎ Prefers older companions or adults
- ✎ Has a wide range of interests
- ✎ Has a great sense of humor
- ✎ Early or avid reader (if too young to read, loves being read to)
- ✎ Concerned with justice, fairness
- ✎ Judgment mature for age at times
- ✎ Is a keen observer
- ✎ Has a vivid imagination
- ✎ Is highly creative
- ✎ Tends to question authority
- ✎ Has facility with numbers
- ✎ Good at jigsaw puzzles

From Silverman, L. K. (2002). *Upside-Down Brilliance: The Visual-Spatial Learner.* Denver: DeLeon Publishing.

May be reproduced.

I want to make it clear that I do not consider all children gifted. As I said in the Introduction, this makes about as much sense to me as saying that all children are "retarded." Once we stretch the term so that it fits everybody, it becomes pointless. There really are children who are so advanced that they need special provisions in order to develop their abilities. There really are children who learn so much faster than the others that they are literally wasting their time every day in school—learning how to underachieve—in classes where they are forced to relearn what they already know. This is a tragic situation, not only for the child, but for our entire society, which has forfeited the gifts these individuals might have contributed to the well-being of the planet.

I also want to clarify that while I see some compatibility between the visual-spatial learner and some of the domains of talent, I have not thrown out the baby of high intelligence along with the bathwater. People with extraordinary general intelligence show developmental differences in early childhood. They develop at a faster rate than other children their age. As adults, they may excel in different areas, but they share the basic characteristics of giftedness listed in Table 4.1, such as high abstract reasoning, rapid learning ability, intensity, sensitivity, perfectionism, curiosity, and concern with justice. These are unusual traits that often alienate children from their classmates or alienate adults from the cultures in which they live. And they are universal: they appear in all societies, all ethnic and racial groups, all socio-economic levels, and both genders. They are culture-fair, and do not depend on the values and recognition of society.

However, having said all that, I think we **miss** identifying many truly gifted children and adults who have hidden disabilities or a visual-spatial learning style or both. We do this by using inappropriate measures or by misinterpreting information obtained through testing. The solution is not to eliminate IQ tests. Without IQ tests, we would never be able to diagnose subtle disabilities. This is a disastrous error in collective judgment that prevents the detection of profoundly gifted children, gifted girls (who often hide their intelligence), gifted children with learning disabilities, and visual-spatial learners. The answer is to develop *better* IQ tests. And that's what we're trying to do. (Can I lure you into glancing at Chapter 8?)

Back to the original question in the title of this chapter. Do I think all visual-spatial learners are brilliant? No. However, I do believe that many dyslexics, many with AD/HD, many who suffer from seizure disorders, many with artistic talent, many who are highly imaginative, many rapid learners from different ethnic backgrounds, many who are underachieving—many who are obviously very bright but cannot read, spell, calculate, memorize, or write well—are hidden gifted learners with a visual-spatial learning style. In addition, many scientists, mathematicians, architects, cartoonists, cartographers, musicians, dancers, mechanics, engineers, photographers, actors, directors, story-tellers, designers, artisans, sculptors, visionaries, humanitarians, moral and spiritual leaders, psychics and creative thinkers are VSLs. There are thousands of VSLs out there who think they are dumb because they were not successful in school, when actually they are among the most brilliant minds on the planet.

In 1983, John Dixon wrote:

Research on the nature of spatial ability has come such a long way in the last century that one would expect it to have considerable impact on the way educators understand giftedness in children. Yet, with few exceptions, when one looks at the spectrum of programs for gifted children, one senses that the accumulated knowledge on spatial ability has been given little if any consideration and has no impact on the planning of these programs. ...*[The Spatial Child]* has been written for the purpose of addressing this shortcoming. Spatial ability is one of the primary ways in which giftedness is manifested in many children. We can hardly move forward in our understanding of giftedness until we have focused on the implications of this. (p. ix)

Gifted programs and school in general have not changed much since John wrote this powerful book two decades ago. School success still depends on left-hemispheric strengths. It emphasizes "well-roundedness"—the ability to perform moderately well in all subjects. However, real genius—brilliance—is often narrowly focused, with large gaps between strengths and weaknesses. It is frequently argued that the cream will rise to the top, despite all obstacles. But in reality, enormous potential is lost from lack of discovery and development, and giftedness can be turned against a society that does not appreciate it, or worse, makes fun of it. In a 2-part special, on the Arts and Entertainment channel, on "The Mystery of Genius: Masters and Madmen" (which, indeed, was all about men), the announcer said, "A gift that has no outlet in the mainstream forges underground, seeking validation in mischievous ways." There are risks in ignoring high abilities.

Giftedness implies developmental advancement, exceptional abstract reasoning/problem-solving ability, and high general intelligence. For me, **brilliance** includes all of these and something more: *unusual creativity or awareness—a spark of magic!* Brilliant people light the way for the rest of us. We will never know how many brilliant children are missed—children whose abilities are more visual-spatial than auditory-sequential. Among them is another Bill Gates, Marie Curie, Gary Larson, Thomas Edison, Mother Theresa, Robin Williams, Oprah Winfrey, Albert Einstein, Whoopi Goldberg—waiting to be discovered.

Notes:

Different Strokes for Different Folks

> I ran across your web page and after reading a few paragraphs knew this was me. I've always called myself a visual person because I picture everything in my mind and am good at spatial concepts. I never knew there was more than one learning style!

Once upon a time, only boys from affluent families went to school. They sat in straight-backed wooden desks, and learned the same rote lessons as all the other students in the classroom. And when they messed up, they were hit sharply on the knuckles with the teacher's ruler. Education for all children was a revolutionary idea, but for hundreds of years the methods remained the same.

Times have changed. Today's teachers must be superhuman and adapt to the children, instead of the other way around. To be a modern teacher, you must be part entertainer, part social worker, part special educator, part police officer, part ringmaster (to accommodate the range of abilities and learning styles and backgrounds and needs of all your students), and, oh yes, part enthusiast—knowledgeable of your subject matter and of the fine art of teaching. And no matter how much the violence in schools escalates, teachers do not receive hazard pay. There has to be an easier way to make a living. (Have you thanked your child's teacher lately? How about flowers??)

Individual differences in the classroom

For the last 40 years, teachers have been urged to plan strategies that take into account the diverse personality types, intelligences, learning styles, and talents of all their students. Here are some of the models they've learned about in workshops. In 1962, Isabel Briggs Myers constructed the prototype of most of the personality style models in use today. Her *Myers-Briggs Type Indicator* (MBTI) generates 16 different personality types. The MBTI is used in business organizations and education. Howard Gardner's *Frames of Mind: The Theory of Multiple Intelligences*, which came out in 1983, generated a revolution in education. Howard proposed 7 intelligences—linguistic, musical, logical-mathematical, spatial, bodily-kinesthetic, interpersonal, and intrapersonal. He has since added naturalistic and existential. Teachers are expected to develop all of these intelligences. But in 1967, Joy P. Guilford, founder of the study of creativity, proposed the largest number of intelligences: 120. In his later years, he expanded his model to 150 intelligences.

The most popular learning styles inventory was developed by Rita and Kenneth Dunn in 1975. It consists of 4 environmental, 4 emotional, 6 sociological, 7 physical, and 3 psychological elements. The combination of these 24 elements results in more than 41,472 possible learning styles! And the number of different talents children might have is endless. All of the various models of personality, intelligence, learning styles, and talent development have succeeded in sensitizing educators to the diversity of the student body—an admirable undertaking. However, the task of planning for all these learning differences is staggering.

There's an easier solution. Research at the Gifted Development Center over the last two decades suggests that there are essentially two basic learning styles to be addressed, and that teachers are already reaching one of the two. Auditory-sequential learners are more likely to be counted among children for whom school is a positive experience. Visual-spatial learners are more often counted among the under-achievers, the creative nonconformists, the highly gifted drop-outs (some of whom are being homeschooled), the mathematically talented children who hate arithmetic, the scientific geniuses who struggle with reading, the technological wizards whose learning occurs after school hours at their computers, the musically and artistically talented, the day-dreamers who can't focus when the pace is too slow, and bright children from culturally diverse groups. The teaching strategies in this book should enhance learning for all of the students in the class, because they activate the right hemisphere, which is critical to attention. As Jerre Levy says, "Unless the right hemisphere is activated and engaged, attention is low and learning is poor." (For more on this, go back to Chapter 2.)

There are two main modalities for receiving information: vision and audition. Most children favor one over the other, and some are equally strong in both modalities. Kinesthetic learners (who use physical movement and muscular feedback) are usually stronger visually, so the term "visual-kinesthetic" is often used. In our experience at the Center, children who suffer from both visual and auditory weaknesses are more likely to be called *kinesthetic* (body awareness), *tactile* (touch) or *haptic* (movement and touch) learners. These children would definitely profit from the techniques developed for VSLs.

It is possible to be a visual-spatial learner even with impaired vision, and an auditory-sequential learner with impaired audition. It sounds confusing, but I've even met blind VSLs. The "visual" part refers to the primary use of visualization in thinking and the auditory part refers to the primary use of *auditorization* (self-talk) in thinking: thinking in images vs. thinking in words. Blind spatial learners can visualize and deaf sequential learners can talk to themselves.

There are two major information processing modes: sequential and spatial. Children who are more left-hemispheric tend to be verbal, sequential, analytic, and time-oriented. Children who favor the right hemisphere tend to be visual, perceptive, synthesizing, and spatially oriented.

> The difference [is] primarily between a sequential way of perceiving the world and a simultaneous way. In computing terms, this is very similar to the difference between serial or parallel processing. ...These two modes would well underlie analysis and synthesis as ways of cognition. The sequential left hemisphere would be good for analysis and would underlie language and reason, and the right hemisphere would see things all at once, good for spatial perception, movement, and the like. (Ornstein, 1997, p. 157)

An underlying assumption of this book is that much of school instruction is auditory and sequential, and that children who learn in these ways, regardless of their level of intelligence, are fairly well served by the current system. Modifications that make curriculum more accessible for visual learners and spatial processors should meet the needs of children with greater right-hemispheric strengths. This group seems to be missed in the current system, and it is a sizeable number—at least one-third of the student population.

Since we only have two hemispheres, it seems likely that instruction geared to both hemispheres ought to cover most of the ground in the classroom. So if you're a teacher, relax a little. Compared to what you've been trying to do, this is going to be a piece of cake. And if you're a parent, don't assume that your child's teacher ought to know all about VSLs. This is new information. Please be gentle in sharing it.

Born for success: Auditory-sequential learners

Children for whom school works are really nice people. I hate hearing them described in negative ways by people who are trying to sell a different model. These students pay attention, they want to succeed, they take school seriously, they remember to do their homework, they turn it in on time, they're studious, they're agreeable, and they're kind to teachers and other living things. If it weren't for these bright young faces, it would be really hard for teachers to get up in the morning and face another day.

Successful students have good sequencing skills. They learn step-by-step the way teachers teach and the way the curriculum is designed. They are able to show their work easily because they took a series of steps to get there. They are orderly. An "order" is a series. Orderly, well-organized children understand the sequence of events that leads to peace and harmony. They care about preserving order in their belongings and relationships. They grow up to be good, responsible citizens. These are admirable qualities in admirable people.

Most successful students have greater left-hemispheric strengths or are well-balanced between their left and right hemispheres. We all need our left hemispheres. We wouldn't survive in the world with only our right hemisphere! Individuals with stronger left hemispheres also have right hemispheres, and the highest functioning individuals are those who integrate information well from **both** hemispheres. So the visual-spatials aren't the good guys and auditory-sequentials the bad guys. It doesn't work that way.

> The right hemisphere specializations develop to their fullest when informed by a fully developed left side. Otherwise we get form without content. (Ornstein, 1997, p. 95)

Auditory-sequential learners learn best auditorally. Phonics works for them because they have excellent phonemic awareness—an auditory skill. They are good listeners. They can make sense of oral instructions. They can listen to the syllables of a word in their head and spell it the way it sounds. They can remember what they hear, and follow complex sets of directions. They can memorize easily—even rote information, like multiplication tables. They are comfortable with step-by-step approaches to instruction, tend to be rapid processors of verbal information, and are generally able to express themselves well verbally.

Children with excellent auditory-sequential abilities can access words easily, efficiently, and quickly. Their verbal fluency gives them greater ease at public speaking and impromptu presentations. It also enables them to be more verbally assertive—to get their ideas heard in a group. Gifted auditory-sequential learners are more likely than equally gifted VSLs to be high achievers in academic subjects, to be selected for gifted programs, to be recognized by their teachers as having high potential, and to be considered leaders.

Another strength of many auditory-sequential learners is timing. Children with good audition and auditory processing have a good sense of timing and of time. They are punctual, they manage their time effectively so that they can get their assignments turned in when they are due, they're able to work within time constraints, and they often know when to say things (and when not to).

An appreciation of linear time was the crucial precondition for linear speech. A conversation can be understood only when one person speaks at a time. In contrast, one's right brain can listen to the sounds of a seventy-piece orchestra and hear them holistically. (Shlain, 1998, pp. 22-23)

Visual-spatial weaknesses

Auditory-sequential learners of all ages usually think in words. Words become their medium of thought. For them, thinking and inner dialogue may be so closely intertwined that they might have a hard time understanding how some people think differently. Visualization may be hard for them. Meditation may be laborious. It is as difficult to silence a relentless verbal production machine as it is to lasso a bull in an open field: it basically goes wherever it wants.

While most auditory-sequential learners have adequate visual-spatial functioning, their nonverbal reasoning probably is not as highly developed as their verbal reasoning. They may get lost easily in unfamiliar surroundings. They may have less facility with jigsaw puzzles, map reading, making mental maps, drawing, physics, and higher level mathematics. Physical skills may take longer to master. There is also a segment of auditory-sequentials who have impaired right-hemispheric abilities. These are surfacing as "Nonverbal Learning Disorders." They include difficulty with social judgment, inability to read facial expressions and body language, unusual emotional reactions, and failure to understand some forms of humor. Individuals with nonverbal learning disorders tend to talk at people instead of having a give and take communication. They may have difficulty with motor coordination, particularly on the left side of the body. But aside from these more serious impairments, mild weaknesses in the visual-spatial system do not appear to interfere very much with daily life or school success.

> I am not very good at spatial tasks, yet because these tasks are not emphasized, I was never given a negative label. (Except in phys. ed. Art, I could usually muddle through). Sequential learning is emphasized, therefore those who aren't [sequential] are given the label, "learning disabled." It doesn't seem fair to me.

Let's face it. Parents and teachers do not wring their hands in despair and lose sleep over the child who cannot visualize well. All the skills that VSLs excel at to a higher degree than auditory-sequential learners are considered *optional* rather than essential. In fact, constructing, reading maps, doing jigsaw puzzles, musical ability, and drawing are all thought of as special talents, not as necessary life skills. Physics, higher level mathematics, and meditation are all avoidable. While good intuition is actually a powerful life skill, you aren't graded on it in school. But the value of right-hemispheric skills varies in different cultures and in different eras. Poor visual memory would result in illiteracy in cultures with a pictographic form of language, and a poor sense of direction could result in death in the jungle. Lack of artistic ability would be a serious handicap in some Island cultures. Who knows? In the not too distant future, the visual skills needed to become technologically proficient may become far more important than they are now.

Tom West predicts that in the "post-literate" society, visual skills will become more and more marketable, and the weaknesses of the visual-spatial learner may be viewed as inconsequential:

> It seems reasonable to expect, sooner or later, the gradual development of a very different way of doing things, one in which the ready recognition of larger patterns, intuition, a sense of proportion, the imaginative vision, the original and unexpected approach, and the apt connection between apparently unrelated things are the salient abilities.... Consequently, before very long, the new market for ability and skills might increasingly devalue the conventional literate accomplishments that have carried such high prestige for hundreds of years. (West, 1991, pp. 88-89)

Those VSLs who struggle to master the written word are often placed in remedial reading courses. Is it possible that in the near future we will have remedial visualization courses to enhance the marketability of auditory-sequential learners in a technological world?

The other half (or third): Visual-spatial learners

What's it like to be a visual-spatial learner? To think in pictures instead of words?

> I think the first time I recognized that I could do something other people couldn't readily do was when I was taking calculus in high school and doing some 3d integrals. The teacher said to the class "Don't worry if you can't visualize it, most people can't." I thought to myself, "How odd, seeing that [this] is as natural as walking."

> I know I have always been this way, but it wasn't until the past couple of years (age 29-30) that I started really noticing that I "think in pictures." Whenever I try to understand a concept, I see it as shapes in relationship to each other. I often draw flow charts of ideas, and when I work on my own problems, I draw them out in some form. Not like art, but like visual diagrams of how things relate to each other. The best way to describe it is, when I think of a concept, especially one I am trying to understand, one that is complex, the way I understand it is in visual forms and shapes, where the shapes and the relationships between the shapes yields the essence of the concept. I have a hard time remembering details even though I understand many complex subjects and concepts. When I read, unless I make notes, the details escape me. I have felt frustrated by this as an adult and I only just stumbled on your

concept of visual-spatial learner today, even though I have been identified as gifted since I was a child. Also, I have a strong capacity to
remember phone numbers and directions, even if I have just written them
down once. The way I remember them is they appear as an image in my
mind. It's not really remembering, its like a picture pops into my head.

When I'm thinking about something, it appears as a physical system in
my mind, much like if someone were to look at a pinball machine. In the
system of the pinball machine, one knows intuitively that certain things
will happen if you, say, hit a certain part with the ball. Working with these
models in my mind is like seeing a system from a god's-eye-view. You can
just know how things are going to work out because you know the system
and certain inputs produce certain consequences. My intuition builds
these models for different things in my environment, and when I find that
it is representing something inaccurately, I can modify it.

As these website responses illustrate, visual-spatial learners have
minds especially equipped for pattern recognition. They are able to see
things from different perspectives, hold their images in their mind's eye,
and manipulate them. This allows them to see relationships that others
miss. They are excellent at detecting inconsistencies in the way things
ought to look. Their enhanced ability to image fuels imagination.
Creativity may follow, manifested in different ways. Some are artistic,
some are musical, some are mechanical, some are technological
wizards, some are scientific inventors, some are empaths, and some are
extremely intuitive—tuning in to channels of information inaccessible to
most of the world.

For boys, enhanced spatial reasoning takes the form of creating
maps in their heads of every place they've ever been, fascination with
Legos™, excelling at geometry and physics, taking things apart to see
what makes them work, and facility with computers. For girls, it may
involve extraordinary memory for details, aptitude for reading facial
expressions and body language, the ability to tell what something is
when they can only see a part of it (visual closure), and the gift of deep
awareness and understanding of others. Both genders show facility with
puzzles, mazes, and numbers.

There are probably a number of different subtypes of VSLs, each of
which differs from the others in some fundamental ways. However,
I want to concentrate on their similarities. Perhaps it's a mistake to
lump them all together, but there are many ways to divide up the pie of
human abilities, and I fear that those who have made painstaking
attempts at differentiation have inadvertently made the job of teaching
more complex than it need be. Basically, I've come across two distinct

groups of gifted VSLs: *high spatial, high sequential* and *high spatial, low sequential.* The exceptionally gifted have highly developed visual-spatial **and** auditory-sequential abilities. It is interesting to note that they tend to be ambidextrous as well (indicating strong development of both hemispheres). The children who are brighter than they appear at school often have highly developed visual-spatial abilities, but poor auditory-sequential abilities.

High spatial, high sequential

G is a happy child, nearly always wearing a smile! He is friendly and outgoing after a brief acquaintance time. He is eager to please and tends to be compliant with authority. He is a quick learner, he readily learns new concepts and grows weary of repetitious learning activities; because of his compliant nature, it appears that he is enjoying the process when actually he is daydreaming or just "putting up." He enjoys helping others learn, but grows weary of being the "buddy" to slower learners in the classroom.

Exceptionally gifted VSLs can learn by auditory-sequential methods, but learning that way often feels boring. They prefer to learn all at once, in great intuitive leaps, where they see the pattern, and everything fits together for them into a coherent whole.

The exceptionally gifted child grasps abstract material by finding the underlying pattern. Once that pattern is understood, the child knows the concept behind the material and further practice is unnecessary. In fact, the whole is comprehended so quickly and thoroughly, the child cannot break it down into component parts to show the steps used to build the concept. ... Many exceptionally gifted children learn in a non-linear manner in which they take in large amounts of information and integrate it into an underlying big picture. (Lovecky, 1994a, pp. 117, 119)

They lead with the spatial system, and if they can't get the concept that way, they will resort secondarily to more tedious, sequential processes. Learning in a step-by-step fashion seems painfully slow in comparison to grasping an entire idea all at once—seeing it and understanding it completely in a lightning flash. (Ron Davis believes that nonverbal thought may be thousands of times faster than verbal conceptualization.) Because they integrate information well between the two hemispheres, highly gifted individuals usually can translate their pictures into words and explain how they got there. They rebel against drill and repetition, because they don't learn from these processes. Once they see it in their mind's eye, there's a permanent change in awareness and understanding that is not improvable by practice. While some students need many examples and much directed experience in order for a concept to sink in, these students get it the first time, and are maddened by the slow pace of instruction in the classroom and the seemingly needless (from their perspective) repetition of information.

Unfortunately, there are teachers who feel that it is good for gifted students to sit and wait for students who are struggling to learn. This is supposed to build character and prepare them to adapt to the "real world," which can be boring sometimes. However, this can actually foster bad habits of underachievement and inattention, as well as undermine motivation to learn.

It makes more sense to give these students difficult enough material so that they, too, have to struggle to learn. As Carol Morreale of the Lake Forest School District in Illinois says, "No student should be deprived of the right to struggle." It is only through working hard to master a sufficiently challenging skill or concept that true learning occurs and children learn the value of hard work. This is the kind of practice that really pays off. If the work is too easy, students become afraid that they can't handle the more challenging work as they get older, and they shy away from it because they haven't had much practice exerting effort to learn.

> Many argue that the real world demands exceptionally gifted children to learn to meet deadlines, do tasks others assign [etc.]... They argue that it does a disservice to gifted children to change task demands... However,... only by understanding their own thinking styles and learning how to use their minds can they ever harness that great mental energy. It is those who are forced at too young an age into others' molds who spend the rest of their lives rebelling or so crushed by the pressure of the tiny box that they never accomplish anything. (Lovecky, 1992, p. 3)

Dee Lovecky's warning about what happens when exceptionally gifted children are "forced at too young an age into others' molds" needs to be heeded. I have counseled many exceptionally gifted VSLs who turned off their innate way of knowing in order to fit in better with the mainstream. Some lost all interest in learning, underachieved, and eventually dropped out of school. Some forfeited their strong suit and became rigid auditory-sequential learners, allowing their visual-spatial abilities to atrophy. Some faced a lifelong battle between their artist and their logician. Some could not control their hungry minds, and ended up on medication. And some had periodic meltdowns because they could not force themselves to concentrate on work that was too easy. All of them surrendered a vital part of themselves that was deemed unacceptable, and suffered for it.

She has talked about seeing "pictures" in her mind. We think she has close to a photographic memory, although she seems less like this since being in first grade... She was very enthusiastic to enter first grade, within 3 weeks was bored, eventually seems to have "dumbed down."

J told me she does logic problems when she needs a break from all the schoolwork because she finds it relaxing and it "rests her brain." How could she feel it rests her brain when most people would have to stretch their thinking skills while solving multiple step deductive reasoning problems; hence, the name "brain teasers." But to J, she finds a natural sense of relaxation and a rest from the lower level brain function that her schoolwork forces her to use. It is too hard for J not to work on material that is too hard... It is imperative that J have the opportunity to work on thought provoking material because her emotional stability depends on it.

High spatial, low sequential

The other type of visual-spatial learner, high in spatial abilities and low in sequential abilities, poses an even greater challenge to educators. Reading, writing, spelling and calculating—the basic curriculum of elementary school—may be difficult for them to master. Children who struggle with the "3 R's" are not perceived as very bright and often feel dumb. It helps them to know that VSLs usually get smarter as they get older, and that their time will come.

My husband is 43 years old and truly never knew his learning style had a name to it, until my daughter (age 7) was recently tested through the school district and found to be a visual/spatial learner. He is a Dental Technician (creates porcelain crowns/bridges) and one of the best known by dentists in our area for producing high quality/detailed teeth. He was considered a slow learner at school, until approximately the 4ᵗʰ grade, when his testing showed him in the 99% for math/science.

Instead of learning step-by-step, these children are whole-part learners, who need to see the big picture first in order to learn. They can't hold too many details in short-term memory. They get confused if they don't see how these details relate to each other or to previous learning. They get lost if they can't make a picture in their minds. They need an outline of that picture first—a structure—into which they can paint the details.

> I find that for me, the way to come to understand something new is to
> perceive it more and more clearly. There comes a point when structures
> become obvious, and only then, I will be able to start articulating the new
> concept.

For some VSLs, audition itself is weak. Others may have acute hearing, but impaired listening skills or poor auditory short-term memory.
When I was on the faculty of the University of Denver, I worked with a
student whose dissertation was on deaf and hearing-impaired gifted
students in a residential center. I noted that the writing errors made by
bright deaf students were very much like those made by the visual-
spatial underachievers I had worked with—particularly underachievers
with a history of chronic ear infections in early childhood.

They often left out endings of words and soft sounds (e.g., the "d" in
"gardener") because they couldn't hear those sounds. They mixed up
small words, like "a" and "an," "the" and "they." They confused singular
and plural. Tenses were not always correct. Extremely creative ideas
might be buried in poor grammar, syntax, punctuation, spelling, and
organization. For VSLs with auditory issues, content needs to be graded
separately from format, so that the student's self-esteem as a writer isn't
crushed due to mechanical difficulties.

Children who have extreme discrepancies between right- and left-
hemispheric functions are twice exceptional—both gifted and learning
disabled. The only way to determine if a child is learning disabled is to
obtain a comprehensive evaluation. If the child seems to have unusual
strengths, the examiner needs to be knowledgeable about both
giftedness and learning disabilities, as the profiles of these individuals
are difficult to interpret. Even minor impairment of the left hemisphere
can lead to writing difficulties in a right-handed child, since the left
hemisphere controls the motor planning of the right hand and arm.
Birth trauma, such as excessively long labor, a cord wrapped around
part of the body, or too much pitocin during the delivery, may result in
fine motor delays. (More on this topic in Chapter 9.)

The most difficult children to identify are visual-spatial learners with
visual processing issues. These children don't test as high as expected
on visual-spatial tasks. Some of them are very mechanically inclined,
love Legos™, and are crazy about math, but they can't do jigsaw puzzles
and they rotate block designs.

> Our daughter got only a 106 on the first IQ test that she was given. She
> "flunked" 3 of the block activity test sections, because she reversed all of
> the block designs, and it wasn't until after the test that the tester realized
> what she had done! The tester thought my daughter was playing a game
> with her, transforming the designs as she had done. She recommended

retesting her at a later date, and predicted that our daughter would score above 135. Six months later, she was given the WISC test, and got a 150 IQ score, having hit the ceiling on the spatial parts of the test!

VSLs with visual processing issues do well with simple mazes, but when the mazes get too visually complex, they get lost. They may be able to read books with large print, but not ones with small print. They may play an instrument beautifully by ear, while being unable to read music. It's extremely difficult for a child with a visual-spatial learning style to have his or her major modality of learning blocked. Vision therapy can make a tremendous difference in the success of these children. (More information on vision therapy can be found in Chapter 9.)

He was first identified as a "visual" learner...in 1st grade. After the initial testing, they used a program that presented 8-10 vocabulary words with visual cues. After about 10 minutes of studying the words with the cues, he then studied them absent the cues and read them in a story. He has never forgotten the words that he learned in those first 10 minutes, although he will often read the word as a synonym: ...small instead of little.

The classroom can become VSL-friendly by using visual aids and visual cues. Overhead projectors need to be a staple in every classroom, used frequently. Videos, computers, demonstrations, hands-on experiences, all bring the material to life for the visually oriented learner. Visualization is a major facet of the learning process for these children, so they need to be guided to see with their mind's eye. Paint vivid pictures with words. Have them close their eyes and create images in their minds and then share their pictures with the entire class or with a partner.

VSLs who struggle with school can only function well with certain teachers, in certain subject areas, with certain instructional methods. A good match for them is a visual-spatial teacher, who thinks the way they think (that is, if the teacher has accepted and honors his or her own learning style). Teacher selection according to learning style can produce more successful students. Another good match is a highly flexible teacher who appreciates students' different learning styles and tries to adapt the curriculum and methods to the diversity of students. However, all teachers can learn methods that enable VSLs to be more successful in their classrooms.

Learning styles of teachers

Auditory-sequential teachers are likely to reach auditory-sequential students more effectively than VSLs. But if you're aware that you may be missing your visual-spatial students, you can easily reach the entire class with a few basic modifications in instructional strategies. Such modifications as the use of an overhead projector and manipulatives do not interfere with the learning of auditory-sequential students. All students appreciate visuals and hands-on learning, and find instruction more exciting with these enhancements. If you teach elementary school, you're probably incorporating many of the methods already. Chapters 6 and 13 were designed specifically for teachers. The next chapter offers instructional tips for each of 27 characteristics of VSLs. Chapter 13 covers different subject areas, such as reading, writing, spelling, and mathematics, and offers a general set of guidelines for teaching VSLs.

If you're a visual-spatial teacher, you'll recognize your own learning style throughout the pages in this book. Most likely you're already working effectively with auditory-sequential learners because that's how you were taught to teach in your teacher-training program. Unfortunately, those training programs may have suppressed your own visual-spatial abilities, neglecting them or worse—making you feel ashamed of them. You may have some unlearning to do so that you can appreciate your own learning style. This is essential so that you don't unconsciously suppress these abilities in your students.

When you've been wounded for being different, it's natural to want to protect your children and students from the pain you've experienced. You're more likely to emphasize the skills they need to help them to adapt to the world of the majority. Close your eyes and remember when you were an energetic child, filled with the wonder of the world. How did you learn best? How do you wish teachers would have taught you? What strengths do you wish teachers had recognized and developed in you? The answers to these questions will lead you to be a superb teacher, mentor, homeschool Mom, or role model for your visual-spatial children.

I loved arts and crafts because I could manipulate the space, be creative, and "see" the end results. Math and English I hated with a passion. I couldn't "see" what it was that was being taught.

6

Two Different Food Groups: Which One are YOU?

SEQUENTIAL   SPATIAL

Are you still wondering if you're visual-spatial or auditory-sequential? This chapter should answer that question. The list on the next 2 pages contains 27 sets of somewhat overlapping characteristics that distinguish the two groups. After the list, I discuss each pair separately, incorporate anecdotes about adults and children, and give some suggestions about how to deal with that particular aspect of the VSL profile in the classroom. (*Be prepared. This is a **lonnnngg** chapter! Read it in segments.*)

We talk of people being either right-handed or left-handed, as if they were two separate groups. Actually, there are degrees of handedness, just as there are degrees of hemispheric strength. We all have two halves of our brain, so we all have some competence in both auditory-sequential and visual-spatial realms. As we discussed in Chapter 2, both halves work together, particularly for complex tasks. Therefore, no one will fit every single item in either category.

The highly gifted often fit both sides and many individuals have mixed dominance. There most likely are some visual-sequentials and auditory-spatials as well. So these categories should not be looked at rigidly. Instead, it's more useful to think of the pairs in each column as ends of a continuum. Some items on the visual-spatial side may be extremely true for you, others on the auditory-sequential side may be extremely true, and some may be in the middle, depending on the circumstances.

If you fit more of the auditory-sequential items than the visual-spatial items in the list below, then you're probably more of an auditory-sequential learner. And if more of the visual-spatial items fit, then you're more of a visual-spatial learner. If you relate to about the same number of items in each column, then you're probably a well-balanced learner with strengths in both hemispheres. To learn more about your learning style, please try the quiz at the beginning of the book. To learn more about your VSL students, please read, "The Visual-Spatial Learner in School" (Appendix A). The following list of characteristics would be good to share with students so that they can identify and understand their learning styles. (It's all on one page in Appendix C.) Or, obtain our *Visual-Spatial Identifier* at **www.gifteddevelopment.com.**

Table 6.1

Characteristics Comparison

The Auditory-Sequential Learner	The Visual-Spatial Learner
✇ Thinks primarily in words	✇ Thinks primarily in images
✇ Has auditory strengths	✇ Has visual strengths
✇ Relates well to time	✇ Relates well to space
✇ Is a step-by-step learner	✇ Is a whole-part learner
✇ Learns by trial and error	✇ Learns concepts all at once
✇ Progresses sequentially from easy to difficult material	✇ Learns complex concepts easily; struggles with easy skills
✇ Is an analytical thinker	✇ Is a good synthesizer
✇ Attends well to details	✇ Sees the big picture; may miss details

The Auditory-Sequential Learner	The Visual-Spatial Learner
✤ Follows oral directions well	✤ Reads maps well
✤ Does well at arithmetic	✤ Is better at math reasoning than computation
✤ Learns phonics easily	✤ Learns whole words easily
✤ Can sound out spelling words	✤ Must visualize words to spell them
✤ Can write quickly and neatly	✤ Is much better at keyboarding than handwriting
✤ Is well organized	✤ Creates unique methods of organization
✤ Can show steps of work easily	✤ Arrives at correct solutions intuitively
✤ Excels at rote memorization	✤ Learns best by seeing relationships
✤ Has good auditory short-term memory	✤ Has good long-term visual memory
✤ May need some repetition to reinforce learning	✤ Learns concepts permanently; does not learn by drill and repetition
✤ Learns well from instructions	✤ Develops own methods of problem solving
✤ Learns in spite of emotional reactions	✤ Is very sensitive to teachers' attitudes
✤ Is comfortable with one right answer	✤ Generates unusual solutions to problems
✤ Develops fairly evenly	✤ Develops quite asynchronously (unevenly)
✤ Usually maintains high grades	✤ May have very uneven grades
✤ Enjoys algebra and chemistry	✤ Enjoys geometry and physics
✤ Masters other languages in classes	✤ Masters other languages through immersion
✤ Is academically talented	✤ Is creatively, technologically, mechanically, emotionally or spiritually gifted
✤ Is an early bloomer	✤ Is a late bloomer

Thinking in words vs. images

My husband is an electronic engineer. He read your list and said he was definitely a visual-spatial learner. (In fact, he was quite astounded that anyone would think in "words." I believe "Whoa, that's weird" was his exact comment.)

When you ask M what reading or being read to was like he says it's "like a movie shooting by on the screen really, really fast." He doesn't think in words, it's pictures. Also, if he is reading and does not get a description of the character he gets frustrated and has to come up with his own physical description.

[My grandson and I] started talking in pictures. He became so excited that I was "seeing what was happening," he talked so fast, his face alive, as we exchanged pictures. I wish I could help him find the right place to "learn" now that I see it is a "talent." His "gift" is dormant until someone "sees" with him.

Most people think in words and some theorists even think it is impossible to think without words. But the first language of an increasingly large segment of the population is images. When you think in words, it permits rapid processing of verbal information. You can carry on a fast-paced verbal interchange, get your ideas heard in a lively discussion, field questions easily after a presentation, handle cocktail party conversation, and participate in debate and other verbal contests. All of these are difficult for the person who thinks in pictures. It takes longer to translate pictures into words. In her book, *Thinking in Pictures*, Temple Grandin writes:

> I THINK IN PICTURES. Words are like a second language to me. I translate both spoken and written words into full-color movies, complete with sound, which run like a VCR tape in my head. When somebody speaks to me, his words are instantly translated into pictures. (p. 1)

> To pull information out of my memory, I have to replay the video. Pulling facts up quickly is sometimes difficult, because I have to play bits of different videos until I find the right tape. This takes time. (p. 31)

Temple has observed that those scientists who maintain that language is essential to thought are often highly verbal thinkers with poor visualization skills. "They excel at verbal or sequential thinking activities but are unable to read blueprints."

Imagistic thought is more difficult to evaluate, since the person has more difficulty explaining his or her thought process. But it is important to understand that the emphasis on verbalization and speed in school (like Mad Minutes—*aargh*) prevents us from recognizing the strengths of the visual-spatial child. To reach students who think in images, encourage them to create pictures in their mind, give them time to think, and give them even more time to turn their pictures into words.

> Words are *really* difficult, even with a large vocabulary.... I wind up having to "talk around" concepts, and the "talking around" gets me distracted from the concepts momentarily and then I get lost and forget details (does this sound familiar? :)) that I could "see" when I was seeing the concept. I really try to get words to point to/from an existing concept, but that is not an easy thing to do. It's easy to overfocus on the words temporarily, and get lost in their structure, and then come back to the concept, and bounce back and forth and get frustrated and then wind up with a spiky picture of the concept where maybe it was originally a round picture but the pieces got missing when I tried to convey it.

Auditory vs. visual strengths

> G is highly visual. He often speaks of the movies he makes in his head while reading and writing. He readily visualizes spelling words and math story problems. He has a vivid memory with many details.

> I'm a college student and a visual-spatial learner... it makes lecture classes pretty pointless, but since I go to a large university, that's what I get.

> My 7-year-old son is, I believe, a v.s. learner. He has difficulty hearing in a crowd. I often touch his arm when I need him to listen to me.... If anything was lost in our home or misplaced we asked S and he always knew where everything was.

> I don't even bother learning the stuff for exams until a week or so before them, and then I go through the books and notes and make diagrams and flow charts and pictures of it all, and then it makes sense and I know it and that's that. When I listen to lectures, it can be interesting and all, but I usually absorb very little and have a hard time stringing all of the bits of information together unless the lecturer is trying hard to present things on lots of different levels (e.g., drawing the reactions out in colored chalk... I didn't understand gene rearrangement when I only

heard about it in a lecture, but it made sense instantly when my biology professor did a demonstration).

We all know that some learners are stronger auditorally, while others are stronger visually. Auditory learners can take in copious amounts of information from a lecture. Visual learners have an easier time when the teacher uses visual aids, like overhead projectors, computers, diagrams, demonstrations, manipulatives, or draws pictures of the concepts on the chalkboard. VSLs remember what they see and forget what they hear.

People are often misled into thinking that if a child is musical, then she must be an auditory-sequential learner. However, lots of VSLs are musical, as music appears to be processed primarily in the right hemisphere. In fact, visual-spatials often learn better when information is set to music. Many VSLs appear incapable of memorization in school but can remember the lyrics to countless songs. Sara writes:

> The only auditory thing I am good with is learning song lyrics. I can hear a song once or twice and know a lot of its lyrics, but there would be no way I could sing you back the whole melody unless all of it had words. I zero in on the words the person is singing and hear them and as I hear each word I see it in my head because to me that is what a word is... a sound that lets me "read" the word in my mind's eye. Words don't seem to have meaning to me unless I can "see" them; that's why reading the book works for me so much better than hearing the lecture. Normally in a lecture I'm not able to pay attention intently enough to "translate" all of what the professor is saying into something I can read in my head, but something about the music in songs cements the words in place.

Awareness of time vs. space

Time is the quintessential attribute of the left brain. All of the functions of this hemisphere proceed temporally. (Shlain, 1998, p. 220)

Weaknesses: a disregard of time (clock, calendar and timetable time) which is, of course, exasperating for schools, though perhaps it may also have a plus side in that there can be an appreciation of history and the future on a large scale—as a whole. The point being that time (everyday clock time) is one-dimensional so, like reading and writing, can be difficult for the 3-dimensional thinker to come to terms with. (Sue Parkinson, Director, Arts Dyslexia Trust, London, 1997)

The auditory-sequential thinker is profoundly influenced by time and is less aware of space; the spatial thinker is preoccupied with space at the expense of time. Time is important in school—being on time, taking timed tests, turning in work on time, finishing activities in a timely fashion, and moving on to new activities in a set schedule. This time-based managerial system is comfortable for auditory-sequential learners. But all of this seems quite foreign to VSLs. They often lack any concept of time. They may be late for school, behind in their work, or reluctant to move on from one activity to another. They freak out during timed tests. Time seems to be their worst enemy.

My 8-year-old son fits your visual-spatial profile. He remembers *where* he was when something happened, but has no concept of *when* it happened (if he remembers at all!) This is almost funny. He has no idea whether something happened weeks or years ago, but can tell you where everyone was seated at the time.

At home, the threat of being timed creates more dread than the threat of being grounded.

No concept of the passage of time: T can spend 20 minutes tying a shoe, or chew a mouthful of food, very slowly, 50 or 60 times. He can hurry, if it's to do something with a friend, but this is extremely rare.

Both of my children really require time to delve deeply into a subject. The typical school day, with interruptions every 45 minutes, annoys them. They need time to ponder, to consider, to think, to visualize, to experience. By the time they settle into a subject and begin to explore, the traditional school structure demands that they disengage.

My sense of time is atrocious. ... I can be really slow at the initial picking up and processing of information (particularly if I am expected to communicate at the same time), but when it's in, it's in.

On the other hand, VSLs have extraordinary awareness of where they are in space, or how the elements of design fit together in space. They are natural artists and map-makers, love puzzles and mazes, build with anything available, see the underlying structure of things, understand perspective, and recognize visual patterns. It is important to value these spatial skills as much as temporal ones, and to provide opportunities for their development in the classroom.

Step-by-step vs. whole-part

I've found he does best when he can learn wholistically about a subject. For instance we'll

1) watch a dinosaur video,
2) read aloud about dinosaurs,
3) make a dino model,
4) and then he'll draw and write a dino story.

When we follow this procedure he learns a tremendous amount with great recall.

But mostly, what strikes me as different is that she seems to learn things in chunks or moments instead of steps.

I've also got a lot of problems with sequential tasks, and with putting steps and things in order (note that this post was written completely out of order :)) ...Even the thought of alphabetizing brings to mind barely concealed frustration.

Auditory-sequential learners often learn best when a task is broken down into a series of small steps. Mastery of a skill takes place one step at a time, with sufficient practice and reinforcement. VSLs learn best if they understand the goal (which means seeing the whole picture in their minds) and then attach the parts in the right places. If you're visual-spatial, and I said to you, "First do this, then that, then this…" without telling you the point of the instructions, you would probably give me a blank look and be unable to follow me. You would quickly run out of short-term memory in which to store the independent steps, and become hopelessly lost. However, if you can form a picture of the desti-nation (e.g., "This is where we are going…"), you can handle lots more information—it visually becomes part of your map.

Once VSLs see how the whole system fits together, they seem to teach themselves. This is quite evident with computers. See if this scenario sounds familiar. You just got a new computer in the classroom. You've been struggling to follow the "user-friendly" directions (often written by VSLs for auditory-sequentials; they never quite get how the rest of us learn) and you just can't get it to do what you want it to. This kid walks up to the computer, says, "Here, let me help you," and in two minutes the machine responds as if by magic. You ask, "How did you know what to do?" He (it's usually a he) gives you a blank look, shrugs his shoulders, and says, "I dunno." It's as if he can place himself right *inside* of the computer and see how all the parts inter-relate, while you are outside the beige box, trying to follow step-by-step directions, without any clear understanding of how the machine is processing the information.

Our computer is another field he loves to tinker in. We never know what we may find staring at us when we boot up. When I ask him how he knows how to do these things, his reply is "I just know, no one has taught me."

Trial and error vs. all-at-once

He learned by observation rather than by trial and error. While his gross motor skills were not advanced, N mastered skills the first time he tried them.

He learns things all at once, and finds it next to impossible to break a process into steps to explain it.

From the time they're toddlers, sequential learners teach themselves new skills by trial and error. They take their first step, fall down, pick themselves up, try again, fall down, pick themselves up, try again, fall down, until they master walking. Some VSLs never take their first step. One day, much to their parents' surprise, they just break into a run. When sequential children teach themselves to speak, there's a fairly predictable sequence to their mastery of communication. After the babbling stage, they communicate with one word, then two-word strings, gradually mastering longer and more complex clauses. Not so with some visual-spatial children. They seem to understand everything, but may not speak until they've mastered the entire language. One child's first words were, "Charlie, will you please pass the salt?"

A six-year-old girl who came to the Center for assessment refused to ride her two-wheeler. Her parents tried everything they could think of, even bribery, but nothing worked. For six months, she watched all the other children in the neighborhood riding their bikes, and finally she got on her bike and rode perfectly. She had practiced all the balancing in her head. Several years later, we had a six-year-old boy who did the same thing, but he didn't practice braking. His first time out, he hit a tree!

My "visualness" made it possible for me to "mentally practice" physical things... I just visualized doing them. I visualized different positions on the bike, for example, and if the visualized me fell off, I knew I would in real life too if I tried that position.

At age 5, we bought her a two-wheeler bike for her fifth birthday. She had never ridden a bike without training wheels. She wouldn't ride it. I figured she was afraid. Then one day, I looked out the window and there she was riding up and down the driveway, by herself. (Without any of us knowing, she had gone to the neighbors to borrow knee and elbow pads and was wearing them.)

At one time I had a pilot in my counseling practice. When he was in flight training, he would sit in his overstuffed armchair after each lesson, and imagine himself in the plane, re-experiencing the lesson.

His flight instructor said that he learned twice as fast as any other student he had had. That's because he had twice as much flying time— only half of which was in the air!

Not all VSLs have such dramatic stories, but they all have extra-ordinary capacity to learn from observation. Once they create a picture of it in their minds, it's theirs—permanently. They perceive the inter-relatedness of the parts of any situation. Their learning occurs in an all-or-none fashion. They are most likely to experience the "Aha!" phenomenon, when all of a sudden they "get it." You can watch the light bulb go on.

> With that "light bulb" comparison, I'm thinking, "Yes! Exactly!" I can look slow, but every piece of information comes into me, I don't really miss anything (even if I seem to in the short term), and then it all connects together and once I can see the connections ("light bulb" right there) it's all there, permanently.

This type of learning does not take place through a series of steps. If VSLs are asked to retrace the steps of the learning process, they usually cannot. Introverted VSLs have the greatest capacity to practice physical skills mentally, because mental rehearsal is characteristic of an introvert. (More on introversion in Chapter 10.) Let these children observe first before attempting new skills, and allow time for the "Aha!" to happen.

From easy to hard vs. easy is hard and hard is easy

> I ALWAYS struggle on the EASIEST material in my classes and I'm always one of the first students to understand the most complicated material. For example, on practice SAT tests I consistently got the "easy" analogies wrong while usually getting most of the medium and hard correct. I often get the easiest questions incorrect on tests and the hardest correct.

> I've always been somebody who could do hard things all at once (like just knowing how to do leathercraft with decorative beading – no intermediate steps, just jump into the hard one).

> She does not want to learn the basics. These are all very boring. Her interest is captured when the information is more complex. She can often go from the complex backwards to "basics" but turns off when going from basics to complex. She gets very frustrated when she discovers she has to learn basic skills first.

The scope and sequence of education is set up on the supposition that all children progress in their learning from easy to difficult. It's a strongly held conviction that knowledge is accumulated, one step at a time, in a fairly predictable order, with complex concepts building on the foundation of simpler ones. This is a logical assumption, and it fits nicely with the learning pattern of auditory-sequential learners, who make up the majority of students. However, we have dozens of cases on file at the Gifted Development Center of children who consistently fail the easy, sequential material, but are highly successful when the work becomes sufficiently challenging. Although I had seen this phenomenon for years in my clinical practice, the first time I encountered it in print was in Tom West's book, *In the Mind's Eye*. Apparently, some of the most creative physicists, mathematicians, statesmen and poets were similarly afflicted. For them, complex was simple and easy was hard:

> Some people are so deeply accustomed to a linear view of intelligence and potential that they find it impossible to believe that certain persons may find advanced subject matter quite easy while they find some elementary subject matter quite difficult. Yet, among some of the most brilliant and creative minds, this general pattern is precisely what we do find. (West, 1991, p. 8)

This confusing aspect of visual-spatial processing can be best understood if one realizes that what our society considers "easy" is usually sequential, and what it considers "hard" depends on the ability to coordinate many complex variables simultaneously. Therefore, individuals who excel at sequencing will master simple sequences with ease, but may have difficulty visualizing how all the parts work together. The opposite is true of individuals who are sequentially impaired, but who visualize complex systems with no difficulty.

> When I was doing the "advanced math" I thought it was a game. When I do "simple math" I tend to get confused, go slowly, and get things mixed up if I don't watch myself (I tend to opt for calculators). When I was little, infinity was "fun." Arithmetic was occasionally interesting (when presented right) but often more like painful. So I would say (half-jokingly) that most people's ideas of "easy" and "difficult" are simply reversed :)

The solution is to give gifted VSLs advanced work, even if they haven't mastered the easier material. This may sound illogical, but it works. I remember tutoring my 9-year-old niece, Arlene, in mathematics. She couldn't remember her addition facts, her subtraction facts, her multiplication facts or her division facts. However, I had no trouble teaching her fractions, because I could show her a pie chart and she could visualize the pieces. Soon she was adding, subtracting and multiplying fractions, even when she was unable to do so with whole numbers.

High intelligence plays an important role here. The gifted child has advanced abstract reasoning skills that may not be accessible in rote, sequential tasks. Complex tasks depend more on abstract reasoning, so the bright student has a better chance of being successful when the work gets complicated than when it is easy. Experts find that gifted children with learning disabilities, who have AD/HD, or who are under-achieving (failing), are more successful when they are accelerated than when they're forced to master grade level work before they can proceed to "harder" work. (Confused? Re-read Chapter 2!)

Even though it may seem that the difficult concepts are "built" on the easier ones, *the spatial learner often grasps simple concepts only in the context of more complex ones.* For example, I once had a bright fourth grader who had never learned his multiplication facts. I gave him a sheet of difficult number patterns to solve, many of which required multiplication for their solution. He taught himself to multiply in one afternoon so that he could solve the problems. (This idea works! Try it.)

Analysis vs. synthesis

The right hemisphere integrates feelings, recognizes images, and appreciates music. It contributes a field awareness to consciousness, synthesizing multiple converging determinants so that the mind can grasp the senses' input *all-at-once.* (Shlain, 1998, p. 18)

The analytic, left hemisphere approach has been very successful with problems amenable to simplification—the basis, really, of the success of Western science over several centuries. However, we are coming to realize that there is another whole class of complex, large-system problems that cannot be split into pieces and simplified in this traditional way. Some things must be considered all together and at the same time, with all parts simultaneously represented; what is important is the continuous interaction of all parts with each other and with the whole. ...it happens that simultaneous consideration of all aspects of a complex system seems to be the distinctive visual-spatial mode of operation. (West, 1996, p. 9)

The student who excels at analysis is good at comparing and contrasting individual components of a whole. That process comes in handy in English literature classes, social studies, and some science courses. Synthesis can mean taking all the parts and fitting them together in a traditional manner, such as synthesizing all the research on a given topic into a report. Or it can mean taking the parts and creating something original. Like designing a vehicle with Legos™ without using a model. The second kind of synthesizing ability is great in Odyssey of the Mind, in the advertising field, in creating new computer programs, or in a research and development team. It seems to be less useful in school than in some professions in adult life, so it tends to receive less emphasis than analytical skills. However, thematic units, interdisciplinary studies, creating new ideas and products, formulating hypotheses, discovery learning, inquiry training, constructivist approaches, and problem-based learning all give students practice in synthesizing.

At one time, a counselor I was seeing listened to me describe a certain situation, and commented: "Your approach to problem solving is like taking a whole page of mathematical equations, and instead of approaching them one line at a time, you concentrate on the entire page until the whole equation comes together simultaneously." He said this with some exasperation, because he was a former engineer.

My intellectual way is extremely synthetical, in the meaning of Hegel—thesis and antithesis lead to a synthesis. I try to find out what connects several things and then collapse it into a more general rule. Maybe other VSLs also do this—they would be very good "inductivists" then.

Details vs. big picture

Looking at the trees would cause me to miss the forest. It's from the point of view of the whole that details can be seen in a meaningful way.

I was struck by the concept that visual-spatial learners grasp the big picture and then go back to the details. That's exactly true. I have so many instances of sitting in class or reading some material that just seemed to be a bunch of unrelated facts and details and one day a key concept instantly unified them all and it made sense. At that point it was possible to go back and review the details and comprehend the many implications of them in the big picture.

M is highly visual with a vivid imagination. His ability to see the whole picture and cut through the details to see the fundamental concept is amazing.

Very gifted socially, A can see the big picture in another kid's behavior. Understands that there may be underlying reasons for a kid acting out in class. Very much the defender of underdogs, will take on teachers and call them on inappropriate treatment of other kids. This began by third grade.

Some people naturally miss the forest for the trees, while others see the forest and miss the trees. Detail-oriented auditory-sequential learners may be very good at doing all the assigned work, and yet fail to grasp the implications of what they're learning. Visual-spatial children often grasp the big picture and the significance of what they're learning, but mess up on the details, such as spelling, punctuation, misreading the addition and subtraction signs, forgetting to answer all the parts of the question. They know far more than they show in class because of these kinds of errors. They do poorly on the mechanics, but they seem to preserve the basic concepts in long-term memory. In written assignments, it's important to grade their ideas separately from their handwriting, spelling, grammar and punctuation. In mathematics, note if they understood the concept, but read a sign wrong or calculated incorrectly. Allow them to retest until they demonstrate mastery.

In order for visual-spatials to learn, they must visualize how the parts are related to the whole. If the learning is doled out in small increments, they don't understand what's going on. They may ask a great number of questions because they can't grasp the meaning of an isolated fact or activity until they've grasped the whole structure. Once they get the big picture, they can fill in the details.

Clearly, the predominant contemporary world view tends to favor the specific and the particular—the world view of the specialist, who may have difficulty seeing the whole. In contrast, most of the individuals [described in *In the Mind's Eye*] seem to have held a world view preoccupied with the general and the whole, although they may have occasionally muddled some of the parts. (West, 1991, p. 15)

Oral directions vs. maps

One of M's remarkable gifts is that he carries a map in his head of the entire world. He has only to travel a route once and he knows the entire thing perfectly. He could walk a bus route after riding it once. He never gets lost. Once, when he was about six or seven, we were in St. Louis, where my husband grew up; my husband got lost by getting turned around on the freeway. M kept insisting he knew how to get us back, and my husband wouldn't listen until we were so lost he decided he had nothing to lose. M told him how to turn, which exits to take, and backtracked us all the way back to the original spot.

Last summer I took him to England and Ireland, and M is the one who repeatedly kept us all from getting lost on the subway or in the confusing labyrinth of London streets, even our own little neighborhood. My mother, who was sure M couldn't always be right, resisted at first and he just shrugged. "You'll see," he said, following behind us as we headed the wrong way, shaking his head. When we got to the end of the street and were wrong, he said, "Now can we go my way?" And of course he was right. That map of the world is mighty handy to have around.

If I were going to give you directions to my house, which is up in the mountains, would you prefer that I tell you where to turn left and right and which landmarks to look for, or would you rather I drew you a map? Auditory-sequential learners are better at noticing landmarks and following left and right directions than they are at reading maps or having a sense of North, South, East and West. (I've been known to read maps upside down and get totally lost!)

VSLs, on the other hand, excel in reading maps:

Don't give a lecture that includes all the information I need in the auditory portion, but only part of it in the visual portion. I can't learn that way (and I'm not sure why). This is a big problem when people are trying to give me directions.

Speaking of which, if you must give spoken directions, go slowly (so I can visualize the route), be willing to repeat (if I miss something while I'm still visualizing the previous thing), and include map directions (north, south, etc.). Give up on landmarks, I'm never going to get them.

This vignette also reveals why visual-spatial learners have difficulty understanding oral directions in the classroom. They can't understand and retain what the teacher is saying unless they can visualize it.

Visualization is the key to their learning. Auditory-sequential children have no difficulty following multi-step oral directions. While their visualization skills may be weak, they have excellent listening skills. Encourage VSLs in the class to visualize and assist them in doing so by using more visual presentations and examples.

Computation vs. math reasoning

A couple of traits suited me so completely that I was saying, "yes"... the "math reasoning exceeds computational skills" was why I hated my calculus class. I would get all of the fancy, hard math 100% right and understand why, but I wouldn't do that great on the tests because I would lose points for "20 - 20 = (-40)" or "3X + 4x= 12X."

He scores very highly in math reasoning tests, but still can't seem to remember his multiplication tables.

Arithmetic was hard (and was also my lowest score when I was tested – the testers asked my parents if I was uninterested in math, and they said "Oh no, she's interested in positive and negative infinities and base 6 numbers and stuff!" :) and I was, and was able in those things, just not so much in arithmetic.)

Auditory-sequential learners excel in arithmetic and algebra, and they may do brilliantly on timed calculation tests. But higher-level mathematics, such as geometry (except for deductive Euclidean proofs), trigonometry, calculus and integral functions, depend on visualization skills. The A-students in elementary arithmetic may have difficulty with geometry, and opt out of more advanced math courses. VSLs have the opposite pattern. They have a terrible time memorizing their addition and multiplication facts. (See Chapter 13 for some secrets about how to get VSLs to learn their math facts in under 2 weeks.) They do poorly on timed math tests, because it takes longer to translate their pictures into numbers. Due to these early defeating experiences, they often think of themselves as "dumb" in math. It comes as a great shock to them when they get to geometry and discover that they're actually mathematically talented. I'm fond of telling the arithmetically downtrodden that anything that begins with an "a" isn't "real" math, and when they get to the "good stuff," they're going to be amazed at how well they do. (Some VSLs begin to do well in algebra, if they have an excellent algebra teacher.)

School is painful. I have had all kinds of problems. I just discovered my visual-spatial abilities this year in geometry. I was coming up with answers easily that a lot of other students were having trouble with. I was wondering why they were having trouble, when it was really obvious to me. I thought everyone else thought like me.

We need to infuse more geometry into the math curriculum throughout elementary grades, as is done in Russia and Japan. And we should allow children who cannot master calculation to take more complex math with the use of calculators. You will be shocked at how many mathephobics (math-fearers) turn into matheholics (math-lovers).

Visual-spatial learners are natural mathematicians. They often have a love affair with numbers from the time they are very young. Some have been known to count everything in sight. Sir Francis Galton was a case in point. He used to count the nodding heads at the theater as a measure of how entertaining the program was. And Isaac Asimov used to count the holes in ceiling tiles when he was bored.

My son counts how many dishes he has to wash or dry! He counts everything.

I count everything! When my children were babies, without meaning to, I counted the clicks on the baby swing. I can tell you what time it is in the middle of the night if there is a grandfather clock, because I count the chimes, even in my sleep.

My children counted all of the station wagons they saw for days after we bought one for our family. When I was little and my family went on vacation, I would always count things on the trip when looking out the car window (how many trailers we passed, how many Corvettes I saw, how many different state license plates I saw, dead animals on the side of the highway). I still "count" things. When I am driving I often find myself counting in my mind how many Saabs or other types of cars we pass (I own a Saab). I never understood "why" I counted, I just did it.

Phonics vs. sight words

I am a strong sequential learner. My son, J, read at age 4—I easily taught him phonics (I guess since we're both sequential learners, it was a natural, seemingly straightforward process and he was exceptionally motivated and excited by reading.)

She never learned phonetic reading, and memorizes whole words as patterns, which makes her a great speller on weekly spelling tests, but overall poor to mediocre on day to day spelling in writing assignments.

As she got older her reading became memorization. She did not like phonics and had extensive phonics tutoring, but still relied on sight reading. Her decoding is still weak.

Phonemic awareness (the isolation of individual speech sounds) is all the rage now in teaching reading. And it is certainly true that children with excellent phonemic awareness become excellent readers. However, Jerre Levy indicates that only the left hemisphere has the capacity for phonics. The right side of the brain can understand semantics—the meaning of either written or spoken words—but it cannot recognize tense or syntax. Jerre warns against assuming that a good educational method is good for every child. "Is whole word better or is phonics better? For most children phonics is better, but for some children whole word is better. There is no ideal method because there is no ideal brain. Diversity is probably what makes a social species possible."

Auditory-sequential learners master phonics quite easily. They can analyze a word into various phonemes and then put the phonemes together to make words. But a child who has had numerous ear infections may not have sufficient auditory discrimination to be able to hear the subtle differences in phonemes. And if the child is non-sequential, it is difficult to remember how to combine the phonemes in the correct order. Sight words, particularly those that represent nouns and verbs, are meaningful units that can be visualized. They are often more accessible to VSLs than phonemic analysis.

Phonics instruction does not need to be eliminated altogether, but sight vocabulary needs to be built first. Then whole words or syllables can be compared and the pattern recognition capacities of the visual-spatial learner can be brought to bear. In fact, VSLs often read and spell better in languages that are entirely phonetic, such as Spanish. Once they see a pattern, it applies in all cases. But English is a nightmare to learn, because it's composed of words from so many different languages that consistency is the exception rather than the rule. The memorization of the endless exceptions is what often makes VSLs such poor readers and spellers.

Teaching. What an experience! Rewarding and stressful, but I love it. I teach special needs students. ... When one of my second grade students failed to improve at all in his reading after over a year in my program, I was frustrated and worried. What else was there for me to do? ... I turned to the reading specialists and special education ... I was disappointed to learn that they recommended more phonics training. Not that I was against the use of phonics, far from it; I taught those skills regularly and intensely. My disappointment came from the fact that they were recommending something that had not worked at all for my student. (Ringle, Miller, & Anderson, 2000, pp. 6-7)

Sounding out vs. visualizing spelling words

Mostly school was no problem. Spelling was a problem. I was terrible at spelling. There are no visual patterns to grab hold of and no logic there to derive the correct answer from... I have always struggled with spelling and always will.

I can't spell worth anything. I have horrible spelling. Never could spell.

Another trait that suited me completely was "must visualize words in order to spell them." I'm an excellent speller, but I can't sound out words to save myself. I see them and then I write them... even when I type, there are certain patterns that my fingers make on the keys to make each word. I don't spell them out letter by letter; I sort of string them together in chunks.

I am very grateful for spell check. It has gotten me through a lot of papers in college. I am not a very good speller. I have been like this all my life.

In reading over a hundred email messages from VSLs in the last year or so, I've come to the conclusion that most visual-spatial learners are bright people who can't spell. I sure have corrected a lot of spelling errors in the anecdotes in this book. Even people who think they are great spellers misspelled several words in their messages!

Contrary to your report, I've *definately* been a very good speller *every* since I started reading at age 4.

But some VSLs are excellent spellers. They tend to have photographic memories. They remember everything they see; however, they may not be able to sound out words they've never seen in print. We once tested a six-year-old girl who scored 156 (highly gifted range) on the Spelling section of the *Wide Range Achievement Test*. She spelled perfectly every word she had seen, but when she tried to spell words she hadn't seen, the words were completely undecipherable. There was no relation between the letters she wrote and the sounds in the word.

B is an excellent speller for all words that he sees in print, but he is not a phonetic speller.

Sounding out words is easy if you have good auditory-sequential skills. Spelling ability is correlated with the Digit Span subtest, which assesses a person's ability to recite strings of random numbers forward or backward. Digit Span measures auditory-sequential short-term memory for non-meaningful material, so spelling must be an auditory-sequential skill. And since it involves "non-meaningful" material, it's not easily accessible to the right hemisphere, which only processes units of meaning.

However, it's possible to make spelling both visual and meaningful. Have visual-spatial Zach visualize the word and then make a picture out of it—the sillier the better. Silly pictures are easier for the right hemisphere to remember. Once he's created a picture, have him look at the picture in his mind's eye, with his eyes closed, and spell the word backward. Then forward. As there is no order to a picture, backward and forward are equally accessible. If Zach can spell the word backward as rhythmically as he does forward, you know that he's formed a good visual image. This technique works for visual-spatial children and adults who are poor spellers. (For more details, see Chapter 13.)

> I have begun to use some of the teaching methods I have read of on your website—in particular, spelling: visualizing the word and spelling it backwards. This makes her learn the word usually the first time, but she doesn't like to do it this way, because the other kids and the teacher don't do it that way.

Neat, fast handwriting vs. keyboarding

> Handwriting disastrous.

> Her handwriting is so terrible they have created an IEP so she can keyboard.

> Handwriting was really hard. I type now. Speaking was hard too. I type for that too a lot of the time.

In Chapter 3, I talked about children who had frequent ear infections, which blocked out the higher frequencies. The higher frequencies appear to organize speech and the fine motor sequences of handwriting. The twin deficits of speaking and writing are often seen in average children who have suffered recurrent ear infections. In advanced children, however, the effects on speech and language development are far less apparent, because a bright child can use abstract reasoning to figure out words that are not heard clearly. As there is very little correlation between general intelligence and handwriting or spelling (Aren't you glad to hear that?), abstract reasoning doesn't help much. Therefore, a gifted child who had many ear infections in the first few years of life may develop speech on schedule, but perform very poorly on written tasks.

Not all VSLs, though, have poor penmanship. Do you happen to have anything written in your grandmother's hand? Do you remember how beautiful penmanship was in that generation? When writing is taught as an art form, *with plenty of time*, artistic VSLs develop beautiful handwriting. In fact, some children with terrible handwriting improved considerably when they studied calligraphy. The secret is slowing down and allowing sufficient time to create beautifully formed letters. In our fast-paced world, writing is supposed to become automatic, a means to an end, rather than an end in itself. So instead of just practicing penmanship, children are supposed to use the skill in the service of learning, which means doing two things at once. This coordination is extremely difficult for many VSLs.

I'm not against the teaching of penmanship, when it is taught for its own sake, like our grandparents learned it. Certain handwriting techniques actually help integrate the two hemispheres. It's when handwriting is considered in the grading of other subjects that I get bent out of shape. *Grades should be based on mastery of information, not on handwriting skills.* If we want VSLs to be skilled note-takers, it makes more sense to teach them to use a keyboard, which will be much more useful in their adult lives. One father told me that the only time he needs to write by hand is when he signs checks. (Please see Chapter 15 for a glimpse of what will become of handwriting in the future.)

The keyboard allows an individual to access both hemispheres, so a VSL's powerful right hemisphere can assist his weaker left hemisphere. If Leonard Shlain's hypothesis is accurate, allowing a student to use a keyboard not only helps the individual, it also helps raise the consciousness of the planet. (I'm for that!)

> Since the 1970s, ...males have rushed in droves to learn what their fathers and grandfathers contemptuously dismissed as a skill for women and sissies—typing. Unlike all the scribes of past cultures, men now routinely write with both hands instead of only the dominant one. The entry into the communication equation of millions of men's left hands, directed by millions of male right brains tapping out one half of every computer-generated written message, is, I believe an unrecognized factor in the diminution of patriarchy. (Shlain, 1998, p. 417)

A visual-spatial child should be taught to use a computer as early as possible. I've had consultations with two sets of parents who taught their toddlers to use the computer when they were a little over a year old. Keyboarding skills are essential for today's VSLs: they enable these students to have greater school success and prepare them for the technological fields that many of them will enter in adult life. If a child is unable to master keyboarding, then a voice-activated computer, such as Dragon Naturally Speaking, is recommended. This is likely to be the way computers operate in the very near future.

There probably are great benefits in perfecting one's handwriting, but I always tell parents that if their children's penmanship is abysmal, encourage them to become doctors. It seems to be a pre-requisite for the medical profession!

> As a physician, I am often criticized for my handwriting, but perhaps it is being a visual-spatial learner as opposed to being a physician that resulted in the illegible script.

Organized vs. organizationally challenged

Hah! Disorganized? Me?

Organization is a nightmare for me. I've gotten better at it over time, but not much. In school I was always the disorganized kid with the messy desk and the messy locker and so on (not to mention the messy handwriting). I got yelled at a lot for that, but I could never change it. ... I can't command my mind to do things on a schedule; it has its own, and if I mess with that schedule there are problems.

Problems would include a lack of organizational skills and an inability to sit through dull meetings or classes without scribbling wild notes or otherwise keeping the mind busy.

My wife has for years been frustrated with my lack of attention to time and with my lack of organization (at home and at my office). Now she may actually believe there is a reason behind it all.

Not all auditory-sequential learners are organizational wizards, but they have a fairly good idea of the sequence of tasks necessary to bring an assignment to completion. One of the greatest complaints from teachers about visual-spatial children is that they are hopelessly disorganized. Highly organized parents and teachers are not usually successful in reforming them, because they don't understand the problem. Organizationally impaired adults stand a better chance. They've been there. And, if they've managed to maintain gainful employment in adult life, they've probably developed some compensating strategies that they can teach organizationally challenged children. Making lists, for example, is not an innate skill. It needs to be learned. Other memory joggers can be mastered early in life: (a) carrying around a daily planner and actually using it; (b) writing assignments on sticky notes and attaching them to books; (c) voice memos; (d) color coding; (e) drawing flow charts. VSLs need direct instruction in organizational techniques.

Try enlisting a helper (student, volunteer, or aide) to guide the organizational process through questioning rather than doing the work for his or her partner.

"Where would be a good place to stack your books?"
"What would be a good place to put assignments that need to be done so you don't forget them or lose them?"

"What should you do with finished assignments?"

"Here are some paperclips. Why don't you clip the parts of the assignment together?"

"Let's make stacks of all the things in your desk and see what goes together."

"Is there anything in there you don't need anymore that you can throw out?"

Showing one's work vs. just knowing

I was always one of those pupils who could arrive at the right answer instantly but could not show the workings, as there weren't any!

I can't show my work easily, except with algebra or something where I need to make myself write out each step in order to not mess up the arithmetic.

He is now in seventh grade and has pre-algebra. He is failing this class. Not because he does not have the correct answer, but due to the fact he can't show all the "steps" on how he came to the answer. His teacher will ask him how he came to his answer and he can't tell her. So, in a teacher's mind, he is *cheating*. At this point he has been broken down to the point he is getting into trouble at school. [emphasis added]

It's quite a simple matter for auditory-sequential learners to show the steps they took to arrive at their conclusions, because, they do, in fact, take a series of steps. There are educational theorists who believe that unless children can verbalize how they arrived at their answers they don't understand the concepts. The theorists who emphasize verbalization are, themselves, auditory-sequential learners, who think in a linear, step-by-step fashion, and assume that everyone else does too—or at least they *should*.

Being required to show their work is nearly impossible for some visual-spatial children, because they see it all at once, rather than arriving at answers through traditional steps. They just know. They don't know how they know and they can't explain to anyone else the route they took to the knowing—they just see it.

VSLs are often penalized in classes that demand that they retrace a series of steps that they never took. And the new emphasis on showing your work in standardized tests is crippling to VSLs. Whenever possible, allow VSLs to get credit for correct answers, even without the steps, and never accuse them of "cheating" unless you have proof. That does life-long damage to self-esteem and assures that you will remain a lasting memory—a very unpleasant one.

Rote memorization vs. seeing relationships

I cannot learn by rote. I think in pictures. When I read Shakespeare it is on two levels: I am simultaneously at the Globe Theatre milling amongst the audience and also taking part in the events of the story as a participant.

My child was fascinated with patterns by kindergarten, calling them "patterens." Compared to linear sibling, this child feels stupid because doesn't learn as fast. Terrible speller. Doesn't memorize well. Learned times tables immediately after I showed patterns.

Rote memorization is torture. I could always figure out the answer. It just took time and the school wanted speedy spit-out answers from memory. I couldn't stand to say the answer unless I was sure it was right. No guessing. I didn't like history, unless the teacher related what life was like for the people who lived then. Dates and names and fussy details were boring, but did they have cars? Electricity? Telephones? That's what I wanted to know. Learning geography was tedious. Still is. They should teach where the mountain ranges and deserts are, then the places would have form. Math was only fun if it was applied math. Give me word problems, a reason to solve it. I can picture that. I can use reasoning skills.

Rote memorization may not be much fun for any learners, but auditory-sequential children seem to be able to do it much easier than their counterparts. For VSLs, learning is understanding a complete network of relationships. They remember meaningful material beautifully, but struggle severely with non-meaningful material. Therefore, in order to reach them, it's important to make each lesson as relevant to their experience as possible, and allow them to visualize the concepts. What questions do they have about the material to be learned? If they can raise a series of questions that they're curious about, and then start fishing for answers to their questions, they're much more likely to retain the information. This activates the right hemisphere.

> I can see connections between things that other people often can't. I can put together patterns really well; my absolute favorite feeling in the world is probably the one where things "connect" and "fit together" and it happens a lot. ...Patterns will fit together whether I have any say in them or not, and they're going to do that in my head. ... I guess my biggest hobby is watching connections fit together (I think in spatial connections) and the feeling when they do fit is extraordinarily beautiful. (Not so, if they are false or force-fitted, when the feeling is ugly.)

Auditory short-term vs. visual long-term memory

> I lose track of things in my short-term memory but I have an amazing long-term memory. I got to use it in biology this year and it helped me out a lot. At the end of the year there was a test of what you remembered for the entire year, a list of 80 questions. Almost half of the questions hadn't even been covered in class. I got the highest grade in the class.

> His memory is very short for snippets of unconnected information which he is not interested in. When he cannot get his questions answered, it is as if the machinery stops and he cannot proceed.

> I have to learn things the round-about way. Lots of the time, I won't do particularly good in a course because I make mistakes in calculations or something, but *I'll know the material for longer and better than a lot of people.* [emphasis added]

Smart auditory-sequential learners usually have well-developed auditory short-term memory. They can repeat a string of 6 or 7 unrelated numbers or remember a three-step direction. They can remember phone numbers without necessarily writing them down. They can listen to lectures and take notes of the important points without missing much of the information. And most of them do not suffer too much from auditory distractibility. They can hear the teacher in an open classroom, bustling with activity. In high school and college, they rely on their short-term memories to cram for finals. But getting an A on the final does not guarantee that the material is stored in long-term memory. They may forget almost all that they learned as soon as the course is over, unless they have some reason to continue to use the information. (This certainly was true for me. I got A's on my exams, but you couldn't ask me the questions a week later!)

Visual-spatial learners tend to have poor auditory short-term memory. Their strong suit is definitely long-term memory. The college student who said he remembered things longer and better than most other people is correct. It may take longer for them to learn a concept, but once it is stored in long-term memory, it appears to be accessible to them indefinitely. My colleague, George Dorry, writes:

> My father was a supervisor for the construction of several of the build-ings being erected for the 1964 World's Fair in New York City. I was a junior in high school at the time. We reviewed the blueprints, and I began to understand that he and I could turn the flat paper diagrams into three-dimensional models in our heads. We were mentally able to rotate the view we took of the finished building before it was even built...
>
> It is also interesting to note that both he and I can choose a building, such as the "Top of the Fair" heliport-restaurant, and still do the same visualization and rotation of the plans. He will be 86 in December. Recall of well-learned visual-spatial memory appears to last a lifetime, or at least over thirty-five years.

Repeating a series of random numbers tends to be very difficult for VSLs, unless they develop a strategy of seeing the numbers as if they were being written on a whiteboard in their minds. They often forget three-step directions. Developmentally, a three-step direction should be mastered by the age of 5. However, there are many adults who still can't do it. Case in point: You're dashing out the door on the way to work, and you say, "Honey, please put the wash in the dryer on permanent press for 60 minutes, oh, and don't forget to clean the lint screen." You come home from work, and Honey says, "What wash? You didn't say anything about wash." Before you begin thinking you've lost your mind, next time try writing it on a sticky note and placing it where Honey is most likely to notice it, like the mirror, the refrigerator, the TV set, the computer, the phone—whatever Honey is into at the moment. You only stand a 50-50 chance that the wash will actually get into the dryer, but at least you won't think you're crazy. Instead of "What wash?" you're likely to hear, "Oh yeah, I saw that note." (By the way, my "Honey" is my husband. Some things don't change with age.)

Note taking can be a nightmare for VSLs, because they don't have the processing speed to be able to coordinate listening, extracting the main points, and writing simultaneously. Some take a tape recorder to class and play back the lectures, stopping and repeating the sections several times if necessary, so that they get the concepts. But this is time intensive, and puts a tremendous strain on an already overwhelmed auditory system. Others learn to pay very close attention in class, photographing in their minds where the teacher was standing, facial expressions and body language—all of which blends together when they recall the information. Still others draw visual sketches and diagrams to jog their memories, instead of taking notes in words. VSLs should be encouraged to explore all of these different techniques. (See Chapter 13.)

> I have difficulty studying from notes. …When I do take notes in class, I don't look at the teacher. Without eye contact with the teacher, the notes are useless, because when I read them later, they make no sense. If I am not actually engaged in the lecture, I miss the whole thing.

Many VSLs suffer from auditory distractibility. They have trouble concentrating in noisy settings because they cannot block out background noise. They can't carry on a conversation in front of the television set. They're more comfortable doing one thing at a time. Open classrooms may be very difficult. They need to learn to sit close to the teacher and away from as many distractions as possible. Help them to develop mnemonic techniques to enhance short-term memory (e.g., "Every Good Boy Does Fine"—EGBDF and "FACE" are used to remember musical lines and spaces). Emphasize long-term retrieval of meaningful information rather than the cramming of data in short-term memory. Exam questions that require students to apply knowledge, contrast, synthesize, or evaluate (ala Bloom's Taxonomy) make better use of long-term memory than questions that assess rote memorization of knowledge.

Drill and repetition vs. a permanent picture

> Once he conquers an item, he wants something different or new. With school, trivial drills annoy him to (literally) tears.

> Once I understand something, I understand it completely, and repetition is useless. Therefore, my note-taking abilities are poor, my notebooks are empty. The information goes into my head, or it doesn't.

I'm not a great fan of drill, but it's possible that repetitive practice is necessary for associative pathways to be formed in the left hemisphere. The auditory-sequential learner depends on some drill for concepts to stick. It can be argued that the amount of practice built into the textbooks is based on careful study of what is needed for average students to grasp and retain information. When you teach these same concepts to a child just one standard deviation below the norm—around 85 IQ—you find that a much greater amount of repetition is needed for retention of the information. If you were to teach these concepts to a child two standard deviations below the norm—around 70 IQ—you might need 20 times as much practice as recommended in the text. Bright children, one standard deviation above the mean—around 115 IQ—need considerably less drill than is recommended, and gifted children, two standard deviations above the mean—around 130 IQ, usually get the concept the first time it is presented. Most of them hate drill and repetition—even the gifted auditory-sequential learners.

Figure 6.1

Theoretical Curve of Distribution of Intelligence

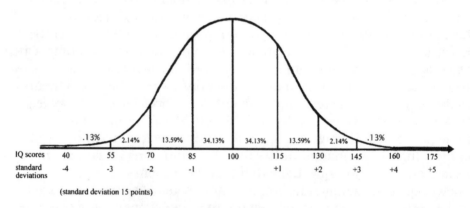

I'm reminded of stories of two six-year-old gifted girls. The first one came from Sharon Stockero, the gifted coordinator for the Dickinson-Iron Intermediate School District in Upper Peninsula, Michigan.

A little girl came home from school one day and said:
"Mommy, is two plus three five?"
"Yes," said her mother.
"Mommy, was two plus three five yesterday?"
"Of course!" responded her mother.
"Mommy, is two plus three going to be five tomorrow?"
"Certainly!" said her mother.
"Then why do they keep teaching it to us over and over and over again?"

The second story is on loan from Jerre Levy. Her friend's daughter was coloring a worksheet she brought home from school. It contained two puppies and three puppies, two giraffes and three giraffes, and two bears and three bears. She tried to explain to her mother that it was all the same, but her mother kept pointing out that the puppies, giraffes, and bears were all doing different things. "What difference does it make if they're puppies, giraffes, or bears?" wailed the exasperated six-year-old. "Don't you see, it's all the same!" and she ripped up the paper and refused to do it.

Have you ever renovated or redecorated your home? Before you did it, were you able to picture in your mind what it would look like when you were finished? Would that picture be improved in any way by drill and repetition? Can you still remember that picture? If the way you learn is to create pictures in your mind, those pictures are not enhanced in any way by practice. Now you can see why visual-spatial learners balk at drill and practice; such exercises do not enhance their understanding. Once they have a visual representation of the basic concepts, the learning is permanent, and they're ready to go on to something new. The solution is to give them a few of the hardest problems or exercises in the unit. If they succeed, skip all the rest.

> I was particularly interested by "Learning is usually permanent: is turned off by drill and repetition" because I think I've noticed that phenomenon when I've studied for tests this past semester. My roommate, who is very much an auditory-sequential learner, always uses flashcards for organic chemistry studying, so I decided to try it, and (much to my dismay, though I got an A in the class anyway) it didn't work at all for me on the final. I did much better going through the reactions a time or two by writing them out. *Drill and repetition seemed to almost make me forget things that I'd learned earlier in the semester,* if that makes any sense. It was like the little bits of information were pulled out of their little categories and piled up into a big lump of meaningless facts when I tried to do it that way. *It misorganized my whole way of thinking...and stole the meanings of some of the things I had previously learned.* A similar thing happened with my bacteriology class when I was trying to learn how the various toxins worked. *I made a bunch of flash cards, but all that did was "unsort" things.* If I think about how the diptheria toxin works, for instance, I sort of picture a body and at the same time the page that the stuff about diptheria toxin was on, and my mental picture sort of zooms in on the throat area of the person, where the pathology takes place. *But after sitting there the night before the exam with the flashcards, it got harder to remember* what part of protein synthesis which toxin interfered with and how, or whatever, *because I couldn't picture anything.* [emphasis added]

What if the college student quoted above speaks for other VSLs as well? Is it possible that drill can be detrimental, not just to motivation, but to learning itself, if it interferes with a student's ability to form pictures?

Learning from instruction vs. developing own methods

One of the most sequential tasks a teacher can attempt to teach is long division. You could get very gray trying to teach some VSLs long division by traditional sequential methods. Auditory-sequential learners can master long division by watching the teacher demonstrate the process and following the steps. Or they can look at the model in the pink box in the book and copy the sequence of steps. Visual-spatial learners may never get it that way.

Long division can be taught to both groups of learners simultaneously. First, put a simple divisor, dividend and quotient on the board without any of the steps. Tell the VSLs to figure out their own way to arrive at that quotient. "Don't show me your work! If you figure out a system that works for you, I'll give you a harder problem and see if it works for that one, too."

$$7\overline{)490} \quad \text{quotient } 70 \qquad 6\overline{)264} \quad \text{quotient } 44$$

While the visual-spatial students are inventing long division, teach it in the traditional way to the auditory-sequential students. Having the students figure out their own methods of problem solving is a lot like a video game. The students know what the goal is and they have to discover on their own how to get there. If they succeed, the video game automatically gets harder. Visual-spatials love video games. They teach inductively. (See Chapter 13 for more inductive strategies.)

Learning in spite of emotions vs. learning dependent on emotions

C is very reactive to teacher attitudes. We are moving her...into a more nurturing school because of this.

❧ ❧ ❧

My seven-year-old son is a highly compassionate, sensitive, and emotional child who doesn't easily open up to others. He generally has a hard time in school when he doesn't like the teacher. He can't easily separate the learning process from his emotional system. They're highly connected. When he's open and happy, he learns much better and he feels good about himself, even though he is a divergent, visual learner. When he doesn't like his teacher, his poor self-concept comes creeping back in and puts a damper on learning anything at all. My son sees himself as stupid. He calls himself that at home where it's safe to let out his real feelings. He thinks he's fooling everyone into thinking he's kind of smart at school, but he struggles to learn things way more than his peers do (or so he believes). He's really very bright which is why he can hide his struggles at school so well.

Liking the teacher is essential. The teacher has to respect her personality.

As I learn more about visual-spatial learners, I have images that float up concerning my own education. I'm in 5th grade. I was taught by Mrs. Humphry. She was *very* attentive to me. I got straight A's! As my education continued, I noticed when a teacher or instructor exhibited compassion, my grades excelled. …My education has been a roller-coaster ride.

Emotions are very complex, and involve many parts of the brain, but apparently the right hemisphere plays a critical role in processing certain aspects of emotion. Jerre Levy says, "The right hemisphere is superior to the left hemisphere in discriminating and expressing emotional information and probably in emotional empathy, but both hemispheres are involved in emotional experience."

Auditory-sequential learners can compartmentalize their emotions better than visual-spatial learners. If they're upset, they can put their feelings on hold during class. Not so with VSLs. They become their anger, their joy, their sorrow. They may be extremely sensitive to how they're perceived by the other students or by the teacher. If you're having a bad day, or a migraine, Zach may interpret your facial expression as indicating that you "don't like him." If he comes to that conclusion, he may not be able to learn in your class. However, if Zach feels that you really appreciate his silly sense of humor, his creativity, his far out ideas, he'll be highly motivated in your classroom. Never underestimate the power of genuine appreciation in teaching children.

Convergent vs. divergent thinking

She is in dire need of divergent assignments that are not tedious and give her an opportunity to show in her own way that she understands concepts.

I always tell him that you have to have a different learning style in order to be a divergent thinker. It's the divergent thinkers in our society who are the true movers and shakers. They are the inventors and the great thinkers. Take Einstein for instance, who couldn't speak until he was three, and who couldn't do simple arithmetic when he was a child. Since my son wants to be a scientist when he grows up, these kinds of examples make him feel a lot better.

I don't like things that can only be done one way. There's only one way to spell a word. If you're doing geometry, if you're supposed to draw a perfect square, there are many ways to do it. You use your mind more. It's more creative.

You can expect auditory-sequential learners to give the right answers to the questions in the books, on the exams, and in the classroom. But you never know what visual-spatial students will come up with. They often give unscorable answers on standardized tests, seeing possibilities that the test constructor never imagined. They see commonalities in uncommon things. The ability to free associate, to see patterns, and to look at things from a different perspective, enhances their creativity.

Brain research suggests that the left hemisphere is better equipped to handle routine tasks, such as the motor requirements to produce speech (convergent production), and that the right hemisphere has a greater capacity to deal with novelty, complexity, and multiple ways of viewing a situation (divergent production).

Neuropsychologists Elkhonon Goldberg and Louis Costa... hypothesized that the left hemisphere is highly efficient at process-ing....well-routinized codes, such as the motoric aspects of language production, and that the right hemisphere is crucial for...more novel situations.... Areas devoted to sensory- and motor-specific functions are greater in the left hemisphere, whereas the right hemisphere is characterized by greater areas of...(higher level, integrative) cortex.... As a result of these anatomical differences, *the right hemisphere has a greater capacity for dealing with informational complexity and for processing many modes of representation within a single task, whereas the left hemisphere is superior at tasks requiring detailed fixation on a single, often repetitive, mode of representation* or execution. (Springer & Deutsch, 1998, pp. 308-310, emphasis added)

Therefore, instruction that leads to one right answer (convergent thinking) is comfortable for auditory-sequential learners, but confining to the thought processes of visual-spatial learners. Children with greater right-hemispheric strengths thrive in classrooms where the teacher asks more open-ended questions (divergent thinking).

Here are some examples of convergent questions:

Water is composed of which chemicals?

Who was the third president of the United States?

Where are the Galapagos Islands?

Here are some examples of divergent questions:

How many unusual ways can you arrive at the answer 20?

What are all the reasons you can think of for homelessness in our society?

What would happen if it were illegal for anyone to own a gun?

Develops evenly vs. asynchronously

As she became school age, we noticed that she was not reading as well as her brothers at that age, but her comprehension level was extremely high. Her vocabulary was extensive, but she had trouble expressing it in writing. The teacher thought her memory was phenomenal because she was reading three grade levels ahead using memory. Her comprehension was even higher. She began to excel in games like SET™ or Mastermind™. Spelling was difficult. She tended to use easier words in her written expression rather than tangle with a more advanced word in her vocabulary.

My scores...have that characteristic "spiky" pattern (distributed over a 60-point range, with everything either at the top or the bottom of it) but they're all so high nobody bothered noticing the spikes. To me...the spiked pattern jumps out at me more than the quantitative numbers next to it....

We're not "delayed" or "advanced" and...we don't really have "internal discrepancies" in our abilities the way people sometimes say we do. It's more like we are headed in a different developmental direction, that doesn't go on the standard developmental chart at all. Does not intersect. *Different direction.*

The average auditory-sequential learner sets the standard for expected development for his or her age group. Development is fairly even—mentally, physically, emotionally, and in terms of skill development. While there is some variation, it tends to be within set limits. Teachers and curriculum developers know what most 7 year olds are ready to learn. Pediatricians know from growth charts what is normal for 7 year olds. And psychologists can compare one child's intellectual development and skills in reading, mathematics, spelling, and writing to the norms for 7 year olds.

Gifted children develop more unevenly and often feel *out-of-sync* with children their age. We call this *asynchronous* development. The higher the child's intelligence, the greater is the gap between mental abilities and physical skills. The child may have trouble fitting in with classmates and may feel out-of-place with grade level expectations. So even a gifted auditory-sequential learner is asynchronous to some extent. But a gifted visual-spatial learner is *really* asynchronous. This child develops in an entirely different manner from other children. (As the young woman quoted above stressed, *"different direction."*)

Children whose right hemispheres develop faster than their left hemispheres often acquire block-building skills earlier than children their age, while speech may be delayed. They are considered "late developers." Math skills may be way ahead of reading proficiency. A child may understand concepts very well, but not be able to express those concepts in writing. There are usually marked inconsistencies between strengths and weaknesses in VSLs. When these discrepancies are severe enough to cause the child to be frustrated, he or she needs to be referred for comprehensive evaluation to determine if there are learning disabilities. (See Chapters 8 and 9.)

Flexibility is the key to meeting the needs of asynchronous children. They need to be accelerated in subjects in which they are advanced, work with children their age in areas where they have age-appropriate development, and have therapy in skills in which they lag behind. If the child is both gifted and learning disabled, an Individual Educational Plan (IEP) should be created to guarantee differentiated services to enhance the gifts, as well as remediate the weaknesses.

> The discrepancies in my abilities have persisted. When I took the Graduate Record Exams (GRE) at the completion of undergraduate school, my mathematics score was in the top 2 percent, while my verbal score was just barely in the top quarter. This difference has continually resulted in what to others may seem like an uneven performance. To the extent that tasks depend on a careful understanding of the spatial-mechanical world around me, I usually do quite well. To the extent that it depends on quick verbal analysis, my performance can seem debilitated.

> As a child I thought of my problem as personal, and I endured it in silence. Now I cannot be so generous. I see no reason that children who have considerable ability of a distinct kind should be taught that they are inadequate, if not stupid. (Dixon, 1983, p. 8)

Consistent high achievement vs. erratic grades

I did my worst at subjects like Government, English, History,...and excelled in classes such as Geometry, Algebra, and Advanced Placement Physics. Without these classes, graduating would probably have been questionable.

I don't like school that much. I get in trouble in a lot of subjects in school, like English and typing. I don't like the workload, I don't like deadlines, having to get things done at a certain time. I wait until the last minute on just about everything—even the classes I do well in like geometry. I like geometry. I'm starting to like English a little bit for the first time 'cause I got a great teacher. I like gym class. And I like cooking class. I don't like everything else.

Subjects that were fun were music, science, cooking, art class. I liked English but often got in trouble for poor spelling. I have trouble with spelling things the way I think they should be and often spell a word consistently wrong (it's right to me)... It was hard to memorize the multiplication table.

Asynchronous development leads to uneven performance in school subjects. If the curriculum is designed to fit the developmental schedule of auditory-sequential learners, it makes sense that they will be more successful academically. Visual-spatial learners, by way of contrast, get more erratic grades. They do well in certain subjects and poorly in others. They succeed with certain instructional strategies and struggle with others. They get A's with certain teachers and may get F's with others. They're clearly more vulnerable as students and need more adaptations, since school is designed primarily for children who learn in a different manner. Their success is so dependent on the relationship they're able to form with the teacher that it makes a huge difference if they're placed with teachers who really like them.

It helps to teach visual-spatial learners strategies for success. Many of them don't realize that they learn differently from others. They just feel stupid when they can't master a subject and confused when they grasp concepts that are difficult for others. If they know something, they think everyone else must know it, too.

They need:
- to be given early success experiences in school;
- to be placed with teachers who appreciate their strengths;
- to learn about their unique learning style;
- to meet role models of successful visual-spatial adults;
- to know in advance which subjects will be easy for them;
- to learn visualization strategies; and
- to have adaptations in their classes to enable them to succeed.

Algebra and chemistry vs. geometry and physics

When I was a sophomore in high school we moved and I started in a new school a month late. They had to fit me into the available classes and I got put into a geometry class with seniors who needed math credit to graduate. I took to geometry like a bird takes to flight. I rapidly grasped the whole concept and the rest of the year was just filling in the details. This was a 100% visual class! In no time at all I was helping the seniors with their problems.

In my sophomore year in high school I "aced" geometry very quickly such that the geometry teacher had time to go over algebra problem solving techniques with me (one on one) that I had struggled with from the previous Freshman year.

I had an awful time trying to deal with the algebra. I'm in trigonometry now and its actually easier because I can rotate, flip, turn triangles without problem. I can "see" why the math works.

He did okay in school, but never really excelled until he reached college and was able to take physics, math, engineering, etc. He loves engineering and has a talent for it. (Definitely, geometry and physics are more his cup of tea than chemistry. He hated chemistry, I loved it!)

Arithmetic and algebra are suited to auditory-sequential learners. But if they have difficulty visualizing, like I do, they may find geometry, calculus, trig and physics overwhelming. More advanced mathematics courses usually depend on visual-spatial abilities. While most VSLs are inherently mathematical, they may have a terrible time in arithmetic, and come to view themselves as poor at math—even if they have the potential for mathematical genius.

This is an exercise I often use with groups of teachers:

Suppose you're in high school during a severe budget crisis and I'm your school counselor. It's been decided that due to lack of funds, half of the students will get algebra and chemistry and the other half will get geometry and physics. It's my job to assign students to these two strands. Which of you are going to bribe me to put you in the algebra and chemistry strand because you know you won't succeed in geometry and physics? Which of you will bribe me to place you in geometry and physics? Which of you won't bribe me at all because you could do equally well in either strand?

I find that about 2/3 of any group I've worked with has a definite preference. Algebra and chemistry usually depend on left-hemispheric abilities, while geometry and physics depend more on right-hemispheric abilities. (Of course, teaching methods can have an impact on this, as well.) In my own case, I excelled in arithmetic, attained 98% on the New York State Regents Examinations in both algebra and chemistry, barely passed geometry with a 65, and dropped out of physics (the only course I ever dropped in my life) after 6 weeks of utter confusion. I think my experience of which subjects were hard and which were easy may be fairly typical of auditory-sequential learners.

Mastery of foreign languages in class vs. immersion

I had a terrible time taking languages.

Auditory-sequential learners often have an easier time learning foreign languages than visual-spatial learners. (Although I have met a couple VSLs who have a natural propensity for languages.) It takes a fine-tuned auditory system in order to discriminate the nuances of pronunciation in a language other than one's native tongue. Children who are late talkers have enough trouble just learning one linguistic system, without confusing them with a second one. It may be particularly difficult if the second linguistic system is very different from their own (e.g., Hebrew or Chinese). However, the world is getting smaller and smaller, and being monolingual may be a handicap in a shrinking world.

Several years ago, I gave a keynote address on visual-spatial learners at a state conference in Montana. A man came up to me after my presentation and said, "I know a person who fits every single description of a visual-spatial learner, but he's fluent in Spanish. How would you explain that?" I figured out that he must be talking about himself, and responded, "How did you do it?" He answered, "Total immersion." That was how I learned that visual-spatial learners *can* learn to speak other languages; they just have to learn them differently.

Some methods that work are:
- being born in Europe (I know, it's too late for you to do that);
- having bilingual parents who speak to you from birth in two languages;
- having a Nanny or housekeeper who doesn't speak any English;
- going to a camp (such as Concordia) where they speak nothing but the language you are trying to learn for an entire month;

❧ being an exchange student and living with a family that doesn't speak English;

❧ watching many films in a foreign language (you can do this with DVDs) after gaining an elementary knowledge of the language;

❧ spending a couple months in a non-English-speaking country; or finding some other creative way to become totally immersed in a different linguistic environment. (At first, it's maddening, but somehow, by osmosis, the music of the language starts to make sense.)

Speaking of music, learning songs in another language stimulates the right hemisphere, as does reading books. The combination of seeing the words, hearing the rhythm, and having the absolute necessity of mastering some of the language in order to communicate your basic needs, seems to do the trick.

Academically talented vs. creatively gifted

As early as age two, A was suggesting new and innovative uses for his father's tools to solve particular concrete problems. The solutions were correct and were ideas parents had not thought of. By age 11, A's suggested applications became more ambitious: Use virtual reality systems in repairing spacecraft to replace hazardous space walks by astronauts; utilize buried magnetic field source to compel traffic to slow down or stop at intersections.

Traditional school success is often the province of auditory-sequential learners, or visual-spatial learners with well-developed auditory-sequential abilities. As auditory-sequentials tend to demonstrate their abilities through high academic achievement, teachers are more likely to nominate them than VSLs for gifted programs. The sporadic achievement of the visual-spatial child is not as commonly recognized as evidence of giftedness.

Some children who are extraordinarily creative are focused elsewhere than academics. The following excerpts of my conversation with Dana describe the kind of inventive capability that occupies his mind. In Chapter 13, Dana's enrichment teacher shares, "What's paid attention to is what he *can't* do, instead of what he can do."

When I was nine, I had an idea about bridges 'cause they were always getting knocked down by ice. My idea was to make a wedged-shaped bridge support that was slanted with a metal edge on it; the pressure would cut the ice in half around the bridge. It would operate like a big ice skate. You know how the pressure melts the ice a little bit and creates a thin layer of water, so when you push down on it, your weight melts the water underneath the blade and you're riding on top of that. It would work even better because the blade would be slanted like a slanted knife. There's a lot of pressure behind the ice. The more pressure, the faster the ice would cut.

Dana went on to say:

Recently, I had this idea for a tent stake that won't pull out as easily. It's a tent stake with three prongs. The prongs spread out beneath the dirt so it holds it in better. Like if you open up your hand, it kind of does that under the ground pushing against the dirt.

In addition, he shared:

In geometry, at the beginning of the year we had to make a perfect square with a compass and a ruler. The teacher taught us the regular way to do it. The way I did it was to have two lines bisect each other, so it looks like 4 rays coming out, then measured it equally on all the lines so that there was a point that was equidistant from the center on each ray. Then I connected the dots. It would look like a diamond if you had the rays up and down and you would have to turn it to look like a square.

I like to make up problems for myself and solve 'em, like physics problems. Just this morning I was thinking if you had a sphere spinning in one way like the earth and it can spin in a million different ways, what if it was spinning in all those different directions at the same time. Would it be spinning or not? What would it be? It takes energy to spin something. It wouldn't be moving, but it would be giving off energy.

Academically talented children are more comfortable with the structure of school. But children who are highly creative, technological wizards, mechanically gifted, or emotionally and intuitively attuned, may not find school relevant for the development of their abilities. They often develop these gifts outside the classroom. Wouldn't it be wonderful if these kinds of gifts were acknowledged as legitimate forms of giftedness and consciously developed as part of the school curriculum?

I know that you worry that these children won't be successful in adult life unless they have at least minimal competency in the traditional subject areas. But in adult life, success depends on finding your own niche, finding out what you're really good at, and pursuing it. You don't have to be great at every subject you studied in school to be a successful adult. Who's going to demand that you tell them what 8 x 7 is (and give you 10 seconds to respond), or require you to recite a poem, or insist that you know the capitals of the states, when you're a grown-up? Some of the skills that we think are absolutely essential for children to learn are obsolete by the time they become adults. We've got calculators, computers, dictionaries, spell checkers, and some of us even have secretaries. Instead of worrying about the "basic skills," it's more important that we honor the unique strengths of all students, and help them to appreciate the special gifts that they have to offer the world.

Outstanding spatial ability often manifests itself in children who are mediocre, sometimes debilitated, in other important academic skills—most often in language skills. The cases of persons of historical genius who had a natural inclination toward spatial ability, but a deficiency in other academic skills, are so striking that they suggest we should more often than not look for spatial genius to be unrelated to more conspicuous academic skills (Dixon, 1983, ix).

Early vs. late bloomers

When my daughter K was very little we worried about her. She frequently fell and walked into doors. My nickname for her was "Crashtest." When I spoke to her I got a blank stare. It wasn't until Kindergarten that I was relieved to find out that the wheels were turning in her head. I watched her play educational games on the computer. She was, indeed, very smart. She was excellent at solving the various puzzles and problems presented to her that she had previously not been very interested in.

As she grew and could do more things, she became interested in taking things apart to understand how they work or to fix them. She can solve iron puzzles my husband has had since before I met him....puzzles that he cannot solve! She is definitely a hands-on learner. I love the way her mind works; it is very different from mine. I fell in love with my husband because I admire his ability to build or fix anything and understand practical, useful things. My daughter inherited this from him and now I admire them both!

I did poorly in school, and at 40, I decided to go back. I adjusted because of life learning. I knew I wasn't "stupid" and I have mostly A's and B's, something I thought I would never achieve.

My younger brother did poorly in school. My parents always maintained that my brother was very smart, and that schools were not teaching him right, but they had trouble convincing others. Even I felt that they had to say he was smart because he was their son, and they had to maintain positive feelings about him. My brother was a late-talker and was always very coordinated. (He could ride a two-wheeled bike with training wheels at 18 months and could ride without the training wheels before he was three years old. I can remember him trying to teach me how to ride my bike without training wheels. I was 8 and he was 5.)

> My brother was always very good with computers and had one as a young man. All his computer skills are self-taught/learned-on-the-job. He now works as a senior systems engineer for a major telephone/internet provider and manages a group of people. All this without any college degrees.

Auditory-sequential learners bloom early and visual-spatial learners bloom late. This pattern begins in early childhood. Children who are early talkers are often auditory-sequential. Children who develop speech later are often visual-spatial. The early bloomers have an advantage for school tasks. They shine in the early years and show great promise. Visual-spatial learners may not look so promising in the primary grades.

Over the years, I have asked parents of visual-spatial learners if they got smarter as they got older (not more knowledgeable, experienced, or wise, but actually more intelligent). I had a hunch that late maturation and integration of the hemispheres ran in families. Many parents responded, "Yes!" Different patterns emerged. Some reported that they failed or were at risk of failing in the primary grades, started to take off in the intermediate grades, did fine in high school, started cooking in college, and really shined in graduate school. There was a gradual increase in their cognitive abilities. Others reported that they were constantly in trouble in elementary school, barely made it through high school, and suddenly became smart in college or when they got out into the work force. The literature is filled with examples of what appears to be a kind of spontaneous remission of learning disabilities or attention deficits in some boys at puberty. One father told me he didn't learn to read until he was 36. I worked with a young man who failed chemistry in high school and later went on to get a Ph.D. in chemistry!

One reason for late blooming might be that advanced work becomes more challenging and demands more abstract reasoning, which is a strong suit for bright visual-spatial learners. Or maybe it involves more visual learning. Or perhaps these students learn more compensation techniques as they get older. Or maybe they have more choice in subject matter, so they can select courses they will succeed at, and avoid the ones in which they know they will do poorly. Or maybe they learn study skills, and gain control over their distractibility. Or maybe as they get closer to adulthood, they become more determined to be successful. Or maybe some brains just mature late. Or maybe all of the above.

My own family really fits the late blooming phenomenon. My father went back to college while I was in high school and earned his B.A. the same year I graduated high school. Following in his footsteps, my sister became a certified public accountant (CPA) when she was 44, my brother became a lawyer at 42, and I became a psychologist at 38—all within a few months of each other! My brother had a great deal of difficulty with auditory distractibility, poor short-term memory, spelling, and calculation in elementary school. He felt really dumb. In high school, he discovered that he was a whiz at history and chess. He was highly successful in college, and in graduate school his teachers directed most of their lectures to him as he was the most promising student in the class. He definitely got smarter as he got older.

Our children were also interesting. Independently, they both came up to me when they were sophomores in college and said that they literally felt their brains expanding. Before this experience, they both sounded like high school kids. Afterwards, they spoke like mature adults. I think there's something to this late maturation.

> It may be a good thing when the maturing process takes a little longer than usual. Parents are usually pleased when their children mature quickly, become more independent, more organized, and more self-directed in advance of their peers. What is not generally known is that late maturation can be useful, although it seems to contradict conventional belief.

> Later maturity may be seen as desirable in at least three ways: First, the plastic, absorbent world of the child may be experienced longer, giving the adolescent a deeper store of real seeing and feeling experience of the world to draw on—and to build intuition on—before the adult world of fixed, literate, learned knowledge takes over. Second, there is a real possibility of significantly increased neurological capacity, at least in some cases and in certain areas, which may more than compensate for earlier awkwardness and some lingering areas of relative disability. And third, the late developer may be able to retain some aspects of the child's view throughout life, such as a sense of wonder, or a comparative freshness and lack of preconception, making the expression of creativity much more probable. Although the clock of maturation follows its own beat, it is good to know that a slower pace may have, under the right circumstances, notable advantages. (West, 1991, p. 25)

How Early Can We Tell if Our Child is Visual-Spatial?

I first noticed there was something "different" about my daughter when she was 6 months old. She was not yet crawling and it was her first Christmas. She was laying in a patch of sunlight on the floor, playing with a toy that had a detachable piece with a mirror on it. This little baby was manipulating the mirror to reflect sunlight onto the wall and was moving the reflection around the wall onto a painting. When one of the dogs barked and startled her, she dropped the mirror but picked it up and repeated the activity. She had made the connection between the mirror in her hand and the reflection on the wall!

I first noticed my son's unique visual abilities when he was 10 months old. He could recognize when a non-picture book was given to him upside down. He would then turn it right side up. This was with the book open, so he wasn't going by the cover. (My mother quizzed me in disbelief.)

Doctors believe in genetics. That's why they take family histories. Our grandson's doctor told us that the best indicator of high intelligence in children is high intelligence in parents. He's right. The same is true of learning style. To paraphrase my friend, Stephanie Tolan, when a Mommy Cheetah and a Daddy Cheetah have a baby, do they say to each other, "Do you think it's a cheetah?" If you're an artist and you married an architect, or you're both engineers, guess what? Is one of your parents an inventor? Do you have a brother or sister who is a musician? Is there left-handedness in your family line? Dyslexia? Are you a computer junkie? All of these would be predisposing factors, likely to create visual-spatial children.

On the other hand, if you're a lawyer and you married a bookkeeper, maybe not. But seriously, while there are engineers and computer programmers with greater left-hemispheric strengths and lawyers with greater right-hemispheric strengths—and even handedness does not necessarily indicate hemispheric preference—certain fields attract more VSLs than others. We've found that parental occupation is a pretty strong indicator of visual-spatial abilities in children. Of course, there are always exceptions to the rule, like visual-spatial accountants. If you're one of those, why did you go into that field? Wouldn't you be happier as a potter??

The following fields attract lots of visual-spatial learners:

- art
- music
- theater
- mathematics
- science

- technology
- architecture
- photography
- cartography
- aeronautics
- engineering
- mechanics
- design

These would be good fields to encourage children with strong visual-spatial abilities to go into in adult life. Life is much more fun when your occupation allows you to use your strengths.

Early signs of visual-spatial abilities

We begin to see the signs of VSL abilities very early in life. The two anecdotes above are about visual-spatial children who were under a year old. Late talking *compared with their siblings* is certainly one of the earliest signs. I emphasized "compared with their siblings" because gifted children are too often compared with the norms established for average children instead of with their own norm group. The development of other family members—brothers, sisters, parents, cousins—is the best norm group for a particular child.

> C is highly creative, observant, advanced in reasoning ability, and she reached developmental milestones early, but suddenly stopped talking until she was well past two, and has been much slower than her brothers and sister at developing her verbal abilities. She seems very bright and creative, but also lags significantly in verbal skills. She said "Mama," "Dada," and "no" at 9 months, then gave up speaking until well after 2 years of age, when she suddenly yelled, "Look! It's a truck—a really big truck!"

Late talking compared to siblings means that the right hemisphere is leading right now in your child's development and the left hemisphere is taking its time. This may or may not be cause for concern. It's wise to have a comparatively late talker thoroughly checked out by an audiologist to be certain that the auditory channel is not blocked. Watch carefully for some of the signs of visual-spatial precocity described in this chapter. Who knows, you may have a visual-spatial prodigy on your hands. (Maybe you're raising an Einstein?)

Vivid imagination; excellent visual memory; attraction to puzzles; drawing; building with Legos™, Construx™, K'nex™, Zometool®,

Lincoln Logs™, blocks and anything else they can get their hands on; taking things apart and trying to understand how everything works—all are early signs of this learning style. You know you have a visual-spatial learner when she tosses her Christmas, Chanukah or birthday presents and starts creating something with the boxes, paper, and ribbon.

> C's play was always imaginative and creative. He did not play with toys but rather enjoyed string, rope, boxes and water. He talked to himself and his "friends."

This chapter is chock full of amazing stories parents have shared with us about their young children's preoccupations, along with a few anecdotes from adult VSLs about their childhoods. I've purposely selected the most astonishing anecdotes to demonstrate what brilliant VSLs are capable of doing at a very early age. Most people wouldn't believe such feats are humanly possible. That's what makes them brilliant!

The following stories speak eloquently about what to look for in trying to determine if your child is a visual-spatial learner, so I have let the stories speak for themselves, rather than elaborating on them. If your child engages in similar activities, but not at such a young age, be assured that you still have a visual-spatial child—perhaps not quite as precocious. In the request that we placed on our website for anecdotal information from VSLs, the first question was: "When did you first notice that you or your child had unusual visual-spatial abilities?" These are the early signs of visual-spatial ability in order of the frequency with which they occurred in the website responses:

- puzzles
- artistic talent
- construction
- numbers
- excellent visual memory
- spatial perception
- maps and geography
- vivid imagination
- mechanical interest and ability
- taking things apart
- music
- mazes
- computers

Most of the stories in this chapter are abou
are organized chronologically by age. Some of
profoundly gifted and have gone on to become
subject areas, while others have had miserabl
accompanied by losses in self-esteem. In my c
close attention to developmental histories. The
about a child's abilities than current school pe
that teachers collect information from parents
development and interests to gain a fuller pict

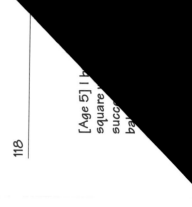

✧ Puzzles

Extraordinary ability to do puzzles is one of the most telling signs of visual-spatial talent. If a child adores puzzles and does very advanced puzzles early in life, undoubtedly he or she is visual-spatial. Puzzles come up more often than any other indicator of early visual-spatial ability in both girls and boys.

K whipped through the tasks at the greatest speed [the psychologist] had ever encountered. He was exceptionally quick at the puzzles he laid out, finishing them almost before the guy could start his stopwatch. When I said that he had been able to do such puzzles easily since the age of 15 months I was told that they were designed for an eight year old. I hardly dared tell him that my daughter had also been doing them at such an early age. As they had both done this, I thought it quite normal!

When my son was 18 months old, his older brother was three and had many wooden puzzles (you know, Sesame Street, animals, etc.). We used to get 4-6 puzzles, mix up all the pieces and set the boards they fit into right side up. It was amazing the way he could pick out each piece and put it in the correct spot on the correct board in such a short amount of time. It looked like it was just the easiest thing for him. He looked as though he didn't even have to think about it.

I first discovered her spatial abilities at the age of three when she worked for two days to put together a 300-piece puzzle—alone. My inclination was to help, but my husband said hands off—let P do it. I never imagined that she would be able—did a perfect job. And to watch her piece the puzzle together—it was amazing. P would eye the puzzle, pick up a piece, and place it perfectly. I thought it was wonderful, but my thoughts were confirmed when her preschool teacher mentioned that P's spatial abilities were extremely high.

...rought home one of those 9-piece puzzles that makes a ...when completed. I gave it to my son; he did not have much ...ss with it. I tried it, unable to complete it, I gave it to the ...ysitter to try. She couldn't do it. M asked what I would give her if she could do it. I told her I would give her 5 dollars. Not 3 minutes had passed when she came running up to me to collect her money. I started bringing home all kinds of visual puzzles and games. She could beat all of us!

It interests me how many of these puzzlemaniacs enjoy putting puzzles together upside-down. I guess it must increase the challenge. Or maybe they're so intrigued by the shapes that the colors don't matter to them. What are your hypotheses?

My son is a visual-spatial learner. He only spoke five words at age two but he could put 100-piece puzzles together on the brown side. He would pick up a piece and look for a piece that matched the pattern of the one he was holding. He never put the edge pieces together like most people do. He just had little parts that he hooked together until the puzzle was completed. He would work diligently until the puzzle was finished.

My daughter will be 3 in July. Right before her second birthday we were at a garage sale and I saw some 24-piece puzzles. I thought, this is a little early, but may as well get them (they were a great deal!). L insisted on doing them as soon as we got home. After she mastered the 3 puzzles (the following day) she started putting them together upside down (with the picture facing down). This ended up being one of her obsessions. Next came 50-piece puzzles, and now she does a 100+ piece puzzle independently (in about 15 minutes if it is her puzzle, ½ hr. if it is brand new).

My son [4½] can do a new 100-piece puzzle in under 15 minutes, and can see three pieces lying anywhere on the table and grab them and put them together. He has never worked on a puzzle in the traditional way, from the outside in, and can see a piece lying upside-down and face down and flip it in his head to see if it fits. He doesn't even need to see the picture on the puzzle face.

I find puzzles extremely diagnostic. If a child hates puzzles, or loves puzzles during the early years and then loses interest in them, he or she could still be visual-spatial. Children who go to the other ends of the earth to avoid puzzles usually have a good reason: visual processing issues. Fortunately, these can often be improved with about 6 months of vision therapy. It's vital that visual-spatial children have optimal visual skills, since their learning is so dependent on vision and visualization. (See Chapter 9 for more information on vision therapy.) If a child likes puzzles that are age appropriate and is sort of puzzle-neutral, it doesn't tell me anything. They have to either love 'em or hate 'em for puzzles to be diagnostically significant.

✤ Artistic talent

Perhaps the most obvious visual-spatials are artists, since they see the world in a different way from the rest of us and can express their aesthetic sensitivities in such remarkable ways. Both girls and boys are blessed with artistic talent, and oftentimes this talent is noticeable during the preschool years. My first year of teaching, I taught 2nd grade, and I happened to have in my class the niece of one of my dearest friends. Bonnie's mother was an artist, and, at the age of 7, Bonnie's drawings demonstrated an incredible awareness of perspective—well beyond any child's art I had ever seen.

Artistic talent is one of the few visual-spatial abilities that are deeply admired in young children, and even developed—at least in families that can afford to develop them. But unless a child also succeeds at sequential tasks, art alone cannot save a young person from feelings of shame engendered by poor reading, spelling or calculation skills.

There is also some question as to whether the development of left-hemispheric competencies (e.g. speaking, reading, writing, etc.), can interfere with prodigious artistic talent. That appeared to be the case for Nadia, a savant whose artistic abilities disappeared as she developed greater facility with language. Is it possible that the great emphasis that we place on left-hemispheric skills in school results in the loss of other abilities, such as artistic talent and spatial genius? Scary! Unfortunately, this may well be true.

> She drew her first Mr. Potatohead man at 1.8 years and continues to show unusual skill in this area.

> When she was two, I asked my daughter if she could draw a square and she did! ...At three or four in the German kindergarten she dazzled her teachers with her gift of observation. In copying a real snow drop by cutting paper and gluing it together, our daughter was the only kid who had the leaves attached the way the snowdrop really showed! At four she also drew a cat by one continuous outline which amazed her teachers as well.

When my son was 3 years old, I was a graduate student at Rice University working towards a masters degree in architecture. One evening, as I crouched over my drawing board at home, T crawled up into my lap and asked me about my drawing. I very briefly explained architectural cross-sections, gave him a hug, put him down and sent him off to play. In less than thirty minutes, T was back. He had found a piece of paper and a pencil, and had created a cross-sectional drawing of our house, through his bedroom and the floor below. He had no help or further instructions, but every detail was amazingly correct—T had visualized and drawn toilets, door knobs, walls, floors and all, in cross-section, in an architectural style, and placed them in their proper locations.

My son draws with strong, firm lines, not little soft sketches, hardly ever using the eraser. I once asked him how he could draw this way and he said, "I don't draw, I have a photocopy machine in my head and I just copy."

When he was between 5 and 6 years of age, he had a phase when he often performed big drawing projects. They used to be pictures of whales and dinosaurs, but once (aged 5) he also made a skeleton almost his own size. The way he worked was always the same: He took A4 blank photocopy papers one by one and drew the relevant parts of his respective project while marking the finishing points of the lines on one piece of paper as starting points on the next. After that he taped all the papers together and voila, there was the whale, dino or skeleton.

M likes to oil paint and draw. When she draws things, she draws from strange perspectives. She drew a playground slide from the perspective of the ladder behind it. ...She makes potions with stuff from the kitchen.

Her hobbies include drawing and coloring, cutting stuff up with scissors (her hair twice and a couple of dresses), clay, friends, stuffed animals, collecting things, jokes, magic, going on walks, music. ...Her list to Santa included: A set of drums, a carpenter's tool belt, an accordion, a snowboard, craft kit, clay, and handcuffs.

⚘ Construction

Another frequently mentioned indicator of visual-spatial abilities in children—young and old—is a penchant for construction. The stories about construction toys, especially Legos™, are so rampant that I'm beginning to sound like a Lego™ commercial (unpaid, of course)! More boys than girls are builders, and girls' constructions tend to be different from those of boys. Kindergarten girls have been observed to work together in block centers to create communities, whereas boys tend to work alone and are more focused on the construction of objects, such as towers and buildings. Boys get emotionally attached to their creations and are likely to get very upset when they're knocked down. So try to find a safe place for them to build. Take pictures of their architectural wonders.

He was intensely interested in "construction"...first blocks, at around a year of age, and on to Legos™. He started playing with the smaller-sized Legos™ at three, rapidly progressing to larger and larger sets. He still plays with Legos™.

≋ ≋ ≋

Before two she was using Construx™ and Legos™, building unique and detailed pieces without help.

≋ ≋ ≋

Our daughter was the Lego™ princess of her preschool.

≋ ≋ ≋

My son [4½] adores Legos™ and any other building system, and makes elaborate and highly imaginative creations. The odd thing is that he seems to be able to think of them from the inside out, and will suddenly rearrange big chunks of them to make something entirely new, which he calls "transforming."

≋ ≋ ≋

As a 5 year old he constructed a time-line of the history of architecture with his blocks (Stonehenge, Pyramids, Parthenon, medieval castle, American log cabin, Eiffel Tower, Empire State Building).

≋ ≋ ≋

M [age 5] is obsessed with building. He builds constantly and with any material around him. ...I can clearly see when I'm around other children that he perceives the world differently ...The first time we went over a big bridge, we said, "M look at the ocean, look at the ships." He said, "I wonder how they built this?" This was when he was 3.

⚘ Numbers

A love affair with numbers may begin when children are just toddlers. Not all VSLs are natural counters, but children who love to count are often visual-spatial. Two of these anecdotes are about 5 year olds who invented their own systems of multiplication, which always generate the correct answers even though no one else can understand how they work. One mother called it "fast adding." The brightest child we tested at the Center developed her own method of rapid finger calculation in place of multiplication before she was 7. Her system worked perfectly, but no one else was able to decipher it.

At 2 years, 1 month, his favorite gift was a Mickey Mouse calculator. He'd sit for an hour or more pressing the buttons, adding and subtracting by one. By 2½, he was counting to 100 forwards and from 100 to 0 backwards. Then he started counting by 10's.

J was able to add three-digit numbers by 2 years 6 months; and mastered multiplication and division by the age of 3.

When M was 3, I would ask her such things as, "If you had 97 dollars and someone took 8 of them, how much would you have left?" Her eyes would go up to the ceiling, her lips would stay still – no fingers moving. She would bring her head down and look straight at me, giving me the correct answer. The sicker she was, the better her math skills got! One day I asked her what she sees when she looks up there at the ceiling. She said she sees, "just numbers."

When she was 4, I caught her buying ice cream from the ice cream truck that was cruising our neighborhood. She apparently had seen other kids give their money to the ice cream man, recognized what correct coins were needed for the treat she wanted (an Incredible Hulk ice cream bar). And went through the junk drawer to collect the right amount of money.

When T was in kindergarten, his brother was in third grade, learning to multiply. T wanted to multiply, too, but his teacher wouldn't consider it. So he figured out his own computation system. He tried to explain it to us, but we never understood how it worked. T always arrived at the right answer, though!

S received Nintendo for his fifth birthday. In the game of Zelda he learned to collect and save 294 coins to buy a magic ring. From watching the coins tally on the screen, he figured out the number line. He asked how far numbers could go. What happens when you get to 999. He learned to add and subtract. He figured out "fast adding" which was his own unique way of multiplication. He was doing things with numbers that he had no vocabulary to talk about. He wanted to know what the ten number was, and the thirteen number. It took us some time before we realized he was talking about million and billion. During his Kindergarten year, one of his favorite things to do was to pull out the unabridged dictionary and look up "number" to find the names of all the "really big" numbers.

In Kindergarten, A asked can you subtract infinity from infinity? "Is the answer zero because any number take away itself is zero or is it impossible because since you can't get to infinity you can't turn around and come back?"

✤ Excellent visual memory

Excellent visual memory is a visual-spatial ability that appears as often in girls as in boys. We need to pay closer attention to visual-spatial talents in girls, which may be masked by their advanced verbal abilities. Visual-spatial skills underlie advanced mathematical talent. Encourage girls with these skills to enter mathematically oriented fields, where they are likely to shine (as well as make a considerable amount of money!).

At 8 months, A could operate the TV and VCR to watch her Spot videos. She would insert the cartridge correctly, rewind the tape, hit play. Incredibly, she would hit pause/rewind to replay parts of the video that were amusing to her. She would chortle during these funny parts. At age

2, A got a 64-pack of Crayola crayons. She memorized all 64 of the colors. At age 4, she knows all 50 states and 50 state capitols. Given one, she can produce the match.

At 11 months, N could select the car key from 10 keys on my key ring and fit it into the car or trunk, never making a mistake. (None of my keys were color-coded.)

At one year old, he was not very verbal. At a stoplight in our city, he started yelling from his car seat, "Wehbot? Wehbot?" He was getting very anxious and straining in his seat to look out windows. He cried and repeated "wehbot" all of the way home. The next few times we were at that intersection he would say the same thing. Finally, we realized there used to be a boat for sale on the corner and it was now gone. K had been saying, "Where boat?"

When he was two, he looked at a slice of kiwi and said "chromosomes," which is exactly what the seeds looked like. Apparently he had noticed the picture of a cell I had shown his brother several days earlier.

I can remember two early incidents, where he remembered places that we had been 10 months before, and before he was talking, seeing the place again, and asking questions or making the appropriate comments. J was probably around 18 months old when we drove by these two places, and around 2½ years old when he saw them again. He would say, "that was the toy store that went out of business, they were closed," or "Mommy, that's where you went to get your driver's license but we had to go because the line was too long."

I have a four-and-a-half year old who demonstrated incredible spatial and visual abilities before he could even talk. He thinks in three dimensions. ...He never forgets anything he sees, and noticed the tiniest details, which drove us crazy while driving. He'd see a little carved owl on the facade of a building on a visually packed city street and would get very upset if we couldn't find it, so we spent a lot of time frantically searching before the light changed. ...He loves mazes. The other day he astounded me by working a word find puzzle without me telling him how they work—he found the words "unity," "environment" and "responsibility" (backwards) and he does not read.

✣ Spatial perception

Children who have a better sense of direction than you do are easy to spot as VSLs. They can tell what rooms are above and below them. They make mental maps in their heads and remember every place they've ever been—even if they've only been there once. It's maddening to hear a 3-year-old voice pipe up with, "Mom, you just turned the wrong way." You try to argue, saying, "You don't know that. You were only here once when you were 2." And guess who's right?

" MOM, YOU JUST MISSED YOUR TURN."

When he was less than a year old, he would recognize when we'd reached our driveway (we lived in a wooded area, and it was not that easy to tell).

As a toddler, he could consistently point out the direction of home, grandma's house, etc., even if we were many miles away, in a totally unfamiliar place! It was a little eerie.

After his second day of preschool, when he was 2½, I drove in the direction of the school (a direction we seldom drove in) but then turned off to go someplace else. He started pointing in the direction of the school and shouting "No - 'at way, 'at way!"

She was selected as the lead role (Clara) in her ballet troupe's Nutcracker performance due to her good technique and ability to know exactly where she is in space during the dance routines.

His teacher explained to me how he has an ability to see in and through things rather than just head on. For example: The children were learning about Indians. The children's drawings reflected a teepee and maybe an Indian. M's was quite different. He explained that the circle in the middle of the drawing was him from inside the teepee looking up into the sky. The circle was surrounded by stars!

His passion has always been roads, traffic signals, roller coasters (high speed, narrow roads!!) and all things related to these areas. When he was three, we started noticing from his comments that he seemed to remember routes taken, even if only taken once. Matters came to a head one day when his grandmother, who was caring for him and his sister while my husband and I were out of town on business, having successfully picked up my son at the park after a preschool outing, took a wrong turn and couldn't figure out where she was. Our son, then 4, successfully directed her back to the main road by indicating with his thumbs, visible in the rear view mirror, which way she should go and when she should turn. The story has become family legend.

✂ Maps and geography

Some visual-spatial children have a natural fascination with maps, globes, capitals, and the location of things. Two of these children munch geographical shapes out of food. Jonathan Estrada's abilities are the most remarkable I've encountered.

Jonathan received a jigsaw puzzle of the United States on his first birthday. At first he needed help to put together the puzzle, then, by the age of 16 months, he was reading and able to put the puzzle together by himself. Before the age of 2, he spontaneously started biting slices of American cheese in his father's deli into shapes that closely resembled states. First Utah, then Pennsylvania, then Texas. Then he began imprinting a tooth mark where each state capital belonged. By the age of 3, he was constructing entire maps of the United States from cheese slices in one hour. This landed him an appearance on Letterman.

When Jonathan was 3, he went into a toy store with his mother and she was about to buy him a ball in the form of a globe when he suddenly burst into tears. "It's broken," he cried. The manager tried to reassure him that the ball was fine—that it would bounce perfectly. But Jonathan insisted that it was broken. "See, the Galapagos Islands are missing. They're supposed to be there, near Ecuador." The manager checked, and, of course, Jonathan was right. The manager gave Jonathan the globe.

Geography has remained only one of Jonathan's many interests. He is fascinated by computers, mathematics, science and music. And he is demonstrating prodigious talent for the piano. He qualified to play at Carnegie Hall before he was 9. He is also a remarkably loving, sensitive, morally aware human being.

From 9 months, [he was] increasingly interested in spending time with books, also love of music, and interest in world map—which began a continuing interest in maps. As a 3 and 4 year old, he often used to bite his crackers and other food into shapes of Greenland or India or Australia or Antarctica.

At 3½, N could put a U.S. puzzle together with no borders. He taught himself all of this from his placemat. He could recognize the shapes of all the states upside down, backwards. He memorized his U.S. flags and countries placemat at age 4. At 4½, he knew all his states, capitals and their locations on a blank map. He also knows the location of the capital within its own state (blank map again). Just before his 5th birthday, he learned all the continents and countries. [At 5½] he can tell you what colors are in every flag and identify them readily. (There are probably 100 on his placemat.) His state map placemat shows the states in 5 varying colors. N can tell you, without referring back to the map for days, what color any of the states are on his map. He pictures it in his mind.

All of these stories are about boys, but I have also come across girls who are deeply attracted to maps. "At 3½ she mastered a U.S. map puzzle." And Anne, discussed in Chapter 1, traced around all the states when she was in preschool and created a map when she was only 4 years old. She went on to say:

Once, in 3rd grade, I found a booklet about topographical maps in the classroom. I read it while the teacher was teaching something else and could read topo maps that day.

✧ Vivid imagination

All children are imaginative to some degree, but visual-spatial children have extraordinarily vivid imaginations. For them, there is a very thin line between reality and fantasy, and they may insist that other family members honor their worlds. Marty Rogers studied the incidence of imaginary playmates among gifted and average students. He found that while an average child might create one imaginary playmate, a gifted child was likely to have a greater number of imaginary friends, and the relationships were often complex. Some had such elaborate fantasy lives that they were regular little Tolkiens.

> One child's imaginary friends included, "Jesus as a young boy. He appeared most often when 'B' was afraid, lonely or frustrated. They carried on lengthy conversations." Another child had a "family that lived in the pan cupboard: David, the father; Kookoo, the mother, and Baby Dew. They later had another baby, Rose. David died. She also had a teenage sister, Hallelujah." One parent wrote, "Being an only child, 'C' had "Imaginary Friend" (that was his name) to play board games, etc. Not surprisingly, Friend always lost!" (M. Rogers & Silverman, 1988, p. 16)

One little girl we assessed had an entire family of mice. A friend of mine from Auckland, who writes and illustrates children's books, had a family of pegs (the kind you hang clothes on). She would get very upset if her father tried to put anything in the back of the car because it was completely filled with her family of pegs and she didn't want them to get crushed. I once tested an 11-year-old boy and asked his father if the boy had ever had any imaginary companions. His son had never talked about them, so he asked him, and the boy replied, "What do you mean 'Did I?' I still have nine of them!" Charlene Davis used to have her middle-school gifted students in Casper, Wyoming discuss their "Fantasy Friends" with each other and then write about them. It was a fascinating exercise for the students to discover that they weren't the only ones who were deeply attached to imaginary friends at some point in their lives.

When it comes to imagination, girls appear to have as much of it as boys, if not more, if the following stories are any indication.

> T started daycare at age 2.5. ...She began telling the daycare and her parents very imaginative and convincing stories that often entertained and sometimes frightened us. She told me that her teacher took the entire daycare to the store and bought them all chocolate, but nothing for her.

> ...T was convinced she could fly and to this day (age 9) has trouble distinguishing fantasy from reality. She constantly saw unicorns, she loves elves, fairies and still strongly believes in Santa. ...In kindergarten T continued with her fantastic stories; they were convincing until we pressed her for details, then they lacked credibility. ...She was very imaginative and advanced with her crafts. ...Our home is cluttered with crafts and inventions of all kinds. We have a joke in our home, every time someone

tries to throw something in the garbage we say, "Don't throw that out!! T can make something out of it!!"

[Age 4] She came into my room with a blanket and in the space of a few minutes turned it (and herself) into a turban, a veil, hair, bats' wings (and told us how the bat sleeps upside down with the wings wrapped around). She will actively be in a conversation with no one else in the room. C loves drawing and painting, being read to, singing and rhyming games, and rock collecting. The scientist in C comes out in unpredictable ways. She is always experimenting. Nothing is safe. The carpet suffers from her experiments.

At kindergarten graduation, M had to tell what she was going to be when she grew up. She couldn't decide between a spy or a comedian. Since then, she has informed me that she will be a tooth fairy, but is a little worried about who will be teaching her how to fly.

She wanted a slumber party with 10 girlfriends... She made them all laugh telling ghost stories off the top of her head about a ghost named Peter.

He can make anything just looking at a picture or creating out of his imagination. He also builds things out of odds and ends around the house. Many rolls of Scotch tape have been sacrificed in the name of science. One time my husband had some little scraps of wood left over from an outdoor project and he asked J (then age 4) if he would like them to build with. Enthusiastically, J ran for his shoes to head out to the garage. "What are you going to make?" I asked. J stopped and looked at me like I was crazy. "I don't know that yet," he replied, "I have to see the wood first!"

⚜ Mechanical interest and ability

Mechanical ability is one of the best indicators of visual-spatial abilities and least recognized signs of giftedness. In previous eras, boys who were good at woodshop, engine repair, or mechanics were funneled into vocational training and perceived as less intelligent than the college-bound, academically talented students. But various high-level fields today, such as mechanical and electrical engineering, the computer industry, and aeronautics, depend on mechanically inclined students. These gifts need to be recognized and developed. They may appear early in life, as is readily seen in these stories about young technical wizards who were obsessed with mechanical objects. Given that most of these anecdotes are about very young boys makes me wonder if the love affair between males and their power tools is innate! I've included a lot of these stories, because I think they're hilarious.

> [At 5 months] M's first word was fan (ceiling fan—began interest in electrical things). Knew all shapes from circle to trapezoid and parallelogram before 2½ years. He loves electronics—builds working and semi-working electronic gadgets. Made 1st electromagnetic generator at age 4. Wanted a ground fault interrupter for 3rd birthday—this meant that he could now safely plug things in one outlet in our new house. Made 1st amplifier at age 5 (assembled electronic Heathkit 1-watt audio amplifier). Always asked the details of how things worked. It used to amaze me that what he learned one day (even during that 1st year) he could still know the information the next morning. I worked with him several hours a day (to the detriment of the housework, but who cares) teaching him language, shapes, alphabet, numbers, sounds, etc. When he asked a question we tried to answer it with all the knowledge we had about the subject (appropriate for his age level and language) and he retained much of what we told him.

We tested M at the Center when he was 5. When he was asked to draw a person, he drew a diode circuit and a transformer with a built-in plug!

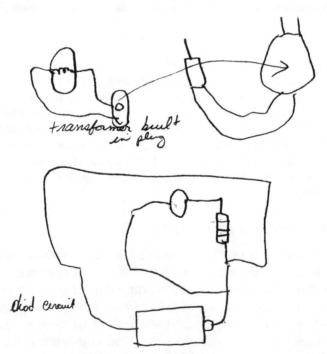

transformer built in plug

diod circuit

M's answers to our incomplete sentences test were a riot:

I dream of "roses, I meant electronic circuits."

I hate "when my brother gets into my electronics and destroys it."

When I get older I'm "going to be somebody who does a lot of electronics."

My mother and father "help me with electronics."

I think most about "electronic circuits."

Talk about single-mindedness! If this kid doesn't grow up to be an electrical engineer, an inventor of electronics, or some related field, I'll eat my hard hat.

At about 11 months B could thread a nut onto a bolt or off of a bolt. [At age 3] B can identify almost *every tool* in the shop (and describe what they do). He can identify almost every piece of heavy equipment made and what they do. At age 2½ B could turn on the TV, the VCR, put in a tape and completely operate the VCR.

From the age of 14 months, E had a total preoccupation with electric and mechanical apparatus. His first phrase was "Big light in living room shock you." As a tot he would follow exposed wiring and cords to find plugs and/or hook-ups. When 3 years old, at Elitch's, he was much more interested in how the merry-go-round worked ("Where is motor, gears, etc."?) than riding it. He also has a real eye for detail in these areas. [At age 7] his favorite activities with Dad are designing and building electrical motors or things attached to electrical motors that go, or light up, or make noise.

[At 2½] Clocks and gears entered our life around this time. M got clocks for gifts and we'd sit on the bed watching them. He wanted to know about gears and had to see the engine of the car. We'd be riding and he'd be listening for the gears operating. The summer when he was 2½, we'd go to the amusement park, and the kids loved the rides but I was a nervous wreck. He would lean way over to see how the ride operated. On the merry-go-round his head was always up watching the poles to see how they operated or else he was leaning into the center of the ride to see the gears. On one of the little car rides, he started crawling under one of the cars. We ran with the attendant and when we got there he looked up and asked, "What makes this thing run, anyway?"

Heh. Yeah, I am probably one of these. My first memory of "programming" was when I was 3 and my dad showed me how the Rain-Bird sprinklers are adjusted. I went around to all our neighbors' yards reprogramming them to water the street. It didn't go over too well with the neighbors!

[Age 4] J loves building, constructing, taking things apart, all facets of building (plumbing, electrical, mechanical things, phone systems, air conditioning systems). His favorite activities are to build these systems out of his collection of materials from Ace Hardware, Builder's Square, Office Depot, our old appliances, computers, telephones, etc. He loves to act out whatever he has seen, refrigerator repairman, sound system installer, gardeners, salespeople, etc. ...His favorite books are Home Improvement books, *The Way Things Work*, *Amelia Bedelia*, *How Thing Work in Your Home* (appliances), *How Things Work* (general), Science books (Electrical, Chemistry). At approximately 3½ years old, J began reciting the dialogue of a home improvement video that he loved to watch (it's about 30 minutes long). It's filled with really technical stuff. J is constantly making keen observations and analogies. When he was about 3, he said the slide at the park looked like an auger bit, so he called it the "worm gear slide."

During the assessment, J completed two incomplete sentences in the following manner: *I want to go to* "Ace." *My mother doesn't* "go to Ace." Ironically, his mother said that the reason they wanted their child assessed was to use the test as a "tool" for selecting the right school for J!

By shortly after age five, he was displaying unusual mechanical ability working alongside his father in our home workshop. A learned to use a mini-lathe and occasionally made remarkably apt tool choices, displaying a gift for mechanical problem-solving.

A's inventions:

Apple juice grinder – preschool age

Pump using straws – preschool age, built without help

Eavesdropping device (for listening to girls on the playground) – age 6, built with Dad

Hovercraft – age 6-7, powered by vacuum cleaner motor, built with Dad from A's concept

Electric vehicle – age 8, built with PVC pipe; project involved substantial parental involvement

One or two smaller electric vehicles – age 9, built with middle-school aged neighbor

Car art-assemblage – 5th grade

Electric race car — begun at 12 or 13, conversion from golf cart, built with Dad's advice and assistance

Electric scooter — age 13, built with Dad's advice

Car assemblage 2 — age 14

Band saw air cleaner — age 14, designed and built entirely by A

Assorted band saw tools — age 14, designed and built entirely by A

❧ Taking things apart

Related to mechanical ability is visual-spatial boys' penchant for taking things apart. Sometimes they even put them back together again accurately. Other times they take the parts and turn them into something more creative. You had better hide anything you don't want taken apart, because that's what some of them do—whatever they can get their hands on. But I did find one girl who fit this category:

From an early age, C knew how to and was interested in fixing things, with or without the fine motor control required. When she was 18 mos., I was fixing a cabinet and said out loud that I needed a Phillips screwdriver. She got her stool, pulled it over to the drawer, opened the drawer, extracted the correct screwdriver and handed it to me. C was always very interested in how the garage door worked. When she started talking at age 2.5, she described in detail how the garage door worked. I didn't even know it was chain operated. ...C was always interested in flashlights. As soon as she could take them apart and put them together, she lost her interest and moved on. ...When C has figured something out or mastered a skill, she is very reluctant to do it again.

Tool Boy

Since C could get around at all he's been taking everything apart, from the kitchen chairs to toys that he received for his first birthday. At my parents' house, I painted a child's desk chair for my youngest brother. My son, then 15 months, discovered the chair and fell in love with it. At that time he was really interested in any and all tools, especially screwdrivers. The chair was held together with 4 screws in the seat, 1 screw in each leg and 4 screws holding the back on. One day, my father had been working on something in the kitchen and he left his tools out, forgetting about our "Tool boy." The tools had been left alone for less than ten minutes. My father had returned to pick up his tools, but was missing one screwdriver, a Phillips head. C had also disappeared. Everyone went in search of my blonde-headed little boy. We found him in my 8-year-old brother's room, with the chair totally disassembled. This all transpired in about 15 minutes. The chair was put back together, with locking nuts, and all tools were then supervised or put away well out of reach. The funny thing was, C dismantled the chair with the correct tool, a Phillips head screwdriver, and did not strip the screw heads.

As early as two, he would take apart the telephone.

I pretty much took apart everything in the house to see how it worked. Around 10 or 11 I started to have the ability to put it together again so it would still work. Even today (at age 36) most of the excitement of buying something new is that I can take it apart and see how it works, and of course put it back together again. Cars, motorcycles, lawnmowers, computers, VCRs, telephones, printers, refrigerators, watches, furnaces, space heaters, and plumbing. You name it, I've probably taken it apart to see how it works. Of course, I read books about theory of operation too, and metallurgy and electricity. I've dabbled in locksmithing, but only to find out how they work. Heck, doesn't everyone carry a set of pliers on them on a business trip, so they can get a decent shower in the morning (bypass the flow restrictor in the shower head)?

✤ Music

Music is a spatial field that receives attention in early childhood, particularly in musical families. Some speculate that there is a critical period for the development of musical talent, and if a child doesn't receive musical training during this period, the talent may not develop to its fullest potential. Of course, if a family perceives music as just a hobby, rather than as a future profession, then this critical period is not of primary concern. But musical children often learn better when information is made rhythmic or put to music. There are as many girls as boys who demonstrate early talent in music.

Noted from about 4½ months on his rhythmic keeping in time with music, with his arm, bouncing in his baby chair and so on.

At 6-7 months (before crawling) he would deliberately hit each key on a toy piano and listen to it before hitting the next note. Before he could talk he would babble recognizable melodies. Now [age 2½] he quickly picks up songs and can reproduce them at will.

H loves to sing. She learned the first verse of the Star Spangled Banner before she was 2 years old. She also loves to make up her own songs when she sings.

Before 2½, she could sing a tune. At 2½, she began cello lessons. I had no plans to start her on cello until she was 5, but she began asking for a cello at age 2. The incident that convinced me that I'd better give in occurred one afternoon when I found her sitting in the living room in my cello practice spot with two toys which served as a pretend cello and pretend bow, announcing her selections (favorite family songs), and then making playing motions while singing the song. I saw then that she *needed* to learn to play the cello. At 3½, she sang a short phrase of music, then told me the rhythmic notation (correctly). At 4½, she composed a phrase or two of music. She has always been perfectly at ease with my junior high and high school aged cello students. [At age 5½] some of her musical abilities (such as sight singing) are at early college level.

She began taking [piano] lessons at the age of five, and her piano teacher said she had great talent—genius ability. Strengths with [visual-spatial] ability include a love of math, science, music, and the ability to excel at foreign language comprehension. And now you want to know what P wants to be when she grows up? The first female president! I know she can do anything she puts her mind to and I'll be proud of her no matter what—I'm already her biggest fan!

⚜Mazes

Many visual-spatial children who love puzzles also love mazes. I once worked with a 5-year-old boy who could solve any adult maze. But there are a lot of VSLs who have never been exposed to them. It would be a good idea to try them with a visual-spatial child and see what happens. Like puzzles, mazes can be affected by visual processing issues. So a visual-spatial child with visual issues may find them frustrating. These stories all happen to be about boys, but I've also seen some girls who excel at mazes.

I took my son to the local hands-on museum when he was three years old. We went to a room to watch a demonstration, then we were handed some shamrock mazes. Our son had finished his even before some of the adults finished. He said, "Look, Mom, I know the secret, you start from the end."

I bought my son, R, a workbook—not my usual sort of thing to do, but he'd seen these little mazes in a freebie book we had and really liked them and I saw a preschool Maze book in the store and picked it up. We sat down together and did about half of it in twenty minutes or so. It was really interesting to see how his mind works. ...He glanced at the picture, saw immediately what path to take, and did it. Of course, he's only three...but this was how I learned that he was a visual-spatial learner!

Zelda™ [a Nintendo game] is a maze. There are hundreds of screens in the game. S [age 5] never got lost. He would come into the living room when someone else was playing, and instantly know where they were, and how to tell them how to get wherever they wanted to go. He knew the contents of every room in the game. He could play for hours.

⚜Computers

I haven't collected as many stories as I would have anticipated about precocious abilities with computers, but the ones I have are choice. Parents who are nervous about computers, lack computer literacy themselves, or fear the damage that their toddlers can do to expensive computer equipment, are less likely to expose their young children to word processing or computer programming. I imagine that as more parents start to recognize how early their children can develop computer competence, the anecdotes in this department will come flooding in. As these stories indicate, today's girls can be just as fascinated with computers as boys.

> At 1 year, A got some computer CD's. She learned how to insert and play the CD's over the next 3 months. She could fully use the mouse (selecting by clicking, dragging and dropping, etc.).

> At age 4, M surprised me again one day with a love letter that she composed and printed on our computer. I never taught her how to turn on the computer, find the word processing program, turn on the printer and print.

> I taught myself the BASIC programming language at age 6. I later developed a fascination with fitting things together and taking things apart, which is still evidenced by various computer peripherals lying around my desk in differing stages of assembly.

There may be other early signs of visual-spatial abilities, but these are clearly the ones that appear with the greatest frequency. If you see any of these characteristics or interests in your child, it would be wise to obtain an evaluation of his or her learning style. You are likely to have to become your child's advocate in the educational system until methods of teaching visual-spatial learners become common knowledge.

It's also advisable to gain a comprehensive evaluation of your child's strengths and weaknesses. Some of the children described in this chapter are profoundly gifted. Others have processing difficulties involving the left hemisphere. Early diagnosis permits early intervention. The next chapter describes how we formally assess visual-spatial abilities, and Chapter 9 addresses gifted children with learning disabilities. Visual-spatial children with attention deficits are discussed in Chapter 11. For more about parenting visual-spatial learners, be sure to read Chapters 10 and 12. And Chapter 15, the grand finale, has something for everyone.

Notes:

How Do You Assess
Visual-Spatial Abilities?

Thought you might be interested in an overview of our daughter, a 10 year old visual-spatial learner (our suspicion was validated on an IQ test she took at age 8 where she maxed out the Block Design and Comprehension tests and was told she had "superior strengths in abstract reasoning and visualization" by the administering psychologist).

The Stanford-Binet 4th edition given to him at age 5 showed: verbal reasoning-103: abstract/visual reasoning-144; quantitative reasoning-118; short term memory-112. The final IQ was 123. Each teacher continued to nominate him for our gifted program until he was tested again in third grade at age 8 years. The WISC-III showed: Verbal 129 and Performance 135, giving an IQ of 135. His highest subtest was in Block Design at 19 and lowest was 11 at Picture Completion. The others ranged 14 to 17. B's CAT tests are decreasing in numbers every year. ...His highest is always in math concepts and vocabulary.

Are you curious about what all these test scores mean? This chapter is for those of you (1) who want to know how testing can determine if a person is visual-spatial; (2) who are wondering if you or your child might have a learning disability; or (3) who are trying to get a VSL into a gifted program. If none of this applies, just skip it and go on to another chapter. (This message is for the auditory-sequential reader. If you're visual-spatial, you undoubtedly skipped around the book anyway, probably reading the last chapter first, or just reading those sections that grabbed you.) Psychologists should definitely read this chapter. It tells you how to identify VSLs through test data.

WARNING: This chapter is a prerequisite for understanding Chapter 9 on learning disabilities, so if you plan to read the next chapter, at least skim this one. OK?

What do these test scores mean?

We didn't test the children in the anecdotes, so all I have is the information you just read above. High Block Design scores show up in both stories. That's because Block Design is the best measure of visual-spatial abilities on the Wechsler scales *(WPPSI, WISC,* and *WAIS)*. In this subtest, examinees are shown pictures of designs, and asked to reproduce them with blocks. The blocks have sides that are all red, all white, and red and white triangles that make a square. They start with 4 blocks, then 9 blocks, and the items get harder and harder. In the first description, the girl "maxed out"—achieved the highest possible score (99.9[th]%)—on both Block Design and Comprehension. This tells me that she's gifted (both of these tests are good measures of abstract reasoning), and a highly gifted visual-spatial learner. No evidence is given of learning disabilities.

In the second situation, the boy achieved a composite IQ score of 123 on the *Stanford-Binet Intelligence Scale-Fourth Edition (SB-IV)* when he was 5 years old. This is in the superior range, but not high enough for him to qualify for most gifted programs. At the age of 8, he obtained a Full Scale IQ score of 135, in the gifted range, on the *Wechsler Intelligence Scale for Children-Third Edition (WISC-III).* **Bravo** to his astute teachers who continued to nominate him for the gifted program despite his earlier test scores!! His score of 144 on the Abstract Visual Reasoning section of the *SB-IV* is nearly in the highly gifted range. That's the section that measures visual-spatial abilities. However, the other parts of the test were all in the average range, and pulled down his composite IQ score. On the *WISC-III,* his Performance IQ was 135, solidly gifted, and higher than his Verbal IQ (129), which is one point below the gifted range. This is a classic visual-spatial profile. His Full

Scale IQ was the same as his Performance IQ score (it's not an average), and this time he probably qualified for the gifted program. YEA!!

Here's how I would interpret the test data on this boy. He is unquestionably gifted, highly gifted in visual-spatial abilities and mathematically talented. But he has significant weaknesses, which are lowering his achievement scores. His *SB-IV* profile when he was five revealed a 41-point difference between his visual-spatial and auditory-verbal skills. This is huge! His auditory short-term memory was weak. He probably has difficulty with auditory processing. On the *WISC-III*, his subtest scores varied from about average on Picture Completion, which measures attention to visual detail, to the highest possible score on Block Design (99.9th%). Most of his scores are in the superior and gifted ranges (91st% to 99th%). However, his *California Achievement Test (CAT)* scores are in the high average range and decreasing every year. So, while he is an excellent candidate for the gifted program, he might be booted out if they place too high a premium on achievement.

I would call him "twice exceptional"—gifted with learning disabilities. He is exactly the kind of kid who falls through the cracks in the school system, as we shall see later on in the chapter and in Chapter 9. None of his scores is below average, so he will not qualify for special education support. He might be seen as a bright boy who doesn't try hard enough, when he is probably trying twice as hard as other students. I would recommend that he have a central auditory processing battery and that his parents do the "Activities to Enhance Auditory Processing" with him at the end of Chapter 3.

In these next two chapters, I will be discussing assessment profiles of many other children like the two described above. Hopefully, their stories will help you have a better understanding of how to interpret test data on yourself, your children or the students in your classroom.

Visual-spatial tasks on the *SBL-M*

When I first started thinking about VSLs in 1981, we were using the *Stanford-Binet Intelligence Scale (Form L-M) (SBL-M)* for our assessments. I noticed that some children performed extraordinarily well on visual-spatial items on the *SBL-M*. The test taken by the second child described above, the *Stanford-Binet, Fourth Edition (SB-IV)*, came out in 1986 and replaced the *Stanford-Binet L-M*. Unfortunately, the *SB-IV* had too low a ceiling so it was not as useful for testing gifted children as the *SBL-M*. Examiners who assess highly and profoundly gifted children continue to give the *SBL-M* as a supplemental test when children top out on the newer tests.

Otherwise, it's like measuring six-foot tall people with five-foot rulers.

The visual-spatial items on the *SBL-M* included counting a number of blocks in an array with some of the blocks hidden; drawing abstract designs from memory that had been shown for only ten seconds; following complex sets of directions involving north, south, east, west, left and right; and visualization of how a folded and cut piece of paper would look unfolded. Children who did well on these items also seemed to do well on mathematical logic items, which require visualization. This was true even for children who had relatively low grades in arithmetic. The test contains more visual-spatial tasks for older children. Many of the visual-spatial items for younger children, such as mazes, drawing, and copying shapes, depend heavily on pencil/paper skills, so they are hard for those VSLs who have difficulty with fine motor coordination.

Table 8.1, on the next page, shows the main items on the *SBL-M* that seemed to fit into one category or the other. Notice the uneven distribution of items that measure auditory-sequential and visual-spatial abilities at different age levels. Assessment of both factors is only possible at ages 10, 13, and the Superior Adult II and III levels.

When I first began looking at VSLs who were high spatial/high sequential, I did *not* find more boys. During the first ten years, using the *SBL-M,* we found as many girls in the highest IQ ranges (above 160, 170, 180) as boys, even though nearly 60% of the children referred for testing were male. However, when I started to focus on VSLs with high spatial abilities and low sequential abilities—mostly underachievers, I was over-loaded with boys. It appeared that girls had high visual-spatial abilities, but less difficulty sequencing. Similarly, Norman Geschwind found

Table 8.1

Analysis of Auditory-Sequential and Visual-Spatial Tasks at Each Age Level on the Stanford-Binet Intelligence Scale (Form L-M)

Year	Auditory-Sequential	Visual-Spatial
IV-6	3 Commissions	
V		Paper Folding Patience Rectangle
VI		Maze Tracing
VII	Repeating 5 Digits	
VIII	Memory for Stories Naming Days of the Week	
IX		Paper Cutting Memory for Designs
X	Repeating 6 Digits	Block Counting
XI	Memory for Sentences 2	
XII		Picture Absurdities
XIII	Memory for Sentences 3	Plan of Search
XIV		Orientation Ingenuity
AA		Orientation
SA-I		Enclosed Box Problem
SA-II	Repeating Passage 1	Ingenuity
SA-III	Repeating Passage 2	Orientation

(AA stands for the Average Adult level; SA for Superior Adult.)

that dyslexic males often possessed remarkable spatial talents, and that their sisters usually had the talents without the dyslexia.

Speed tests vs. power tests

I expected it to be much easier to find VSLs with the *WISC-III*. The Wechsler scales were developed specifically to find individuals with high intelligence in the nonverbal realm. During World War I, David Wechsler had been assigned the task of testing recruits who could not pass the written *Army Alpha* and *Beta* tests. He found that they did better on nonverbal tests. So, 20 years later, when he began developing IQ tests for adults, he made sure that half the items were nonverbal. Eventually, he developed tests for children, using the same format. Until 2003, all Wechsler scales were divided into Verbal and Performance (nonverbal) items. The Verbal items were presented auditorally and the Performance items were presented visually. It was generally believed that individuals with visual-spatial strengths were able to demonstrate them better on Wechsler tests than on the more verbal *Stanford-Binet* scales (*SBL-M* and *SB-IV*). This is what I assumed would happen. It just didn't work out that way.

To my dismay, our visual-spatial learners actually performed considerably better on the old *Stanford-Binet L-M* scale than they did on the newer tests that supposedly were designed with them in mind. The main reason for this was that the Performance items were **timed**, and visual-spatial learners often need more processing time than the tests allowed. By way of contrast, the *Stanford-Binet L-M* is largely an untimed test of intelligence. The *WISC-III* and the *Wechsler Preschool* and *Primary Scale of Intelligence, Revised (WPPSI-R)* were the most problematic, because they increased the bonus points for speed much higher than they had been on previous versions of these same IQ tests. Alan Kaufman, the major interpreter of the Wechsler scales, reported that emphasis on bonus points for speed penalizes gifted children who are reflective or slower in motor coordination:

> Giving bonus points for speed to preschool children seems silly from every developmental and common-sense perspective. ...The new emphasis on response speed on the *WPPSI-R* will be especially damaging to children referred for gifted assessment. ...

> The main point is that there is great variability in the ability levels of speed, and that variability is undoubtedly due largely to non-intellective factors such as poor motor coordination or a reflective cognitive style. Whenever personality, behavioral, or motor variables enter into a child's scores on an intelligence test, then the role assumed by "pure" intelligence becomes less. The children who are

most affected by the intrusion of "irrelevant" variables are invariably the ones who are referred for gifted assessment.

It is well known that gifted children, as a group, don't excel quite as much in sheer speed. Coding, largely a measure of psychomotor speed, commonly emerges as a valley in the subtest profiles of gifted children. ...

The *WISC-III* allots three bonus points for solving one Block Design item in one to five seconds, and does the same for a Picture Arrangement item. I have only one label for a person who responds to a problem in five or fewer seconds: foolish. (Kaufman, 1992, pp. 156-157)

So now one had to be fast to be considered smart. This new trend really made visual-spatial learners invisible.

I served on the Advisory Panel of the fifth edition of the *Stanford-Binet Intelligence Scale (SB5)*, released in 2003 by Riverside Publishing Company. The project directors and test constructors sought input from the Gifted Development Center staff in constructing the new instrument. We submitted items for consideration; we participated in the item trials in the summer of 2000; and we helped to validate the new test with gifted and exceptionally gifted children in the summers of 2001 and 2002. In July of 2000, Project Director John Wasserman hosted a "gifted summit meeting" in Denver so that the test constructors could spend a few days listening to the special concerns of those of us who work with the gifted. There are more visual-spatial items in the *SB-5*, and the new test, thankfully, is largely *untimed*. So we are hopeful that VSLs will be assessed more accurately on the *SB5*. And it is permissible to use the *SBL-M* as a supplemental test.

WISC vs. Binet scales

The way the *SBL-M* was designed, if you passed one item at an age level, you could go on to a higher age level, which made it possible for visual-spatial learners to demonstrate their abilities well into the adult ranges, even if they only passed the visual-spatial and mathematical reasoning items. Their IQ scores weren't penalized much by the auditory-sequential items that they missed. The test has a very high ceiling, all the way up to Superior Adult III. And it is so rich in abstract reasoning that gifted VSLs can use their abstract reasoning abilities to solve complex items way beyond their age level.

The *WISC* only goes up to age 16, and a child has to be good at most of the subtests in order to obtain a high IQ score. Poor performance in auditory sequencing or defining terms or eye-hand coordination or attention to visual detail knocks down their IQ scores so that they appear less intelligent than they really are. Only one of the subtests on

the *WISC-III* measured visual-spatial abilities extremely well: Block
Design. So if Zach obtained the highest possible score on this subtest
(19), but he was slow at copying symbols, his low score in Coding
canceled out his high score in Block Design. (See the subtest scatter
profile in Figure 9.4, in Chapter 9.) The other Performance subtests
ought to be of some help here, but they all relied heavily on attention to
visual detail and speed. Lots of visual-spatial children don't have these
strengths. So we actually saw higher Verbal IQ scores in our VSLs than
we did Performance scores.

"Niles," a nine-year-old boy, is a good case in point. Just looking at
his *WISC-III* scores would lead one to believe that Niles is an auditory-
sequential learner, since all of the items on the Verbal side are all
presented auditorily. (See Figure 8.1 on the next page.)

Niles' Verbal IQ was significantly higher than his Performance IQ.
His Performance IQ was in the gifted range, but his Verbal IQ was in the
highly gifted range. Notice that his Block Design score was 19, at the
ceiling of the test (99.9[th]%), and that his Picture Arrangement score was
also at the 99th%. We regularly retest on the *SBL-M* children who obtain
two or more subtest scores at the 99th percentile on any current test.
Niles had five scores in this range. His Binet profile is revealing. (See
Figure 8.2 on the next page.)

Niles obtained an IQ of 161 on the *SBL-M*, 20 points higher than his
Full Scale IQ score on the *WISC-III*. His verbal abilities only took him as
far as the 12-year-level, but his spatial abilities took him all the way to
Superior Adult II, accounting for most of his 161 IQ. He was able to
pass orientation problems (north, south, east and west), mathematical
reasoning, and all the visual reasoning items seven years above his age.

Niles

Verbal IQ:	146	Highly Gifted
Performance IQ:	130	Gifted
Full Scale IQ:	141	Gifted

Figure 8.1

WISC-III

Name: Niles   Age: 8 Years, 6 Months

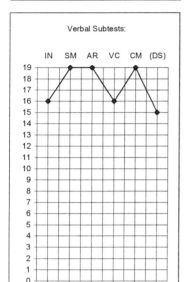

Verbal Subtests:		
Information	**IN**	16
Similarities	**SM**	19
Arithmetic	**AR**	19
Vocabulary	**VC**	16
Comprehension	**CM**	19
Digit Span	**(DS)**	15

Performance Subtests:		
Picture Completion	**PC**	12
Coding	**CD**	12
Picture Arrangement	**PA**	17
Block Design	**BD**	19
Object Assembly	**OA**	12
Symbol Search	**(SS)**	15
Mazes	**(MZ)**	12

( ) Not included in calculating the IQ score.

Figure 8.2

Stanford-Binet L-M

TEST SUMMARY:

Chronological Age (CA): 8-6   Mental Age (MA): 14-3   IQ: 161

			yrs.	mos.
Basal	Year 11	XI	11	
	Year 12	XII		6
	Year 13	XIII		8
	Year 14	XIV		10
	Average Adult	AA		6
	Superior Adult 1	SA I		4
	Superior Adult 2	SA II		5
Ceiling	Superior Adult 3	SA III		0

I would classify Niles as a highly gifted visual-spatial learner, mathematically talented, who does not exhibit sequential deficits. He exemplifies the high spatial, high sequential child. There were four sequentially loaded items on the *WISC-III:* Arithmetic, Digit Span, Coding and Picture Arrangement. Niles scored the highest possible score in Arithmetic, since he loves numbers. He scored in the highly gifted range in Picture Arrangement, which involves putting cartoon pictures together in a logical sequence. These are both meaningful tasks to Niles. He scored in the superior range in Digit Span (the ability to hold unrelated numbers in auditory short-term memory) and the high average range in Coding (the ability to quickly copy a series of symbols)—both of which involve *non-meaningful* material. Niles scored considerably higher on meaningful material than he did on boring, non-meaningful material.

So what brought down Niles' score on the Performance portion of the *WISC-III?* In his case, it was neither eye-hand coordination nor speed that lowered his scores. There is no evidence of a learning disability. His three lowest scores on the *WISC-III* are all in the high average range: Picture Completion (seeing what is missing in pictures of familiar objects), Coding (eye-hand coordination and speed) and Object Assembly (puzzles). All three require excellent visual perception and attention to visual detail. The clue was puzzles. With his visual-spatial strengths, he should have easily obtained a highly gifted score on Object Assembly. He also should have done considerably better on Picture Completion, another visual-spatial task. But Niles was an eight-year-old budding mathematician and research by Camilla Benbow and her associates has shown that mathematically talented children often become somewhat myopic by eight or nine years of age. Niles was following a classic pattern and probably needed glasses.

Constructing an operational definition

I wanted desperately to come up with an "operational" (numerical) definition of the visual-spatial learner so that I could crunch some numbers for the journal editors. Our Visual-Spatial Learner Study Group looked at different visual-spatial instruments, including the popular *Mental Rotations Test*. These figural tests measure how quickly a person can rotate images, see figures from different viewpoints, perceive which shapes can be turned into a box, etc. It would have been simple to define a VSL as someone who obtained a high score on one of these tests. However, nearly every measure of visual-spatial abilities that we could find, including the Block Design subtest, suffered from two major weaknesses: they were timed and they definitely favored males.

To some degree, these are related, because the discrepancy between males and females on spatial tasks decreases substantially under untimed conditions. Yet, women related as well as men to the characteristics of VSLs that I've described. So I didn't want to use these measures, which underestimate the spatial abilities of many females.

I had tons of *Binet* and *WISC* data, so I thought I would be able to define the visual-spatial learner by comparing performance on visual-spatial items with performance on auditory-sequential items. But the *SBL-M* posed a serious challenge, because children of different ages are administered different items. Some age levels have several visual-spatial items (such as age five), whereas other age levels (such as age six) have none. (See Table 8.1.) It was too hard to compare children who had taken different items. The *WISC* looked like it would be a breeze, by comparison. All children from six to 16 take exactly the same items. So, in 1991, when the *WISC-III* came out, I decided to try to use *WISC* subtest scores to define the visual-spatial learner.

My first attempt at an operational definition was in the paper, "Strategies for Gifted Visual-Spatial Learners." I wrote it with Jeff Freed right after the *WISC-III* was released. I defined the gifted visual-spatial learner as *a student who attains a score of 16 or higher on the Block Design subtest of the WISC-R or WISC-III and a Digit Span score that is at least seven points lower.* I liked it. It looked neat and tidy. Unfortunately, the studies we conducted with the *Visual-Spatial Learner Identifier* didn't give me a whole lot of confidence in this definition (see Chapter 14). It was a good starting point, but as we tested more children, we discovered VSLs whose Digit Span scores were not that much lower than their Block Design scores.

Now that we've been using the *WISC-III* for over ten years with thousands of children, I am seeing several different patterns of VSLs. High Block Design remains an important indicator. A Block Design score of 16 or higher signifies gifted visual-spatial abilities. So would a gifted range score on any other spatial measure, such as the Abstract Visual Reasoning section of the *SB-IV*, the *Universal Nonverbal Intelligence Test (UNIT)*, the *Naglieri Nonverbal Abilities Test (NNAT)*, the Matrix Reasoning subtest of the *Wechsler Adult Intelligence Scale (WAIS-III)*, the Johns Hopkins' *Spatial Task Battery*, the *Mental Rotations Test* the *Raven's Progressive Matrices,* the nonverbal sections of IQ tests, and tests requiring spatial visualization (e.g., embedded figures, cubes, formboards, etc.).

In terms of *WISC-III* scores, if the Performance IQ is 130 or above and surpasses the Verbal IQ (like the boy in the anecdote at the beginning), or Block Design is in the gifted range and at least three points higher than Digit Span (one standard deviation) or the Perceptual Organization Index score is in the gifted range (130$^+$), I consider the child a gifted VSL.

The Perceptual Organization Index was composed of four Performance subtests: Block Design, Object Assembly, Picture Arrangement, and Picture Completion. If a child's performance on spatial tasks is higher than his performance on other tasks, but not in the gifted range, the child would still be visual-spatial—just not as advanced.

Only one of these criteria is necessary and Niles fit two out of three. While his Verbal IQ was higher than his Performance IQ, he achieved a 19 on Block Design, compared with a 15 in Digit Span and his Perceptual Organization Index was 131, in the gifted range. When the Performance IQ score of a bright child is slightly higher than the Verbal IQ score—even by only a few points (as in the second anecdote at the beginning of this chapter and in the case of Tripper described later in the chapter), the child qualifies as a visual-spatial learner. Most of the gifted children we assess have the opposite pattern—Verbal is higher than Performance (see Adam, and Children A, B and C in Chapter 9). I don't have enough experience with scores in the average range to be certain, but I suspect that all children who obtain Performance IQs higher than Verbal IQs are more visual-spatial. This certainly would make an interesting study.

Using the *SB-IV*, a visual-spatial learner is someone whose Abstract Visual Reasoning score is superior and significantly higher than the other subtests (as the boy at the beginning of the chapter). With the *SBL-M*, I assess the pattern of strengths and compare it with the pattern of weaknesses. If visual-spatial and mathematical items are among the highest scoring items and auditory-sequential items are among the earliest items missed, I consider the child visual-spatial.

"Rebecca": A case study

I would like to tell you about a girl I'll call "Rebecca." She was the youngest subject in our second visual-spatial pilot study, only six years old. Yet, she attained one of the highest scores on an early version of our *Visual-Spatial Identifier*. On a scale of 1 to 5, Rebecca marked 5 for the following items, indicating that they were "very true" for her:

- ❖ I understand ideas all at once and worry about details later.
- ❖ I think mainly in pictures instead of words.
- ❖ I often lose track of time.
- ❖ I am a visual learner.
- ❖ I learn better if I see the big picture first.
- ❖ I have a wild imagination.
- ❖ I like to take things apart to find out how they work.

These items were given ratings of 4 ("true"):

- ✂ I am inventive.
- ✂ I can easily find places I have been to only once.
- ✂ I daydream a lot.
- ✂ I know more than others think I know.
- ✂ It's hard for me to learn if the teacher doesn't like me.
- ✂ I don't do well on tests with time limits.
- ✂ I see how things are connected when others may not.
- ✂ I hate writing assignments.
- ✂ It's much easier for me to tell you about things than to write about them.

Her mother's ratings of Rebecca were even stronger, confirming Rebecca's self-evaluation.

Rebecca could be the visual-spatial poster child. Her interests were classic: "drawing ability," "likes to use her imagination," "learning to sew and knit," "loves crafts and science experiments," "won't sit and listen to a book unless she can look at pictures on every page," "always sees everything going on around her," "great interpersonal skills—everyone loves Rebecca," "special rapport with animals."

In the last section, I operationally defined a visual-spatial learner in terms of *WISC-III* scores: (1) Performance IQ even a few points higher than Verbal IQ; (2) Block Design in the gifted range (significantly higher than Digit Span); or (3) Perceptual Organization Index in the gifted range. Rebecca's Block Design score was 19 (the highest possible score), while her Digit Span score was 11—an eight-point discrepancy. Her Performance IQ of 146, in the highly gifted range, was 14 points higher than her Verbal IQ of 132 (nearly a standard deviation). Her Perceptual Organization Index was 141, solidly in the gifted range and her Full Scale IQ score was 142, solidly in the gifted range. While Rebecca's and Niles' Full Scale IQ scores were very similar, their Verbal and Performance IQ scores are reversed in strength. (See Figure 8.3 on page 153.)

Rebecca achieved the highest possible score (19) in three other subtests as well: Similarities (one of the best indicators of abstract verbal reasoning), Picture Arrangement (a series of cartoons that create a story), and Symbol Search (a new subtest measuring visual discrimination and processing speed). In addition, she scored an 18 (99.6th%) on Coding (eye-hand coordination and speed) and a 17 (99th%) on Vocabulary (the subtest with the highest loading on general intelligence). These scores are all at or above the 99th percentile, and indicate that Rebecca is smarter than these IQ scores. Had there been harder items to give her in these subtests, she undoubtedly would have scored higher.

As Rebecca attained 6 subtest scores at or near the ceiling of the WISC-III, we also administered the old Stanford-Binet (SBL-M), with its higher ceiling. Her Binet IQ score of 147 matched her Performance IQ on the WISC-III, supporting her high levels of giftedness. Her highest scores were in visual-spatial items. She passed the difficult Block Counting item at the 10-year-level, which presents arrays of blocks, some of which are hidden. She passed a very complex Memory for Designs task at age 11, accurately duplicating one of two abstract designs shown to her for only 10 seconds, and coming fairly close on the second design. The Plan of Search item at Year 13 was perfectly executed, and she was able to pass a difficult mathematical-logic problem at Year 14. (Remember, she was only 6!) Obviously, Rebecca is highly gifted intellectually, mathematically gifted, and a brilliant visual-spatial learner. However, there's more to the story.

The Binet also confirmed suspected auditory processing problems, which depressed her total score. Rebecca could not repeat 5 digits forward at the 7-year-level; she could not remember the details in a short paragraph or understand the verbal absurdities (jokes) at the 8-year level—all of which tax auditory short-term memory. Compare these to her ability to do complex math problems at the 14-year level. These deficits echoed her lower Digit Span score on the WISC-III.

It's interesting that while Rebecca failed the verbal absurdities at the 8-year level, she was able to pass the more difficult verbal absurdities at the 9-year-level. The pattern of failing the easier items and passing the more difficult ones of the same type signifies giftedness combined with learning disabilities, AD/HD, or a visual-spatial learning style. Rebecca has a documented hearing loss in her left ear due to scarring after an ear infection. In addition, she appeared to have some relative weaknesses in visual perception, as her Object Assembly and Mazes scores were both in the high average range. As most visual-spatial learners do well on Object Assembly, and there was a marked discrepancy between Rebecca's Block Design and Object Assembly scores (like Niles), we recommended a vision evaluation by an optometrist. Directionality,

Rebecca

Verbal IQ:	132	Gifted
Performance IQ:	146	Highly Gifted
Full Scale IQ:	142	Gifted

Figure 8.3

WISC-III

Name: Rebecca   Age: 6 Years, 6 Months

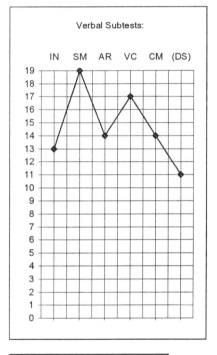

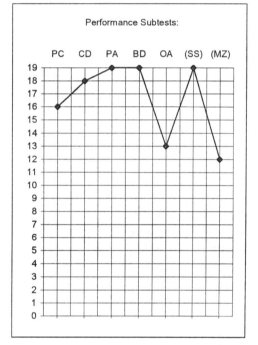

Verbal Subtests:		
Information	**IN**	13
Similarities	**SM**	19
Arithmetic	**AR**	14
Vocabulary	**VC**	17
Comprehension	**CM**	14
Digit Span	**(DS)**	11

( ) Not included in calculating the IQ score.

Performance Subtests:		
Picture Completion	**PC**	16
Coding	**CD**	18
Picture Arrangement	**PA**	19
Block Design	**BD**	19
Object Assembly	**OA**	13
Symbol Search	**(SS)**	19
Mazes	**(MZ)**	12

visual-form perception, and tracking weaknesses were detected, in addition to reversals suggestive of dyslexia. There's a family history of dyslexia, and Rebecca's mother suspected that Rebecca might be dyslexic as well, since she was having difficulty mastering reading.

Rebecca's Broad Reading score on the *Woodcock-Johnson Achievement Battery-Revised (WJ-R)* was 109 (average), while her Broad Math score was 151 (highly gifted). Despite her astonishing strengths in mathematics, Rebecca perceived herself as "dumb" because of her difficulties mastering reading. Sadly, her kindergarten teacher reinforced this impression by saying repeatedly to Rebecca's mother, "She's just average, and it's OK to be average." Rebecca's intelligence was judged on the basis of her average reading ability, rather than on the basis of her mathematical talent. And Rebecca believed these judgments.

Neither of Rebecca's IQ test scores reflects the full strength of her abilities, as they were both depressed by her auditory-sequential deficits. The best estimate of Rebecca's abilities is actually her Broad Math score of 151 on the *WJ-R*. If we just look at her 147 IQ on the *Binet L-M*, her 146 Performance IQ score on the *WISC*, her 151 on the Broad Math, her 99.9[th] percentile scores in Similarities, Block Design, Picture Arrangement, and Symbol Search, and her ability to pass a math reasoning item at the 14-year level on the *Binet*, it's clear that Rebecca is highly gifted—even with weaknesses depressing her scores. Her general intelligence is at the .001 level of the general population—1 in 1,000. Yet, Rebecca is convinced that she's "dumb." This is typical of the plight of gifted visual-spatial learners—even highly gifted ones—with auditory-sequential deficits. From the time they enter school, they're often perceived as less capable than they really are. Our next case study, considered an "underachiever" by his teachers, faced similar issues.

Tripper: A second case study

When Tripper was two, we started our walks to the library. Our purpose was to find out "what was wrong"—if anything. Tripper was so inquisitive and high energy, it was as if I were raising 2 children—or 3 or 4! This being my 1st child, I wasn't sure if this was normal or not, but I "just had a feeling" that some little thing wasn't in place. Anyway, after reading every book offered on illness, phobia, trauma, retardation, I still had no answer and found one book offered on gifted children. To me, Tripper fit the profile. I thought if this were true "it" would come to be seen at some time. I wish then I had had the information offered by you—I would have understood so much sooner and feel everyone's life, especially Tripper's, would have been easier.

Tripper was 15 years old when he came to M.I.T. to hear me give a lecture on visual-spatial learners. If teachers were only given Tripper's Verbal, Performance and Full Scale IQ scores on either his WISC-III or WISC-R, they would think he was "plain vanilla gifted." He was anything but.

WISC-III at age 14			WISC-R at age 10		
Verbal IQ:	135	Gifted	Verbal IQ:	127	Superior
Performance IQ:	139	Gifted	Performance IQ:	139	Gifted
Full Scale IQ:	140	Gifted	Full Scale IQ:	132	Gifted

Tripper was never identified or served as a gifted student. He was miserable in school, struggling fiercely to keep up. He had no confidence whatsoever in his abilities. I show Tripper's test profiles whenever I have the opportunity. Once we understand how to interpret VSL subtest patterns, we'll be able to recognize children like Tripper and help them fulfill their potential.

Tripper's highest scores, all at the ceiling of the test (99.9th%), were in Comprehension (social and moral awareness), Block Design (visual-spatial reasoning), and Object Assembly (puzzles). These are probably the best estimates of Tripper's abilities. Most of his high scores were in the subtests that measure gifted abstract reasoning. In addition to the highest possible scores in Comprehension and Block Design, Tripper scored at the 98th% in Information, 98th% in Vocabulary, and 95th% in Similarities. His Object Assembly score was highly gifted and his Picture Completion (attention to visual detail) was in the gifted range (98th%). Notice that his Performance IQ score was only 4 points higher than his Verbal IQ score, and that he attained the highest possible score on the two most powerful indicators of visual-spatial abilities: Block Design and Object Assembly. All of this signifies that Tripper is not only gifted, but a highly gifted visual-spatial learner.

Tripper's four lowest scores were in Arithmetic, Digit Span, Coding, and Picture Arrangement, the four *sequential* subtests, indicating that he's a VSL with sequential deficits. His two lowest scores were Digit Span and Coding, which involve sequencing of non-meaningful material. Picture Arrangement (91st%) and Arithmetic (91st%) entail abstract reasoning and visualization, so he did considerably better with these subtests.

While none of Tripper's scores was below the average range, there was a dramatic discrepancy between his strengths and weaknesses, which is completely hidden in the Verbal, Performance and Full Scale scores. The discrepancy between his Block Design score of 19 and his Coding score of 10 was 9 points. A nine-point discrepancy is usually indicative of learning disabilities. Handwriting, which correlates with Coding, was very difficult for Tripper, causing most of his problems in school.

Tripper

WISC-III at age 14			*WISC-R at age 10*		
Verbal IQ:	135	Gifted	Verbal IQ:	127	Superior
Performance IQ:	139	Gifted	Performance IQ:	139	Gifted
Full Scale IQ:	140	Gifted	Full Scale IQ:	132	Gifted

Figure 8.4

WISC-III

Name: Tripper   Age: 14 Years, 0 Months

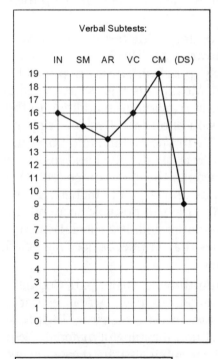

Verbal Subtests:		
Information	**IN**	16
Similarities	**SM**	15
Arithmetic	**AR**	14
Vocabulary	**VC**	16
Comprehension	**CM**	19
Digit Span	**(DS)**	9

Performance Subtests:		
Picture Completion	**PC**	16
Coding	**CD**	14
Picture Arrangement	**PA**	19
Block Design	**BD**	19
Object Assembly	**OA**	11

( ) Not included in calculating the IQ score.

Figure 8.5

WISC-R

Name: Tripper   Age: 10 Years, 0 Months

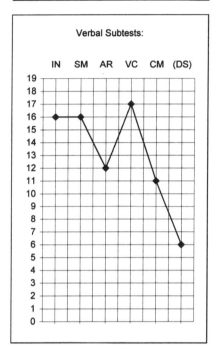

Verbal Subtests:		
Information	IN	16
Similarities	SM	16
Arithmetic	AR	12
Vocabulary	VC	17
Comprehension	CM	11
Digit Span	(DS)	6

Performance Subtests:		
Picture Completion	PC	6
Coding	CD	11
Picture Arrangement	PA	18
Block Design	BD	19
Object Assembly	OA	17
Mazes	(MZ)	7

( ) Not included in calculating the IQ score.

Tripper's Digit Span scores on the *WISC-III* and his previous *WISC-R* provided the best clues as to the source of his problems. His score of 9 was 10 points lower than his Comprehension score of 19. There was an 11-point discrepancy between his visual-spatial strengths (Block Design and Object Assembly) and his auditory-sequential weakness (Digit Span). When he was 10, his score on Digit Span was only 6 (9th%) on the *WISC-R*; however, his Block Design score was still 19 (99.9th%). This represents a difference of 13 points between his visual-spatial reasoning and his auditory-sequential skills (more than four standard deviations).

To give you an idea of how great that discrepancy is, 4 standard deviations (s.d.) is the difference between a gifted IQ (130) and an IQ in the special education range (70)! The most likely cause of this enormous discrepancy was an undetected central auditory processing disorder.

What I found most amazing about this young man was how hard he had worked to improve his weaknesses. In addition to his 6 in Digit Span on the *WISC-R*, he obtained a score of 6 in Picture Completion, 7 in Mazes, 11 in Comprehension, and 12 in Arithmetic. He wasn't given the Mazes subtest on the *WISC-III* four years later, but his Digit Span score improved a full standard deviation (3 points), his Arithmetic score came up 2 points, his Comprehension score went from high average (11) to the ceiling of the test (19)—an 8-point jump, and his Picture Completion score shot up more than 3 standard deviations (10 points). This is miraculous improvement! It demonstrates that visual-spatial learners do bloom late, becoming measurably brighter as they get older, and that they can improve in their weak areas through practice of compensation strategies. Despite these amazing gains, Tripper was perceived as "lazy" by some of his teachers.

In the Intake Interview, Tripper's mother endorsed 21 of the 25 characteristics of giftedness (84%), and said that the following were extremely true: "reasons well," "gets feelings hurt easily," "has a vivid imagination," and "loves jigsaw puzzles." She said that she wanted advice about her "highly spatial son." For instance, he gets his math answers correct, but can't show the steps and is in deep trouble with his math teacher. "In fifth grade, Tripper cried often and did not want to go to school. In the 7th grade, he was late every day. In 8th grade he is on time but failing pre-algebra." Given the strength of Tripper's visual-spatial reasoning, mathematics ought to have been his best subject, but pre-algebra is highly sequential.

The Developmental Questionnaire indicated that Tripper had had 8 ear infections, beginning at the age of 5 months and lasting until he was 4. He never had tubes inserted in his ears to relieve the pressure. Ear infections may have been the hidden culprit again. In describing her son's development, Tripper's mother wrote the following:

> Tripper loved the outdoors and was not just dirty but filthy within an
> hour. By nursery school his questions were types I couldn't answer and
> his stories to me about space, etc., were so long and complicated
> I would lose interest. He was fussy in the respect that clothes had to
> "feel" right and [he] seemed to me to be stubborn. Tripper was marching
> to the beat of a different drummer. When he talked, he said, "See the
> pretty ball" and when he began to walk, he walked—across the floor and
> through the house. He read *The Very Hungry Caterpillar* to his nursery
> school class. (I thought he had memorized the book.) His 1st tooth was

at 2 months and by 6 months he had 6 teeth. He was always drawing, painting, and creating, and had a collection of every piece of our world. He was intense. Projects would last days and became elaborate.

Sounds like a gifted VSL to me! But Tripper was held back between kindergarten and first grade, and was clearly unhappy with school ever since second grade. Painfully shy, it was hard for him to relate to his classmates, and he tended to be lonely. He was teased a lot by the other children when he was younger. He did better with really hard teachers than with easy teachers. He got mostly A's and B's in school, but a C in his French class, and it was his French teacher who referred him for assessment. His mother wrote: "He likes the language, but it is the writing (spelling) that is hard. His favorite class is social studies, because he likes the teacher and the subject. His least favorite class in math; it's boring, too easy. He participates in no sports."

Tripper was referred for a special education evaluation in eighth grade because of problems with academics and difficulty with organization, and it was also noted that he did not seem to have many friends. He had erratic performance on quizzes and tests, and his math notebook brought his grade down from an A to a B. He had "outstanding understanding" of the material in his social studies class, but his "written work is not up to his verbal understanding." In language arts, he completed an 85-page adventure story, but he was "weaker in essays. Has a solid B."

Achievement testing consistently showed strengths in mathematical reasoning (97th%) with weaknesses in computation (25th—79th%) and spelling (45th—67th%). As spelling correlates with Digit Span, it's not surprising that Tripper had difficulty with spelling. While he ranked between the 90th and the 91st percentile in his overall reading achievement, there was a significant difference between his reading of single words (61st%) and his reading comprehension (98th%)—typical of VSLs. His Social Studies and Science achievement scores were at the 99th and 97th percentiles, respectively.

Tripper's *Bender Visual-Motor Integration* test revealed no weaknesses. "His Bender designs were copied perfectly." (In the materials sent to me was a note from Tripper's pre-first grade teacher: "I do not remember ever having a pupil who can draw like Tripper.") He excelled in drawing, but handwriting was quite another story. It took him three times as long as his classmates to do a written assignment.

In my evaluation, I saw Tripper as a highly gifted visual-spatial learner with left-hemispheric learning disabilities in auditory-sequential processing and visual-motor planning. This view of Tripper was substantiated by an evaluation from a psychologist outside the school district when he was in third grade. The examiner reported that "he was very bright and was compensating for a learning disability." She saw Tripper as a "global learner" (another term for spatial learner). However, the special education staffing team at his school did not come to the same conclusion.

After copious testing, all they had to say was that Tripper was "not identified as special needs because there is not a severe discrepancy between ability and achievement on standardized testing. He appears to lack organization and could attend summer school for study skills if parents requested it." Like so many gifted visual-spatial learners, particularly those with sequential weaknesses, Tripper was not clearly understood. No services were made available to enhance his strengths or to remediate his weaknesses. He was a casualty of the system. Thoroughly discouraged, Tripper joined the Marine Corps right after he graduated high school. Hopefully, he will find himself one day and realize his true potential to become the scientist he has always wanted to be.

Recognizing visual-spatial learners

While the analysis of subtest patterns tells me a great deal about visual-spatial learners, most of the time I rely on the children's interests. They seem to be more reliable than any particular constellation of subtest scores. Visual-spatial children usually love Legos™ and other construction toys; they are attracted to creative endeavors, such as art, drama, music, dance, Destination Imagination (Odyssey of the Mind), constructing computer programs or scientific experiments; they often enjoy math, science and computers; and they dream of going into artistic or scientific fields. I also look at the careers and interests of parents, and examine the ear infection history of the child. If the child has had more than 8 ear infections in the first few years, there is a good chance that he or she will be visual-spatial. Is this a child who is particularly astute socially? Empathic? Morally sensitive? I look at the whole picture of the child in determining his or her learning style. And we now have the *Visual-Spatial Identifier* (see Chapter 14), allowing teachers and parents an easy, valid method of locating VSLs.

Finally I have found someone who understands my son! He is seven years old and in the second grade. He was identified by his first grade teacher as possibly having ADD. He learns new concepts/facts easily and quickly grows bored with repetition of things he has already learned. He has always had a wonderfully creative imagination and delights in problem solving. He is INCREDIBLY talented with spatial/design tasks. He spends (literally) hours building complex creations, often with perfect symmetry, with LEGO™ blocks. No other child we know (or adult, for that matter!) can match his uncanny ability in this area. He was tested with the *WISC-III* and scored a composite 126. Interestingly, his Block Design subtest score was a 19. Guess which subtest was his lowest?? He scored a 9 in "Picture Arrangement," which measures SEQUENCING skills! Is this beginning to sound familiar? I believe that he is gifted (academically and creatively) but that his weakness in sequencing is lowering his IQ score and masking the true extent of his abilities. We intend to have him retested in the Spring to see if anything changes. He needs to score 130 to qualify for the school district's gifted program. He is delightfully "visual-spatial!"

Notes:

9

Visual-Spatial, Learning Disabled, or Both?

A works at lightning speed on his own projects and diligently though slowly on schoolwork. He has difficulty with decoding what is required by preprinted worksheets. (These often have inadequate or confusing instructions.) Some nights, he may spend four or five hours on a single subject. This doesn't leave time to get everything done. ...A sees himself as a "normal, average kid who fails."

A will *do fine* as an adult. Our concern is that the public school system may make him miserable and demoralized in the interim, without acknowledging and building on his gifts.

J is a very active 6 yr old [who] excels in gymnastics.... She spelled all the family members' names the other day, first writing them correctly left-to-right (she's right-handed for the most part), top to bottom. She stated that this was the "hard" way of doing it. Then she did it the "easy" way. From right-to-left from the right hand side of the page (yes—it was mirror image). She did write it with her right hand, however I have seen her use both on occasion, left hand getting less and less usage with more schooling. I did not tell her that this mirror image writing was wrong; I simply said, "That's very good to be able to write both ways, I bet not very many people can do that!!" She seems to know that her "hard" way is the way everyone else writes and the way the teacher wants it. But she can show you it's simpler for her to do it her "easy" way.

How can you tell if a child has the typical learning differences of a visual-spatial learner or if he or she actually has a learning disability? Visual-spatial can be a preferred learning style, or it can be so pronounced that a person has difficulty learning any other way. Many highly gifted children have superb visual-spatial abilities, without the deficits. Only when these strengths are accompanied by serious weaknesses is the child considered learning disabled. It takes diagnostic testing to determine the extent of those weaknesses.

In the last chapter, I presented three cases: "Niles," a highly gifted visual-spatial learner with no sequential deficits, "Rebecca," a brilliant little girl with powerful visual-spatial abilities and hidden learning disabilities, who was perceived as average, and Tripper, a gifted visual-spatial underachiever who has sequential weaknesses. The last two children should be kept in mind while reading this chapter.

"A," the first child described above, is one of our clients. He is both dyslexic and dysgraphic. He reads slowly and with some difficulty, has problems with spelling, and definitely struggles with handwriting. (See A's writing sample on the next page.) His remarkable mechanical ability was noticeable from an early age. (A's inventions are listed in the section on "Mechanical Interest and Ability" in Chapter 7.) But he can't absorb knowledge auditorally and he's a poor test taker. His standardized test scores range from the 98th percentile in his ability to express himself in creative writing to the 9th percentile in handwriting. "A" functions better in school if he's given projects rather than worksheets.

On the face of it, "J," the child who engages in mirror writing, might seem to be learning disabled. However, there are no indications in the anecdote that she is struggling to learn. Three cheers for the Mom who supported her daughter's differences rather than correcting her! This story reminded me that my mother has always been able to do mirror writing. She would write something for us and we would have to run to the mirror to figure it out. It was a fun game, and I tried to learn how to do it, but I was never very good at it. Mom probably had some dyslexia that kept her from doing well in school, particularly in arithmetic, but she has always been a reader, she has beautiful handwriting, and her spelling is fine, too. J may have a unique ability without accompanying deficits or she may run into problems later on in her school career.

Figure 9.1

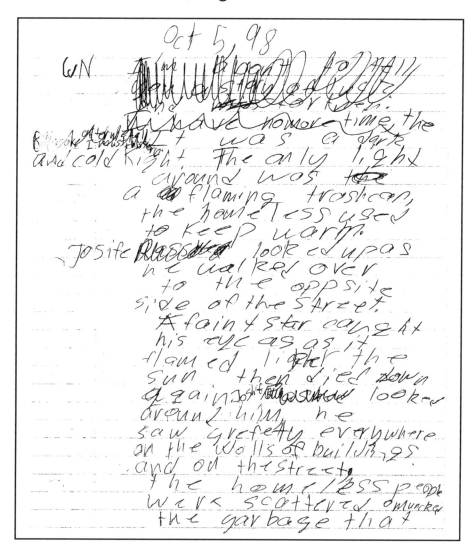

J's family has a history of dyslexia, and dyslexics often have the ability to do mirror writing. In this case, I would want to test J to see if any visual or auditory issues emerge that can be helped by therapy. If no weaknesses surface, I would adopt a wait and see attitude, monitoring her progress.

Each child is different. Each one needs to be seen within the context of his or her family history, life experience, strengths and weaknesses, passions and frustrations, to determine if learning differences are actually learning disabilities. A case study approach allows you to look at all the variables in a child's life and see the full diagnostic picture.

Visual-spatial learners with disabilities

Lots of people balk at the term, "learning disabled." They're more comfortable discussing learning differences, and feel that we should broaden our conception of what's normal to include a greater range of individual differences. "Visual-spatial learner" is acceptable—it's nice, neutral territory. But it isn't always enough. First of all, if a child has a set of symptoms that cause frustration and can be helped with some kind of therapy, you need to label the weakness, so that you can get the child needed services. Second, the way schools currently work, unless there's a formal diagnosis, it's unlikely that there will be any modifications to enable the child to be more successful. And third, without the label (which places the blame *outside* the child), children are likely to blame themselves for not succeeding in school. Most of the children we've worked with were *relieved* to find out that there was a real problem preventing them from reading or writing, rather than a character flaw or a lack of effort on their part. Being called "learning disabled" did not lower their self-esteem at all; in fact, it often raised it.

The problem of labeling gets intensified when you start applying multiple labels to the same human being. Apparently our left-hemispheric labeling system can only deal with one name at a time. The notion that a child can be both gifted and learning disabled sounds ridiculous to some people. How can you be both "learning abled" and "learning disabled"? This doesn't compute. There are two basic misunderstandings here: that the learning disabled aren't smart and that giftedness means high achievement. If someone thinks learning disabled means "dumb," and that the gifted are "smart," you can't be smart and dumb at the same time. However, federal and state definitions of learning disabilities specifically limit the term, "learning disabled," to children *of at least average intelligence*. So you have to be smart to be learning disabled!

At least one-sixth of the children who have come to the Gifted Development Center for assessment of giftedness had various types of learning disability—usually undetected before the testing. This is close to the general incidence of learning disabilities nationally and internationally. "It is estimated that 10 to 15 percent of the school-age population in North America and Europe shows evidence of a learning disability of one form or another" (Springer & Deutsch, 1998, p. 272). These disabilities continue into adulthood. Karen Rogers and I found that one-sixth of the fathers of 241 children above 160 IQ suffered from dyslexia or other learning difficulties.

The second source of confusion is the belief that giftedness equals high achievement in all subject areas. Therefore, if a child can't read, or can't remember her math facts, or can't write well, she can't possibly be gifted. While many high achievers are gifted, many gifted children are *not* high achievers. They may be completely turned off to schoolwork or they may suffer from unrecognized learning disabilities, like Tripper and Rebecca, which prevent them from being successful. One way to clear up these misunderstandings is to ask, "Can a blind person be gifted?" "A deaf person?" "Someone in a wheelchair?" "Would these people be able to demonstrate their giftedness in all areas?" Learning disabilities are physical impairments, similar to deafness, blindness or paralysis.

There are many kinds of learning disabilities. The types that show up most often at the Gifted Development Center are:

 Auditory processing weaknesses
- Sensory integration dysfunction
- Dyslexia
- Attention deficit/hyperactivity disorder
- Visual processing deficits
- Spatial disorientation

There's considerable overlap between the first four of these disabilities and the visual-spatial learning style. Children with weak auditory skills often develop stronger visual skills as a means of compensation, so they're more likely to be VSL. Low scores in Digit Span, Comprehension, and Arithmetic may indicate a central auditory processing disorder. (If you want to know the meaning of these subtests, go back to the last chapter. Maybe you shouldn't have skipped over it after all!) A complete audiological evaluation, including an exam such as the *Central Auditory Processing Battery*, is needed to be certain.

Sensory integration involves fine motor development (e.g., writing and drawing), gross motor development (e.g., riding a bicycle and catching a ball), and making sense out of sensory information (sound, touch, light, smell, and taste). Many VSLs are excellent athletes, but struggle with handwriting. Children with obvious delays in gross motor coordination are usually referred to an occupational therapist for sensory integration therapy. But those with only fine motor weaknesses may not be detected until they're unable to keep up with the writing demands in school. (For more information about sensory integration issues, see Chapter 14.)

Much has been written about the right-hemispheric, visual-spatial strengths of dyslexics (e.g., *In the Mind's Eye* and *The Gift of Dyslexia*). Many disabled readers can't distinguish the sounds of similar phonemes (e.g., *da* and *ga* or *de* and *be*). Jerre Levy explained that the right hemisphere cannot generate phonetic images or hold them in working memory. Paula Tallal and her colleagues suggest that dyslexia may be a failure to rapidly process subtle auditory distinctions. They have had considerable success in increasing the rapidity of auditory processing through a computerized process called "Fast ForWord."

While most research on reading difficulties focuses on phonemic awareness, which is an auditory skill, Professor John Stein, at the Oxford University Laboratory of Physiology, has found strong evidence of visual issues in dyslexics at the magnacellular level. Letters move, wobble, seem to float, and are blurry. A typical report from a dyslexic was that "the letters moved over each other so I couldn't tell which was which." Guinevere Eden and her research team lend support to John Stein's work. They found that dyslexics had visual processing deficits as well as deficits in processing speech sounds. They suggest that both the speech sound and visual difficulties have in common the processing of temporal properties. In other words, dyslexia may be connected to *visual and auditory timing*, which can be improved with practice.

This sure beats the ideas they had about dyslexia when I was studying special education. They used to call it "minimal brain dysfunction" and thought it was related to structural issues, such as lesions in the brain.

Children with attention deficit/hyperactivity disorder (AD/HD) tend to be non-sequential thinkers, sometimes with visual-spatial strengths. They share many of the symptoms of children with central auditory processing disorder and sensory integration dysfunction, and some are dyslexic. (Chapter 11 provides a fuller discussion of attention deficits.)

The two disabilities in this list that seem least related to visual-spatial abilities are visual processing deficits and spatial disorientation. And yet, there are VSLs who suffer from one or both of these problems. Visual-spatial learners with poor visual processing skills are often much smarter than they appear on tests or in school. (See Child A, Child B, and Child C in this chapter.) Children need good visual skills in order to demonstrate their visual-spatial strengths. When these skills are weak, they're handicapped in their strong suit. Some indicators of visual processing issues are a significant discrepancy between Verbal and Performance IQ scores on Wechsler scales, in favor of the Verbal IQ (e.g., Adam and Bill, described later in the chapter), a low score on Object Assembly, and avoiding puzzles.

The strategies for visual-spatial learners work even for visually impaired children who are strong visualizers. And while the ability to visualize comes with the territory of being a visual-spatial learner, some VSLs need to be taught how to use their visualization skills more efficiently in learning. Some rapid processors or children with attention deficits have a difficult time holding an image for a long enough period so that they can really study, understand and retain the image.

It's hard to wrap your mind around visual-spatial learners with visual deficits; it's even harder to imagine a visual-spatial learner with spatial deficits. But many dyslexics have difficulty with left and right, get lost easily, and have trouble orienting themselves in new situations. They still exhibit most of the strengths of VSLs. And I've noticed that many women who relate to the basic ideas of the visual-spatial learner have some difficulty with certain types of spatial perception.

The more severe forms of spatial deficits are not related to visual-spatial strengths; on the contrary, they may indicate right-hemispheric disorders. However, it's possible to have right-hemispheric giftedness combined with right-hemispheric disabilities. We tested one boy who had the highest possible score in Block Design, was composing sonatas at the age of 5, and came up with a unique proof of the Pythagorean Theorem at the age of 7. His brilliance was in visual-spatial fields associated with right-hemispheric development. However, he had difficulty recognizing anyone outside his immediate family and he put the lips above the nose in the face puzzle in Object Assembly. A neuropsychological evaluation revealed an abnormality in an area of the right hemisphere.

The mystery of compensation

Learning disabilities can be very difficult to detect in extremely bright individuals. This is because more abstract reasoning ability is available to compensate for weaknesses. When there is injury or less efficiency in the part of the brain that normally controls a function, compensation enables another part of the brain to take over that function. The more brain power, the greater the potential for compensation. This is good news and bad news. The good news is that learning disabilities can be more easily "overcome" or worked around when a person is smart enough to use other strategies to achieve desired goals. The bad news is that compensation makes it nearly impossible to diagnose the full extent of a disability. So if people can compensate for disabilities, why is it important to diagnose them? Because compensation is unstable. Sometimes it works, and sometimes it doesn't.

Compensation breaks down when you're stressed, tired, ill, injured, anxious, or encountering new situations. When compensation works, you feel like an imposter, and when it fails, you feel incompetent. Am I smart or am I stupid? Not a great basis for building self-esteem or setting high aspirations.

Have you ever cheated on your driver's test, closing one eye so that you could see through the little machine what you're supposed to be able to see with both eyes? That's compensation. Do you carefully write down phone numbers because there is no way you can keep them in your head even for a few minutes? That's compensation.

Some forms of compensation are conscious and intentional. Did you learn to read music by memorizing "Every Good Boy Does Fine" for E,G,B,D,F? When you're driving to some place you've never been before, do you make mental notes of landmarks whenever you turn a corner, otherwise you won't be able to retrace your path to get back home? Do you always add columns twice to prevent "careless" errors? Do you always put your keys in one particular spot so that you'll know where to find them? Are you are addicted to your Daytimer?

Other forms of compensation are unconscious. The brain takes over the job automatically. If, as a toddler, you kept bumping into the doorframe because you saw it an inch to the left of where it really was, your brain would make the adaptation and teach you to shift your perception one inch to the right. If you started out reading and writing backward more readily than forward, you retrained your brain so that you could see and perform with the same orientation as everyone else. (This is probably what's happening with "J," the mirror writer described at the beginning of the chapter.)

If you had lots of ear infections as a child, you might develop the unconscious habit of looking at people when they talked—partially lip reading, without even knowing it. These unconscious adjustments can prevent even serious problems from being detected and corrected. One gifted toddler would turn his mother's face toward him when she spoke and intently study her face. Later, when he went to school, he sat in the front row and watched his teacher just as intently. He was in second grade before it was discovered that he had a 98% hearing loss (C. June Maker, personal communication, July 8, 1998).

In our assessments, we often see children with visual weaknesses who talk their way through visual tasks, using verbal abstract reasoning in place of vision to solve visual problems. They're usually successful, but it takes longer, and the extra time costs them in bonus points, which lowers their IQ scores. Some children consistently rotate blocks 45 degrees when matching them to a picture, and when they're finished constructing the pattern, they straighten the whole set of blocks to correspond to the picture. Are they seeing everything tilted 45 degrees? If so, how much work does it take the mind to correct every perception by 45 degrees? No one even realizes that the child is rotating images unless it happens to be observed and noted by the examiner during an assessment.

Compensation strategies that you practice a great deal usually become automatic, which means that you don't even realize you're compensating, but that doesn't mean that they're necessarily consistent. Once a compensation has been mastered, you expect to be able to count on it all the time, and so does everyone around you: parents, teachers, friends, colleagues. I've been studying learning disabilities for more than 30 years, but it didn't dawn on me until recently that compensation usually requires more time and always requires additional physical, emotional and mental energy. When I'm tired, my eyes cross. I'm completely unaware of how much energy it takes to keep my eyes straight.

When your body is fatigued, when you're dieting excessively and not receiving proper nutrition, when you suffer an illness or injury, there's often insufficient physical energy to compensate. Likewise, when you're emotionally wounded, you have less emotional energy. After exerting a tremendous amount of mental energy concentrating all day when concentration is difficult, you may feel "brain-fried"—unable to take in any more information. At all these times, disabilities may be more evident or appear more severe. Sometimes you can have a surplus of mental energy, but not have enough physical energy to do anything but watch TV. You can't borrow from one energy source to replenish another. All three sources of energy must be present for functioning to be optimal (Marlo P. Rice, personal communication, July 13, 1998).

Age is another variable that affects compensation. A gifted visual-spatial child may be sort of spacey in elementary school and still maintain a B+ average. However, by junior high school, when hormones kick in, and the work becomes more difficult, the student's grade point average may drop to C. The compensation strategies that the mind developed for coping before age 12 may not work as well during the pre-teen years, and this adversely affects motivation.

During the second half of life, most people experience "senior moments," when they can't access a word or a name. Learning disabled adults are often mortified when they have a similar loss of short-term memory, since it conjures up humiliating memories of childhood. But if they're able to shift their perspective, they realize that they're no longer alone—most individuals in their 40s or 50s are facing what they have had to cope with their whole lives. As Marion Downs says, "you're having a *junior moment!*" Compensation can also be situation-specific. It works in some situations and not in others. New strategies may need to be consciously developed when the automatic mechanisms no longer do the job.

Unfortunately, since compensation occurs at an unconscious level, individuals rarely appreciate their own heroic achievements. Instead, they chide themselves for their weaknesses or inconsistency of perform-ance. They expect the compensatory mechanisms to work all the time, and they *blame themselves* if they don't. This undermining of self-esteem is often the by-product of the lack of understanding they received as children from the significant adults in their lives. I worked with a highly gifted teen who is dyslexic and dysgraphic. Her well-mean-ing English teacher set standards for her based on what she demonstrated she could do on one occasion. If she failed to repeat her previous performance, he punished her for "not trying hard enough."

Individuals with learning disabilities need to be prepared for fluctua-tions in energy that cause fluctuations in their ability to compensate, leading to fluctuations in their performance. There will be "good days," when they have sufficient energy so that their compensation strategies work well, and "bad days," when compensation mechanisms work poor-ly, if at all. On those days, they won't be able to think straight or perform anywhere near their true level of ability. Remind them that we all have bad days, that everyone experiences ups and downs as a nor-mal part of life, and that good days will come again. Encourage them to believe that their performance on their good days is the true reflection of their abilities, not their performance on bad days. When you've spent most of your life seeing it the other way around, you need a great deal of support to heal the wounds and see yourself in a positive light.

The importance of early identification

Disabilities need to be diagnosed as early as possible. Early detection enables early intervention—imperative for certain disabilities because there's a critical period during which efforts at correction will be effective. The auditory-sequential skills involved in hearing, speech, and fine motor development, and eventually reading and writing, appear to be under a tight time schedule for correction. (That figures, since the left hemisphere, the seat of auditory-sequential skills, is also the home of our time sense!)

It's extremely important to detect hearing issues in the first six months of life. Deaf and hearing-impaired infants who are provided with amplification of sound within the first six months have significantly higher IQ scores than children whose detection and intervention occurred after six months of age. Communication lags need to be attended to early, as well. This is a prickly area for VSLs, who tend to be late talkers. When does "late" become an issue?

Is your child able to communicate at the same level as other children in his or her playgroup? Is your child developing expressive abilities at the same rate as siblings? As first cousins? Find out about your own early development, and compare your child's development of speech with your own. Family members or close relatives are a better comparison group than norm charts, which tend to be very broad. Does she respond to her name if she can't see you? If you call her from another room, does she know what direction to go to try to find you? If not, an audiological evaluation should be scheduled.

Does he understand what you're saying? Can he bring you things that you ask him for? Is he able to let you know his needs? If so, then his receptive language is fine. Does he have siblings who talk for him? Are there late talkers in your family line who show no other problems? Some introverted children will not communicate until they have the entire structure of language mastered. Their first words are entire sentences.

Are you noticing any other delays, such as lack of interest in other children or lack of responsiveness to you? Does your child have unusual mannerisms, rituals, or obsessions? Does he or she have difficulty making eye contact? Do you have a nagging feeling that something isn't quite right? Listen to yourself. Obtain a comprehensive neuropsychological evaluation to rule out all possibilities. Even if the diagnostician gives your child a label you disagree with, *forget the label and try the therapy to see if it helps.* Intensive sensory integration therapy, speech pathology, and behavior modification, when done early enough and consistently, can often change a dire prognosis, and enable a child who started out impaired to overcome the deficits.

Motor delays must also be attended to early, since the best time period for their correction is under the age of eight. Too many educators and pediatricians adopt a "wait and see" attitude with children who seem advanced in other areas. They notice that the children are "not that far behind" the norms for children their age in fine motor or gross motor development, and they assume that the children will simply "outgrow" the delays, and "catch up" with their agemates. Unfortunately, the window of opportunity for correcting sensory integration dysfunction may be over before anyone takes the problem seriously. A pediatric occupational therapist should be contacted to evaluate any signs of clumsiness, switching hands when engaging in activities, inability to cross the midlines of their bodies, or difficulties with writing or drawing.

We've found a surprising number of gifted children with sensory-motor delays at the Gifted Development Center. Many of these children were the product of very long labors, emergency C-sections, a cord wrapped around part of the body, or needing oxygen at birth. Recently, another potential culprit has emerged. One of our staff psychologists, Helen McVicar, noticed a relationship between long hours of pitocin and sensory integration dysfunction in children. In her research, Helen learned that pitocin was developed to be used for up to three or four hours to induce labor, but it's commonly used for longer periods. Gifted children tend to have larger heads. These heads are difficult to get through the birth canal—especially firstborns. Many mothers of under-achievers who hate handwriting reported exceptionally long labors, sometimes with as much as 20 or 30 hours of pitocin, before emergency C-sections were performed. Pitocin causes harder contractions. What does hour upon hour of hard contractions do to an infant's brain? We don't know, but we want to find out, so we've started collecting data from all our clients on how much pitocin (if any) was used to induce labor. Eric Hollander of New York's Mount Sinai School of Medicine is also investigating the effects of pitocin. Several years ago, he observed that 60 percent of the autistic patients in his clinic had been exposed to pitocin in the womb. He's now studying 58,000 children whose mothers were monitored during pregnancy.

Challenges in assessing twice exceptional children

The best way to determine the presence of learning disabilities is with comprehensive assessment. But even assessment can be misleading, because of traditional methods of interpretation. Often, children who are twice exceptional—gifted in visual-spatial abilities and disabled in sequential skills—are misdiagnosed because:

✿ their scores are averaged, masking both their strengths and weaknesses;

✿ they are compared to the norms for average children instead of to their own strengths;

✿ their lower scores may not be significantly below the norm;

❖ their ability to compensate often elevates their lower scores; and

❖ the magnitude of the disparities between their strengths and weaknesses is not fully taken into account.

Here is a typical scatter profile of a gifted VSL with sequential disabilities:

Figure 9.2

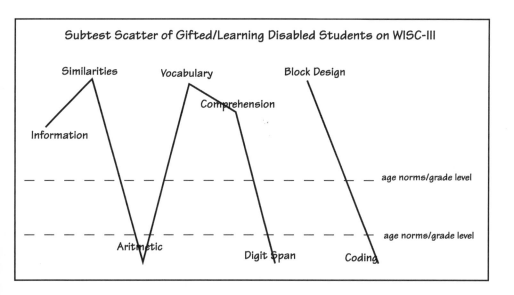

IQ scores are derived by averaging abilities in many different areas. Note that Similarities, Vocabulary, Comprehension and Information are high. These measure abstract reasoning. Block Design, which measures both abstract reasoning and visual-spatial ability, is also high. Arithmetic, Digit Span and Coding—all strongly sequential—are low. The high subtest score in Similarities is offset by the low subtest score in Arithmetic. The high subtest score in Block Design is cancelled out by the low subtest score in Coding. When such dissimilar scores are averaged to produce a Full Scale IQ, the person appears less capable than she really is and less disabled than she really is. Like Rebecca, she may be perceived and treated as "average."

A learning disabled child of average intelligence will have some scores above the norm for average children (the top line in Figure 9.2 above) and some below the norm. Let's say that the child's highest score was 13 and the lowest score was four. The nine-point discrepancy between strengths and weaknesses would obviously signify a problem. A gifted VSL with learning disabilities could have exactly the same scatter of subtests, only higher on the chart (using the bottom line in Figure 9.2 above.) In this case, let's say that Similarities and Block Design are both 19 and Arithmetic is 10. The difference is still nine points, which is significant. But since the child's lowest score is in the average range, this student fails to receive services. The low scores "aren't a problem" because they're in the average range. At least one of the scores has to be significantly below average for the child to be recognized as disabled.

Gifted VSLs with sequential disabilities need modifications for both of their exceptionalities, but rarely qualify for any special provisions. The following three children are typical examples of twice exceptional children who fall through the cracks, receiving no services for either exceptionality.

Child A has extremely high abstract reasoning ability and auditory-sequential skills. Her Block Design score on the *WISC-III* is also in the gifted range, indicating that she's a gifted VSL. In her school system, the cut-off score for the gifted program is a Full Scale IQ score of 130 and she misses it by only a few points. There is an enormous gap between her Verbal IQ of 142 and her Performance IQ of 106—36 points. In such a case, it's inappropriate to use the Full Scale IQ score to estimate the child's abilities. The same principle applies to highly discrepant index scores on the *WISC-IV*.

Her highest subtest score is 19 in Information and her lowest sub-test score is six in Picture Arrangement. This is a huge discrepancy—13 points! (A four-point scatter is significant.) Yet, she will not qualify for special education services, because her lowest scores are still in the average range. (Yes, even the six, at the ninth percentile, is considered "low average." Average is defined verrrry broadly!) With auditory-sequential skills as high as hers, she's likely to get passing grades in her classes, which further masks her learning disability and disqualifies her from any support services.

Child A has a very low score in Picture Arrangement, coupled with a low score in Picture Completion, both of which pull down her IQ score. These subtests rely heavily on attention to visual detail. Her visual processing is suspect. Does she need glasses? She should be evaluated by a behavioral optometrist to see if she would profit from vision therapy.

Child A

Verbal IQ	142	Gifted
Performance IQ	106	Average
Full Scale IQ	127	Superior

Figure 9.3

WISC-III

Name: Child A   Age: 11 Years, 10 Months

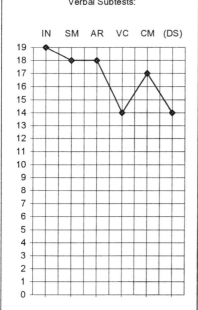

Verbal Subtests:		
Information	IN	19
Similarities	SM	18
Arithmetic	AR	18
Vocabulary	VC	14
Comprehension	CM	17
Digit Span	(DS)	14

Performance Subtests:		
Picture Completion	PC	9
Coding	CD	11
Picture Arrangement	PA	6
Block Design	BD	16
Object Assembly	OA	12
Symbol Search	(SS)	14

( ) Not included in calculating the IQ score.

The next profile looks like bad news in the stock market! Like Child A, Child B has a gifted Verbal IQ and an average Performance IQ, with a discrepancy of nearly 40 points! He has extremely high abstract reasoning ability, and fairly well-developed auditory-sequential skills. But his score on Object Assembly (puzzles) is extremely low, at the 2nd percentile, indicating severe visual processing problems. Would you believe that even that low a score is called "borderline" rather than "disabled"? Similarities (verbal abstract reasoning) is at the ceiling of the scale, at 19, while Object Assembly is 4 (representing a disparity of 15 points—5 standard deviations. (This would be equivalent to the difference between an IQ of 130 and an IQ of 55!) However, the average of his Performance scores is 98, right in the middle of the average range. So, like Child A, he probably will not qualify for either gifted education or support services for children with special needs.

The two tests of visual-motor planning—Coding and Mazes—are lower than his other scores, indicating that writing tasks are very difficult for him. Picture Arrangement (visual sequencing) and Symbol Search (visual discrimination) do not trail very far behind. All the visually presented subtests are extremely low with the exception of Picture Completion and Block Design, two visual-spatial tasks, suggesting that he has visual-spatial strengths. But even these are pulled down by his visual issues. Visual processing issues prevent the full expression of his visual-spatial talent.

Child B

Verbal IQ:	137	Gifted
Performance IQ:	98	Average
Full Scale IQ:	121	Superior

Figure 9.4

WISC-III

Name: Child B

Age: 8 Years, 4 Months

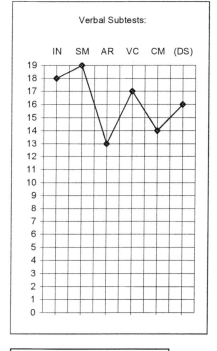

Verbal Subtests:		
Information	**IN**	18
Similarities	**SM**	19
Arithmetic	**AR**	13
Vocabulary	**VC**	17
Comprehension	**CM**	14
Digit Span	**(DS)**	16

( ) Not included in calculating the IQ score.

Performance Subtests:		
Picture Completion	**PC**	16
Coding	**CD**	7
Picture Arrangement	**PA**	9
Block Design	**BD**	12
Object Assembly	**OA**	4
Symbol Search	**(SS)**	9
Mazes	**(MZ)**	8

Child C also has a very large gap between his gifted Verbal IQ and his average Performance IQ: 37 points. Yet, the pattern of his weaknesses differs from the other two children. He is severely disabled in visual-motor skills, and somewhat deficient in visual sequencing, visual discrimination, and visual perception. His Coding score is 3, at the 1st percentile, which does qualify as disabled (finally!). He has a miserable time with writing, and he can't even master a keyboard. He is at the 3rd percentile for processing speed, but at the 99th percentile for verbal comprehension. There is also a relative weakness in auditory processing, as evidenced by his lower scores in Arithmetic and Digit Span compared to his other Verbal scores. But notice how, similar to Child B, Picture Completion and Block Design, two visual-spatial tasks, appear as peaks on the Performance side. He definitely has visual-spatial strengths and visual-motor weaknesses. He will need to have his writing requirements cut down, and he would profit from the use of a voice-activated computer for note taking, assignments, and tests. He will need more time for standardized tests and in-class assignments. A sensory-integration evaluation, vision evaluation, and *Central Auditory Processing Battery* would all provide additional information about his weaknesses.

All three of these children are twice exceptional VSLs. They all have much higher Verbal scores than Performance scores, making it hard to see their learning style from test scores alone. As mentioned in Chapter 8, many VSLs have higher Verbal scores because the *WISC-III* is so heavily timed.

Psychologists, optometrists, audiologists, speech pathologists, and occupational therapists are all trained to compare a child's scores to the norms for children his or her age. The question they ask is, "How does this child's performance compare to the norm?" If the child scores within the average range, they say that the child does not have a disability. I call this the *normative perspective* of test interpretation. It's very useful for determining delays in children of average or below average abilities. It's not helpful, however, in revealing disabilities in extremely bright children. A twice exceptional child can have "average" or "adequate" performance and still be disabled. This sounds impossible unless you compare the child's strengths with his or her weaknesses.

A child with an IQ of 150 who struggles with handwriting, or who can't keep the teacher's directions in short-term memory, is definitely disabled—even if his lowest scores are in the average range. To recognize learning disabilities in advanced children, it's necessary to ask an entirely different diagnostic question: *"To what extent does the discrepancy between this child's strengths and weaknesses cause frustration and interfere with the full development of the child's abilities?"* I call this an *intrapersonal perspective* of test interpretation.

Child C

Verbal IQ:	131	Gifted
Performance IQ:	94	Low average
Full Scale IQ:	114	High average

Figure 9.5

WISC-III

Name: Child C   Age: 12 Years, 6 Months

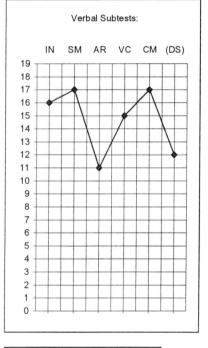

Verbal Subtests:		
Information	**IN**	16
Similarities	**SM**	17
Arithmetic	**AR**	11
Vocabulary	**VC**	15
Comprehension	**CM**	17
Digit Span	**(DS)**	12

Performance Subtests:		
Picture Completion	**PC**	15
Coding	**CD**	3
Picture Arrangement	**PA**	6
Block Design	**BD**	12
Object Assembly	**OA**	9
Symbol Search	**(SS)**	6
Mazes	**(MZ)**	7

( ) Not included in calculating the IQ score.

" VISION THERAPY "

The impact of vision therapy

Of all the disabilities, visual weaknesses appear to be the easiest ones to correct. When visual processing issues are apparent in either children or adults, we recommend an evaluation by a behavioral optometrist and six to nine months of vision therapy. We've seen enormous improvement in visual perception when these exercises are practiced faithfully at least 15 minutes a day.

Here's an example of a highly gifted boy with both verbal abstract and visual-spatial strengths, whose visual processing issues significantly lowered his IQ score. Adam was tested on the *Wechsler Intelligence Scale for Children-Revised (WISC-R)* when he was 7 years old. Note the 43-point disparity between his Verbal and Performance IQ.

The only peak on the Performance side was Block Design, which was in the gifted range, despite Adam's visual difficulties. Adam went through two sets of vision therapy, each for six months in duration. He was retested on the *WISC-III* six years later, and dramatic improvements were seen in all subtests except Coding.

Adam's Performance IQ increased 23 points and the difference between his Verbal and Performance IQ scores is now only 7 points. The lower Verbal IQ score is not significant because the *WISC-III*

Adam at 7 on the *WISC-R*

Verbal IQ:	154+	Highly gifted
Performance IQ:	111	High average
Full Scale IQ:	138	Gifted

Figure 9.6

WISC-R

Name: Adam   Age: 7 Years, 2 Months

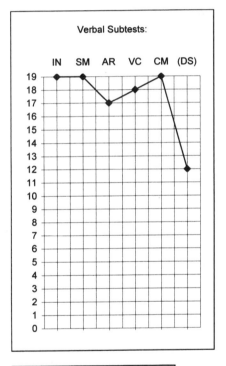

Verbal Subtests:		
Information	**IN**	19
Similarities	**SM**	19
Arithmetic	**AR**	17
Vocabulary	**VC**	18
Comprehension	**CM**	19
Digit Span	**(DS)**	12

Performance Subtests:		
Picture Completion	**PC**	12
Coding	**CD**	9
Picture Arrangement	**PA**	11
Block Design	**BD**	16
Object Assembly	**OA**	10
Mazes	**(MZ)**	

( ) Not included in calculating the IQ score.

Adam at 13 on the *WISC-III*

Verbal IQ:	141+	Gifted
Performance IQ:	134	Gifted
Full Scale IQ:	144	Gifted

Figure 9.7

WISC-III

Name: Adam   Age: 13 Years, 4 Months

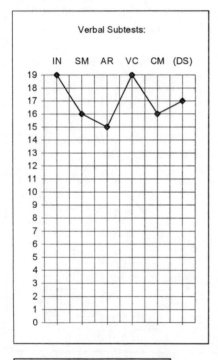

Verbal Subtests:		
Information	**IN**	19
Similarities	**SM**	16
Arithmetic	**AR**	15
Vocabulary	**VC**	19
Comprehension	**CM**	16
Digit Span	**(DS)**	17

Performance Subtests:		
Picture Completion	**PC**	18
Coding	**CD**	9
Picture Arrangement	**PA**	17
Block Design	**BD**	19
Object Assembly	**OA**	16
Symbol Search	**(SS)**	18
Mazes	**(MZ)**	12

( ) Not included in calculating the IQ score.

generates lower scores than the *WISC-R*. But the gains in the visual subtests are even more remarkable, since scores on the Performance section of the *WISC-III* are usually considerably lower than *WISC-R* scores, due to the increased bonus points for speed which penalize 13 year olds to a much greater extent than 7 year olds. Adam's Picture Completion score jumped from 12 to 18 (2 standard deviations); his Picture Arrangement score went from 11 to 17 (2 s.d.); his Object Assembly went from 10 to 16 (2 s.d.); and his Block Design went from 16 to 19, the highest possible score (1 s.d.). He also obtained a highly gifted score on Symbol Search, a new test of visual discrimination.

It's possible that the improvement in Adam's scores is a function of maturity alone—"late blooming"—but most children do not show such dramatic and consistent gains without intervention. The *WISC-III* provides a truer reflection of Adam's abilities than his previous *WISC-R*. His score in Coding did not improve at all, and his fine motor coordination remains significantly weak. Adam's biggest problem in school is writing.

Bill

Bill, a 41-year-old gifted man, discovered that the discrepancy between his Verbal IQ and his Performance IQ on the *Wechsler Adult Intelligence Scale (WAIS)* was 55 points. He wrote to 150 experts in several different fields, and took several neuropsychological batteries, trying to find out why. I referred him to Carl Gruning, OD, FCOVD, for a vision evaluation. It seemed logical to me to rule out vision issues first. After a few months of vision therapy, Bill wrote that serious difficulties had been identified with his eye focusing and teamwork, depth perception, and peripheral vision. On some assessments, he scored in the bottom 20th percentile. Here is an excerpt of his letter to me:

> For the first time in my life I have normal functional vision. For the past twenty-seven years I have worn eyeglasses when I drove a car, but now I don't need them anymore. I haven't taken the Wechsler again but it is likely that my performance scores would be significantly higher. ...Did my poor vision really have a major impact on my life? Although many would disagree I believe that it has, in the words of a Harvard neuropsychologist back in 1996, had a rather profound effect on my development as a person.
>
> I have noticed subtle but no less real changes in my life. My eyes are more alert and I can concentrate better on visual tasks. I am more aware of my daily surroundings. In the past I have generally acquired and evaluated information by reading and solitary reflection. By not focusing on people and visual-practical methods of dealing with the world I have definitely shortchanged myself. I hope that my new found visual skills will enable me to perceive the world in a more balanced manner.

Obtaining services

All children with learning disabilities should have Individual Educational Plans (IEP) that take into account both their strengths and their weaknesses. However, it's difficult for gifted visual-spatial learners to qualify for IEPs under the Individuals with Disabilities Education Act (IDEA). To be considered eligible under IDEA, the child must have a significant discrepancy between ability and achievement, as measured by standardized tests and not be receiving reasonable benefit in regular education. This immediately poses problems for gifted VSLs with learning disabilities. "Reasonable benefit" is usually interpreted as the child achieving near grade level (special education students are usually two grade levels below). Gifted VSLs may be performing well below their own potential, but within grade-level norms. Second, as seen in Tripper's case, they may not be able to prove that they have significant discrepancies between their ability and achievement. IQ tests are often heavily timed, while the achievement measures usually have generous time limits. Catch 22! How is a visual-spatial learner with a processing speed deficit supposed to qualify for adaptations?

Another alternative is requesting accommodations under Section 504 of the Rehabilitation Act of 1973, which serves the same purpose as the Americans with Disabilities Act (ADA). IDEA has more benefits for learning disabled children and is more strictly enforced than ADA, but it only goes up to age 21. And one of its objectives is to return the child to the regular classroom. Bright VSLs with learning disabilities have an easier time qualifying for support under Section 504, particularly if they have AD/HD symptoms, processing speed issues, or sensory integration dysfunction (problems with handwriting). Child C above would definitely qualify for a Section 504 plan. This legislation is helpful throughout the lifespan, as it's assumed that the disability will not go away over time.

Section 504 enables the individual to have adaptations in the classroom and on standardized tests, such as more time, use of a computer, use of a calculator, a note taker, a quiet place to take the test, handscoring, etc. In most cases, this is exactly what VSLs with learning disabilities really need, rather than access to a resource room. The main problems with Section 504 are that it's difficult to implement, loosely enforced, and there's no funding attached to it. Teachers don't usually receive training in accommodating students with special needs, so they may not know how to do the adaptations. And they may not be held accountable by their districts. This leaves the child more vulnerable.

Parents of children with learning disabilities should make every effort to work collaboratively with the schools, rather than taking an adversarial role. Strong parent advocacy is essential, and so is parental support of teachers. Volunteer in the classroom to lighten the teacher's load. Teachers want to do a good job, but they may not have the time to research teaching strategies needed for a particular child. Parents need to work closely with teachers, providing information about what works in a clear, practical way that can be easily implemented. (Be careful not to overload the teacher with too much information all at once.) The following section may be helpful for this purpose.

Keys to Success

Early detection and intervention, while the brain has a great deal of plasticity, enables the development of new pathways. Any unusual developmental patterns should be assessed as early as possible, because early intervention is essential. Most corrective efforts should be put in place before a child is nine. There are many types of therapies available for different disabilities. One common element in all of them is that the earlier they're begun, the greater the improvement. A second common element is that the more they're practiced, the greater the success. Like the body, the brain responds to exercise. New neural pathways are formed through practice. After the age of 9, compensation strategies are needed, as well as modifications in teaching techniques.

The following adaptations work wonders for twice exceptional VSLs:

Keys to Success For Twice-Exceptional VSLs

- Show them, don't just tell them. Teach them to picture concepts.
- Use hands-on learning experiences.
- Don't make them show their work. Let them find answers their own way.
- Avoid timed tests. Arrange for more time for standardized tests (e.g., SAT).
- Allow them to use a computer for all written work.
- If they cannot master the keyboard, use a voice-activated computer.
- Use visualization techniques in all subject areas.
- Give them advanced concepts even if they haven't mastered easier work.
- Expose them to role models of successful twice exceptional adults.
- Teach them to use a day planner.
- Teach them to make lists.

- Allow use of a word processor with spell check for written assignments.
- Arrange a quiet study center at school and at home.
- Let them tape record lectures.
- Use earphones to block out auditory distractions.
- Have a place in the classroom where they can retreat when overstimulated.
- Provide a Franklin speller or *The Bad Speller's Dictionary*.
- Practice visualization as a memory aid. Ask them to picture concepts in their minds.
- Have them estimate answers before calculating.
- Shorten written assignments.
- Substitute oral for written tests.
- Allow use of a calculator when necessary.
- Allow them to dictate assignments to a scribe when necessary.
- Avoid rote memorization. Use more conceptual approaches.
- Use computer-assisted technology in some subject areas.

Consult with the resource teacher for more suggestions for adapting to a specific student.

Visual-spatial learners who are learning disabled often feel like failures in school, and usually suffer from low self-esteem. Even if they're brilliant, they tell themselves that they're "stupid." It's important for them to have a Greek chorus of supporters who believe in them and continuously reassure them that they'll get smarter as they get older. VSLs tend to bloom late. Financial success allows a disabled adult to hire a support team with the skills that the person lacks. The natural inventiveness that enables the person to compensate for weaknesses has a positive value in the world. With the right support services, twice exceptional VSLs become some of the most creative, productive innovators—people who change the world.

Disabilities as gifts

> J is a well-developed, very healthy young lady, polite, with no signs of
> ADD that I can see. Just very athletic with a quirky ability to write
> easily in mirror image. (Yes, I may be dyslexic, but never been tested.
> I very often confuse right and left and typically stop to think which
> hand my wedding ring is on). So I plan to talk to her teacher and show
> her what J wrote [mirror-writing] and see if she suspects anything. If J
> does test positive for dyslexia, I plan to make it more of a gift than a
> disability.

This anecdote is a continuation of the one at the beginning of this
chapter. What a remarkable Mom! She plans to make dyslexia, if it's
diagnosed, "more of a gift than a disability" for her daughter. Right on!

The idea that a disability may actually be a gift is yet another
paradox with these paradoxical learners. When the left hemisphere, the
source of school success, is disabled, it may enhance the functioning of
the right hemisphere, the source of inspiration. Tom West suggests that
left-hemispheric deficiencies, such as dyslexia, are fundamentally
linked to right-hemispheric strengths, such as visual thinking, spatial
ability, pattern recognition, problem solving, heightened intuition and
creativity. Dyslexia forces the brain to solve problems in different ways,
increasing the likelihood of creative solutions. In discussing eminent
individuals, he hypothesizes that many achieved greatness because of,
not in spite of, their apparent disabilities. "They may have been so
much in touch with their visual-spatial, nonverbal, right hemisphere
modes of thought that they have had difficulty in doing orderly,

sequential, verbal-mathematical, left hemisphere tasks in a culture where left hemisphere capabilities are so highly valued" (West, 1991, p. 19). He enumerates the talents that often accompany dyslexia:

- High talents in spatial, mechanical, and related right hemisphere skills, with early development of sophistication of these skills.
- Love of construction toys, models, and craft work.
- Love of and great skill at drawing (although the same person may have poor handwriting).
- An especially good "musical ear."
- An especially good ability to visualize and manipulate images in the mind (this may or may not be linked to good drawing skills; alternately, this might be associated with a propensity to develop a visual analog of things that others do not think of in visual terms). (West, 1991, p. 93)

Ron Davis (1994), in *The Gift of Dyslexia*, also describes the benefits of dyslexia. He lists the basic abilities that all dyslexics share:

- They can utilize the brain's ability to alter and create perceptions (the primary ability).
- They are highly aware of the environment.
- They are more curious than average.
- They think mainly in pictures instead of words.
- They are highly intuitive and insightful.
- They think and perceive multi-dimensionally (using all the senses).
- They can experience thought as reality.
- They have vivid imaginations. (p. 5)

Like J's Mom, look for the gifts, the unusual abilities, in visual-spatial children who have sequential deficits. They may show up in artistic talent, mechanical wizardry, a knack for computers, genius with puzzles and mazes, inventiveness, creative ideas, an intuitive grasp of the essential rather than the superficial, uncanny empathy, profound spirituality, or in other ways that aren't currently valued in childhood (even psychic abilities). When the mind's incessant chatter is quieted by left-hemispheric deficits, it seems to allow more access to the intuitive gifts of the right hemisphere. Be on the look-out for remarkable insight and extraordinary wisdom from these children. They know a great deal more than others think they know. If they feel safe enough to tell you what they know, you'll be amazed.

VSLs with learning disabilities who are seen as defective, in constant need of repair, come to view themselves with shame and doubt. They're unable to value their gifts when the significant others in their lives pay more attention to fixing their deficits. When parents and teachers are overly focused on making them more like everyone else, they become victims of their disabilities. But when those closest to them honor their strengths and believe in their ability to fulfill their dreams, they're able to mobilize their will to succeed against all odds.

Notes:

The Inner World of Introverts

D accomplishes physical tasks by watching and perfecting them in his head before he'll try them independently. He is acutely aware of looking foolish, falling, or getting hurt.

The first time I observed this was when he was learning to walk. From 11 months of age, he would always use an adult hand, a table edge, the couch, etc. and it was clear he wasn't using it for balance. It was just "Dumbo's feather." At 13 months, he finally took off when I put something attractive to him at the other end of the room when there was excitement and activity going on. He forgot to use the "feather" and just sauntered across the room. He rarely fell down as a toddler.

He chose "George Brett Teaches Baseball" at the video store when he was two. He watched intently, absorbing every detail. He has been an amazing hitter and pitcher for his age since that time.

D has been riding his bike without the training wheels touching the ground since last summer. The only time they hit the pavement was when he'd turn a corner. This summer I finally took the training wheels off, saying it was because they were slowing him down in his turns. "O.K.

Mom, but if I fall, we're putting them right back on!" I agreed that I would after six falls. So after a month of riding his bike, D had the first skinned knee of his life.

He has had very few injuries because he rehearses mentally (and he is coordinated and extra cautious.) We have not gone through a full box of bandages in his six years of life on this hard, bumpy earth.

P.S. My husband ... also uses mental rehearsal frequently, ...especially with his skiing.

J is quick to tire when around people too much, and insists that week-ends be kept as free of planned activities as possible. She seems very refreshed if she can spend a couple of uninterrupted hours in her room drawing or reading.

M is very shy in large groups of people, more open in one-on-one encoun-ters. M is cautious and reserved when he's encountering new situations—he will observe, rather than participate.

L is a very polite child away from home. She is angry and disagreeable in her home environment. She is unable to express her feelings... L has had one good friend... L plays by herself at school and does not enter into a group unless she is invited and is interested in what they are doing.... She resists change and does not react well to changes in plans. She needs plenty of advanced warnings of new events, changes to methods or changes to her "expectations."

The anecdotes above illustrate different facets of introversion. I mentioned earlier that VSLs are often introverts. John Dixon and David Lohman also found some confirmation of the relationship between introversion and visual-spatial abilities. So what exactly is introversion?

Basically, introverts are oriented inward toward the subjective world of thoughts and concepts; they get their energy from inside themselves; and they're inclined toward reflection. Extraverts are oriented outward, become energized through interaction with people and things, and are directed toward action. Whereas introverts feel drained by too much interaction with people (like J in the second anecdote above, who is quick to tire if she's around people too much), extraverts are energized by interaction—the more, the merrier. The slogan of introverts could be Greta Garbo's "*I vant to be alone,*" while the theme song of extraverts should be Barbra Streisand's ♪♪ "*People—people who need people...*" ♪♪

Most people think of introverts as "quiet"; if that's what you think, you haven't been alone with one in a car after school. They're only quiet in large groups, like classrooms. One-on-one, some of them can talk your ear off. They save up all the things they wanted to say until they're with someone "safe" and then it's magpie time.

Introverts are often called "shy," but this is an initial reaction to new situations that usually wears off when they feel comfortable. A more accurate depiction of shyness is being easily overstimulated. Introverts have very powerful emotions that can quickly overwhelm them. Kazimierz Dabrowski called this "emotional overexcitability." Because they have so much internal stimulation, introverts are not stimulation-seekers. They're cautious in new situations until they're sure of what to expect so that they feel in control of their emotions. When they're bombarded by too much stimulation, they feel out of control and just want to escape.

Are you an extravert or an introvert?

The term, "introvert," was invented by Jung, and it was self-descriptive. He viewed this personality trait positively. It only seems negative to some people because America is such an extraverted society. The American dream is to be extraverted. We want our children to prefer to play outside with their buddies rather than retire with a good book. Our concept of being "well-adjusted" means making friends easily and having lots of them, liking parties, being eager for new experiences, being good risk takers, being open about feelings, being trusting, and loving to be with people all the time. Anyone who doesn't fit this gregarious pattern is viewed with some concern. In addition to "shy," we call them "withdrawn," "aloof," "loners," "secretive," "unfriendly." Introverts must feel very misunderstood and unacceptable in an extraverted world.

The value of introversion depends a great deal on the cultural context. In many Asian countries, introversion is the norm, and extraverts would be seen as odd. Most Americans (about 70%) are extraverts. When I talk about introversion in Miami, they think it's a disease. But when I discuss introversion in Burlington, Vermont, or Fairbanks, Alaska, I feel waves of gratitude from the audience. (I get a few half-smiles and nods—introverts aren't big on giving speakers feedback, but afterwards they line up to tell me how affirmed they felt.) So there are pockets in the United States where introverts flourish. Try Montana.

You can't always tell when you meet someone if the person is intro-verted or extraverted. Introverts are capable of acting very much like extraverts in public settings. They're excellent observers and often can imitate extraverted behaviors. Like any other minority group, they adopt the customs of the majority in order to blend in and be accepted. Some become class clowns, actors, musical performers, and public speakers. They carefully prepare and rehearse, and the more practice they have, the more natural they appear. But when the performance is over, don't invite them to the cocktail party afterwards. They hate chit-chat with people they don't know. They want to go back to their room, close the door, put on their favorite music, open the book they're in the middle of reading and recharge their batteries—alone. (Introverts are always in the middle of reading at least one book. They read ten times more than extraverts. It was probably the only way they could get any privacy as children, since reading isn't a group sport.) Extraverts, on the other hand, can perform all day and party all night. Our batteries are charged by the audience reaction during the performance. The bigger the audience, the more jazzed we are.

I do a lot of public speaking and I can always tell if my host or hostess is introverted or extraverted. The introverts assume I need alone time to prepare for my presentation (including dining alone), and quiet time to recover afterwards. The extraverts think my coming to town is a big party, and they want to invite all their friends to have dinner with me either before or after I present. They would consider alone time inhospitable, and do everything in their power to make sure I'm entertained every minute. (Works for me! Do introverted speakers go nuts with extraverted hosts?)

In the following table are the major differences between introverts and extraverts of all ages:

Table 10.1	
Introversion and Extraversion	
Introvert	**Extravert**
Gains energy in solitude	Gains energy from interaction with others
Focused on inner thoughts and feelings	Focused on people and things around them
Is reserved	Is outgoing
Needs privacy	Is usually open and trusting
Is contemplative and thoughtful	Is action-oriented
Can mask feelings	Usually shows feelings
Is reflective	May be impulsive
Mentally rehearses before speaking	Thinks out loud
Learns by observing	Learns by doing
Avoids attention	Seeks attention
Is uncomfortable with change	Adapts quickly to new situations
Is loyal to a few close friends	Makes lots of friends easily
Is quiet in large groups	Is a risk-taker in groups

Everyone has some introversion and some extraversion in his or her personality, so it's really a matter of the degree to which you exhibit traits on one side or the other of the continuum. Some people (like me) are rabidly extraverted, some are intensely introverted, and some are a happy combination of both. Like handedness, these personality preferences become apparent early in life, and are relatively stable throughout life, particularly if you are strongly introverted or strongly extraverted.

Many introverts perfect their public appearance, so that they behave one way in the world (e.g., school) and another way at home. This public face is what Jung called a "persona." We all have a private and a public self, but introverts are masters at crafting personas that may bear very little resemblance to their private selves. The persona plays a vital role in the lives of introverts, protecting them from too much intrusion and stimulation from the outer world. But it's also a burden to have to put on a personality like a girdle every time you leave your home. Many actors are introverted. Acting is second nature to them; they've been practicing acting since childhood in order to survive in an extraverted society. Teachers might only get to meet personas in the classroom, and never know the real person behind the façade.

Contrary to general opinion, introverts can be extremely skillful socially and quite popular. The downside is that while the extraverted persona has dozens of acquaintances, the introverted person inside may be lonely in the crowd. We give children the Harter *Self-Perception Inventory*, and I've seen the following scenario many times. Janie gives herself the highest possible ratings for scholastic self-concept, but considerably lower ratings for social self-concept. Janie's parents are shocked, exclaiming, "How is that possible? Are you sure you don't have our child's self-concept test mixed up with someone else's? Our daughter is so popular. The phone rings off the hook. Everyone in the neighborhood wants to play with her." I explain how it's common for a popular child to be lonely. Janie is very bright and has superb social skills. She attends to the other children's needs, solves their problems, and gives everyone what they want, but she isn't getting anything back from all those other children. She feels drained. What Janie desperately craves is a soul-buddy like herself, someone with whom she can have a real give-and-take relationship.

I find that many gifted women are "closet introverts." With their astute social awareness and imitative abilities, they've learned the language of extraversion very well, and the face that they present to the world is quite outgoing. Gifted women may be so good at feigning extraversion that they believe their persona is who they really are. The feminine role is incompatible with introversion. Women are supposed to be other-oriented, to be caretakers, to be aware of what other people want even if unspoken, to be selfless. If you'd much rather read a book than talk on the telephone, there must be something wrong with you.

It's perfectly OK for a man to be introverted. The strong, silent Marlboro man only talks to his horse (until he and his horse die of emphysema...). And it's all right for a scientist to work 16 hours a day and sleep in his laboratory. But an inward-oriented woman is denying her feminine duties. Ironically, one of the strongest portrayals of this dilemma was offered by John Stuart Mill, over 100 years ago. In his last work, *The Subjection of Women,* he wrote:

> Independently of the regular offices of life which devolve upon a woman, she is expected to have her time and faculties always at the disposal of everybody. If a man has not a profession to exempt him from such demands, still, if he has a pursuit, he offends nobody by devoting his time to it; occupation is received as a valid excuse for his not answering to every casual demand which may be made on him... [However, a woman] must always be at the beck and call of somebody, generally of everybody. If she has a study or a pursuit, she must snatch any short interval which accidentally occurs to be employed in it. (Mill, 1869, pp. 138-139)

Raising introverted children

The *Introversion/Extraversion Continuum* I developed for our clients at the Gifted Development Center is provided on page 201. We have each parent complete it separately, and if the child is old enough, we have him or her complete it as well. The items on the left side represent the traits of introverted children and those on the right, extraverted children.

We find that parents often have very different perspectives of their children, with mothers endorsing more of the introverted characteristics than fathers. Remember Tripper, in Chapter 8? On the *Characteristics of Introversion in Children* scale, his mother rated him as extremely introverted, checking 11 of the 16 characteristics of introversion.

His father saw him exactly opposite. He marked only two of the introversion items as descriptive of his son: "needs time to observe before trying new activities" and "thinks through ideas before sharing them with others." Tripper's self-evaluation matched his mother's perceptions more closely than his father's. Tripper and his mother agreed that the following items described him:

- Needs time to observe before trying new activities
- Has intense need for privacy
- Desires one best friend rather than many friends
- May try to be "perfect" in public, then vent negative feelings and frustrations at home
- Can mask feelings
- Is slow to respond to people and situations, needing time to think
- Reticent to talk about his feelings or problems

Introverted children tend to show more of their introverted side to their mothers. Maybe it has something to do with having been in the mother's womb. Or maybe it's related to the fact that mothers are usually the child's primary caretakers, so they get to see more of the inner core of the child and working fathers get to see the next layer of the child's personality. For some children, being alone and being with Mom are virtually the same thing. They become their mother's third leg and never let her out of their sight. But we've had some introverted fathers who see more of the introversion in their children than the mothers do, perhaps because they identify with their child.

Introverted children, such as L in the last anecdote at the beginning of the chapter, show their best side when they're away from home and their worst side with the person they love and trust the most. Here is another typical scenario. Jeffery goes to your neighbor's house for dinner, has the best manners your neighbor has ever seen, says "thank you," "please" and "yes, Ma'am," compliments your neighbor on her cooking, takes his dinner plate to the sink, and asks if he can help with the dishes. Your neighbor calls you and raves about how you are raising a "model child." Model Child comes homes and screams at you because you put his socks on the right side of his drawer when you know they go on the left, and you've lost one of them besides. Are you raising Dr. Jekyll and Mr. Hyde? No, Jeffery is just showing you how much he loves you.

Table 10.2

Introversion/Extraversion Continuum

Please check the ☑ indicating how close your child is to one of the descriptors within each pair:

Needs time to adjust	❑	❑	❑	❑	❑	❑	❑	Adapts quickly
Embarrassed by own mistakes	❑	❑	❑	❑	❑	❑	❑	Laughs at own mistakes
Mentally rehearses	❑	❑	❑	❑	❑	❑	❑	Thinks out loud
Prefers one close friend	❑	❑	❑	❑	❑	❑	❑	Prefers many friends
Hates being interrupted	❑	❑	❑	❑	❑	❑	❑	Doesn't mind interruptions
Keeps feelings private	❑	❑	❑	❑	❑	❑	❑	Shows feelings readily
Needs time alone	❑	❑	❑	❑	❑	❑	❑	Needs social interaction
Learns by observing	❑	❑	❑	❑	❑	❑	❑	Learns by doing
Reflective	❑	❑	❑	❑	❑	❑	❑	Impulsive
Explores topics in depth	❑	❑	❑	❑	❑	❑	❑	Prefers variety to depth
Cautious	❑	❑	❑	❑	❑	❑	❑	Risk-taker
Uncomfortable with change	❑	❑	❑	❑	❑	❑	❑	Prefers novelty
Slow to respond, needs time to think	❑	❑	❑	❑	❑	❑	❑	Quick, verbally assertive
Concentrates intently	❑	❑	❑	❑	❑	❑	❑	Easily distracted
Reserved	❑	❑	❑	❑	❑	❑	❑	Outgoing
Needs to control environment	❑	❑	❑	❑	❑	❑	❑	Flexible, "goes with the flow"
Focused on inner world	❑	❑	❑	❑	❑	❑	❑	Focused on social life
Avoids attention	❑	❑	❑	❑	❑	❑	❑	Likes attention
Questions own abilities	❑	❑	❑	❑	❑	❑	❑	Confident
In a new situation, prefers to listen	❑	❑	❑	❑	❑	❑	❑	In a new situation, prefers to talk
Likes to concentrate on one activity at a time	❑	❑	❑	❑	❑	❑	❑	Can focus on many ideas at once
May appear different at home and in public	❑	❑	❑	❑	❑	❑	❑	Same in public and at home
Is (has been) tantrum-prone	❑	❑	❑	❑	❑	❑	❑	Expresses anger freely
Prefers a book to a party	❑	❑	❑	❑	❑	❑	❑	Prefers a party to a book
Holds in negative feelings in public, and vents them in a safe environment	❑	❑	❑	❑	❑	❑	❑	Vents negative feelings when they arise

(Gee, thanks.) It takes a whole lot of work to be perfect in public, and the anxiety builds up inside like a volcano, so Jeffery erupts over any little thing, just to release the tension. He waits until he is with you, because he feels safe with you. You are his escape valve.

Children who don't have an escape valve can be headed for trouble. Small flare-ups are a lot safer than building up to huge explosions. Children like Jeffery are tantrum-prone. They become easily overwhelmed by the emotional tension in their systems and blow up with little provocation when they're in the safety of their homes. It helps to know that this is a typical facet of introversion. You aren't a bad mother, and you aren't raising a lunatic. But it doesn't mean you have to put up with being the object of Jeffery's affectionate venting. It's perfectly fine to send him to his room until he calms down. He's likely to calm down faster there than if you attempt to talk to him. Introverts are mortified to be seen when they're out of control, so even Mom becomes part of the problem by just observing the melt-down. If he can't leave the room, you can. Some children do better when they're held and soothed during a tantrum. Just don't talk. Introverts of all ages are incapable of processing verbal information during an eruption.

How to care for introverts

- ✤ *Respect their need for privacy.* When an introvert tells you a secret, you need to take an oath of confidentiality as if you were a psychologist. They never forgive you if they find out you've blabbed what they've shared with you in confidence. Knock on an introverted child's bedroom door and wait for permission to enter instead of barging into his or her space. After all, you want your child to knock before entering your bedroom, don't you? This is a courtesy that makes the child feel respected.

Introverts and extraverts should never share bedrooms. Introverts are possessive of their belongings and they believe that wherever they put something before they went to school, it should still be in the same place when they come home. Extraverts, especially extraverted younger siblings (like cats), believe that everything in sight is mine to play with. So they basically have different philosophies, and life on the home front can deteriorate to a war zone unless the introvert has his or her own space. If you can't buy a bigger house, convert part of the garage or the dining room into a private corner for your introvert (complete with a handmade **"KEEP-OUT"** sign).

❧ *Never embarrass them in public.* Introverts are easily humiliated, and they can relive in glowing detail every real or perceived humiliation for the rest of their lives. If you have to reprimand them, do it privately and quietly, rather than loudly in the middle of the supermarket or in front of their friends.

❧ *Give them time to think.* Don't demand instant answers. If you're an extravert and you're upset with a family member, you want to talk about it **right now**, because that is how you discharge your angry, negative feelings. If you don't get the chance to discuss what happened and how it made you feel, you just get angrier until you can get it out. (That's what I do!) It just doesn't work when you're arguing with introverts. They need time to think, to process, to sort out their feelings, and to calm down inside before they can hear you or respond rationally. If you demand that they process the situation out loud, with you, right now, on your time schedule, you're asking for a melt-down. It's best to wait about 24 hours until both of you calm down before you discuss things, so that you stand a chance of being able to resolve the situation and prevent it from happening again in the future. If you need some

way to vent your anger immediately, put your feelings in a letter
and then sleep on it before you share the letter. See if you still
want to say it in that same way in the morning.

- Similarly, when you've shared a deeply moving, positive
  experience, if you're an extravert, you want to process it immediately. After you've attended a breathtaking performance or seen an
  incredibly moving play with your introverted partner, you're dying
  to talk about it. But if you start probing, "Wasn't that
  phenomenal? What did you think of it?" your loved one is probably
  wishing you'd shut up. Introverts can't talk about their strong
  feelings, positive or negative, until their emotions have settled
  down. Try again later. That line is busy right now.

- *Plan more time for transitions.* Have you ever hollered, "Dinner!" and
  no one came to the table? Did you begin to wonder if your family was
  deaf? If you live with introverts, they can't switch gears that fast.
  Introverts usually like to do one thing at a time, and they can get
  completely engrossed in whatever they're doing. They like to finish up
  one activity before they move to the next. It works best if you give the
  introverts in your family 15-minute warnings, such as "Dinner will
  be ready in 15 minutes," or "We have to leave in 15 minutes."

- *Give them advanced notice of expected changes in their lives.* If
  you're planning on moving or you want to place your introverted
  child in a new school, it's wise to take her to visit the school as
  early as possible. Introduce Janie to her new teacher, show her
  where the bathroom is, show her the route from home to school.
  Find a classmate she can make friends with over the summer
  before school starts.

  If you aren't certain which school to place her in, have her visit
  two or three schools for half a day, and allow her to have some
  input in the decision. Discuss the pros and cons of the different
  schools, including costs (if relevant), distance, facilities, and anything that is important to your child. Let her think about it for a
  couple of days before she tells you which one she would prefer and
  why. This gives her a feeling of some control over her life, and
  reduces the anxiety and tension that can escalate into tantrums.
  We've found that even four-year-old gifted children can be very
  astute observers and make wise choices in their selection of
  schools. They notice how the children treat each other on the
  playground. They imagine themselves in different settings and
  intuitively know which one will be most comfortable for them. In
  my experience, children make very positive adjustments when they
  have helped to select the school they will attend.

Introverted adults aren't keen on sudden surprises either. "Look, Honey, we just won two tickets to Hawaii, but we have to leave tomorrow!" may not get quite the response you were hoping for.

⚘ *Don't interrupt them.* One of the qualities introverts find the most difficult to deal with in us extraverts is that we interrupt them all the time. We don't mean to be impolite. Half the time, we don't even know we're doing it. We even interrupt ourselves. It comes from thinking out loud and getting very excited about our own thoughts. When two extraverts carry on a conversation, they both talk at once. (You must be wondering, "Then who's listening?" We talk and listen at the same time - honest!)

I had no idea how much I interrupted until I was invited to Missouri to make professional videotapes in the state telecommunications department. At my request, they invited a dozen people to be on the set with me so that I could interact with them in a natural way. A teacher in the front row was an extravert like me, and, naturally, we both talked at once. When I was invited to help edit the videotape, I realized that the viewers couldn't hear what either of us was saying and all of that dialogue had to be edited out.

It helps to set up some kind of a signal system that acts like a stop sign so that the extravert knows that the introvert hasn't finished talking yet. Each time an introvert pauses to think about what he's going to say next, the extravert thinks it's an invitation for her to speak. "Oh, it must be my turn now!" (I should be wearing a T-shirt that says, "I'm talking and I can't stop!")

❖ *Teach them new skills privately rather than in public.* Introverts like to learn things privately and then show their finished product when it's perfected. In Chapter 6, I talked about children who didn't speak until they had mastered complex sentences; children who didn't take their first step until they could run. These are children whose learning process is introverted.

If you want to teach Janie to roller skate, take her to a deserted parking lot at 9:30 PM on a summer evening several miles from home and let her fall down where you will be the only one who sees her until she learns how to maintain her balance. If you want to teach her to swim, don't enroll her in a swim class. Take her to a private pool, if you can find one, and let her sit on the side of the pool and observe you swimming for as long as she needs to until she feels ready to go into the water. If you want to teach Janie to ski, don't take her to Vail over Christmas break and hire a ski instructor. Instead, take her to a less populated ski resort in March and let her observe the skiers on the bunny slope until she gets the hang of it and is willing to give it a try. Introverts' powers of observation are awesome.

❖ *Help them overcome their fear of making mistakes.* Introverts are very perfectionistic. So are the gifted. A gifted introvert is a perfectionist squared. In addition to setting high standards for themselves, gifted introverts are failure avoidant. Annemarie Roeper (of *The Roeper School* and *Roeper Review*) explains that from the time they're toddlers, gifted children are capable of understanding consequences better than children of average intelligence. If an average toddler manages to get to the top of a flight of stairs unsupervised, he might tumble down the stairs and have to learn by trial and error to be careful of stairs. But a gifted toddler would be more likely to back away from the stairs and not get hurt. This means that bright, introverted children have less experience with failure all through their childhood than less capable children, and because of this, may come to fear making mistakes. They're much more likely to engage in an activity in which they're certain they will be successful than in an activity they've never tried before.

I recommend that parents become good role models for surviving mistakes. If you've never ice skated before in your life, take the whole family ice skating so everyone can fall down together, look silly, laugh at themselves, pick themselves up, and try again. Treat mistakes as learning experiences, and ask yourself out loud, "What did I learn from that?" This is a healthy way to view mistakes instead of beating yourself up with statements such as, "I should have known that would happen." (While you're at it, scrap "You should have…" and "Why didn't you…")

One parent came home from work every day and asked her young son for advice on how to help her fix her mistakes, so that he would understand that mistakes were fixable. "Oh dear, I forgot to thaw the chicken for dinner. Now what should I do?" If she hadn't made a mistake that day, she and her husband made up mistakes for their son to help fix. After six months, the boy was less afraid of making mistakes. Encourage your child to try something new, and praise the effort instead of focusing on the result. (When my sister made her first cake, following a recipe, she had never heard the word "dash," so she put a dish of salt in the cake. That was a hard mistake to swallow…)

✂ *Help them find one best friend who has similar interests and abilities.* It takes an introverted child a very long time to make a true friend—someone with compatible interests and values. It's not easy for Jeffery to find someone he feels can accept him exactly the way he is so that he can take off his mask and show his real self. Until he can connect with another person at that level, his relationships tend to be superficial and unrewarding. He'd rather play Nintendo by himself than put the energy into inviting over someone with whom he has little in common.

If Jeffery does find a soul-buddy, and that child moves away, he'll be heartbroken, experiencing the loss as if a family member died. It may take him a year to recover and believe that he can find another friend. It's important to keep the connection between him and his soul-buddy alive (thank goodness for email), because once an introvert has made a friend, he will be loyal to that friend for life. It doesn't matter if the friend moves to Mars and they have no contact for 20 years. The only thing that destroys friendships between introverts is betrayal of trust. If an introvert feels betrayed by someone he trusted, he never gets over it. The pain is forever.

⚘ *Don't pressure them to make lots of friends.* Introverts do not need hordes of friends in order to be happy or well adjusted socially. Throughout their lifetimes, they will probably have only a few really close friends who know the inner person rather than the façade. Janie shouldn't be pushed into going to parties or dating a lot of boys in high school. She'll need lots of alone time to think and the company of one close friend with whom she can share her soul without pretense. Let's face it. Janie is never going to be a budding socialite. In fact, too much social exchange is actually unhealthy for her. She knows that she's different. She's highly sensitive, and she may feel socially awkward—knowing she's putting on an act in order to be accepted. If she's put in too many of these uncomfortable situations, it will increase her anxiety to the point where she might become physically ill. Too much energy and tension is involved in trying to be the party animal she isn't, blending in, and hiding her true self.

⚘ *Respect their introversion. Don't try to remake them into extraverts.* In parenting introverts, it's essential to respect their natural mode of being in the world. Understanding their need for privacy, solitude, and reflection is essential. Trying to turn an introvert into an extravert is as unhealthy as forcing a left-handed person to be right-handed. When a child spends lots of time playing with his friends, his parents don't usually wring their hands in despair and say, "If only he would spend more time in his room reading." We aren't busy trying to make introverts out of extraverts. So why does it bother us so much when Janie would rather read than play?

Your introverted children may have a hard time if you're an extravert who doesn't understand them. But they may have even a harder time if you're an introvert who does understand them. You may have experienced so much pain due to your own introversion being misunderstood that you'll go to any lengths to prevent your child from experiencing the same pain. It would be wise for you to come to terms with your own introversion so that you can be a good role model for your son or daughter. I recommend the book, *Please Understand Me,* by David Keirsey and Marilyn Bates. It makes good family reading, deepening everyone's understanding of the different personality types in the family and promoting self-acceptance and family harmony. *Discover the Power of Introversion* by Cheryl Card is also helpful.

The introverted child in school

A major difference between extraverts and introverts is that extraverts think out loud, while introverts mentally rehearse everything before they say it (and wish everyone else would, too). Introverts would never dream of thinking out loud. It would be like hanging out their dirty laundry for everyone to see. Extraverts are happy to share all their thoughts with anyone within earshot. (I have such a wonderful time talking that it doesn't matter if anyone is listening!) When you ask a question, the extravert raises her hand before you've finished the question, second-guessing the rest of your sentence. The introvert is not as forthcoming. When you call on an introvert, you always hear a pregnant pause while he rehearses the perfect pearl to share with the class. And when he's finished, you sigh in amazement, "Oh, that was beautiful."

Sometimes primary teachers underestimate the abilities of the child who stands on the periphery of the group and watches the others rather than participating (like Craig in Chapter 1). These "sideliners" seem less certain of themselves. The confidence of the extravert can be mistaken as evidence of higher intelligence. The slow-to-warm-up child is often terrified of looking foolish. While the other children are freely experimenting, learning by trial and error, eagerly engaging in interaction, the introverted child observes, experiments mentally, and is not comfortable engaging in the activity until he is absolutely certain he knows how to do it perfectly. By then, the children have moved on to another activity, and the opportunity to participate is lost.

More high school than elementary school teachers are introverted, and introverted students are able to demonstrate their knowledge in the work they turn in rather than through class participation. Colleges are havens for introverts, and introverted students often excel with their introverted professors. So, like visual-spatial learners, introverts may appear smarter as they get older.

Imagine that a group of teachers has been divided into introverts and extraverts and given a task to do with markers on butcher paper in a set time limit. The extraverts immediately start drawing on the butcher paper while they talk and decide exactly what they want the finished product to look like. We are doers—we process actively. The introverts are very quiet at first, thinking about the task, then they talk about it together and plan how to execute it. No marks are made on the butcher paper until around 15 minutes before the time is up. The difference between action and reflection!

The greatest fear introverts have is public humiliation, and they will go to nearly any lengths to avoid it. Some students sit as far away from the front of the class as they can, and hope that you won't notice that they're there. They fear that they will be called on to answer a question and will get it wrong. Some are so anxious that they panic when they're put on the spot or asked to read aloud to the class. Their minds go blank. If another child fails to answer a question correctly and the class laughs, the introverted child viscerally responds as if it had happened to him. He experiences the embarrassment more than the child who made the error. It's imperative to create a classroom environment where students are not allowed to make fun of each other, so that all the children, especially the introverts, feel safe. The only rule I had in my classroom was "No put downs." They only had to remember three words and they were non-negotiable. I explained that creativity can only flourish in an environment in which everyone feels safe to contribute and everyone's ideas are valued. (See Chapter 13 for more about this.)

Tips for teaching introverted children

    ❖ *Let them observe.* Introverts have an amazing capacity to learn from observation. They're not "cheating" when they watch the other children before they begin to work. They're using their best method of learning.

       At exactly one she held a pencil correctly after observing her uncle intently. At two she tied her shoelaces, again after observation. Later when she could talk I would sometimes ask her how she knew how to do something involving a manual skill. Every time she would answer: "I just watched you do it" as if this should be obvious to any idiot. There is rarely any trial and error involved. …She started the violin last year and the teacher was amazed that she learned to manipulate the bow in the first lesson, something he claims usually takes up to a year. She probably "just watched him do it." She continues to show unusual skill in this area.

    ❖ *Incorporate more wait time between questions and answers.* You might remember the research of Mary Budd Rowe in the seventies, who observed how much time teachers wait between asking a question and accepting answers from the students. In analyzing taped classroom discussions, she discovered that teachers tended to wait *less than one second* for students to reply to their questions. Only extraverts would be able to respond that fast. It's a good idea to initiate "think time" (longer pauses) after questions to students to give the introverts in the group time to think and reflect. If the silence is uncomfortable for the class, tell them you want them to really think about the question before they respond, and that you are going to give them a little time to do that before calling on anyone.

I spoke at a conference in Arizona and a teacher came up to me afterwards and asked, "Weren't you the one who did a presentation on introversion a few years ago?" I said yes. Then she relayed what had happened when she taught her students about introverts and extraverts. Her class was involved in small group projects and one group really wanted to hear the ideas of a particular student who was quite creative but also very introverted. She overheard one of them excitedly go up to the boy and say, "We really need your input on this. Think about it and get back to us."

- *Give introverts a place to think.* Think time can be encouraged in other ways as well. In an elementary class, you can set up a corner of the classroom with pillows, away from too many distractions, as a quiet place to think. (Maybe with a little Rodin statue of *The Thinker??*) Children who are distracted or easily overstimulated could escape there to do their work until they feel ready to rejoin the group. It's necessary that the corner not be used as a form of punishment, and that children can choose to go there when they feel the need to get away from it all and regroup.

- *Form dyads for greater participation.* After presenting an idea or a new concept to the whole class, have the students discuss with a pre-arranged partner how they personally relate to the concept. Do this activity for about ten minutes before initiating a discussion with the whole group. This gives the introverts an opportunity to talk about their feelings and experiences one-on-one. After they've had a chance to see how one person reacts, they may be more willing to share their thoughts with the entire class.

- *Have students write ideas down before brainstorming as a group.* Brainstorming is a wonderful way of enhancing creativity in the classroom. The only problem is that it tends to be dominated by verbally assertive extraverts. Here's a twist that provides think time and increases the likelihood that introverts will participate. First have the students write down their ideas for 5 or 10 minutes, then let everyone who wants to participate have an opportunity to share his or her ideas.

❧ *Use a signal system to involve more introverts in group discussions.* It's very difficult for introverts to get a word in edgewise in a rapid-fire class discussion when exuberant extraverts have the floor. Introverts hate interrupting. They may have something important to share, but before they can get it out, another extravert has interrupted the first one and gotten the attention of the group. One method that seems to work is having students who want to add something to the discussion raise their hands while another student is talking. You can nod your recognition to all of them, one at a time, so that they know they will have a chance to speak, and the order in which they will speak. Your nod is a signal that you have seen them, and that they should put their hands down. If too many raise their hands, you can write down the names of the students who wish to contribute, in the order in which you noticed them, and then let them know when it's their turn to have the floor.

❧ *Correct and praise them privately.* Introverts often do not like public attention for any purpose—positive or negative. They're just as upset at a teacher singling them out for praise as for punishment. "Oh, look at Janie's picture! Isn't it wonderful?" As the teacher holds up Janie's work, Janie is wishing she could crawl under the table. Introverts much prefer teachers to talk to them privately with any kind of feedback in a voice that can't be heard by the other students.

❧ *Help them overcome their fear of making mistakes.* Introverts hate making mistakes; yet, mistakes seem to be part of learning any new skill. A computer is an excellent tool for introverts, because they can learn new skills without anyone seeing their mistakes. Children can also practice new skills at home rather than in the classroom as another means of protecting themselves from embarrassment. Encourage them to try new activities and praise them for their efforts.

I often play the game *Bagels* with students to help them overcome their fear of errors and see mistakes in a more positive light. You think of a 3-digit number and the students take turns shouting out 3-digit numbers to see if they can guess your number. For each accurate digit in the right place, you write "Fermi" on the board. For each accurate digit in the wrong place, you write "Pico." If they get no digits right, you write, ✍"BAGELS!!!"✍

But don't tell the students these code words before you start playing. Tell them as they play.

Here's an example:

Say your number is   192.

A student shouts: 123   You write: Fermi, Pico and say, "That means one of your numbers is correct and in the right place and one is the right number in the wrong place."

128   Fermi, Pico

216   Pico, Pico

798   Fermi

875   ✳✦♀♟♗BAGELS!!♞♟♛✦✳

You make as big a deal as possible out of Bagels. At first, the students think they guessed the right answer. Then you tell them with tremendous excitement that "Bagels" means they were **absolutely wrong** and ask what's wonderful about being completely wrong? They soon figure out that they can now eliminate 8, 7 and 5 and get close to the correct answer much faster. The strategy is to go for Bagels. (*Jotto* and *Mastermind* are logic games similar to *Bagels*. *Jotto* uses 5-letter words with no position clues and *Mastermind* uses colors.) After you've played *Bagels* with them a few times, you can remind a student who is getting upset at having made a mistake, or panicking over the fear of making a mistake, of the lesson of *Bagels*.

✂ *Have them practice public speaking with a video recorder.* For many introverts, the fear of public speaking is greater than the fear of death. They can be traumatized by having to give a formal presentation to the entire class before they're ready to take on the challenge. Children do not get over their fears by being thrown into situations they feel unable to handle. Try having the introverted student speak to a video recorder and submit the videotape in lieu of speaking to the class. The videotape can be erased and corrected as many times as the student wishes until he feels it's presentable. Then have the student give a presentation to a small group of friends with whom he feels comfortable. Gradually, the size of the group can be increased until the student feels able to handle speaking to the entire class.

✂ *Allow students to do independent projects.* Group projects are very popular in schools today, particularly in cooperative learning groups. Cooperative learning groups are great for extraverts, but they can be a nightmare for introverts. Many times the gifted introvert ends up doing all the work for the group because no one else does the work up to the level of his standards. And he fumes if he gets marked down because of someone else's behavior.

Our job as educators is to accept children's personalities, just as we accept their learning styles. We don't try to make right-handed children more left-handed and, hopefully, we've stopped trying to "correct" lefthandedness in young children. Ambidexterity is not the goal. The same is true for introversion and extraversion and for visual-spatials and auditory-sequential learners. They blossom if they're appreciated for who they are instead of being pressured to be more "well-rounded." Success in adult life comes from self-acceptance and from finding one's own place in the diversity of life.

Introversion and visual-spatial learning

Both visual-spatial abilities and the tendency toward introversion appear to increase with IQ. Highly gifted children are more likely to favor visual-spatial thinking than moderately gifted children, and they're more likely to be introverted. Whereas about 60% of moderately gifted children are introverted and 40% are extraverted, 75% of the highly gifted children we have studied are introverted and 25% are extraverted. Both introverts and visual-spatial learners are reflective, needing extra thinking time before entering into tasks. But there are many introverts who are not VSLs, and I'm sure there are some VSLs who are extraverts.

In *The Spatial Child*, John Philo Dixon offers a comprehensive summary of the studies linking introversion to spatial abilities. The studies extend from the 1920s to the 1980s. Spatially gifted people, such as engineers and physicists, tended to be withdrawn, slow to warm up, absent-minded, continually absorbed in thought, inhibited in their reactions, self-sufficient, independent, reclusive, reserved in the expression of emotion, self-critical, and anxious. David Lohman suggests that thinking in images influences personality type. "Children who showed a preference for imagistic processing were much more likely to be introverted whereas those who showed a preference for verbal elaboration were more likely to be extraverted" (1994, pp. 256-257). On the other hand, Jerre Levy cited research that appeared to link introversion with left-hemispheric development, and extraversion with right-hemispheric development.

Overall, I believe that most of the visual-spatial learners I've come across were introverted to varying degrees. It also makes sense to me that imagistic thinking would be internal and private. Thinking in images is not a group process; it requires alone time to construct a clear picture. This form of thought necessitates focusing on one's own inner world instead of on the distracting social context. In addition, spatial perceptions are difficult to communicate to others. If one's medium of thought is words, that medium is more amenable to social exchange and validation, as the social world is highly linguistic. As I see it, an extraverted child with stronger left-hemispheric activation comes equipped for communication, and an introverted child with greater right-hemispheric arousal is equipped for perceiving more aspects of a situation. Communication with limited perception is empty; perception with limited ability to communicate is frustrating.

The combination of an introverted personality type and a visual-spatial learning style can lead to loneliness and feelings of isolation. Highly verbal, sequential extraverts live in a shared reality; each intro-verted VSL inhabits his or her own reality. VSLs feel more isolated in their perception of the world than their sequential peers. Introverts have to learn how to extravert to some degree in order to survive in an extraverted society and VSLs have to learn some sequential skills in order to survive in a sequential world. Luckily, many sequential skills can be mastered through practice.

But the introverted visual-spatial child lives in a world that is not understood by the extraverted sequential individuals who surround him or her. In the first place, auditory-sequential learners may be unaware that there is another way of knowing. They're able to be successful without much development of their visual-spatial abilities. They're the dominant culture, so they do not have the same motivation to master the spatial domain. Even if they did, spatial abilities are much more difficult to teach. The sequential child can learn to do some visual-spatial tasks, but he or she can't easily learn to see the way the spatial person sees. Artists perceive form, space, color, texture, perspective, and contrast in a way that non-artists do not. Sequentials can visit the world of the spatial person but they cannot live there.

The benefits of introversion in adult life

Introverts need to learn about the positive benefits of their personality type. They need to be taught that reflection is a good quality, that the most creative individuals sought solitude, and that leaders in academic, aesthetic and technical fields are often introverts. Parents need to know that more National Merit Scholars are introverted than extraverted, and that introverts have higher grade point averages in Ivy League colleges than extraverts, because they're less distracted by their social lives.

Contrary to public opinion, success in life is not dependent upon extraversion. Many introverts become leaders in their adult lives. Extraverts attain leadership in public domains such as the political arena and business, but introverts dominate theoretical and aesthetic fields. Leadership is not just the charisma to lead groups; it also occurs in more solitary forms--in scientific breakthroughs, the creation of philosophy, and the writing of profound books. Scholastically achieving introverts frequently gain prestigious positions at universities and research institutes, are valued for their knowledge and skills, and have excellent opportunities to rise to positions of leadership through scholarly efforts and creative contributions to their fields.

The personality profile of introversion, less focused on the values and attitudes of the mainstream, allows for creative introspection. Those giant figures who created new fields of thought or who rearranged existing knowledge often spent long periods in solitude. For example, Rene Descartes moved his residence frequently so that no one could disturb him in his work. Only one monk knew how to reach him. And Charles Darwin feigned illness as a means of isolating himself. His wife protected him from visitors.

Introverts also have an advantage at midlife in that long, hard journey to the Soul, which heralds the second half of the life cycle. They're more capable than extraverts of retreating from the world, going deep into themselves, and handling the reflective tasks involved in personality integration. Introverts are less influenced than extraverts by the values and attitudes of others, so they're able to develop a personal philosophy, to know what they stand for, and to be self-determining.

As they're a minority in our society, most introverts have had to develop some extraverted behaviors in order to cope, but extraverts rarely are called upon to develop the introverted parts of their personalities. As an extravert, it was difficult for me to introvert (notice that for me "introvert" is a verb) enough to be able to write this book. Although there is no question that extraversion is advantageous in childhood and young adulthood, the full integration of the personality depends on the development of all aspects of the Self—the introverted and extraverted parts of one's personality. The time has come to respect the introverts in our families and classrooms and the hidden introvert in ourselves.

Double Jeopardy:
Visual-Spatial and AD/HD

My son has been a whirlwind since the day he was born. He slept sporadically, infrequently, and often only long enough to recharge. It was like he was afraid he would miss something. My husband and I feared he would be labeled ADD at school. He has calmed down considerably since he turned 4 but still pursues activities that interest him with a voracity and focus that is remarkable. Just like your description; he all of a sudden "gets it."

In grade 1 her teacher felt she was easily distracted, would daydream or not pay attention, always knew the answers but would not necessarily complete the seatwork. It seemed to me that these were classic signs of a bright child who was bored. ... I want her to do well at school, but not at the expense of losing the quirky and imaginative things that are in her brain that she is just being able to express. She is a wonderful child who, from the beginning, marched to the beat of her own drum.

T has a hard time staying in his seat and is constantly chatting with his classmates. His teacher has moved him many times. He tends to sit every way at his desk, except for the traditional way. However when he is called on for information, he always had the correct answer. He has been listening, while upside down in his chair! Chess class has been a great experience for him. He loves the game, and has learned to be patient for his turn. It has taught him to focus for a long period of time and it has given him self-esteem knowing that he is better at something than most of his classmates.

All of these children are visual-spatial. But which have attention deficit disorder (AD/HD)? Your guess is as good as mine! For over a decade, I've been trying valiantly to tell apart AD/HD, giftedness, and visual-spatial learning style, and falling short. The majority of VSLs do not have AD/HD, but many with AD/HD are probably visual-spatial. This chapter is about VSLs who have AD/HD symptoms and how to help them. If you'll come with me on my journey to understand AD/HD, I'll share with you the insights I've gained along the way. The story begins with a discovery that ties in with the last chapter.

AD/HD or extraversion?

Several years ago, I was doing a presentation on Introversion and Extraversion for a group of parents, and the particular list I was using ended with the following three pairs:

EXTRAVERTS	INTROVERTS
❧ Distractible	❧ Capable of intense concentration
❧ Impulsive	❧ Reflective
❧ Are risk-takers in groups	❧ Fear humiliation; quiet in large groups

A father sitting in the front row raised his hand and said, "So what's the difference between extraversion and AD/HD?" I was completely caught off-guard by his question. I looked up at the list on the overhead, read out loud, "distractible, impulsive, risk-takers" and responded, "I don't have a clue. All these years I just thought I was extraverted; maybe I have AD/HD and don't know it!"

Until that moment, I never realized that some of the extraverted traits coincided with major symptoms of AD/HD. As you can see in Chapter 10, I had been using extraversion merely as a backdrop for my discussion of introversion. (You read Chapter 10, right? If not, go back a chapter before you read on.)

My interest in introversion was fueled by observing that a lot of bright children were introverted and the brighter they were, the more introverted they seemed. I became the champion of the Introverted Underdog and talked a lot about introversion in my presentations to parents and teachers. After awhile, the extraverts in my audiences let me know—with all the subtlety that we extraverts have at our command—that they felt neglected. One participant remarked, "Are you saying that you think extraverts **like** being humiliated?" Originally, I had constructed two checklists: *Characteristics of Introverts,* a scale for adults, and *Characteristics of Introversion in Children.* The feedback from disgruntled extraverts motivated me to replace the *Characteristics of Introversion in Children* scale with the *Introversion/Extraversion Continuum.* (See Table 10.2 in the last chapter.)

Now that I was aware of the overlapping characteristics of extraversion and AD/HD, I began to notice that children with AD/HD symptoms usually came out more extraverted than introverted on the new scale. I called my friend, Deirdre Lovecky, author of *Different Minds: Gifted Children with AD/HD, Asperger Syndrome and Other Learning Deficits,* and asked her if all children with AD/HD were extraverted. Dee laughed, "Of course not!"

The interaction of AD/HD and introversion

Then I noticed something else that was curious. Parents of children with AD/HD would often mark several opposing items on **both** sides of the continuum as true, such as:

"concentrates intently" and "easily distracted"

"cautious" and "risk-taker"

"reflective" and "impulsive"

This made it hard to score! I remembered that in our Visual-Spatial Learner Study Group, George Dorry, our AD/HD expert, mentioned that the essence of AD/HD is **disinhibition**—the inability to inhibit (hold back) a response. Impulsivity reigns. There is no "Maybe I shouldn't do that," or "Maybe I shouldn't say that," to restrain behavior. It dawned on me that the essence of introversion is **inhibition**—a strong innate tendency to control responses. Introverts are frequently described as "inhibited." They do not act brashly. Was it possible for people to be inhibited and *dis*inhibited at the same time? If they were introverted and had AD/HD, wouldn't they be in constant inner conflict? How would those two forces interact with each other?

Soon I had an insight about those questions. A child came to the Center for assessment who fit most of the AD/HD descriptors, as well as a mixture of the introverted and extraverted traits on the Continuum. In our Developmental Questionnaire, we also ask a lot of questions about introversion:

- Does your child need privacy?   Y__ N__
- Does your child behave differently at school and at home?   Y__ N__
- Is your child perfectionistic?   Y__ N__
- Is your child sensitive?   Y__ N__
- Is he or she easily humiliated?   Y__ N__
- Does your child prefer to observe activities before getting involved? Y__ N__

Mom responded "yes" to all the above questions. She also mentioned several other introverted traits throughout the questionnaire, such as that her son was slow to warm up in new situations, he was a loner, etc. Yet, she had rated him with a sizeable number of extraverted traits on the Continuum. It occurred to me that maybe he wasn't really extraverted at all—maybe he just appeared that way because of his impulsivity. As we talked, my hunch seemed to be right. I have continued to see this same pattern in many introverted children with AD/HD symptoms. They look more extraverted than they actually are because they don't have much impulse control. (They're in your face a lot.)

Now a related hypothesis began to form in my mind. I had heard from the time I was in graduate school that a lot of boys "outgrow" hyperactivity at puberty. And I had met adults who appeared to have either overcome their AD/HD by the time they reached adulthood or found a way to make it to work for them instead of against them. Was it possible that these people were introverts? Through maturation, would the war between Inhibition and Disinhibition eventually be won by Inhibition? I'm betting that it would. I believe the built-in need for control ultimately conquers those unruly impulses. I have no concrete evidence yet that this is true, but I've checked out the hypothesis with some researchers who have studied attention deficits, and it certainly seems plausible to them. It would be great to do a longitudinal study and see how introverted children with AD/HD develop in adult life. (If you're an introverted adult with AD/HD, how was it for you?) If you have a child who is somewhat introverted and has symptoms of AD/HD, I think the introversion may help provide a built-in check on your child's impulsivity.

Is there such a thing as AD/HD?

For the first ten years of the Center's life, I refused to believe in AD/HD. I thought it was a catch-all term that didn't have any real basis. Now that I think about it, how could I have dismissed the idea for a whole decade? I had been trained in learning disabilities, and I certainly had seen and worked with hyperkinetic children in the '60s and '70s. Wasn't this just a new term for an old syndrome?

My awareness began to shift in April of 1989, when Dee Lovecky invited me to New York to participate in a panel discussion for the American Orthopsychiatric Association. I presented on "Gifted Children with Hidden Handicaps," and discussed gifted VSLs with central auditory processing disorder. Dee talked about gifted children with different kinds of attention deficits. We both had sample WISC-R profiles. I looked at her data, she looked at my data, and we both wondered if we were two blind men describing different parts of the same elephant. The profiles looked a lot alike. There had to be common ground between our two groups.

Eventually, the moment of truth arrived. A couple years after Dee and I spoke in New York, I tested a child who tested my patience to the limit. While she was obviously very bright, it was practically impossible to get her to focus on what we were doing. She alternated between running around the room and crawling under the table. She couldn't keep her hands off the testing materials, she couldn't stay on task, she couldn't keep information in short-term memory, she kept offering toilet humor, and her answers were more like free association. When asked to tell me what certain words meant, she responded "from the wall" several times. (Talk about off-the-wall answers...) I asked her to repeat 5 digits, like 6, 2, 1, 9, 3, and she would say, "1, 2, 3, 4, 5." By the time I was done assessing her, I was exhausted and a nervous wreck. I called Dee, waved a white flag, and conceded that AD/HD really did exist. I had seen the light.

What exactly is AD/HD?

Attention Deficit/Hyperactivity Disorder (AD/HD) has been described by various experts as inconsistent or fluctuating attention, an inability to inhibit responses (faulty brakes), being at the mercy of the environment (distractibility and inability to set priorities), and a problem of motivation. You will hear the terms "ADD" and "AD/HD" used interchangeably. Now they mean the same thing, but they didn't always. Before 1994, "ADD without hyperactivity" and "AD/HD" were two conditions with some intersecting symptoms. In 1994, when the fourth edition of the *Diagnostic and Statistical Manual of Mental Disorders (DSM-IV)* was released (the mental health bible), "AD/HD" became the official name for both the "inattentive type" and "hyperactive/impulsive type."

"ADD without hyperactivity" made a whole lot more sense than "Attention Deficit/ Hyperactivity Disorder without hyperactivity," don't you think? It's an entirely different syndrome from its cousin, AD/HD—hyperactive/impulsive type. It looks more like depression, and is often treated with antidepressants. Many children suffer simultaneously from both syndromes, and are called "combined type." Essentially, AD/HD involves distractibility, difficulty concentrating, poor impulse control, and, in the most obvious cases, hyperactivity. It's commonly diagnosed with the following criteria listed in the *DSM-IV*:

Table 11.1

Criteria for
Attention Deficit/Hyperactivity Disorder

Inattention
↳ often fails to give close attention to details or makes careless mistakes in schoolwork, work or other activities;
↳ often has difficulty sustaining attention in tasks or play activities;
↳ often does not seem to listen when spoken to directly;
↳ often does not follow through on instructions and fails to finish schoolwork, work, chores, or duties in the workplace (not due to oppositional behavior or failure to understand instructions);
↳ often has difficulty organizing tasks and activities;
↳ often avoids, dislikes, or is reluctant to engage in tasks that require sustained mental effort (such as schoolwork or homework);
↳ often loses things necessary for tasks or activities (e.g., toys, school assignments, pencils, books, or tools);
↳ is often easily distracted by extraneous stimuli;
↳ is often forgetful in daily activities.

Hyperactivity
↳ often fidgets with hands or feet or squirms in seat;
↳ often leaves seat in classroom or in other situations in which remaining seated is expected;
↳ often runs about or climbs excessively in situations in which it is inappropriate (in adolescents or adults, may be limited to subjective feelings of restlessness);
↳ often has difficulty playing or engaging in leisure activities quietly;
↳ is often "on the go" or often acts as if "driven by a motor";
↳ often talks excessively.

Impulsivity
↳ often blurts out answers before questions have been completed;
↳ often has difficulty awaiting turn;
↳ often interrupts or intrudes on others (e.g., butts into conversation or games).

(American Psychiatric Association, 1994, pp. 83-84)

Children who exhibit 6 of the 9 indicators of inattention, or 6 of the 9 criteria of hyperactivity and impulsivity, are labeled AD/HD. We regularly give an adaptation of this checklist to our parents, but we've added the direction to think about their child when he or she is *not* interested in an activity, instead of when the child is engaged. Very bright children with AD/HD can be fiercely attentive in self-chosen activities that fascinate them, such as LEGOs™, and unable to pay attention for three seconds when they're not interested.

Central auditory processing disorder (CAPD)

Before I saw the light, I considered most cases of underachievement and attentional issues to be attributable to undetected auditory processing problems. In 1986, Jana Waters and I presented at a National Association for Gifted Children Convention on the topic, "The Hidden Handicap—Auditory Dysfunction in Gifted Children." We shared a list of the symptoms of auditory processing problems we had seen in gifted children:

Table 11.2
Symptoms of
Central Auditory Processing Disorder

✎ *Asks to have directions repeated*
✎ *Misunderstands what is said*
✎ Mispronounces words
✎ Puts hands over ears in noisy situations
✎ Talks very loudly
✎ *Does not hear name called when playing or concentrating*
✎ Mispronounces some sounds of letters
✎ *Cannot sound out words effectively*
✎ Makes letter reversals at eight or nine years old
✎ Spells words according to their shape, not their sounds
✎ *Leaves out endings of words in writing*
✎ *Leaves out small words in writing*
✎ *Has difficulty memorizing (such as math facts)*
✎ *Daydreams after ten minutes of instruction*
✎ *"Forgets" written homework assignments or submits short, sloppy work of much lower quality than is capable*
✎ *Performs poorly or not at all on timed tests*
✎ *Has difficulty with handwriting or handwriting is poor*

I used a similar list in my presentation with Dee Lovecky, and Dee and I spent many phone conversations after that trying to sort out the diagnostic criteria for the two groups. Over two-thirds of these criteria would also fit children with the inattentive type of AD/HD. To complicate matters further, AD/HD specialists often ask for ear infection histories, because so many children with attention deficits have had numerous ear infections. Later on, I learned about a ten-year study that had been done of infants who suffered from recurrent ear infections. The most frequent after-effect was attentional issues! So when is it auditory processing disorder and when is it AD/HD? Not an easy question to answer. We recommend a Central Auditory Processing Battery and an evaluation by a specialist in AD/HD to be certain. Lots of times it's *both*.

Three miracles

Now it's embarrassing to think that for ten solid years I didn't think any of the one thousand children who came for assessment had AD/HD. I probably missed some pretty blatant cases, but I had my own theories. I talked about three "miracles" I had seen that magically trans- formed irritable, acting out, unmanageable children into delights. The first miracle was surgically implanted tubes in their ears. (See Chapter 3.) Toddlers and preschoolers suffering from recurrent ear infections tend to be irritable and may act out in frustration from not being able to hear or communicate clearly. I realize that there are potential dangers involved in this procedure. Many doctors only insert tubes as a last resort, which is wise. But behaviorally, the differences that parents have reported before and after tubes have been quite remarkable: from little demon to pussycat.

The second miracle occurred when advanced children were placed in classes with others like themselves. This phenomenon was particularly apparent when children were wonderful at home, but acting out in school and getting into trouble. In these cases, I would recommend that parents of children with school-based AD/HD symptoms try a different school placement and see if that made any difference in the child's behavior. It's amazing how many bright boys who looked very AD/HD- like when *not sufficiently challenged* had dramatic recoveries in full-time programs or schools for the gifted, where the pace and level of learning were more appropriate.

There is actually support for this observation in the *DSM-IV*. In fact, it's the only place in the manual where high intelligence is recognized as possibly mimicking the symptoms of a disorder. Before a positive diag- nosis of AD/HD is made, the following must be ruled out: "Inattention in the classroom may also occur when children with high intelligence are placed in academically **understimulating environments**." (American Psychiatric Association, 1994, p. 83). Even gifted children who truly suffer with AD/HD are able to concentrate much better when the work is more difficult than when it's too easy. Try it!

The third miracle was dietary interventions. I encouraged parents to take overactive children for allergy testing to see if they might have undiagnosed food sensitivities. I had noticed that a considerable number of bright children had either respiratory or digestive "allergic" reactions. I put allergic in quotes because the medical profession reserves the term for severe, life-threatening reactions, like anaphylactic shock. But parents call even minor, annoying reactions—like hives— "allergies." (Me too!) Colic, asthma, sensitivities to various environmental factors, and food sensitivities appeared so often in my clients that I considered allergies the number one non-intellective factor related to giftedness. Camilla Benbow and her associates also found a higher incidence of allergies and other auto-immune deficiencies in the gifted. I observed that when certain foods were removed from their diets, the behavioral changes for some children were astonishing.

All I did was quit eating wheat and dairy, and my grades went right up to A's and B's.

More about allergies

The most pronounced food allergies or sensitivities that have surfaced in our clients over the last 2 decades are:

- ❖ milk products
- ❖ wheat
- ❖ sugar
- ❖ corn
- ❖ chocolate/caffeine
- ❖ eggs
- ❖ red food dye

Of course, there are also the children who have life-threatening allergies to peanuts, or break out in hideous rashes from seafood or tomatoes. But the foods listed above seem to have an adverse impact on behavior. And guess which is the main offender? Nope, not sugar. Milk products! I assumed it was lactose intolerance, but I've also run across children with strong reactions to casein—the protein base of milk.

In her analysis of the data we collected on 241 exceptionally gifted children with IQ scores above 160, Karen Rogers found that nearly half were reported to suffer from allergies (44%) compared to 20% in the general population. Of the allergic children, over one-third (35.5%) were reported to be sensitive to milk. No other foods emerged in the study. The next highest allergy was to trees: 8.2%. Grass, animal dander, molds, and weeds all affected less than five percent of the sample. Milk products are prime suspects in bed wetting as well, and need to be avoided when a child has a cold or other respiratory infections.

Some children react to a particular combination of foods rather than to a single food. A mother came up to me at a conference and shared that when she took her daughter off of milk, nothing happened. When she took her off wheat, nothing happened. But when she took her off *both* milk and wheat, within 24 hours she "had a new child." And sometimes it's not the food itself, but the food additives that cause the problem. Red food coloring has been identified as a potential culprit in hyperactivity. (Look for it in children's drinks.) Processed foods contain numerous additives, including corn syrup, which can cause AD/HD symptoms in many children who are sensitive to corn. There are also some children who react to the pesticide sprays on fruits and vegetables. Try organic produce.

When I first began to suspect food sensitivities as a cause of difficult behavior, I must have sent at least a hundred children for skin tests. It wasn't until I had the skin tests done myself that I realized how unreliable they were for reactions to food. I tested positive for foods that didn't bother me at all, and tested negative for foods I was positive affected me. After the skin tests, the allergist insisted I try an elimination diet for three weeks to be certain. (So why bother with the skin tests?) Blood tests, hair analysis, biofeedback devices and muscle-testing can also detect food allergies.

Allergists often recommend that you eat only a few foods that you know you can tolerate, and then gradually add one food at a time to see how your body copes with it. For example, you could eliminate all 7 of potential allergens—*milk products, wheat, sugar, corn, chocolate/caffeine, eggs, red food dye*—along with packaged and processed foods, soft drinks and Kool-Aid, for five to ten days. Serve only fruits, vegetables and meats that are not processed, then add the other foods one at a time and note the behaviors that occur. This may work well with highly disciplined adults, but it's really difficult to pull off with children. I have an easier plan.

I recommend eliminating one food at a time from a child's diet, for a three-week period, then re-introducing as much as they want for three days. Here's how it works. Keep a record of everything your child eats for a few days before beginning an elimination diet. See if you spot a relationship between what your child has eaten and outbursts, impulsive behavior, temper tantrums, high activity levels, or distractibility. If you suspect a certain food, eliminate it for three weeks and see what happens. On the next page is a sample diet diary. (Make lots of copies.) Throughout the elimination diet, record what your child eats and when, and any reactions you notice afterwards. You don't need to be obsessive about it. Just keep as good an account as you can. If your child is old enough and scientifically minded, ask him or her to help you with the record-keeping.

Make copies of the Mood Chart and the Diet Diary that follow.

Figure 11.1

☺ **How do you feel today?** ☹

On a scale from 1 (YUCK!) to 10 (GREAT!), rate your mood today in the morning and at night. Were you happy? ☺ Did you get in trouble? ☹

Date_____

	Sunday	Monday	Tuesday	Wednesday	Thursday	Friday	Saturday
AM							
PM							

You and your child complete separate copies of the chart every morning and evening for a few days before you start the elimination diet, and compare your ratings. Rate your child's mood/behavior from 1 to 10, with 1 indicating *terrible* and 10 indicating *wonderful.* Enlist your child's support as the Primary Investigator (Head Scientist?) in a scientific study of his or her own body. Try eliminating one of the seven foods or any other suspected allergen for three weeks. Complete the mood chart and diet diary to whatever extent possible. At the end of three weeks, give your child as much of the forbidden food as he or she wants for three days. (This is a good incentive if your child craves the item.) If your child is sensitive to that particular food, behavior should steadily improve over the three-week period, with more good days than bad days, and take a nosedive during the three-day binge. Once you've located the foods that cause the greatest reactions, your child may choose voluntarily to stay away from them (or reduce intake), rather than continue to experience so many bad days.

Figure 11.2

Diet Diary

Date_____

Time	Food(s) eaten	Reaction

Comments:

_____

_____

_____

Overexcitabilities, creativity and VSLs

There is yet another factor that can make creative visual-spatial learners look like they have attention deficits: overexcitabilities (OEs). OEs come from the work of Kazimierz Dabrowski, a Polish psychiatrist and psychologist. After observing a group of creatively gifted children and youth in Warsaw in 1962, he concluded that creative individuals have different wiring from other people—greater intensity of neural responses. By nature more easily stimulated and excited, creative people respond more intensely in a variety of situations. There are five types of overexcitability: *psychomotor, sensual, imaginational, intellectual* and *emotional.* OEs supply an abundance of physical, sensual, creative, intellectual and emotional energy.

Overexcitabilities can have both positive and negative effects. On the upside, the child may be born with abundant energy, heightened senses, vivid imagination, an insatiable love of learning, and an unusual capacity to care. The downside, however, is that the child may have an inability to sit still; an inability to tolerate noise, clothing tags or certain textures of food; an overactive imagination; intense intellectual curiosity; and extreme emotional sensitivity. Intense intellectual curiosity is a problem when the child's mind insists on journeying wherever it wants to go to answer its questions, rather than allowing the child to pay attention to what's going on in the classroom. It's a difficult balancing act to harness all that energy wisely.

OEs occur in various combinations and strengths. A visual-spatial learner can have a few mild OEs or come equipped with powerful doses of all five. Janie might have high Intellectual OE, moderate Emotional OE, and mild Psychomotor OE. She wouldn't look like she has AD/HD as much as Zach, who has very high Psychomotor OE, high Sensual OE, high Imaginational OE, and high Emotional OE. Visual-spatial learners, like Zach, manifest most or all of the OEs. Heightened sensory awareness makes it difficult for them to focus their attention. They become irritated by sock seams or "itchy" clothing; distracted by the nearly imperceptible flickering of fluorescent lights or the whispering of their classmates; carried off in flights of fantasy by their active imaginations; overstimulated by their own intellectual curiosity and understimulated by the pace of classroom instruction; and intensely affected by the emotional climate of the classroom and their relationships with classmates.

Visual-spatial learners tend to be creative. The higher the creativity, the stronger the overexcitabilities. When these overexcitabilities are very strong and difficult to channel, the child exhibits symptoms reminiscent of AD/HD. However, with maturation, the young person is likely to develop greater impulse control and the ability to manage the OEs. Some children need years of practice to regulate this intense bombardment of inner stimulation. Overexcitabilities are not bad. They lead to creative endeavors in adulthood, and they can also lead to advanced emotional and ethical development. They just make life more challenging for everybody!

It's difficult to tell whether highly creative VSLs bursting with overexcitabilities suffer from attention deficits, as well. Ned Hallowell and John Ratey, authors of *Driven to Distraction*, have found a tendency toward creativity in people with AD/HD, and they consider the creative person with AD/HD a separate subtype of attention disorders.

> Bombarded by stimuli from every direction...people with ADD live with chaos all the time.... For all the problems this might pose, it can assist the creative process. In order to rearrange life, in order to create, one must get comfortable with disarrangement for awhile. (pp. 176-177)

> A third element that favors creativity among people with ADD is...the ability to intensely focus or hyperfocus at times. ...The term "attention deficit" is a misnomer. It is a matter of attention inconsistency. While it is true that the ADD mind wanders when not engaged, it is also the case that the ADD mind fastens on to its subject fiercely when it is engaged. A child with ADD may sit for hours meticulously putting together a model airplane. An adult may work with amazing concentration when faced with a deadline. (p. 177)

> This ability to hyperfocus heats up the furnace in the brain, so to speak, and melts down rigid elements so they may easily flow and commingle, allowing for new products to be formed once they hit the cool light of day. The intensity of the furnace when it heats up may help explain why it needs to cool down, to be distracted, when it is not heated up.

> A fourth element contributing to creativity is what Russell Barkley has called the "hyperreactivity" of the ADD mind. Cousin to the traditional symptom of hyperactivity, hyperreactivity is more common among people with ADD than hyperactivity is. People with ADD are always reacting. Even when they look calm and sedate, they are usually churning inside, taking this piece of data and moving it there, pushing this thought through their emotional network, putting that idea on the fire to burn, exploding or subsiding, but always in motion. Such hyperreactivity enhances creativity because it increases the number of collisions in the brain. Each collision has the potential to emit new light, new matter, as when subatomic particles collide. (p.178)

"Hyperreactivity" sounds remarkably like overexcitability, doesn't it? So how can you tell if it's OEs, AD/HD, or both? Here again, the answers are unclear. But we sure have been trying for years to find the distinctions.

A few summers ago, something funny happened. I invited Michael Piechowski, one of the main experts on Dabrowski's theory, to teach a course on "Emotional Development and Emotional Giftedness." On the first night of the course, he was discussing the overexcitabilities, and, naturally, the question came up, "What's the difference between over-excitabilities and AD/HD?" Not being an expert on AD/HD, Michael opened the question to the group, and the participants offered their opinions. While they were puzzling over the question, three of us from the Gifted Development Center (Helen McVicar, Annette Revel Sheely and me) passed a scrap of paper back and forth, outlining what appeared to us to be the differences. This is what we came up with:

Table 11.3

Overexcitabilities vs. AD/HD

Overexcitabilities	AD/HD
Control of aggression	Inconsistent impulse control; Unintentional aggression
Inhibition (tendency toward introversion)	Disinhibition (appears more extraverted)
Field independent (self-determined)	Field dependent; stimulus bound (at the mercy of the environment)
Focused (especially if one OE dominant)	Distractible; forgetful; disruptive; disorganized
Essential thinking	Tangential thinking
Purposive movement	Repetitive movement, not goal directed

I came home from the class to a phone message that John Ratey was flying into Denver that weekend (spur of the moment decision) and he wanted to come visit the Gifted Development Center. The golden opportunity had arrived: Mr. OE and Mr. AD/HD in the same city! We could finally get the definitive answer to the giant puzzle. I quickly called a bunch of interested onlookers to witness the great event. That Sunday we squeezed about 20 people into our little conference room, and posed The

Big Question to the two authorities (about 10 seconds after they had a chance to meet each other). We wrote our list on a whiteboard. They looked at each other, shrugged their shoulders, and both said, "I don't know. You have to look at each case individually." Swell!

Home remedies for AD/HD-like symptoms

Regardless of all the confusion, AD/HD-like symptoms can cause adjustment problems for many children and adults. When VSLs with these behaviors are placed in challenging, stimulating environments with true peers and loving adults, their symptoms lessen. During times they are engaged in activities that fascinate them, their symptoms often disappear entirely. One-on-one instruction, homeschooling, or computerized instruction may eliminate symptoms that show up in large groups. Annemarie Roeper (psychotherapist and wise woman) advises us to accept each child's individuality, and to adapt our teaching and parenting styles to fit this unique person.

But what can we do to help children whose symptoms are excessive, who engage in impulsive, risk-taking behavior that may be dangerous, or who become distracted no matter how hard they try to pay attention? First, it's important to obtain comprehensive diagnosis with a specialist on AD/HD. Diagnosis does not mean placing your child on medication. It gives you vital information so that you can begin to explore alternatives. Some of the alternatives are dietary interventions, such as those described earlier in this chapter; neurofeedback; Davis Dyslexia training; the Tomatis Ear technique; ear filters, as described in Chapter 3; nutritional supplements; increase in daily exercise; protein powders; and therapy. Read everything you can about AD/HD, and check it out on the Internet. Talk with other parents to see what has and hasn't worked for their children.

Neurofeedback is expensive, but many children have been able to get off medication completely when they tried this method. Individuals with AD/HD spend too much time in theta states, where they are spacey, and they have a difficult time sustaining beta states, where they are focused. With electrodes attached to his head, Zach plays a videogame that can be activated only by decreasing theta levels and increasing beta states, thus "re-setting" how the brain's neurons fire.

Several of our clients are experimenting with nutritional supplements. The most popular of these are: (a) Super Blue-Green Algae: Omega Sun (Cell Tech); (b) Omega 3 essential fatty acids; (c) pycnogenol and acidophilus (Kaire); (d) OPC grape extract, colloidal minerals, and multi-enzymes, along with cutting down considerably on sugar intake (New Vision); (e) Brain Food (Ocean Essentials);

(f) Hawaiian Spirulina (Light Force); (g) Phytobears, a vitamin in the shape of Gummi bears that also helps the immune system (Mannatech); and (g) St. John's Wort.

John Ratey recommends protein powders for adults with AD/HD to help stabilize glucose absorption (which stabilizes attention). We suggest that children have high-protein snacks every few hours. John also advises daily exercise involving a mental component, such as a Martial art. The Davis Dyslexia Correction Program is helpful for both dyslexia and AD/HD symptoms. The Tomatis technique, designed for people with auditory processing deficits, has also been used for some children with AD/HD symptoms. Cognitive-behavioral therapy, socialization groups, behavior modification, counseling, and family therapy are all successful with different children, and AD/HD coaching is popular for adults.

Be open to the possibility that medication may help. A trial dosage of stimulant medication may improve handwriting as well as controlling hyperactivity, distractibility, and impulsivity. John says it leaves the body as quickly as a cup of espresso. It needs to be carefully monitored to be certain it's the right dosage, that it's being administered at the right time, that there are no side effects (such as excessive weight loss, tics, increased anxiety, or difficulty sleeping), that there's not a prolonged rebound effect as the medication wears off, and that "vacations" are taken and other medications attempted.

> My husband and I have been trying to understand M now since he was in preschool. He is now 11 years old... I'm finding this website to be very interesting! M was diagnosed as being ADHD several years ago. Now after trying Ritalin and finding out that it wasn't what he needed, and reading many books, we're discovering that there may be many other things that contribute to his troubles. One being that he seems to be a visual-spatial learner.

Teaching techniques for overactive children

Working effectively with highly active children isn't easy, and with some children it's a matter of trial and error. Ask the child's parents what methods have been successful in the past. Has there been a beloved teacher or mentor who had a magic touch with the child? Seek guidance to increase your chances of success. Following are some general guidelines that may be helpful in your quest:

Teaching Techniques for Inattentive or Overactive Children

• Provide highly stimulating work, along with structure, firm rules, clear expectations, and specific adaptations for AD/HD.

• Give them opportunities for movement in the classroom. They can only sit for just so long. Honest. Let them sharpen a pencil, do an errand, go to a learning center, pace, or whatever, every 15 minutes.

• Some children are able to sit for longer periods of time on a large ball that you can obtain from a back store or an occupational therapist. Or try different kinds of cushions.

• Instead of reprimanding them each time they blurt out an answer, try complimenting them when they demonstrate some self-control. Remember that much of this behavior is not within their control.

• Provide incentives for homework completion or on-task behavior. Maybe they can earn a special privilege by working hard at adapting to the rules in the classroom.

• Try providing a more challenging activity or assignment and see if that helps. If it is too hard, they will give up in frustration, and if it is too easy or too repetitious, they will be unable to concentrate.

• One-on-one attention really helps. Can an aide or volunteer assist the child? This is particularly necessary at the beginning of an assignment, as these children often are uncertain how to get started. They need guidance with organization and elaboration of ideas.

• Remember that attention is variable, so expect inconsistency. An activity that is new and interesting one day may be unappealing the next day. They respond to variety, so be creative.

• They usually have trouble stopping an activity they are engaged in and moving on to something else, so develop a signal (e.g., a tap on the shoulder) or assign a buddy to help them with transitions.

• As most suffer from poor handwriting and racing thoughts, allow them to use a keyboard for written work. A typing tutorial program should be employed, such as Mavis Beacon, Mario Teaches Typing, etc.

• Shorten writing assignments or allow them to demonstrate mastery in some other way.

• Preferential seating is often necessary. Sit the child near you and give frequent eye contact to help maintain attention (as well as reduce disturbance of others).

- Call on them as often as possible during class discussions. Interaction really keeps them focused, and waiting their turn is difficult.

- Have a firm rule in your classroom that no teasing is allowed. These children are particularly vulnerable to ridicule by other students. A class discussion about individual differences helps set the tone for acceptance.

- When behavior becomes problematic, ask the child to brainstorm with you some ways to resolve the difficulties. This will increase self-awareness and improve self-control.

- Develop a good communication system between home and school, so that the child does not get too far behind in homework and the parents are informed on a regular basis about behavior at school. (Thank goodness for email!)

- Have a place in the room where the child can retreat when overstimulated or unable to maintain control. This should be a quiet corner with headphones, and perhaps some relaxing music, puzzles, books, etc. This is **not** a time-out center that the child associates with punishment. Instead, it is a self-chosen retreat when needed.

- A social skills group or "friendship group" can help the child learn skills such as taking turns, not standing too close, not dominating a discussion, finding out what others are interested in, etc. This experience can prevent social rejection.

- If you have a Student Assistance Team or Care Team at your school (an interdisciplinary group that meets to discuss children at risk), brainstorm other ways to accommodate the needs of this particular child and other highly active children in your school.

Do you have AD/HD?

John Ratey and Catherine Johnson's, *Shadow Syndromes,* is about the milder forms of all the mental disorders. I was certain I would find myself under the milder form of obsessive-compulsive disorder, but I'm not a compulsive hand washer. (I just empty trash every day.) But Chapter 5, "Prisoners of the Present," nailed me.

> The distractions inherent in full-time motherhood are extremely difficult for the woman who is even mildly ADD. Looked at from the perspective of ADD, children are full-time distraction machines; their needs are never predictable, and one of their main functions in life is to interrupt their parents.

People with no attentional problems can weather this aspect of parenthood; they can remember where they were before each interruption. But the ADD mother is going to find herself continually, ongoingly, chronically not remembering what she was doing, where she was going, what she was thinking. Worse still, the role of homemaker requires tremendous organizational skills. When you have an attention deficit—even when you do not have an attention deficit—a house quickly becomes one big barn of a place for things to be lost in. Toys, bills, remote controls: to the ADD brain, the amount of sheer stuff to keep track of is overwhelming....

And last, but far from least, the life of the full-time homemaker can play hell with a mildly ADD woman's environmental dependency. She is likely to feel a grating "pull to the stimulus" each time she sets foot in a messy room, and with children and pets (perhaps we should add husbands here, too) underfoot, rooms are always going to be messy. As one woman describes this phenomenon:

> I'll walk in the kitchen and I'll see dirty dishes and I'll think, "Oh, I have to do those dishes, but then on my way out to the garage to get some more dish detergent, I'll pass the laundry basket and think, "Oh, I have to do the laundry and I'll see a torn sock and I'll think, "Oh, I have to mend this sock"...and I feel so bad all the time that I'm not getting any of it done. (Ratey & Johnson, 1997, pp. 192-193)

Did this sound familiar? These passages really hit home for me. To make matters worse, several members of my family of origin, and their children and grandchildren, have been diagnosed with AD/HD, so if it's hereditary...

I remember once asking my daughter what was the most annoying thing I do. (Asking that question takes guts!) She immediately replied, "When you start a sentence and then get distracted in the middle of it and never finish what you were saying!" My kids make fun of the fact that the minute I enter the living room with the TV set on I'm instantly drawn into it—even if it's a commercial. (I don't go in the living room much.) I can't concentrate when I notice any little thing out of place. Another family joke is my straightening the Q-tips when I was late to catch a plane. Thanks to *Shadow Syndromes*, I finally recognize my own mild AD/HD, and I'm trying various interventions. So far, though, nothing has helped. Adderall just made me clench my teeth a lot. I'm living proof that you don't have to be a visual-spatial learner to have AD/HD. Or maybe I'm just a rabid Extraverted iNtuitive Feeler Perceiver (ENFP). Here's the "prayer" for ENFPs that I received by email:

"Please help me to keep my mind on one th – Look! A bird! –ing at a time."

Making AD/HD work for you

Having AD/HD isn't all bad. As John Ratey reminds us:

Hyperactivity does have its advantages: high energy, high enthusiasm, and the ability to hyperfocus, all of which can take a person to great heights in some realms. Emergency-room physicians, high-risk commodities traders, movie moguls: all of these "types" show symptoms of mild hyperactivity, and many may in fact have subtle forms of the disorder. When a job requires that workers spring from one high-intensity situation to another at lightning speed, a little bit of hyperactivity can be a good thing. And his or her penchant for risk-taking may lead to great success as an entrepreneur or a venture capitalist—or in any career that requires a love of high-risk undertakings. (Ratey & Johnson, 1997, p. 180)

When Michelle was 9 years old, she asked her mother if she could volunteer in a nearby nursing home. She loved meeting people and wanted to visit elderly people who never receive visitors. She called the Volunteer Coordinator, and, while her mother accompanied her to the interview, she answered all the Volunteer Coordinator's questions herself. Michelle found on her own a wonderful way to channel her excess energy. She plays cards, reads stories, plays games, and talks with the elderly every week, and they have all fallen in love with her. The same behaviors that were frowned upon in the classroom became a source of joy for the senior citizens. They love Michelle's vivacious energy, her willing hugs, her ready smile, and her endless creativity.

Dee Lovecky (1994b) found additional strengths in her sample of gifted children with AD/HD:

- ❖ spontaneity
- ❖ novel ideas
- ❖ creativity in thinking and writing
- ❖ keen ability to notice what others miss
- ❖ feeling joyful and spreading that joy to others
- ❖ talent in acting, supported by less concern with how they looked to others
- ❖ sweet temperament and trust of people
- ❖ a positive view of humanity, even while being rejected by their peers
- ❖ forgiveness—tending not to bear grudges
- ❖ when motivated, working quickly and producing work of significant quality

Visual-spatial learners with AD/HD symptoms can be highly productive and effective, as long as they are willing to monitor their impact on others in their work and private lives. Hyperfocusing, the manic tinge, the ability to see the world from a different perspective, instantaneous pattern recognition, and the obsessive quality that accompany the syndrome can lead to great discoveries, a powerful zeal for work, and extraordinary accomplishments.

Betty Maxwell has said countless times that any group of character-istics that is correlated with high levels of ability cannot be considered a defect. There must be some evolutionary purpose for these AD/HD symptoms. Perhaps they do not assist children in adjusting to the class-rooms of today or the world as we currently know it, but is it possible that they are needed for the world of the future?

Notes:

The Challenge of Parenting Visual-Spatial Learners

T is quite a character; she is funny and entertaining and we have a strong bond, but I will confess there are days I just tell her to PLEASE don't talk for 5 minutes and I daydream about putting her in an envelope and mailing her to someone else until she is 18.

He does have many of the sensitivity issues mentioned in some of the literature on this subject, and has been a challenge and a joy to parent. He is highly empathetic and persistent, and we have to plan for the smallest transitions in order for them to go smoothly.

Yes, it is a challenge to raise a child who marches to a different drummer. Especially if you care what the neighbors think. Visual-spatial children do everything in their own unique way. You can distract other toddlers from their goals, but these little people have their own agendas, as Annemarie Roeper reminds us, and they're not easily persuaded to give them up in favor of yours. While some visual-spatial children are compliant, the majority are not. They tend to be curious as kittens, iron-willed, and determined to make the world conform to the pictures in their minds—not the other way around. Rules were meant to be contested, or at least stretched. "Why?" may be heard a hundred times a day. "Because I said so," doesn't go very far in obtaining cooperation. They don't respect the authority of adults. They think adults are just overgrown playmates, and they expect you to drop everything and entertain them 16 hours a day. If they're night owls, some of those hours may be in the middle of the night.

Getting up in the morning may be among their least favorite things, ranking right up there with going to bed at a reasonable hour, brushing their teeth, rushing, eating everything on their plates, stopping a building project or a video right in the middle, sitting still, and being quiet. Later on, you can add doing homework, cleaning their rooms, doing their chores (or anything else they're told to do) and practicing piano. Paradoxically, these children are noisy and excitable, but easily overstimulated when in noisy situations or in the company of too many people; they refuse assistance—"I do it myself," but they quickly become frustrated if they're not immediately successful; they hate sameness, but they're often uncomfortable in new situations; and they have zero tolerance for boredom, backbiting, and bigotry (the 3 B's).

How do you raise these delightful, quirky, maddening munchkins? Hopefully, this chapter will give you a deeper understanding of why they are the way they are and offer hints on dealing with some typical issues in parenting all children. Let's start with their atypical sleep schedules.

To sleep or not to sleep—that is the question

> When other babies were getting 12 hours of sleep, I was lucky if he slept 6 hours. I figured he was smarter than other children his age because he had been awake twice as long. (quoted in Silverman & Kearney, 1989, p. 52)

Compared with other children, visual-spatial sleep patterns are "odd." I wonder if the biorhythms of VSLs are more irregular than those of auditory-sequential learners. Children are expected to get sleepy when it gets dark, wake up shortly after dawn, be hungry soon after they awake and be ready to start the day in the morning. Visual-spatial children, however, often have a very different timetable. They may be wide awake at night and difficult to get up in the morning. They may go days on end with very little sleep—especially when they're excited or in the middle of a creative project—and then crash for half a day.

Rhea Gaunt studied highly gifted children (many of whom are visual-spatial) and found that they needed less sleep than moderately gifted children (more of whom are auditory-sequential). And Dee Lovecky suggests that highly gifted children cannot get to sleep if they are either over- or understimulated. I know two families of highly gifted night owls who homeschool their children at night. That's when they and their children are most alert. But when you as parents keep a more regular schedule than your child, how do you survive? A single Mom told me she needs 8 hours of sleep a night, but her brilliant son seems to need only 3 or 4. She's been exhausted for seven years. David Feldman and Lynn Goldsmith describe a similar case:

> I remember Fiona relating how Adam as a two- and three-year-old would be up from eight in the morning until two or three at night, continually chattering away, making observations, and asking questions about this and that. Although Fiona could by no stretch of the imagination be classified as a low-energy individual, she began to find Adam's schedule oppressive and finally explained to him that she was finding it extremely difficult to keep up with his nineteen- and twenty-hour days. She reported that Adam, somewhat surprised and taken aback, asked why she hadn't told him earlier that his nocturnal habits were a burden. He promptly began going to bed by 10:00 P.M., and several days later he asked Fiona solicitously whether she was feeling a bit more rested! (Feldman & Goldsmith, 1991, pp. 100-101)

Creative inspiration often strikes at night. It's quieter then—internally as well as externally. The day belongs to the left hemisphere, and the night to the right. The right hemisphere is easier to access in the dark, when the left hemisphere stops working so hard. Leonard Shlain suggests that the cones of the retina, which need bright light, serve the left hemisphere, and the rods, which perceive best in dim surroundings, serve the right. The cones are central to focusing and concentrating, while the rods play a greater role when the mind is in a state of relaxation.

> Like the brain, the human eye also evolved opposite but complementary functions...

> Rods, named for their cylindrical shape, are extremely light sensitive. Like trip wires, they detect the slightest movement in the visual field. Distributed evenly throughout the periphery of each retina, they see in dim light and appreciate the totality of the visual field, seeing images as gestalts. Rods share with the right brain the ability to perceive reality *all-at-once*...

> Because rods supply the big picture, they are the key component of a visual, physical, and mental state known as contemplation. The rods enlist the entire individual to help them perform. Muscle tension diminishes. The brow becomes unfurrowed. The pupil dilates. The skeletal muscles of the eyes relax, unfocusing vision. These actions serve to let maximum light into the eye. In this right-hemispheric mode, the individual is better able to see the entire visual field rather than any one detail. Looking at nothing, the eye in this state sees everything. This receptivity affects the whole body. Consciousness idles and a person slides into the integrated mental state of being. (Shlain, 1998, pp. 24-25)

Several years ago, I had a conversation with children's author, Stephanie Tolan, about sleep patterns of highly gifted children. When Stephanie's son and his equally gifted buddy were little, they had no trouble getting to sleep and staying asleep—as long as they had had an intellectually demanding day at school. On days when they were not intellectually challenged, they seemed to have a very difficult time getting to sleep or they would wake up in the middle of the night, their minds filled with all kinds of questions. Their being able to sleep served as a litmus test of sufficient stimulation in school. Stephanie pondered if the minds of highly gifted children were wired so that they had to do a certain amount of mental work each day in order to rest. Interesting thought!

At a meeting of our POGO group, a support group for parents of children above 160 IQ, I brought up the question of sleep patterns. I asked the parents if they felt that their children needed less sleep than other children. Every parent there nodded yes. "Your children need less sleep than you do," I joked, "so you need to hire someone to sleep for you!" One of the parents challenged my joke, and asked all the parents how much sleep they needed and how much their POGO child needed. To my surprise, parents and children needed about the same amount of sleep. It just seemed like the children needed less sleep than their parents because they all hated bedtime (afraid they would miss something) and were allergic to mornings. The parents were exhausted all the time by the battles of getting their children to bed, and getting them up in the morning.

What's a parent to do with children who don't sleep? I recommend some limit-setting on child time and less access to adult time. One suggestion is to have a house rule that whether they're tired or not, your children must retire to their rooms at an appointed hour every night. They may read or draw or do whatever they please that's quiet and doesn't require assistance, but they may not leave their rooms. You can say something like, "In order for me to have energy to give you tomorrow, I need time to rest this evening. Otherwise, I'll be crabby tomorrow." Or "This is Daddy's and my alone time. You've had time with me all day long, now it's Daddy's turn." It's more effective to explain that the bedtime rule is for you, rather than because it's good for them. It's also healthy for children to understand that you have needs, too, and to learn to give something to you, rather than expecting that you'll always be available to meet their needs, but that they don't need to give anything in return.

Unusual sleep patterns appear to continue throughout the lifespan. The 9 to 5 job can be an impossible nightmare for the visual-spatial adult. Maybe that's another reason that VSLs developed technology. With the advent of computers, a different biorhythm no longer is a permanent handicap in the job market. Natural night owls can learn at night and even work the night shift in their adult lives in the world of cyberspace. I wonder if cyberspace will change the natural biorhythms of the world!

The creative spirit

Visual-spatial children do not suffer from "functional fixedness." That is, they do not believe that it's necessary for anything to serve the purpose for which it was designed. Some people may think a straw is something you drink with, pot lids are to cover pots so that they don't boil over, and shoeboxes are to be discarded when you get home from the shoe store. Not so for VSLs. A straw makes an excellent pea shooter, a tunnel for ants, a bubble maker in soup, and a periscope for the Lego™ submarine at the bottom of the bathtub. Pot lids are wonderful cymbals: they make symphonic crashing sounds when they collide. They're good for collecting run-off from a drainpipe (you never know what interesting insects you can find in rain water). And they make strong bases for Play-Doh sculptures and hand-made Christmas trees. And a shoebox, ah, now that's inspiration for endless creativity. Not only can you store an infinite number of things in a shoebox, you can also pull it apart to see how it's constructed; you can cut it in squares, strips, or even confetti; you can burn it; you can cut parts and attach them to other parts to see what that will create; you can make a diorama in it for school. Never throw out a shoebox.

From the time they're young children until they reach old age, VSLs look at every object as raw material from which to construct something else. I remember visiting one of my grad students, Kathy, who reminded me so much of my mother. The curtains in front of her tub were made out of sheets. The canopy of her daughter's bed was made from a lace tablecloth. Her oversized coffee table was a dining room table with the legs sawed down! In every room, one could see something being employed in a novel manner, other than its intended use. Just like home!

Our basement was always filled with stuff: boxes, plastic containers, packing materials, wood, things other people would have thrown out. My inventive mother could imagine a use for just about anything. Leftovers were just ingredients from which to create a new dish (which could never be duplicated, of course). And Mom could transform things in her mind in ways that completely baffled me. About a year after I got married, my husband's family had a Halloween party and we were all to come in costume. I mentioned this to my mother, so she went to her favorite place, Good Will, and bought ruby red drapes. I had no clue what she had in mind. Can you guess? All I could see were red drapes.

She put the drapes in the washing machine with her favorite medium of transformation—Clorox—and they came out bright orange. She handed us brushes and shoe polish, and had us paint the fabric with large black spots. A few snips and stitches later, and, voila, the red drapes magically became two Flintstone costumes. Who would've thought...

Luckily, many highly creative children were clever enough to select highly creative parents—people who would rather turn the house into Peter Pan's hideaway than into a showcase for *Better Homes and Gardens*. My friend, Janice, danced with her son in his endlessly creative world. The dining room would be converted temporarily into a tent, complete with scenery. They would make up songs, make costumes, be silly. He was free to decorate his room any way he wished, including painting the ceiling and walls. His artistic talent was fully encouraged at home. Both parents took great delight in their zany son, and he's now blossoming into a fine artist.

Chaos—a nice theory, but I wouldn't want to live there

The biggest problem has been that she is a huge slob. Anyone could tell what she has been doing by following the trail of stuff she was using. When I ask her to put things away...she starts to, but gets distracted on the way. I find her clothes, toys, sometimes even food in strange places. (I found a can of soup in her shirt drawer.)

Her room is typically a "pit" and she seems to be more relaxed in this environment because when we clean it up, she does not play well in this more organized environment.

I'm very disorganized. My room's a total disaster.

Visual-spatial children keep their bedrooms in a condition you can never show company. Their idea of "company clean" is shoving everything under the bed. They may feel that the only purpose of cleaning a room is to rearrange it. Creativity requires a bit of chaos. You have to tear down the known and familiar to turn it into something new. So does that mean you have to live in constant chaos? No. But there are many gradations between making sure that all the hangers in your son's closet are facing the same direction (an utterly hopeless battle— give it up) and being reported to the Board of Health.

You might have a rec room in your home where anything goes. It may look more like a wreck room half the time, but you can put a lock on it to keep company out when it's important to you that the rest of the house look nice. You also can convert part of the garage into space for creative projects. If you live with a whole family of VSLs and you aren't one, you may need to have a sacred space in your home where order rules. Even if it's only your bedroom. You need to have a sane place to retreat and regroup.

When you send them to clean their rooms, they can spend hours accomplishing nothing because they literally don't know where to start. It helps to teach your children how to clean their bedrooms when they're very young, doing it with them, and talking out loud about the process.

"Let's see, what should we pick up first?"

"Where do your dirty clothes go?"

"How about the books?"

"Can you find all the parts to this game?"

"Find all the blocks for me."

"Hey, it's looking better already. How about a hug?"

Later, you can sit on the bed, and walk them through the process verbally, keeping them company while they do the work themselves. Gradually, the steps to cleaning a room may become clear to them. When they forget, you can shout verbal cues from the kitchen. The same process can be applied to doing a report. Work with them at first, teaching them a set of steps to follow. Write the steps down so that they can refer to them in future reports. Be available to lend a helping hand when they get stuck or overwhelmed.

When we had a group care home for six teenage girls, chaos reigned. So I came up with some house rules that made it more tolerable for me. Common rooms, such as the living room, dining room, family room, kitchen, hallways and bathroom, had to be kept picked up. But the girls were allowed to keep their bedrooms in any condition they wished as long as (a) there were no dishes, silverware, cups or glasses in their rooms, as we didn't have enough to have some ferreted away; (b) there was no food that would attract creepy-crawlies; and (c) once a month they picked up everything from their floors and vacuumed. (Our vacuum cleaner had panic attacks at the prospect of going into those bedrooms.)

In order to enforce the rule of clean common rooms, we had a rotating position called, *"The Confiscator."* At 10:00 PM at night, The Confiscator would pick up everything left in the common rooms and hide them until our weekly family council. The bag of confiscated items would be brought out at the meeting, and it was necessary to pay a quarter to the pot for each item retrieved. The only items that could be retrieved before the family meeting were eyeglasses, textbooks, and shoes. But they still had to be paid for. The money in the pot was saved until there was enough to take everyone out for a treat, like ice cream sundaes. Each week a different Confiscator was chosen. The worst offender in our family was my husband, who paid dearly at each family meeting.

The family meeting

Family meetings kept us sane during our group care home era. We held them every Sunday night, and everyone was expected to be there. They began with a delicious family dinner. Afterwards, we would move into the living room for the formal part of the meeting.

A family meeting provides direct experience in democratic decision-making. Everyone is given an opportunity to air grievances, request changes in rules, learn negotiation skills, learn conflict resolution techniques, and practice effective communication skills on a routine basis. Family meetings can also be a vehicle for building self-esteem and family solidarity. We always included a time for compliments, as well as a time for complaints, and our meetings concluded with shared activities, such as reading aloud a book of high adventure. In a family meeting, everyone is treated like an equal and works together to resolve issues equitably.

I'll share with you the format we designed that worked for us, but it can be varied in whatever way would suit your family:

- ✄ Announcements
- ✄ Schedule
- ✄ Meal planning
- ✄ Shopping list
- ✄ Compliments
- ✄ Complaints

- ⚘ Conflict resolution
- ⚘ Redeeming confiscated items
- ⚘ Selecting a confiscator for the following week
- ⚘ Selecting an activity leader for the following week
- ⚘ A shared family activity

We had 11 people living in our home at this time, and only two cars. It was important to let everyone know every week what was happening in each of our lives, so that I didn't hear, "But Mom, I've got rehearsal for the school play tomorrow night," when we had already committed the car to be at soccer practice. Our family consisted of our 9-year-old son, Brian, our 10-year-old daughter, Miriam, 6 girls between 14 and 16, and Cindy, a 19-year-old college student, who assisted us in exchange for room and board. Life was never dull on the home front, and our washer and dryer were tested to the limit.

We developed a master plan for each week at the beginning of our family council. The children announced where they had to be when for the entire week, and we would place all the commitments on a schedule. Then we would decide who would prepare each evening meal and what she or he would serve. Everyone took a turn cooking, including Brian. At first, all he knew how to make was tomato soup and grilled cheese sandwiches, but when the girls got tired of grilled cheese, they bought him a Jr. cookbook and showed him how to make Swedish meatballs with ginger ale, and a few other more interesting meals. Those who cooked did not have to clean up. Meal planning was tackled after scheduling so that we would know who was available to cook on which nights. A shopping list was circulated so that the cooks could write down all the ingredients they would need to prepare their meals, to make sure we bought whatever was needed at the grocery store. (Can you imagine the quantity of food we had to buy and the grocery bills for 11 people each week??)

Next came the compliments. We felt it important to incorporate a time for positive feedback as well as negative feedback. Brian, the youngest member of our family, always started this part of the meeting, and most of the time he would compliment himself! "I played a really good game of football this week." (Brian would also write himself little reminder notes that went like this: "Dear Brian, Don't forget your lunch. Love Brian.") We didn't assign Brian the role of group leader. He just took it upon himself to do it, and he was actually quite good at it. When no one could think of any more compliments, we moved on to complaints, accompanied with groans of trepidation.

With six teenage girls sharing three bedrooms, some of the complaints were predictable. "She took my blouse without asking, and it was the one I was planning to wear today." Brian often forgot to do his chores. (We had a large chart of chores that was laminated so that we could write the person responsible for each chore with an erasable grease pencil.) Sometimes the complaints were more problematic. But, if at all possible, we would ask that rule infractions and hurt feelings be resolved at the weekly family meeting, instead of at the time they occurred. This took us as parents out of the role of disciplinarians, and all of us learned some conflict negotiation skills.

The person offering the complaint would be heard without interruption and the offender would be allowed to respond without interruption. The complainant would then have an opportunity for a rejoinder, and anyone else who had observed the situation could also voice an opinion or observation. But it was never allowed to deteriorate into a shouting match about who was right, and name-calling was forbidden. Often, when the facts, as both parties perceived them, had been fully described, Brian would intervene and ask how we would resolve the situation.

Most of the time, the offender would admit guilt, and offer an apology. (It always amazes me that children accept so much more responsibility for their behavior in a tribunal situation than when a parent—or teacher, for that matter—plays judge. Maybe they just perceive the latter as a game of "My Word Against His" and avoid being blamed at all costs.) The complainant usually would admit to some over-reacting and also apologize. If the disagreement was not resolved by the parties involved, the entire group discussed the matter until a consensus was reached. The guilty party was then asked to suggest a consequence, and the rest of the family determined if the consequence was appropriate. We found that offenders tended to dole out some pretty severe penalties to themselves, and the rest of the group often agreed to soften the punishment.

Hilton and I were not immune from this process. Occasionally, complaints of unfair rules or favoritism would be lodged against us, and we would try to be good role models about listening to viewpoints that disagreed with our own, accepting criticism, apologizing, and changing rules or behavior as agreed upon by the group.

When the yucky part of the meeting was over, the Confiscator of the week would bring out the bag of items collected, and everyone would have to pay a quarter for whatever was left in a common room at 10:00 PM. The Confiscator and the Activity Leader for the following week were determined, and then we would do a family activity, selected by the Activity Leader who had been chosen the previous week. Activities could include games, videos, telling stories, a group dynamics activity (such as Compliment Charts), or taking turns reading aloud.

Compliment Charts was a game I played at a party, and also used in the classroom. We taped a large sheet of butcher paper on everyone's back, and placed thick and thin colored marking pens on the table. We all took turns writing compliments on each other's backs, using different colored pens so that you wouldn't be able to detect who wrote the compliment. The girls really cherished their compliment charts, often hanging them in their rooms for months. By far, the favorite family activity in our home was reading aloud from an adventure story, such as *The Princess Bride*. We all still love being read to.

Even though we live in separate homes now, we all know we can call for a family meeting whenever there is a dispute or hard feelings or a big decision to be made. In recent years, I've asked my family of origin to hold family meetings once or twice a year. We began our first family meeting with statements of gratitude for all our elderly parents had done for us, reminiscing important moments in our lives. Then we all said what we would like from each member of the family. It was a very healing experience. I know one family that conducted family meetings and the children continued to hold them after their parents divorced. Children as young as 7 or 8 can participate well in this type of format, although I know one couple who held them with their preschooler. It's important not to use the family meeting as just a gripe session, or only when there's a problem, or no one will want to come. A regular time for sharing is a time for family renewal.

Everyone helps

All parents want cooperative children. And some children seem to be born that way. It may be the luck of the draw, rather than due to the particular temperament of the parent. Parents who were sweet, cooperative, helpful, parent-pleasing, high achieving students as children, may give birth to hellions. And then, again, hellions may create carbon copies of themselves (in which case, your mother's curse may be more responsible than luck: "You wait until you're a parent. I hope you get one just like you!") I've noticed that there is usually only one cooperative child per family. If your first one is cooperative, quit while you're ahead. I've also noticed that this role can shift. When the sweet one rebels, the rebel suddenly cooperates. But truth be known, most children are a combination of l'il angel and l'il devil at different times under different circumstances. We ask on our parent questionnaires, "Is your child easy to manage or difficult to manage at home?" Many parents respond, "both."

How do you persuade children to cooperate? It helps to explain why you need their cooperation the way you would with a friend. When you're having a problem with your child, wait until you're both calm, and then sit down and discuss it, listening to each other's point of view, with the object of resolving the issue in a way that works for both parties. The more children practice conflict resolution, the more they come to believe that problems can be solved, and the more capable they become at solving problems.

If you have the rule that everyone helps, and your visual-spatial children forget to do their chores, you can put up daily or weekly charts with symbols for their chores. Pictures are far better than words with VSLs. For example, you can copy the trashcan icon on the computer, which stands for emptying the trash; or a magazine picture of a made bed to remind them to make their beds; or a photo of the doggie bowl to jog their memory to feed the puppy; or a flower pot sticker to help them remember to water the plants. Or ask your child to draw a picture for the task to be done or find representative clip-art by surfing the net. They can check off each chore, or give themselves a star or a sticker. You can also reward each task with a hug and a smile. A really good week may earn a bonus in allowance, and a good couple of months may earn a raise.

Another method of handling misbehaviors or forgotten tasks with visual-spatial children is to set up a system of gestures or visual cues. An outstretched hand indicates, "Stop whatever you are doing instantly." A beckoning hand means "Come here now." As a teacher, I used to turn off the lights to get the students' attention. Unplugging the Nintendo is bound to have the same effect at home. One finger, then two fingers, could be the same warning as counting out loud, and they better get their act together before your third finger joins the other two.

If your children are in another room and can't see your hand signals and gestures, you'll have to resort to words, but remember that with VSLs, less is more. They easily tune out too many words. "*Freeze*" is better than "Stop hitting your brother." "*Shoes*" is better than "Put your shoes on." "*Walk*" is better than "Stop running right now or I'm going to get really mad." One mother invented words as reminders of what needed to be done, such as "*jambruwash*," which stood for "Put on your pajamas, brush your teeth, and wash your face." Children can participate in creating the hand signals, shortened sentences, and silly words, which makes the whole process of cooperation more fun.

Some amount of quarreling between siblings is normal, even healthy. But limits need to be set. Physical aggression is never OK. Name calling isn't allowed. Teasing and sarcasm can be quite hurtful and should not be condoned. "No put downs" can be a family rule as well as a school rule. (See the description in Chapter 13.) We had a rule in our home that if you put someone down, you had to pay a quarter to the pot. It quickly became apparent that one child in the family was continuously being scapegoated.

Parents should not always be placed in the role of arbiter. It takes more time and patience, but it's worth the effort if you ask your children to work out the conflict themselves, while you observe. Forcing children to say, "I'm sorry," when they aren't, isn't teaching them manners; it just teaches them to be dishonest. Better to ask them to make amends than to offer false apologies. "What can you do to make it up to your sister for breaking her doll?"

Michael Davis, our Staff Counselor, used a nonverbal technique with his four sons. When one of them would come to him crying, he would hold the boy and imitate his erratic breathing. Then, gradually, he would calm his own breathing pattern, and his son would follow suit. No words were exchanged, no explanation of what happened was given. When the boy felt calmer, he returned to his brothers. Nonverbal methods are very effective with VSLs. They respond to back rubs, shoulder massages, quiet walks, cuddling, wrestling, sometimes tickle wars, watching a video together, playing a computer game, relaxing music, and meditation.

Be on the look-out for signs that your child is tired or hungry. Short naps can change outlooks from stormy to sunny. A protein snack, such as peanut butter and crackers, a protein bar or drink, cut-up fresh string beans, string cheese, or other finger foods, can improve concentration, mood, and family dynamics.

Visual-spatial children respond to metaphor, which is processed in the right hemisphere. If you're creative, you can make up a story about a child who has a problem similar to your child's, and tell how she solved the problem. Or you can ask your child to finish the story, telling you how the central character solved the problem. You can act out the story with puppets. You can also find children's books that cover a variety of family issues and read them to your child. With older children, you both can read a book silently and then discuss it. Bring in your child's favorite fictional characters to help solve the problem (e.g., "What do you think Harry Potter would do?") A good children's librarian can help you find a children's book on just about any topic you can think of, and reference guides are available on the Internet to assist you in locating books on various subjects. You can also consult *The Bookfinder* by Dreyer (1993), an annotated guide to children's literature, organized by common issues children face.

One of my favorite books for young VSLs is *Tacky the Penguin*, by Helen Lester. Tacky is an off-beat, noisy, messy penguin who doesn't do anything like his companions "Goodly," "Lovely," "Angel," "Neatly," and "Perfect." "Tacky was an odd bird" who marched to his own unique rhythm: "1-2-3, 4-2, 3-6-0, 2 ½, 0." Terribly off-key, he would make up songs, such as, "How Many Toes Does a Fish Have?" In subsequent books, Tacky encounters reading, writing, arithmetic, directionality, sitting still, following directions, and being part of the team—all of which elude him. But in each book, the things that are so unique about Tacky end up saving the day, being prized, and make everyone love him. I like Tacky because he's his own person. There are many other books about creative characters who were scorned, but in the end turn out to be admired. Visual-spatial children need to be exposed to books like these as a reminder that they will not always be understood, but that they should still cherish their individuality.

Andrew Mahoney

Reading readiness for VSLs

Visual-spatial children master reading in a different manner from auditory-sequential children. Some VSLs have a difficult time learning to read, while others seem to magically absorb the entire process before they enter school. Perhaps the key here is *before they enter school.* Methods used for teaching reading in school may not work for

VSLs. Because relationship is so important to their learning, perhaps part of their reading instruction should be done in the safe atmosphere of home—maybe with the help of grandparents. Here are some suggestions that can set the stage for your child to become a better reader. These ideas will help all young children to fall in love with books.

Reading Readiness for VSLs

- Read to your children as often as possible. Read anything and everything, not just children's books. Continue reading aloud as a family even when your children are reading independently. (My husband and I read the Harry Potter series aloud to each other even now. Great fun!)

- Put your finger under the word you are reading, so that they see the connection between the written word and the word you are saying. Then, when they are ready, have them do the same.

- Encourage your child to memorize stories or books, especially those with repetitious phrases (e.g., *Green Eggs and Ham* and other Dr. Seuss books).

- Promote awareness of printed words. Point out words in the neighborhood, such as stop signs, road signs, street names, names of stores, names on boxes and cans in the grocery store. Read the names of favorite cereals at home, and point to words in television ads.

- Have a time for reading in your home, when the television is off, and everyone reads silently.

- Tell stories to your children. Have round robin stories, where you start the story and each of your children or their friends continue it at an interesting part and then pass it on to the next person. My mother used to ask us for three things: (1) something that grows in the ground; (2) something manmade; and (3) a person or animal. Then she would weave together a story about the three things we named. (She said that I should be sure to tell you the idea wasn't original, but she can't remember where it came from.)

- Create books with photographs of their favorite people and pets, with the name written under each picture.

- Cut pictures of objects out of magazines and write the names of the objects under the pictures. These can be made into posters for your child's room or into little picture books.

- ⚬ Have your child draw a picture, then dictate to you a caption, sentence, or story about the picture. Write his or her ideas in large letters by hand or on the computer. Decorate the house with these picture stories. Start with just a few words, as fewer words are easier to read.

- ⚬ Borrow books without words from the children's section of your local library (there are tons of them), and have your child tell the story from the pictures. Record your child's stories on the tape recorder, then transcribe them on the computer in large print.

- ⚬ Read children's books that have repeated passages, such as *Chicken Soup with Rice*, by Maurice Sendak, and have your child fill in the repeated word, then the repeated phrase.

- ⚬ Buy rhythmic, rhyming books with tapes, and have your child follow along in the book, while listening to the tape.

- ⚬ *Jumpstart Reading* and *Interactive Reading Journey* are good computer programs for early readers.

- ⚬ Borrow or buy extra large books with very large print. These were developed for classroom use with large groups, but they are fun for beginning readers as well.

- ⚬ There are tiny refrigerator magnets of words that can be made into silly sentences. Find or make large-sized words and take turns seeing who can make a sentence with the longest number of words.

- ⚬ Get books on tape and listen to them in the car.

The crucial factor in being your child's teacher is having fun. If you aren't having fun or your child's not having fun, stop. Make a game out of every learning activity, and don't be attached to the outcome. It's the process that counts, and the enjoyment of being together. Don't compromise that enjoyment by setting achievement goals.

Homework—the bane of our existence

Here's the bad news. We all hate it, but according to meta-analyses, homework works. It has a powerful impact on learning. However, it's the source of the greatest amount of parent/child friction. Most visual-spatial children really abhor homework. Their creative minds would much rather take flights of fancy, read an exciting book, play a computer game, build a Lego™ tower, stage a play, or contemplate their navels.

It probably has to do with the nature of most homework. When homework consists of drill and repetition, it generates the most resistance. Perhaps if homework involved giving children an opportunity to help ease the suffering of the world, VSLs would be more cooperative. And I imagine that creative homework, such as creating a diorama, a computer program, a video, a skit, or a construction would not generate quite as much conflict. But I'm not certain. It may be the very principle of homework that causes such family strife. Visual-spatial children are often annoyed that they have to give up six precious hours a day, five days a week, to do something the world sees as useful, when they could be learning what they want, when they want. To them, homework is just adding insult to injury—highway robbery.

The parent-child relationship is compromised when parents have to don the role of "Enforcer." In our busy world, the valuable time that parents and children have together should be focused on more loving pursuits, such as enjoying each other's company. So what's a parent to do with a homework-resistant child?

A good way to begin is with the family rule described earlier: "Everyone helps." Everyone has work to do. If you grew up on a farm, you know that every pair of hands is needed, no matter how young. When there is real work to be done, children actually enjoy contributing to the good of the whole. They like feeling needed and shouldering some responsibility. From the time they're toddlers, children should be asked to help, given chores in the home, and taught to assume some responsibilities. Little fingers can fold washcloths, put silverware in the dishwasher or the drawer, help set the table, wipe up spills on the floor, throw trash away, put things away on low shelves, etc. Preschoolers feel more grown-up when they have chores to do. By kindergarten, children can take on a specific set of chores and be given a set time to do those chores, with increasing responsibility as they gain maturity and eye-hand coordination.

You may be thinking, "What has all this got to do with homework?" If the first time your children encounter responsibilities is homework, they have no frame of reference in which to place this "extra" work. People who have never had to work before resent having to put forth that energy for someone else's agenda.

Consider giving children an allowance dependent upon their completion of some family responsibilities. A weekly allowance teaches them about delayed gratification. Young children can be given pennies until they gain an understanding of the comparative value of different coins. They learn that five pennies can be traded in for a nickel, ten of them for a dime, and 25 of them for a quarter. They can buy things with their own money instead of asking you for things they want at the grocery or toy store, and they can learn to save up the money each week for things they want that are more expensive. As they get older, they can open a bank account and learn how their money can earn interest. If you're raising a young entrepreneur, you can even invest in their money-making ventures, with the full expectation that you will receive your investment back (and maybe a bit of interest) before they claim any profits for themselves. And if you have a child who loves money (I've met a few of those), and who cannot bear to part with it, you might consider subsidizing a portfolio and teach him or her how to invest in the stock market (if it improves!). Who knows, this child may end up a financial tycoon.

Again, you must be wondering what this money thing has to do with homework. Well, some people work for the joy of working, but there are others who would much rather play, and only work because of the rewards of work. If children begin very young to understand the financial rewards of hard work, they're more likely to invest their time doing their chores and, eventually, their homework. Doing homework, like helping with housework, becomes an investment of time toward a greater goal. The goal may be getting accepted at a really good college, or winning a scholarship, or being able to pursue what you most love doing as a career. I am definitely *not* suggesting that you pay your children for doing their homework or for bringing home A's. I'm suggesting instead that you teach them a work ethic that begins with helping in the household and (hopefully) carries over into the responsibility of schoolwork.

Have a set time each day and a quiet place to do homework. It's a good idea to ask your children each day what homework has been assigned, and if they need your help with it. Some visual-spatial children have a difficult time understanding what is being asked of them. It isn't cheating to explain the assignment to your child, and be available to answer questions. But wait until you are asked before you give assistance. Some of these children need to dictate their answers to you, as the process of writing may be quite difficult. It's also a good idea to check the homework to make sure that it's correct. Immediate feedback from a parent enhances learning to a much greater extent than the delayed feedback received from a teacher. When a long-term project is assigned, it helps to break it down into parts and set up a time frame with your child for getting the segments completed. Give your child plenty of breaks—every 15 minutes—and lots of protein snacks and crunchy foods to keep him or her more alert.

You may have a child who claims never to have homework, and then, when the note comes home, or you get a call from school, or the midterm grades are received, you discover that homework has been assigned all along but not completed. If this sounds familiar, be pro-active next semester. Go to the teachers at the beginning of the semester, explain the problem, and ask for advice to prevent it from happening again. Ask them how much homework you should expect your child to receive from them each week. Are there penalties for turning in the work late? How much time do they expect your child to devote to homework for their classes? Are they available if your child needs extra help?

Some teachers will be willing to set up a regular communication schedule with you, perhaps by email, when your child has assignments due. Or maybe you can collectively come up with a creative way to keep track of assignments—such as a sticky note attached to the textbook. If your child is prone to forgetting to bring the books home, you might need two sets of textbooks, one for home and one for school. (In John Martin's class at the Rocky Mountain School, children never forget their homework, because they do all their work on their laptops both at school and at home.) Ask your child's teachers to inform you immediately after an assignment is missed, so that you can remedy the situation before it becomes too overwhelming for your child to deal with. You can avoid a downward spiral with a good communication system.

If the situation has already become chronic, new tactics might be needed, such as hiring a tutor, taking your child for an AD/HD evaluation (some spacey children get by in elementary school but hit the wall in middle or high school), experimenting with different incentives, or trying an alternative school placement. One thing you do *not* want to do is take away sports, hobbies, or activities they're really good at as a punishment for poor grades or not doing homework. This is counterproductive.

Linda Emerick studied students in various parts of the country who had been underachieving for a period of at least three years and then turned around the pattern and became achievers for at least a year. In all cases, the parents maintained a positive attitude toward their children even in the face of academic failure. They saw underachievement as a passing phase rather than as a permanent pattern, and remained calm, consistent, and objective. They supported their children's interests, recognizing that their children needed to feel successful in some arena. And they did not become the homework police: they placed responsibility for achievement on their children. Some students had to experience failure before they chose to turn around the pattern.

In my estimation, these parents should be nominated for sainthood! But the most remarkable finding in the study was that every one of these former underachievers believed a specific teacher had been the single most influential factor in reversing their underachievement pattern. Each teacher (a) sincerely liked the student as an individual;

(b) treated the student as a respected peer; (c) was enthusiastic and knowledgeable about the topic he or she was teaching; (d) directly involved students in the learning process; (e) engaged the students in independent projects in their areas of interest, so that they could bring their creative hobbies into the classroom; and (f) had high but realistic expectations for the student. Best of all, the teacher was able to show the underachiever how school was a means of turning a creative interest into a lifetime career. Magic!

Everyone gives

> He worries about everyone in the world: people dying, people getting hurt or sick he wants to make them all better. When he was 4 he got his preschool teacher to help him organize a "toy/ food supply" drive. He saw the devastating flood in Southern Ohio on the news. He was very upset that those poor children had "no toys" and he packed up most of his toys and then asked his friends to send toys etc. to the families in southern Ohio who had lost everything due to the flooding. He made the front page of the paper and they ended up with a whole semi trailer full of toys, diapers, food, etc., to donate to the victims of the flood.

As VSL children possess unusual levels of empathy, they want to be of service. Terrorist attacks have instilled determination in young people to do their part to bring about change. This section provides ideas about how children can help heal the world. It extends the philosophy *Everyone helps* beyond the family into the world at large.

Children learn from example that giving is a natural part of being a member of a community. At first, that community consists of individuals with whom the child has personal contact, but gradually it should come to include strangers who are in need anywhere on the globe. Visual-spatial learners who are blessed with the natural gift of empathy need to be able to act on their awareness of the suffering in the world; otherwise they become depressed. Opportunities for community service, both at home and at school, fulfill a deep longing to do their part to help ease the pain on the planet.

Some visual-spatial learners, like Temple Grandin, have great empathy for animals. Her ability to experience what a cow feels when it is confined for vaccinations, or in the slaughterhouse, enabled her to create more humane enclosures for animals that reduce their fear. Temple's inventions are now used in most livestock facilities throughout the world.

There are a few VSLs who have deeper emotional attachments to inanimate objects than to human beings. It's essential for these children to be taught about human needs and to be raised with the expectation that they will do whatever is within their power to reduce human suffering. The more advanced they are in mathematics, science and computer technology, the more they need a strong focus on liberal arts in their secondary and higher education, so that they develop a solid moral and ethical basis for their adult careers. Community service is important for all children, but it's critical for children who have difficulty forming human attachments.

Everyone helps and *Everyone gives* can become family mottos that appear on the refrigerator, guide family discussions, and underpin family values. Babies give their smiles and their love freely to their caretakers. Parents give up sleep, personal freedom, and luxuries, for their children. Children can learn very young to share their toys to make a brother, sister, or friend happy. Our niece, Robyn, goes through her children's toys with them every few months, suggesting that they give toys they no longer use to children who are less fortunate. "I notice that you haven't played with this in awhile. Would you like to give it to a child who has no toys to play with?"

Lisa Novak does something similar on a weekly basis:

Every week we look around at everything in the house. For every item, we ask, "Is it useful and do I use it, or do I love it and it gives me pleasure to see it here?" If the answer is not yes to one of the questions, we move the object on to a better place, to someone who can answer yes. Nearly every Saturday begins with a trip to recycling and charity and anywhere else something needs to go.

Talk to your children about the volunteer work you do, why you use your time in this way, and the good feeling it gives you inside. Take them with you when you adopt a road to keep clean, when you collect money for a charity, when you serve food in a homeless shelter, when you help a political candidate whose values are similar to your own, when you attend City Council meetings to protest and try to change an unjust policy. When you watch television programs, videos or movies that show exploitation or violence, use these as opportunities to discuss, "What can we do to change this?"

Children can make a difference. They need to be introduced to role models of other children who are working to make this a better world. Sara Jane is a visual-spatial learner who was born with unusual compassion for others. She was only 2½ when she saw a news report of an earthquake in Russia that left hundreds homeless. She brought her piggy bank to her mother, and with tears in her eyes begged, "Mama, send my money." The following Christmas, at the age of 3, Sara Jane announced to her parents, "I have everything I need. I wish you would give my presents to some little girl or boy who won't get any." When she was 6, she called a homeless shelter asking what they needed, and then wrote a letter to the children at her school asking them to contribute shampoo, peanut butter, general supplies and gifts for children at the shelter.

Greg Smith, who has appeared several times on the Oprah Show, is an inspirational peace activist who is helping the world see that children can make a difference.

> Greg began his PEACE efforts and mission to protect the rights of children at the age of five by speaking at public events. His first major speech was "Practice what you Preach." That same year he wrote a letter to Congress asking them to ban smoking in public places and any environment where children live, play and learn. He has volunteered at senior citizen centers, playing bingo and socializing with the residents. While living in Florida he would spend free time walking along the beach collecting trash to help clean up the environment. In the fall of 2000 he had legislation passed by unanimous consent in the US House and Senate to designate January 1, of every year as a Holiday of Hope, Peace and Generosity. The new national holiday will be called "OneDay."
> (J. Smith, personal communication, March 20, 2001)

Visiting Greg's website, **www.gregoryrsmith.com,** children can sign a pledge to boycott violent games and movies, and commit themselves to using nonviolent means of conflict resolution. At the time of this writing, Greg is 11 years old.

Jason Crowe began his peace crusade when he was 9. Devastated by the death of his grandmother, Jason turned to Jim Delisle, a warm-hearted leader in gifted education, who suggested that reaching out to help others is sometimes the best cure. So Jason published a news-paper, and donated the proceeds to the American Cancer Society.

> Four months after starting my "By-Kids-For-Kids" newspaper, another awesome friend, Laura Whaley from the Center for Gifted Studies at WKU, sent me an article to read about a cellist in Bosnia who witnessed the massacre of 22 of his friends and reacted by playing the cello for 22 days amidst sniper fire. To me, his musical harmony represented social harmony, and I immediately knew that I had to keep his message alive. Thus, at age 10, I became a peace activist.
>
> Besides organizing local events, I decided to commission a peace statue to be sent to Bosnia from the kids of the world. I wrote to President Clinton and received an encouraging reply, got endorsements from Joan Baez, Pete Seeger, Yo-Yo Ma, U2's Bono, and also received a thumbs-up from statesmen, businessmen, and educators. I found a sculptor and commissioned The Children's International Peace-and-Harmony Statue.
> (Crow, 2001, p. 3)

For more information about Jason's projects, please contact him at **jdc@sigecom.net.**

Introduce your children to Barbara Lewis's books (e.g., *The Kids' Guide to Social Action, The Kid's Guide to Service Projects,* and *What Do You Stand For?*) Barbara highlights projects initiated by children to help others, and provides wonderful ideas for community service projects for children of all ages. With role modeling and encouragement from parents, children can make a difference, and learn the lifelong value of giving.

The key is respect

Whenever I've been asked how we managed to raise so many teenagers, the answer that always comes to mind is one word: *respect.* In many homes, children hear, "Respect your elders." I believe that elders should be respected, but not because they're older. I think they should be respected because *everyone* deserves respect. Respecting only elders leaves the young with little respect, and that imbalance creates family strife.

The family is a microcosm of society. We learn how to be a member of society in the miniature society of our families. A family can be disempowering to its members or supportive and empowering. Either we learn how to compete and manipulate in order to gain advantage over others, or we learn how to cooperate, negotiate and resolve conflicts in ways that serve everyone. In a healthy family, the basic premise is that everyone is of equal worth. Therefore, everyone has a voice, everyone's opinion is listened to, everyone shares in the responsibilities, and every-one participates in decisions that affect the family. In this way, the family becomes a true community in which all members are encouraged to develop to their fullest.

If you were fortunate enough to be treated respectfully and kindly by your parents, it's easy for you to treat your children respectfully. But if you weren't as fortunate, your greatest challenge may be to move beyond the patterns you were raised with. It's worth the effort to become the kind of parent you would like to be. And you help create a better society in the bargain.

We convey respect to children in the ways in which we communicate to them, both verbally and nonverbally. Try this exercise:

> *Close your eyes and imagine that you are asking your mother-in-law (or favorite aunt) to get off the phone. Observe everything you can about yourself.*
>
> *Now imagine that you are asking your child to get off the phone.*

What differences do you notice in your choice of words, tone of voice, facial expression, body posture, amount of wait time, etc., in these two situations? Why does your mother-in-law warrant being treated differently from your child? Your visual-spatial child is extremely aware of your facial expression, your tone of voice, your body language, and all the nonverbal ways you express your annoyance. The words you use are of secondary importance.

There are some cultures where direct imperatives do not exist in the structure of the language; therefore, it's impossible to say, "Get off the phone!" *All* requests are prefaced with a gesture of politeness, such as "please," even to children. These cultures are peace-loving, creative, and cherish their young. We need to be aware that ordering children around is a leftover habit from an era in which domination was revered, and inequality in the family was a given. Thankfully, as we enter the 21st century, we are leaving these values behind. Here are some ways we can show respect to children:

- *Do we listen to children with the same degree of attention that we give to our friends?* Of course, you can't always respond when they want you. But you can say, "I can't give you my full attention right now because I'm making dinner, but I promise you that as soon as I'm finished, I'll sit down with you and we can talk."

- *Do we explain our reasoning to children?* Children are much more cooperative if they understand the reasons they are asked to do (or not do) certain things. You wouldn't demand that your friends or parents do something because you "said so."

- *Do we give children legitimate choices?* Young children can choose which books they want read to them, which foods they like, which outfits they want to wear, etc. Start by allowing them to choose between two acceptable alternatives. As they get older, you can expand their choices. Ask their opinions when selecting a school for them. You'll be amazed at how well they adjust.

- *Do we give children responsibilities?* Young children can help fold laundry or pick up toys and put them in the toy box. Responsibilities should increase with age. Give your children choices of responsibilities or let them choose when to do their chores, but in a community, *everyone helps.*

- *Do we give children opportunities for conflict resolution?* If you jump in and take responsibility for resolving each squabble among your children, they learn little about problem solving. Instead of interrogating to see who is at fault and who should be punished, teach them how to work through inevitable disagreements until everyone is satisfied. When a child cries, "That's not fair!" you can respond, "Fair to whom?" "Fair" doesn't mean getting what he or she wants. It means everybody wins.

- ❧ *Do we refrain from comparing our children to others?* Comparisons breed competitiveness and envy. In a healthy family, everyone takes pride in the accomplishments of each individual member. The uniqueness of each individual is respected and the unique contribution that each member of the family can make to the whole is recognized and valued.

- ❧ *Do we try not to interrupt children?* My friend, Alan Roedell, observed that when a child tries to talk to an adult who is talking with another adult, the child is usually scolded for interrupting. But when a child is in the middle of a conversation with an adult, another adult might interrupt, assuming that adult needs are more important. Alan used to stop anyone who interrupted when a child was talking with him, saying, "I'm talking with this person right now, and I'll be with you as soon as I'm finished." (A. Roedell, personal communication, April, 1990)

- ❧ *Do we teach through example that the ends never justify the means?* This is a universal ethical principle. There is never a "good" reason for humiliating or using physical punishment with a child. Dishonesty in the name of "protection" is also inappropriate. These methods teach children to abuse and lie, because children learn the means we use to achieve our ends. We need to choose respectful methods of attaining our goals.

Fortunately, most parents with whom I've worked over the years appear to reason with their children rather than resorting to punishment and other forms of external power. Children learn to respect all of life by being treated respectfully from birth. This means talking to your children in the same way you talk with adults, asking their opinions, listening to them, giving them a voice in family decision-making, and allowing them choices. Children tend to behave manipulatively or disrespectfully in situations in which they feel powerless or not respected. The antidote is to create an egalitarian family system with a balance of power, in which all members feel supported. The family meeting is one way to achieve this end. It's particularly helpful with teenagers.

Conflicts with adolescents are resolved by accepting them as peers and sharing power. In families in which teens are taken seriously as cherished friends, there is little adolescent rebellion (but not much motivation to move out either...). A healthy family provides a strong foundation for all of its members to go into the world and become their finest selves. It is only through being treated with respect that one truly learns to respect everyone on the planet, and even the planet itself.

Childhood is a small piece of the pie

Your children are angels who have been given into your care for the brief moment called childhood. While you're parenting babies in diapers, it feels like that moment is an eternity. But all too quickly, infants become children with wills of their own and sometimes it feels like a battle of your will versus theirs. You've been told that a good parent has control of his or her children, so that you can take them out in public without embarrassment. And you hope that they'll grow up to be responsible citizens who do the right things. In preparing them for responsible citizenship, you expect that they'll fulfill their ever-increasing responsibilities at school—following the rules, doing their homework, studying for exams, and getting good grades so that they can attend good colleges and lay the foundation for a secure future.

If you buy without question this picture of parenting, you're overlooking something of critical importance. Childhood is but a small portion of a person's life—and it's becoming smaller and smaller as the life span increases. The prescriptions for parenting that have come down to us from our parents and grandparents are based upon the economic survival needs of generations of parents who had much shorter life spans.

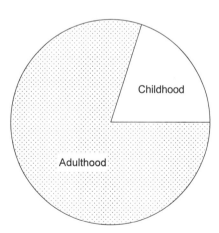

At the age of 61, I'm blessed to have both of my parents alive. At 94 and 90, my parents maintain their own apartment, two doors away from my sister's apartment. My sister has had a relationship with our parents for 68 years. Most of that time she has been an adult. And she has spent more years being responsible for their welfare than they spent being responsible for hers.

If you can look beyond the roles of parent and child, you can begin to appreciate that this presence you have brought into your life is a life-long companion, friend, and fellow traveler on this journey. Look deeply into your child's eyes and you will see a unique individual with special gifts to bring you. Even the challenges they present are gifts to assist your own growth. If you have more than one child, you know how unique each child really is. This journey you are on together will hope-fully last many decades, and, in the end, the roles will be reversed and they will parent you. (So the next time you holler at your child for bring-ing home a B instead of an A, remember that this is the same person who will decide whether or not you go into a nursing home...)

You need to develop a relationship with your child that is robust enough to survive throughout the lifespan and transform as developmental changes transform your roles. You can demand that children be responsible and respectful, but you cannot demand love and genuine caring. These will be given freely by children who have received your love and respect. They can care for you out of duty or because they love you.

When your children become adults, what kind of relationship do you want with them? How would you like your adult children to feel about you? Think about what you need to do now to create that kind of relationship with your growing children. Here are some of ideas:

Creating a Lasting Relationship

- ❖ Recognize their individuality.
- ❖ Accept them for who they are.
- ❖ Do not try to mold them into someone you want them to be.
- ❖ Listen to them. Really listen.
- ❖ Share with them who you are as a person.
- ❖ Be honest with them.
- ❖ Say "I'm sorry" to them when you are wrong, but do not force them to say "I'm sorry." Instead, teach them to make amends.
- ❖ Support their passions.
- ❖ Be their advocates.
- ❖ Enter their world and they will choose to join you in yours.
- ❖ Guide them, be a good role model for them, but do not try to control them.

- ❧ Honor their sexuality.
- ❧ Make time for them.
- ❧ Have fun with them.
- ❧ Respect them and they will respect you.
- ❧ Love them.

And, perhaps most important of all, learn to take care of yourself, love yourself, and do what it takes to make your own life enjoyable. If you're so busy trying to be the perfect parent that you don't take care of your own needs or the needs of your relationship with your partner, you become a poor role model for your children.

There is not a more challenging occupation nor a more fulfilling one than being a parent. Enjoy the journey. With a creatively gifted, visual-spatial learner, you're in for a wild ride!

Notes:

Teaching Techniques that Work

OK, now that you're getting a sense of which of your students fits the visual-spatial profile, what should you do next? Ask your students! Why not try teaching your students about these two learning styles? You can use the list of characteristics in Appendix C or the *Visual-Spatial Identifier* or both. Divide the class into three groups—those who identify with more of the visual-spatial characteristics, those who identify with more of the auditory-sequential characteristics, and those who are both. Have the groups brainstorm how they learn best, selecting a scribe to write down their ideas (an aide with a laptop? Ah, wouldn't that be lovely...), and then report back to the entire class what works for them. This way you can get an idea of what percentage of your class needs these adaptations, and you can find out directly from them what they need. *(If they come up with ideas that aren't in this book, let me know!)*

You can also use this book as a handy reference guide. Practical strategies are imbedded in most of the chapters, particularly in this one and Chapter 6. If you notice a behavior that was on the chart of characteristics in Chapter 6, go to that section, and try the recommendations there. If you see a child who seems to get embarrassed easily, re-read "Tips for Teaching Introverted Children" in Chapter 10. If you've got one who can't sit still, check out "Teaching Techniques for Overactive Children" in Chapter 11. Got a learning-disabled child in your class? Read "Keys to Success" in Chapter 9.

In this chapter, I cover how to teach the basics to visual-spatial learners: readin', 'ritin' (spellin' too), and 'rithmetic. The chapter begins with five sections that span the grades from preschool to college, and highlight key factors in teaching VSLs: relationship, classroom climate, visual aids for visual learners, dealing with time, and inductive teaching strategies. It concludes with a list of instructional strategies for VSLs. You'll also find two success stories sent to me by deeply caring teachers. They warm the heart, and provide some firsthand guidance on living with VSLs in the classroom.

Relationship with the teacher is everything

Visual-spatial learners thrive with teachers who appreciate them. They wilt with teachers who find them impossible to tolerate. Rarely do they elicit neutral responses. Yes, they are certainly a challenge in a traditional classroom. But they can be such a delight as well, with their offbeat ideas, endless creativity, unpredictable responses, great sense of humor, and dazzling array of excuses for not getting their work done. They certainly liven up a classroom.

It helps to have a good sense of humor ("You get extra credit for that excuse—I haven't heard that one before!") Besides keeping you sane, it's one of the main ways of reaching them. Humor engages the right hemisphere, so students with great right hemispheres are fun, funny, and respond positively to teachers who use humor in dealing with them. But be careful to avoid sarcastic humor, because they're very sensitive.

Here's a loving teacher who made a huge impact on a visual-spatial child's life:

"Have I got a visual-spatial story for you!"

This school year I had a highly gifted student...grade-skipped to my Magnet grade 4 classroom. When he came in he was bright eyed, happy, excited about learning. Then we took our first spelling test. I couldn't believe my eyes! His lettering was all over, his spelling terrible...

After a few weeks it was very apparent that there was a "problem with A." A was highly disorganized, inattentive, slow at copying material from the overhead, never handed in assignments and we were both becoming frustrated.... Kathi Kearney did identify him as a significant v-s learner. So now what? Busy me, I read much of the literature but with all the other learners poor A was pretty much on his own (much to my guilty conscience).

I began a "city" unit with my class (from the Interact Company). The students were to create a box city, with each "living" in their refrigerator box home/business. A started out a complete mess. Papers everywhere, never had a pencil of his own (and didn't care! HA!) After a few weeks he suddenly had an organized desk and was handing in assignments and writing more than two sentences! Cool!

Then came the Mother's Day essay. I should mention that A, up until this point, had made little progress in his writing abilities. He had terrible cursive and even worse spelling abilities. A was to write a short essay about "Why I love my mother..." He came to me that day and told me that (as usual) he'd not finished the assignment. I told him he needed to get it done right away, after all it was fairly short and that he could use the resource room if he needed a quiet place to write. (This was prompted because by this time I was so close to his mother through all the e-mails I was determined that she was getting that essay, come what may! She really deserved it!) About 15 minutes went by where I was observing A writing. He then came up to me with a beautifully written little essay all in cursive with only one minor spelling error. I was shocked! Dumbfounded! It was a real miracle!

The only thing that I could see that was done to help him was to allow him to use a "Franklin speller" throughout the year but for this assignment he never used it! ....Just writing for me, or a grade was never enough motivation to get quality work. He had to "buy into it." Whether this is a result of the v-s abilities, motivation, or upbringing I don't know.

I was so excited with this story that I wrote A's teacher and asked for more information about what she felt had worked with A. *(Please send me your success stories!)*

1. A learned to organize his space by first being confined. I noticed that prior to the refrigerator box experience, A kept his materials in complete disarray. He couldn't find a thing and really didn't care at all! Then all of the students were required to move their desk into their refrigerator box to "live." Once A was confined to a 3 ft. x 3 ft. space he started out with papers everywhere, pencils flew, and he received several tickets from the city health officer for safety violations. At that point A recognized that he needed to contain himself in a more acceptable fashion. After a couple weeks I noticed that A had developed his own system for organization, he had his papers in his desk (instead of all over the floor), and had his materials when he needed them.

   A needed some confinement to keep himself organized. I would not recommend the use of a study carrel to isolate him; that would be disastrous as he'd have been humiliated. But the teacher needs to just let him know that he has only so much space and needs to work within that space. Also setting clear expectations is really important.

2. Using the Franklin speller was a great help to him. He was able to type in the large words he longed to write and come up with correct spellings. (BTW, it was also a great way to make friends and influence people. All of the kids wanted to "play" with the Franklin speller!)

3. Constructivist teaching approaches worked best for him. *He was able to go from the whole to the parts. He was totally hands-on and discussion oriented. He needed to have a "big picture" to everything we did before he'd give his heart to it. It works better to give A the product or outcome first and then let him build backwards to explore and determine, based on his own knowledge, meaning.* [emphasis added]

   For example, the class was given the task to create a city... This actually resulted in some pretty comical moments between A and me as he could visualize what the box home would look like while the other kids were asking questions like, "Should the box have a door?" He would practically pull his hair out because he just couldn't believe the others couldn't see it as well as him. We'd just look at each other and laugh. (You'd love him; he's a beautiful boy and a real sweetheart.) Anyway, A had a much easier time than most of the class because he could clearly understand what the city should operate like and would just work backwards such as, "We need a police officer to give tickets to kids who speed down the hall. But we also need a city council to oversee the police officer to keep him honest."

The class learned hand massage and then the kids went to the nursing home and massaged a partner's hand over the course of the semester. A, at first, was kind of lost in this activity until I finally approached it "backwards," telling A what I hoped he would gain from this experience. Then he had a "vision" of what he needed to do and set right to it.

In writing it helped A immensely if I put a finished student example on the overhead and "dissected" it for positives and negatives. Then he knew what I wanted and had no problem completing activities successfully.

4. A did not want to have to "write out" problems in math. He saw no purpose in this. Writing out math problems was one of the questions that the Student Assistance Team tackled. At first the team couldn't fathom why he was so adamant about not wanting to show his work. We hypothesized many reasons, including insecurity.... The strategy the [math] teacher used was to first explain WHY she needed to see his work. I believe she gave him some extra credit for showing all his work and I know that using graph paper instead of lined paper (and also at times they turned the lined paper sideways) helped A line up his numbers visually so it was easier for him to write out the algorithms. I believe that he really didn't use the algorithms he was taught as much as he was able to figure answers intuitively.

The story above reveals as much about the kind of relationship A's teacher enjoys with A and his mother, as it does about the specific techniques she used to help A become a better student (although #3 is packed with great strategies, and the idea in the last paragraph about giving VSL students lined paper sideways to line up numbers is a dandy).

If you keep telling yourself that *they would* do the work, keep their desks clean, write more neatly, not make careless errors, etc., *if they could*, you can help them become better students. I've often seen astonishing, unexplainable improvement, such as A's teacher described: "He then came up to me with a beautifully written little essay all in cursive with only one minor spelling error. I was shocked! Dumbfounded! It was a real miracle!" The miracle was wrought by A's teacher's love of him and appreciation of his mother. A could feel how important it was to her and to his mother that he do a good job on his essay. His teacher's high expectations of him were also important. Her expectations were clear, she assisted him as much as she could (e.g., providing a Franklin speller and a quiet place for him to work), and she showed him her confidence that he could do it.

Sometimes VSLs with very weak sequential skills come to you downtrodden, filled with the pain of failure, and certain that they will fail again. They may not even try, for there is less humiliation in not trying than there is in trying and failing. You may have a hard time finding what lights their lights, when the light of their self-esteem is so dim. If they've been badly damaged, you will not experience them as fun or funny or creative. You will only see the wall of sullenness that they erect to protect themselves from feeling miserably inadequate. When you have such children in your classroom, teaching them is out of the question until you've developed rapport with them. They can't learn from you until they trust that you won't crush them. Girls may show these symptoms or they may become withdrawn and depressed. They are particularly vulnerable in middle school.

> Elementary school was OK, but since middle school...it's like hell for her and she is now suffering from mild to moderate depression. She has even lost her zest for art, which always was her passion! She's all but given up on school! The once bright light that shone from within as a child is now little more than a barely glowing ember!

> My daughter, L, 13 years old, appears to do very well visual-spatially. ...She doesn't like school anymore. ...She has illegible handwriting and not very good spelling in spite of the fact that she can draw well and reads a lot. Her reading level is many grades above her current age group. ...Right now she is at a critical point of accepting school life or totally rejecting it.

These are the students who need to be referred to the Student Assistance Team that A's teacher spoke of in her email. If you don't have such a team, see if you can create one at your school. Or enlist the help of the school counselor.

Help these children to feel safe in your class and you will watch them blossom. Give your heart to them, and you will be repaid tenfold. They need you to be their coach, their cheering team, their Greek chorus, their fan club. When you do this, you will make a lasting difference. They will treasure you for the rest of their lives.

Establishing a safe environment

Creativity flourishes in a safe environment, where children feel that they will not be laughed at or ridiculed for their ideas. To this end, I established one rule in my classroom: "No put downs." It was the only rule I had, but it was absolutely firm. There were severe consequences for breaking it, and no one tried it more than once. We discussed why the rule was in place, and what it meant. It applied to all of us—me included. They were not allowed to put me down (or a substitute teacher), nor was I allowed to put them down. We talked about the importance of creating a classroom atmosphere where everyone feels respected and safe, and how this is a responsibility that all of us must accept. If one person violates the agreement, it jeopardizes the emotional safety of everyone in the class.

"What happens in situations where kids make fun of each other?"

"Have you ever been in situations like that?"

"What did it feel like?"

"Why do you think kids do this?"

"Do you think it's fair?"

"Do you think school would be more fun if you knew that no one was going to tease you in this class?"

"Do you think this is a good rule to have?"

"What do you think should happen if someone breaks the rule?"

The classroom climate is particularly important for VSLs. They not only need to feel safe with the teacher, they also need to feel safe with all of the students in the class. They're more likely to share their wild and crazy ideas, participate in class discussions, and try to master difficult skills, when they're certain no one will be allowed to make fun of them. Emotional safety is as important for high school students as it is for elementary students. In the wake of Columbine, some schools have instituted "no teasing, no bullying" policies enforced by students and faculty alike.

A picture is worth a thousand words

My 9th grade vocabulary teacher (Nila Beard) in Aiken, SC, had us learn 500 words in 9 weeks by using index cards. On the front of the index card, we wrote the vocabulary word. On the back of the card, we drew any picture that reminded us of the word. Our artistic skills didn't count! To this day, more than 20 years later (!) I still remember almost all of those words. A couple of examples follow: for the word "superfluous," which means needless, I drew a needle as my illustration. For the word "enervate," which means to weaken, I drew a rock wall with water pounding on it.

M [age 5] was the only member of her OM team that could not read the script the kids had written. She had a big part in the presentation and the coach was concerned that, no matter how many times they rehearsed, M forgot her lines. I took the script, broke it down into four main parts and drew a picture symbolizing each part. I held up the pictures and read the lines to M one time. Then she tried with the pictures and did fine. I took the pictures away to see how she would do. She had visualized her lines and performed beautifully at the competition.

Presenting the whole system/picture is the best way to go; it lets us start making little models of the system and remember how everything is supposed to work from the start, not try to learn it piece by piece and only afterwards see how it fits in. Instead of working through things in speech, draw it out, make representations of abstract things on paper—anything to create an image.

The most important strategy in teaching visual-spatial learners is to remember that they learn **visually**. The more visuals you employ, the better Zach and Stephanie will learn. When I present to groups—children or adults—I always use an overhead projector. I like to use PowerPoint overheads because they're so colorful. I try to limit the amount of text on each transparency so that the listener doesn't feel overloaded with too much information. Someone once told me that if you just put words on a transparency, the visual learner still has to cope with words instead of images. So I try to put interesting clip art on my overheads to give the audience something to see besides words.

These are nice beginnings for an auditory-sequential learner, like me. But a visual-spatial teacher would do it differently. I realized that when I watched a VSL give a presentation. Diane Farris—an artist, photographer, children's book writer and illustrator, therapist, and expert on personality type—gave a presentation at a symposium we held in Boulder, Colorado on "Personality Type and Giftedness" in 1996. Her slides were all pictures, with no words. Each picture captured an idea she was presenting to the group. Would I ever be able to get to the point where I could present just a series of pictures and have each picture conjure up the words? I wonder...

Obviously, in the classroom, there's no time to create beautiful PowerPoint presentations or photographic slide shows of every concept. But there are some things you're already doing to reach the visual learners in your class, and, if the entire faculty sat down and brain-stormed what different teachers do to reach these students, you would be quite amazed at how many strategies are available within your own building. They just need to be shared.

Please take a few moments to write down what you do now that helps children who learn visually:

_____

_____

_____

_____

_____

_____

_____

_____

_____

_____

What are some additional methods you have seen in other classrooms or presentations that you could incorporate in your classroom?

_____

_____

_____

_____

_____

_____

_____

_____

_____

_____

_____

_____

Here are a few visual aids to plug into your lesson plans:

Classroom Aids for Visual-Spatial Learners

⚘ Overhead projectors	⚘ Computers
⚘ Videotapes	⚘ Movies
⚘ Slides	⚘ Diagrams
⚘ Charts	⚘ Drawings
⚘ Demonstrations	⚘ Visual cues
⚘ Photographs	⚘ Maps
⚘ Atlases	⚘ Globes
⚘ Colored pens on white boards	⚘ Picture books; Books without words
⚘ Cartoons	⚘ Color-coding
⚘ Flow charts	⚘ Colorful posters
⚘ Costumes	⚘ Construction
⚘ Games	⚘ Visualization
⚘ Experiments	⚘ Animals
⚘ Action-oriented activities involving the students physically	⚘ Having students put ideas on poster-size post-it notes all over the classroom
⚘ Dramatizations	⚘ Field trips
⚘ Artists-in-residence	⚘ Manipulatives
⚘ Mind mapping (webbing)	⚘ Three-dimensional forms
⚘ Map-making	⚘ Hand-held graphing calculators
⚘ Models	⚘ Student creations (e.g. dioramas)

While you're clearly the orchestrator of learning in your classroom, you don't always have to provide the visual aids yourself. Children can be asked to create or bring in some needed resources. Parents can also be called upon to share slides of a trip or design an experiment for the class. A district media center can loan equipment to the classroom. Local businesses or national technology firms can be contacted, particularly in low-income areas, to supply computers, color printers, cameras, slide projectors, and other equipment to increase technological proficiency of the students. (See Resources for VSLs in Appendix B for more ideas.)

Even without technology, it's possible to make instruction more visual. When you present a new idea, ask the students to take a moment or two to "picture" it in their minds. Then ask them to describe their images to the class, to a small group, or to a partner. Suggest that visual-spatial students diagram their ideas instead of writing them out in words. Teach them how to take visual notes. Jeanie Goertz recommends that students keep a sketchbook as an easy way to record the flow of ideas so that no idea is lost. She also recommends "visual brainstorming," using drawing as a tool to record ideas.

> Idea sketches can be a personal thinking tool in any subject. Idea sketching is used to clarify thinking rather than to communicate ideas to others. For example, when a learner is having difficulty understanding a concept, a quick sketch will help him clarify the concept. In a history lesson the learner could be asked to design a map of a specific time period in past, present, or future. A concept being introduced in an English lesson could be in the form of a tree diagram—a visual representation of an idea. The learner would need to consider what the concept would look like. During a science lesson the learner could draw the structure of a cell or the veins of a leaf the way he thinks the system or process would look. (Goertz, 1991, p. 12)

Figure 13.1

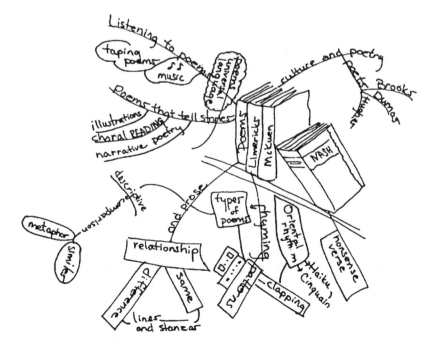

The question of time

In our busy worlds, in which there never seems to be enough time, it's hard to find extra time for students who can't keep up with the others. "If they would only concentrate and work harder, they could get the work done in a reasonable amount of time," we think about these "dawdlers." But many visual-spatial learners panic the minute they know they're being timed and literally can't think straight. They can't access their knowledge and they can't find the words. They need a less pressured learning environment.

If you have a student who shuts down during timed tests, seems to think slowly, is always the last one to complete an assignment written in class, or whose handwriting is slow and labored, refer the child for diagnostic assessment. A student with a processing speed deficit needs accommodations in the classroom such as the following:

- ⚬ No timed tests
- ⚬ More time for in-class assignments
- ⚬ Being allowed to do assignments on a keyboard
- ⚬ Being allowed to complete assignments at home

Record all modifications you make in the student's permanent record, so that he or she can use that documentation to apply for more time on the SAT or ACT. The small adaptation of simply allowing Zach more time for in-class assignments can dramatically change his life's path. Not only will it serve him during the year he's in your class; it may also assist him in gaining acceptance to a challenging college.

Inductive techniques

The higher-level general organizing abilities, understanding the gist of a passage, simultaneous perception, inductive reasoning, and the ability to match shapes and tones, may well later settle down in the right hemisphere because of the earlier settlements of infancy. (Ornstein, 1997, pp. 156-157)

In *Thinking in Pictures*, Temple Grandin says visual thinkers learn inductively. Deductive methods appear to work better for auditory-sequential learners and inductive methods for VSLs. Deduction involves giving the students the general principle and then having them practice various examples of that principle until the rule is learned. Induction involves giving students specific examples and having them figure out the rule through generalization. For example, you can teach the students the commutative principle deductively by explaining that a x b = b x a. Then you can give them several examples of the principle to practice until you're certain they understand it. To teach the same concept inductively, provide several examples and ask them to "Guess the rule!"

$$2 \times 7 = 7 \times 2$$
$$6 \times 4 = 4 \times 6$$
$$8 \times 5 = 5 \times 8$$

What's my rule?

They won't have the accepted name "commutative law," but they'll understand the principle and be able to express it in a formula (e.g., ♥x♣=♣x♥) . (Later, in the section, "Math is Fun," I describe a quick way to teach students their multiplication tables. The commutative principle comes to life when they fold the table diagonally and see that knowing this principle cuts the work in half.)

I learned "What's My Rule?" from Bob Davis, creator of Madison Project Math. Visual-spatial learners love these games, because they're wired to see patterns and relationships. Learning in any subject area can be taught through guessing games. Here's another variation.

Pick the word that doesn't belong and tell why:

sadly   **tightly**   **bully**   **quickly**

The students have to see what the commonality is—the underlying relationship that cements one group together and excludes others. If you ask a VSL to define an adverb, you'll get a blank look, because she cannot visualize this abstract concept. (Remember, "no image, no under-stand?") But she will remember concrete examples like the one above.

Pictures are even better than words or numbers, but it may be harder to find pictorial representations of the concepts you're teaching.

This method can be introduced to primary grade children, using Attribute Blocks. A red circle, a blue circle, a red square, and a red triangle can be placed together, and the children can be asked, *"Which one doesn't belong? Why?"*

Figure 13.2

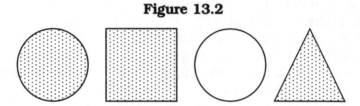

Third and fourth graders enjoy simple logic games, such as Queen Annes:

"Anne loves apples, but she hates pears"

"Anne loves yellow, but she hates blue."

"Anne loves boots, but she hates shoes."

"Anne loves_____, but she hates _____."

Queen Anne

Loves	Hates
Apples	Pears
Yellow	Blue
Boots	Shoes
_____	_____
_____	_____

When the student guesses the rule, he just adds another Queen Anne. In this way, the game can be played until nearly everyone in the class figures it out. (Hint: What do apples, yellow and boots have in common that pears, blue and shoes do not have?)

In Bob Davis' Madison Project Math, this same strategy is used to demonstrate complex mathematical relations, like the Tower of Hanoi puzzle. It has three spindles, with discs of graduated sizes on one of the spindles.

Figure 13.3

Most people just play with it, trying to move all the discs from one spindle to one of the other two, so that they are back in order from largest on the bottom to smallest on the top. (Rule: You can't put a larger one on a smaller one.) But it takes a sophisticated level of mathematical knowledge to answer the question, "What is a rule that would let you know the least number of moves it would take to move **any** number of discs from one spindle to another without ever putting a larger one on a smaller one?" (Hint: Create a "What's My Rule?" chart. Reduce the task to its simplest form and look for the pattern.)

Figure 13.4

What's My Rule?

Number of Discs ■	Least Number of Moves △
1	1
2	3
3	?
4	?
5	?

? ■ = △

Jerre Levy advises that any time you design educational methods to stimulate the understanding of underlying principles, invariants, or abstractions, you're pulling the two halves of the brain together.

Reading for VSLs

My middle son, J, appears to be a Visual-Spatial learner. He is now seven. My oldest son was an Auditory-Sequential learner and reading came very easy. If he looked at an alphabet book he knew his alphabet. It was apparent that this was not so for J. His high abilities were obvious in the math realm, but math concepts at that age are almost all presented using manipulatives. I decided to buy him an alligator alphabet puzzle, which had upper case letters on the pieces and lower case letters in the tray. They would only fit in one way. I helped him do the puzzle twice and that was all it took for him to memorize the alphabet.

You talk about a lightbulb on! I was three and sitting in the rocking chair (the old-fashioned wood kind) with my dad. It was evening, and he was reading to me from Heidi. I was following his big finger under the words with my littler one, and all of a sudden, in an instant, I knew that I understood that the sounds of his voice and the shapes on the page matched. I have never met anyone else that literally remembers the instant of comprehension, but I know that I do and I remember the image of his hand, my hand, and the words on the page.

I have a little guy in the first grade, who we have recently identified as a visual-spatial learner. He is very bright, but having great difficulty learning to read by traditional methods being taught at school. ...As J (now 7) was reading to me recently he came to the word "over." Rather than sound out the word, he stopped and said, "Oh—wait a minute. I know this one. It was in a book I was reading yesterday. It went, 'The monkey went over the bridge...yeah, that's it. Over.'" That gave us a big clue that he is memorizing words in context rather than decoding.

I'm a fast reader. I think I read "from top to bottom" instead of left to right. When I read, it sort of stops being print and becomes a movie. Even instructional stuff, like a software manual (it becomes a movie of what it would look like to me if I were doing it). With fiction, I often can't remember whether it was a book that I read or a movie that I saw.

At age 5, I was a little concerned at her lack of interest in reading and lack of phonetic ability. We practiced quite a bit, as suggested by her teacher. She wasn't remembering the names of several letters and didn't know all the sounds either. It would frustrate me because she would forget just seconds after I told her the sound. One day, I asked her to help me clean out the book cupboard. She pulled out a book—never seen before—opened it to the middle and just started reading away... My mouth dropped. She looked up at me wide-eyed and said, "I can read."

As these anecdotes reveal, visual-spatial learners learn to read in an entirely different manner from the way that reading is usually taught. It's somewhat mysterious—less amenable to direct instruction than with auditory-sequential learners. And the timing is unpredictable. We have noted two distinct patterns in the mastery of reading by VSLs: early readers who teach themselves to read (well, not really—they just "get it") before they enter school, and late readers, who struggle with the printed word far beyond the age when other children are reading fluently. Rarely do we find visual-spatial children who learn to read "on schedule" with their age peers.

The right time to read

When is the "right time" for a child to read? We've seen children who read before the age of 3. On the other hand, Rudolf Steiner, the founder of the Waldorf Schools, felt that children are given formal instruction in reading far too early. Waldorf Schools focus on physical integration, artistic expression, creativity, and community building, well before reading instruction.

In *Annemarie Roeper: Selected Writings and Speeches*, Annemarie shares her philosophy about when children should be taught to read:

> My experiences during the past 30 years have only served to confirm my belief that age and developmental phases are not interchangeable. A three-year-old may read and be eager to read. We would be remiss in not offering that child the opportunity to do so. A six-year-old, on the other hand, may be neither ready nor eager to read. In this case, we might harm that child by forcing him to learn. Both children end up with a lack of skills and interest or develop other emotional reactions if adults are not sensitive to their developmental rhythms. (Roeper, 1995, p. 46)

Why do we begin reading at six? Apparently, most auditory-sequential learners are developmentally ready to sound out words at the age of six. Children who are not ready to read until 9 often feel three years behind, grossly inadequate, and ashamed. Unfortunately, enormous pressure has been placed on primary grade teachers to make certain that all children learn to read fluently by third grade.

As every reading specialist knows, children learn to read in many different ways. It's important for children to feel successful and that reading is as natural as breathing. Annemarie feels that children are most likely to learn to read when they feel accepted and valued, and when they are taught to their learning style.

> Children do not learn to read until they are ready and when they feel accepted as whole persons. Therefore, reading is not a priority in itself. The development of the total person must remain the ultimate priority. ... Both the teaching and expectations must be geared to the individual and not tied to an arbitrary norm. (p. 47)

> What are some of the factors that help children to develop the skills and motivation for reading? [selected excerpts]

> ⚘ An atmosphere which creates a good self-image.

> ⚘ An atmosphere which provides safety and security so that the child's energies can be directed toward growth rather than toward emotional and physical self-preservation.

> ⚘ Adults who are able to provide this atmosphere.

> ⚘ Respect for a child's own learning style, plus teachers who are able to adapt to the particular child's learning style or who can recognize the fact that they are not able to adapt to it and will find another adult who is. (p. 49)

> Creating interests in different fields will motivate the child to want to read. This could be any area of interest ranging from baseball to science, from Superman to social studies—whatever may excite the child. (p. 50)

Some VSLs appear to struggle with decoding simple words and easy readers, and then, one day, without warning, reading just seems to click. The anecdote above about a five-year-old girl is illustrative: "She pulled out a book–never seen before–opened it to the middle and just started reading away... My mouth dropped. She looked up at me wide–eyed and said, 'I can read.'" Another little girl seemed unable to read beginning readers, and her parents were becoming concerned. Would she ever learn to read? One day they came home and found her reading *The New York Times*! We've found young gifted children who would not disclose that they could read. They want to own this part of their experience, and not have their reading (or any other performance) belong to their parents. Beware of "Show Grandma how well you can read, Darling." And many girls who are early readers hide this ability in school so that they'll fit in with their peers. They' ve developed "home reading" and "school reading." At school, they struggle sounding out words: "Th-iss iss a buh-oo-kuh." At home they read fluently, "This is a book."

Whole word reading instruction

Visual-spatial learners often have a difficult time mastering phonics. They tend to be sight readers. Here are Betty Maxwell's ideas for teaching whole word reading:

Whole Word Reading Instruction
Betty Maxwell

- Be sure that the child can retain a visual image. Some children with AD/HD perceive in a blink, but have poor short-term visual memory. Play memory games, such as "I Spy" with eyes closed. Encourage taking "memory snap shots" of favorite words.

- Build a **large** sight vocabulary. Label things. Use picture dictionaries. Have a Treasure Box of great words. Sylvia Ashton-Warner gave children their own pile of words—whatever they wanted to learn. "Treasure Boxes" with favorite words aid the sight word process. It is important to learn lots of sight words, which become stored in visual memory and are available for analytic phonics.

- Play games with Treasure Box words. Pull 2 or 3 random words and make a silly sentence. Pull 3 to 5 words and use in a story. Sort 12 words into categories. Any categories will do, like *words with double letters, 7-letter words (5-letter, 4-letter), action words, words that make pictures in your mind, words ending in "y," words with only one vowel, words with letters all the same size, words*

---

with letters that go below the line (g, j, p, q, y). Have the children make up their own categories.

✂ Pin words behind people and play, "Guess the Word." Others see the word and can answer yes or no questions.

✂ Small, bland words that are not easy to visualize (e.g., "the," "went," and "over") can be learned in fun, colorful phrases, such as, *"The monkey went over the bridge."*

Figure 13.5

✂ Make pictures for phrases, such as "over the bridge," "into the dragon's mouth," "behind his back," " the King of Slobs," "for ME!" etc., to help learn Dolch reading vocabulary.

✂ After you read a story aloud, play Word Hunt on a couple of pages. Ask the child to find an interesting word—never a bland word like "for," "of," "the," etc.

✂ Have all the children make their own books. They can cut out or draw pictures, then dictate captions. Staple the pages together into books. Have fun reading these books. (Now little words are learned in context.)

✂ After the children are reading a bit, use Treasure Words for analytic phonics. Have them sort words into: Same Beginning Sound pile, Same Ending Sound pile; Rhyming Words; Silent E words; etc. Can they make a silly sentence or tongue twister out of some of the words?

✂ Discover word patterns. These will often be rhymes. On the board, play games substituting beginning or ending sounds. Rather than teach short vowel sounds (which are hard for VSLs to learn), teach a rhyming word or the same word "family." Remember that these children are good at recognizing patterns, love seeing relationships, have a superb sense of rhythm, but are poor at memorization.

↲ Teach consonant blends through silly tongue twisters: *"Please play on the planet, Pluto." "Greedy Greta eats green grapes." "Spray the Spruce with sprinkles in the spring."* Read the Dr. Seuss alphabet book to the children, then have them make up tongue twisters of their own.

↲ Teach Greek and Latin roots, prefixes and affixes. See if they can find these parts of words in the additives on cereal boxes, in dictionaries, in books with Latin names of animals and insects, in medical books, at the zoo or botanical garden.

↲ Accompany reading with visualization techniques to assist children in learning to spell words they want to use in their creative writing. (See "A Visualization Approach to Spelling" after the section on reading.)

What to do with late readers

Last year a 9-year-old boy asked me if he was dyslexic. I told him I didn't know for sure, but that there are lots of children who have trouble learning to read at first, and then, when they least expect it, they suddenly discover that they can read. Sometimes it might take a little extra help, like tutoring or a reading program or vision exercises. I told him to be patient and to trust that the time will come when he, too, will be able to read.

When older students are having difficulty with reading, there are several different approaches that can be tried. We have been particularly pleased with the results of Ron Davis' program, outlined in *The Gift of Dyslexia.* (See Chapter 4.) One visual-spatial learner that we sent to Burlingame, California to work at Ron's center gained 4 grade levels in one week, and retained the gain. The program is well-suited to VSLs, because it places such a high premium on visualization—the visual-spatial learner's strong suit. My daughter, Miriam, a language teacher, notes that when VSLs read aloud, they skip over the simpler words. Ron says that these are the words for which there are no images. The child (or adult) makes each letter out of plasticene, and then the basic Dolch words used most often in reading. After sculpting the word, the person creates a clay image to go with the word. For example, "the" might be represented by an arrow.

Jodi Ringle, a special education teacher in Sherrard, Illinois, describes several of Ron Davis' techniques and her own adaptations that were effective with her students:

> Working with clay is educationally one of the soundest ideas I'd come across.... The students use clay (tactile, visual) to make letters and then progress to sight words.... They look up the definitions of the words, discuss the meaning and use the word in sentences, sometimes showing me with body movement what they mean or want their sculpture to show (auditory, verbal, kinesthetic) and make a sculpture out of clay to show the word's meaning (tactile, visual). They then make the word out of clay as well and include that in their picture (tactile, visual). By the time they are done creating a picture of the word's definition in clay, talking about its meaning, and making the word out of clay, they have triggered so many brain cells they have no problem reading the word when it comes up in print. ...I had the students make a drawing of their sculpture on paper and write the word next to it. I called it their picture dictionary, and from time to time had them look at the words and what they meant. (pp. 12-13)

> After working through the letters, we made punctuation marks out of clay, discussed how the various symbols are used and what they mean when they see them in print. Then we searched various types of publications to find all the different forms of punctuation. This helped the students who were forever reading through the punctuation marks....

> Picture at Punctuation is the best technique I have seen for improving comprehension skill.... When they come to a comma, period, exclamation mark, question mark, dash, colon, or semi-colon they stop reading and tell me what they are picturing in their minds about what is happening in the story....

> What makes this comprehension technique so good is it uses their strength of making mental pictures. I'm not drilling them with questions they might not be able to correctly process, I'm simply saying, "Tell me your picture." (pp. 13-14)

Multi-modal, multi-sensory approaches of all kinds are helpful for VSLs who are struggling with the reading process, e.g., Fast Phonics, Lindamood-Bell. Approaches that work with auditory timing are also effective, such as Fast ForWord and Ear-o-bics. Vision therapy helps many children to become better readers. Different children respond to different approaches, so don't expect one method to be effective with all children.

Betty Maxwell, who was a reading specialist earlier in her career, suggests trying the following techniques with VSLs in the classroom or in individual tutoring:

Reading Techniques for VSLs
Betty Maxwell

- Use a sight approach to reading rather than relying solely on phonics.

- Silent reading is preferable to oral reading. Ask comprehension questions and allow them to find answers through reading silently at least part of the time.

- Teach them to use their finger as a visual guide in reading. It keeps them from jumping from word to word around the page. (If this symptom is noted, visual tracking is suspect, which often responds to 6 months of vision therapy.)

- Use a frame that shows only one line of print at a time.

- VSLs respond well to poetry. Use rhyme and rhythm to enhance reading.

- Offer them books—even adult-level books—in their areas of interest. Gifted VSLs can often find answers to the questions that pique their curiosity in very advanced books, even if they can only decode a fraction of the words.

- Give them books with lots of pictures—even comic books.

- Don't require them to read every word on a page. Instead, encourage them to make a photographic imprint of each page. Ask them where on the page they can "see" a particular idea in their mind's eye.

- Try using enlarged print.

- Teach them word patterns, roots and affixes, and decoding as puzzle solving.

- Use books rich in visual imagery (e.g., *The Chronicles of Narnia*, *Harry Potter*, etc.) to enhance interest and ability in reading. (Be aware that some visual-spatial learners may need initial help in learning to visualize.)

The most important factor, as Annemarie cautions, is to keep the child's self-esteem a priority, while developing the skill of reading. Many visual-spatial learners take a longer time for the reading process to gel, but when it does, they become life-long readers. Assure them that they will get there in their own time. Meanwhile, they can get the information from other sources, such as being read to, discussions, videotapes, audiotapes, and textbooks available from Books for the Blind and Dyslexic. And, even if reading should remain elusive, they need to know that there are many ways for nonreaders to be successful in adult life in our post-literate, technological world.

A visualization approach to spelling

Your spelling technique has made all the difference for him.

I learned this technique from Lynn Hellerstein, OD, FCOVD, a behavioral optometrist, and it works with adults as well as with children. Try having the students visualize a word like "dog," and see how clearly they can see a particular dog in their mind's eye. With their eyes closed, have them describe their dogs to a partner, in as much detail as possible.

"What kind of dog do you see?"

"What color is it?"

"How big is it?"

"What is it doing?"

"Where is the dog?"

Try visualizing a car or a house and describing it to a partner. If a child says he can't picture anything, ask him to try to picture a color, then make the color brighter, darker, bigger, smaller, encased in a ball, in a square, etc. If that doesn't work, ask him if he can tell you how to get to his house. Ask him if he is picturing it as he tells you. Can he picture his bedroom? What is in his room? Most people can picture a little bit, even if they don't think in pictures, although they may have trouble holding onto those images.

After this warm-up activity, your students can learn how to picture words in their minds. Ask the students for a word they have trouble remembering how to spell. Some typical words are "because," "success," and "friend." Write the letters of the word 2 or 3 inches high in brightly colored ink. Ask which part of the word is the hardest to remember (e.g., the *au* in because, the double *c* in success, or the *ie* in friend). Color those letters in a different color with a thicker pen, right over the original color. If you're doing this activity with a group, write the word on a transparency. If you're doing this activity with an individual, write the word on a card or sheet of paper. Have the person hold her arm straight out in front of her. Place the word at arm's length, just above eye level, and have her concentrate on the word until she can see it clearly with her eyes closed. (She can put her arm down as soon as you place the card at the right distance.)

Have your students do something wild and crazy to their image of the word, something that will call their attention to the part of the word they have trouble remembering. But their image should contain all the letters. Sometimes they make the letters into little Pacman figures that are eating each other up. Some children see the word better if they break it into syllables. Some see the letters vertically or in different shapes. For "because," one child might picture a bee flying above the be and draw a frightened face in the a, running from the bee, and jumping into a large u-shaped vat. Another might have the ie in friend in a magnifying glass, much larger than the other letters. Or the first three letters might remind him of a fish fry, so he sees a fish, and the last three letters spell "end," so he draws the tail of the fish. Maybe success reminds her of a great victory in her life, so she pictures a giant banner with the word, **"SUCCESS,"** in big capital letters. It has two c's and two s's to extend the experience of success for as long as possible! (Sort of like remembering the difference between *desert* and *dessert*. Dessert has 2 s's because you want more of it.) Have them share their images with the rest of the class.

Your students can draw their representations of words. Artistic students enjoy creating pictures out of words, like making an elephant out of the letters in elephant. Have them share their drawings with the rest of the class, to give some ideas to children who have difficulty visualizing. They can write the word on paper, then trace it with their fingers. They can write the word in the air or on their arms with their finger. Once they have created a picture in their minds, have them place the word somewhere near them, so that when they go back to that place, their word will still be there. Most people place the word somewhere around eye level. Have them point to where they place their word. Later on, have them close their eyes and see if their word is still where they put it.

Now comes the real test. Ask a visual-spatial child to spell this word **backward**. Even your weakest speller will be able to pull off this feat if she has created a good picture in her mind. There is no order in a picture, so all she has to do is look at her picture and name the letters in reverse order. This is easier for VSLs to do than auditory-sequential learners, who are more likely to try to auditorize the word very quickly from beginning to end: "*becaus e, becau s, beca u....*" Everyone will be amazed at the VSL's ability to spell words backward—especially the visual-spatial learner!

After the child has spelled the word backward, have her spell it forward—again, just reading the letters in her picture. You can tell if the person has created a good picture by the rhythm. If she spells backward and forward with an even cadence between the letters, you know she is seeing the letters in her picture. If there is a break in the rhythm, the picture may be in two parts. But if the rhythm is very uneven, she may be auditorizing the word instead of looking at an image.

When the students have spelled their words backward, they can write them once. Young children can trace them in sand or sugar or dry jello. If the whole class participates in this exercise, it will be easier for children who need it to use this technique at home and at school. Teach children to spell prefixes, suffixes, and Latin and Greek roots as well.

The art of writing

Handwriting is difficult and slow for A, and his writing is often too big to fit in the blank spaces provided on the pre-printed worksheets and tests. This is not something he has much control over. We believe it is inappropriate to grade him on either the appearance or size of his hand-written work, as we are thankful he can write at all and do not want to discourage him. A cannot write cursive.

The physical act of writing may be extremely difficult for some VSLs, while their minds are bursting with ideas they want to express. The 14-year-old inventor, A, described above and in Chapters 7 and 9, obtained a 98th percentile score for his age in the Writing Sample subtest of the *Woodcock-Johnson-Revised Tests of Achievement (WJ-R)*, with a grade equivalent 16.9. He scored at the 65th percentile for college graduates! His use of language, his vocabulary, and his style of writing were superb. But he scored at the 9th percentile in handwriting—with a grade equivalent of 2.0; at the 8th percentile in the Dictation subtest—a grade equivalent of 4.6; and at the 14th percentile in the Spelling subtest—a grade equivalent of 4.7. I read a deeply moving story that A wrote about the holocaust from the perspective of a child watching his parents being killed. He dictated the story. If he had had to write it by hand, it never would have been written, or it would have been illegible, like his writing sample (see Figure 9.1 on page 165).

What to do with children like A? It is imperative that they be given the tools of expression that will allow them to demonstrate their ideas. In A's case, I recommended a Dragon Naturally Speaking voice-activated computer. (Information can be obtained on the web at **www.dragon.com**.) Dragon has been a lifesaver for many twice exceptional young people with whom I've worked. It takes time to train the computer to recognize the person's voice, and may need to be supplemented by a voice recognition system, such as the Omni Kurtzweiler. Voice-activated computers allow bright students with disabilities to obtain excellent grades in high school and college. Before this technology was developed, students with these problems often were forced to drop out of high school. Voice-activated computers are likely to be the wave of the future. That will be a blessing!

Why is written work so difficult?

Just as they learn to read in a different manner, VSLs learn to write differently as well: from idea to form. The writing process consists of several inter-related skills: forming ideas; putting the ideas into words; using interesting, diversified language to express the ideas; organizing the thoughts in such a way that they communicate to the reader; spelling; grammar; punctuation; capitalization; correct word usage; sentence structure; and handwriting. Only the first of these skills is easy for visual-spatial learners. They excel at producing ideas— wonderful ideas, novel ideas, fabulous stories, inventions, problem-solving. But the rest of the skills involved can be so overwhelming to them that they completely turn off to the writing process. And so their ideas may be bottled up inside of them, with no way to get them out. This is destructive to the Self.

Visual-spatial learners have a more difficult time putting their ideas into words than auditory-sequential learners who think in words. They may see the image clearly in their minds, but not be able to retrieve the words that go with the picture. It often takes them more time, and school, for them, is often a race against time. When the words fail them, they become anxious, and the anxiety further blocks the translation process from image to words. Timed situations skyrocket their anxiety.

For writing to be interesting, the writer has to be able to express similar ideas in many diverse ways. For auditory-sequential wordsmiths, this is not a problem. If they don't automatically come up with several different ways to express an idea, they push the thesaurus key (shift F7) or pull the thesaurus off the shelf. There are endless ways to say the same thing. This is actually a novel concept for the visual-spatial learner. I learned from Gerald Grow, a professor at Florida A & M University, that visual thinkers tend to use words as labels for pictures. Each picture bears one label. It would no more occur to a VSL to use a variety of ways to express a single idea than it would be to go around and change the names of all the pieces of art in an art gallery.

Organizing thoughts in ways that communicate clearly to the reader is another sequential task that is quite simple for auditory-sequential learners and an utterly mystifying art to VSLs. Pictures come to mind as a whole. They are not sequential. Outlining ideas before writing is totally sequential. Gerald Grow explains that to the visual thinker, all ideas are equally important, and all the details of their picture are inter-related, so it's difficult to decide in what order to express them. Unraveling a picture in some kind of orderly manner so that it can be reassembled and viewed by a reader seems completely undoable.

Then there's spelling, grammar, word usage, sentence structure, punctuation and capitalization—all the elements that make up the Dictation subtest of the *Woodcock-Johnson Achievement Battery*. None of these details have correlates in pictorial thought. It would be much easier for VSLs to learn Japanese or another pictographic linguistic system that does not depend on all these rules and sequences.

And last, but not least, we have the issue of handwriting—the personal nightmare of so many VSLs—even those who are able to draw quite detailed pictures. The fine motor sequences involved in writing may be so difficult to master that they never become automatic and useful as tools of learning and expression. (Whew! I hope you're as exhausted reading this as I am writing it. It's a wonder any VSL learns to write.)

Poor handwriting

His handwriting is unreadable.

I have really messy handwriting, too.

The following list contains the symptoms of what is known to special educators as *dysgraphia*, to occupational therapists as *sensory integration dysfunction*, to optometrists as *visual-motor impairment*, or to psychologists as *developmental coordination disorder*. In more teacher-friendly language, I call it a **writing disability.**

I use the generic "he" because this particular disability strikes many more males than females. If you see half or more of these symptoms in a student you are tearing your hair out over, send the student for comprehensive assessment and provide modifications in the classroom. No matter which label you use, you are looking at a real disability.

Table 13. 1

Diagnostic Checklist of Writing Disability

- ❧ Is his writing posture awkward? (like a scrunched up pretzel)
- ❧ Does he hold his pencil strangely?
- ❧ Can you see the tension run through his hand, arm, furrowed brow?
- ❧ Does it take him much longer to write than anyone else his age?
- ❧ Does he fatigue easily and want to quit? (Are you hearing a lot of groans?)
- ❧ Does he space his letters on the paper in an unusual way? (too close, too far apart, no spaces between words)
- ❧ Does he form his letters oddly? (e.g., starting letters at the top that others would start at the bottom and vice versa)
- ❧ Does he mix upper and lower case letters?
- ❧ Does he mix cursive and manuscript?
- ❧ Are his cursive letters disconnected?
- ❧ Does he prefer manuscript to cursive?
- ❧ Does his lettering lack fluidity? (looks sort of like chicken scratching)
- ❧ Does he still reverse letters after age 7?
- ❧ Is his handwriting illegible?
- ❧ Is his spelling terrible?
- ❧ Does he avoid writing words he can't spell?
- ❧ Does he leave off the endings of words?
- ❧ Does he confuse singulars and plurals?
- ❧ Does he mix up small words, like "the" and "they"?
- ❧ Does he leave out soft sounds, like the "d" in gardener?
- ❧ Is his grasp of phonics weak? (Is it difficult to decipher what he was trying to spell?)

Here are the solutions we usually recommend in our reports at the Center:

- Reduce writing assignments.
- Let the student use a computer for written assignments.
- If the student cannot master a keyboard, allow him or her to use a voice-activated computer, such as Dragon Naturally Speaking.
- Allow the student more time for in-class tests and assignments.
- Encourage the student to use a tape recorder for note-taking.
- Ask another student to act as recorder and take notes during lectures.
- Have the student dictate assignments to an aide or parent.
- Give the student oral tests.
- Enable the student to demonstrate mastery of material by other means besides written tests (e.g., making a videotape, diorama, mural, etc.)
- Grade on content separate from mechanics, with more emphasis on content.
- Try calligraphy! This sometimes works, particularly if the child is artistic.

Poor word retrieval

For visual-spatials, writing is a lot like painting a picture. They may paint with broad strokes at first, filling in the details as they refine their pictures. In a painting, there's no particular order. You can start in the middle and work toward either end, or you can start at the end and work toward the beginning. I know a VSL who is a superb writer (although she says she would much rather be a potter). She cannot show anyone her rough drafts because they are full of holes. These are real gaps in the flow of the writing where the picture hasn't formed yet. Being non-sequential in her thinking, she skips around the text, filling in the parts that are clear in her mind, and leaving large, gaping holes. Sometimes these holes are filled in her dreams, as her unconscious supplies the missing words or missing pieces of the picture. Writing become girder-like, a scaffold on which to flesh out ideas.

Creative ways to reach high school students

I have to share with you a brilliant technique developed by Fred Tierney, a high school teacher in Toronto, Ontario, working with underachievers who refused to do any writing. He was trying to engage them in the process of creative writing. He put all the boys at computer terminals with the monitors off and had them write their stories without being able to see a word of what they were writing. This forced them to keep their minds on their stories instead of on the mistakes they were making. When they had written out the entire story, then he would have them turn on the monitors and use spell check and grammar check to make their work more presentable. It was a wonderful face-saving device for these boys, because all writers would make mistakes if they couldn't see what they were writing! Fred's method also works because it divides the idea generation phase from the evaluation and proofreading phase of writing. These two aspects of the creative process are separated in brainstorming and in professional writing. Fred got boys who had steadfastly balked at writing to compose beautifully creative essays.

Let me tell you what Bernita Grove did at her school. Bernie was teaching honors English to seniors in a highly industrialized school district. When she read the first batch of papers that her students turned in, they were so abysmal that she couldn't get through them. She came into class the next day carrying a large canvas bag. She went to the front of the room, pulled a meditation pillow out of the bag, placed it on the floor and knelt down on it. A hush fell over the room. She extracted a kimono from the bag and ceremoniously wrapped it around herself. Then she drew out a large dagger in one hand and the sheaf of student papers in the other. She looked at the students, announced, "I've read your papers," and then pretended to commit harikari. (Of course, in today's schools, she wouldn't have been allowed to bring in the dagger.) She put no marks on the papers. The next set was appreciably better. For the remainder of the year, Bernie chose not to grade their papers. Instead, she wrote comments and had discussions with each student about his or her work. By the end of the term most had become fully competent writers.

Math is fun

For several years, I demonstrated creative mathematics with advanced learners in a summer creativity workshop. And when I was at DU, I developed a course for teachers called, "Elementary Mathematics for Gifted Learners." At least three-fourths of every class was mathephobic. My job was to transform them into matheholics. And I succeeded! (No one seems to be math-neutral.) Math is really fun. If you aren't having fun, you're doing it wrong. And if you aren't having fun teaching it, you can be sure your students aren't having fun learning it. I'm saying this to you as an auditory-sequential learner, and if I can have fun with math, so can you. Math is not about memorization or drill or speed. It's about patterns: seeing interesting relationships between numbers.

Making quick work of math facts

First, let's get rid of the dreaded multiplication facts. (VSLs hate memorizing their "times tables" and will do anything they can to avoid that task.) We can knock them off in less than two weeks. That should clear the deck and allow you to discover ways in which math can be more fun for you and your students. This is how you do it. Give your students this grid to complete.

Figure 13.6

X	0	1	2	3	4	5	6	7	8	9	10
0											
1											
2											
3											
4											
5											
6											
7											
8											
9											
10											

Here are the instructions:

"Count the number of math facts there are to learn. How many are there altogether? (pause) 121! Boy, that's a lot. That could take forever. (Groan convincingly!) Let's see how we can make this easier. I want you to complete the grid as fast as you can, filling in the easiest rows and columns first. If you have to stop and think about a fact, skip it. If you notice any patterns that are useful in completing the grid, fine. Raise your hand as soon as you've got all the easy ones filled in."

When most have raised their hands, have a discussion of the rows and columns that are the simplest. The first three are 0's, 1's and 10's. Then take a vote and see how many think 2's are easier than 5's and vice versa. VSLs often vote for 5's. The 5, 0, 5, 0 pattern is very visual. Recently, a boy told me that he taught himself to multiply by 5 by taking half the number and removing the decimal point (e.g., For 7 x 5, half of 7 is 3.5; remove the decimal point, and you have 35.) Amazingly, he invented this system at the age of 5½!

Ask if anyone knows a trick for 9's. There are several of them. Have the students teach the rest of the class the tricks they know or the patterns they've observed. One is that the two numbers always add up to nine. Another is that the first number is always one less than the number you're multiplying by. Put those two together, and you've got it made. For example, 4 x 9 = 30-something. What plus 3 equals 9? Just completing the grid, the students may notice some interesting patterns. In the 9 column, the tens go from 0 to 9, while the ones go from 9 to 0. Or they might have seen that the numbers are mirror images of each other: 09 on one end, 90 on the other; 18 and 81; 27 and 72; etc. Or they might multiply by 10 and subtract the number they're multiplying by: 7 x 10 = 70. 7 x 9 = 70 − 7 (63).

You can also teach them the finger method of multiplying by nines. Put both of your hands up in the air. The fingers on your left hand are 1, 2, 3, 4, 5 (1 being your pinky and 5 your thumb). The fingers on your right hand are 6, 7, 8, 9, 10 (6 is your thumb, and 10 is your pinky). If you're multiplying by 6, for example, you put down your right thumb. The fingers on the left of it (your entire left hand) become the ten's column, and the fingers on the right of it (what's left of your right hand) become the one's column. So 6 x 9 = 54. Have the class try it with all of the nines. They'll love it. Then have them fill in the 9's on the grid.

Figure 13.7

Finger Method of Multiplying by Nine

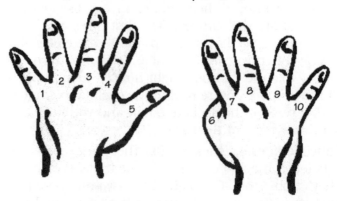

"Are there any other easy ones or tricks or patterns you noticed?" I find that most children can learn 6 x 6 = 36 instantly, because it is rhythmic and rhyming. One child taught me a trick for 7 x 8: **5, 6, 7, 8,** 56 = 7 x 8. Have them fill in 7 x 8 and 8 x 7. At a seminar on Vision and Learning, a teacher taught me a new one she learned from one of her students. "When you're **16**, you can drive a **4 x 4**!" If they know their doubles really well, they might have noticed that the 4's are just double the twos. Or one of them might have learned the little ditty for 3's from the Schoolhouse Rock video, "Multiplication Rock." ♪♪ 3, 6, 9—12, 15, 18—21, 24, 27—Thirteeeeee. ♪♪ If they can count by 3's, they can multiply by 3's. If they can count by 4's, they can multiply by 4's.

If no one points out that each of the facts except the doubles has a mirror image, this is a great time to teach them the commutative principle. If they know 4 x 6, they automatically know 6 x 4. Saves a lot of memorization. To get the point across, have them fold their grids on the diagonal from the multiplication sign to 10 x 10. "Hey, that cuts the work in half!" Now, have them count how many are left to learn. Even if they don't know their 3's and 4's, that only leaves 12 math facts. If they learn to count by 3's, that reduces the number to 7.

This is how to teach them the remaining facts. It works like a charm with VSLs. Trust me. Each night for 7 (or 12) nights ask them to draw a picture to represent one of the facts. The picture must contain something they like a whole lot. For example, if they like horses, and they're trying to learn 4 x 6, they draw 6 horses, and give each of their horses 4 cubes of sugar. They put that picture up on the wall of their bedroom, and it becomes their visual representation of 4 x 6 and 6 x 4. Maybe they love ice cream, and they're trying to learn 3 x 7. They can draw 7 ice cream cones, each with 3 scoops. When they have all of their images firmly in their minds, they take the pictures down.

The reason this system works is that (1) it's visual; (2) it makes use of their natural pattern-finding and abstract reasoning abilities; (3) it relies on imagery and visualization; (4) they have to construct the image, so it's more relevant and meaningful, particularly if it includes something they're emotionally attached to; (5) drawing is kinesthetic; (6) it requires no memorization or drill; and (7) it can be mastered quickly.

Math games

Now that you've got that out of the way, you can knock off long division even faster by using the method described in Chapter 6. Have your VSLs invent long division while you teach it the long way to the auditory-sequentials. So, if you're a third grade teacher, what are you going to do with the rest of the year? Make up games for them to learn everything else you were planning on covering, or, better yet, have them make up the games. I used to have my students bring in all the game pieces they had left from every broken game in the house and put them all in a big box. (This was in the era of board games. I don't know if kids still play board games!) Then I would have my students create new games from the pieces. I would tell them a concept that some of the other students were having difficulty learning, and they would make up a game to teach it.

- ❧ "What would be a fun way to learn about prime numbers?"
- ❧ "How can you adapt a game that's too hard?"
- ❧ "How many different things can you learn with attribute blocks?"
- ❧ "Here are some number patterns. After you solve them, make up some for the other students and we'll place them in the learning center."

Two 4th graders made up a game called "Silverstreak," which was a mathematical version of Stratego. Two sets of different colored folded cards containing math facts represented the two armies that march toward each other on a game board composed of lots of squares with a couple of lakes. The armies cannot see the math facts on each other's cards. If one card challenges its opponent's for the same space, the higher-ranking card wins, and the lower ranking card has to leave the game. For example, if 4 x 8 challenges 7 x 7, 7 x 7 wins the spot. The object of the game is to capture the opponent's report card, which reads, "You Get an A in Math." The report card is the only piece that cannot move. The purpose of the game was practice of math facts. I also had the students carefully write out the rules of the game and watch as their classmates tried playing the game from their rules (without intervening to show them how). If the directions were unclear, they had to rewrite them until the game could be played without them. Great practice in language arts, too. A teacher in my Elementary Math course duplicated the Silverstreak game with cubes, and her students really enjoyed it.

Figure 13.8

Mathematics should be as enjoyable as reading, and school should be a place where students develop a lifelong love affair with mathematics. Use manipulatives, discovery learning, physical movement, estimation, math games, math-art, teams, student-designed math projects, computer software, counting and measuring everything in the school, real-life investigations—whatever it takes to make it fun. (See Resources in Appendix B for all kinds of great ideas.) Boycott timed math tests and contests! Your visual-spatial learners will come alive in an enriched math program.

Instructional strategies for visual-spatial learners of all ages

I always had to adapt my learning style to the teacher. I think that a good teacher should adapt the teaching style to the student. The best teachers I have had were the teachers that gave a general "over-all" preview before going into the specifics. It's just a shame that that has only been 3 teachers out of my 17 years of school!!!

The following guidelines capitalize on visual-spatial strengths. They enhance learning and enjoyment for all your students, because a multi-modal approach (using the visual, auditory and kinesthetic modalities) increases the amount of information absorbed and retained by everyone. Try these strategies one at a time and see which ones work best for you and for your students. If one technique doesn't work, stop and try something else. *Please let me know if you come up with some ideas of your own that aren't in this list.*

- ☙ **Show them, don't just tell them.** These students remember what they see and forget what they hear, so present ideas visually. Use overheads. Draw pictures. Use videos, posters, charts, graphs, and diagrams liberally.

  As to teaching strategies, I think demonstrations and then going back and looking at supporting concepts and details work for me.

  I've always had a terrible time following verbal instructions from teachers.

- ☙ **Use visualization techniques.** Ask them to picture what you are saying. Have them record their images using webbing, mind-mapping, or pictorial notes. Teach the students to visualize spelling words, math problems, "What would happen if…" scenarios in reading, science, and social studies. Employ movie, television, and computer techniques to assist them in visualizing: *zoom-in, split screen, slow motion, superimposition, fast forward, instant replay, etc.*

  In order to do or understand something I have to be able to visualize it.

  She is good at making mental pictures of how things work…like science concepts. She also can recall facts by remembering where she was and what the setting looked like the day they were presented.

- ☙ **Give them the big picture.** Visual-spatial learners learn best if they understand the goals of instruction. Tell them where the lesson is leading, so that they have an idea of the whole, before they try learning the parts.

  I definitely like to see the "big picture." I like to have visual representations of how things relate to each other.

  I've…always had to be able to see "the big picture" before I was able to understand anything about a certain subject.

⋇ **Teach to their strengths.** Help them use their imagination, creativity, as well as their ablities to visualize, recognize patterns,see from different perspectives, build, draw, dance, sing, act, etc., to compensate for their weaknesses.

Follow his lead! He needs teachers capable of understanding the depth of his answers.... Teach to his strengths.

Perhaps I can still succeed if I can identify my learning problems, and capitalize on my strengths.

⋇ **Emphasize creative imagination.** Make use of fantasy. Creativity should be encouraged in all subject areas.

S is very creative... He likes to observe and then take off on his own, usually in a creatively different manner than the one he observed.

He'll draw pictures and write stories all day if I let him.

⋇ **Use discovery techniques.** Play "What's My Rule?" in different subject areas. VSLs are good at discovering rules and principles. Have them discover their own methods of problem solving instead of teaching step by step. Employ inductive reasoning and inquiry training.

Show patterns and relationships.

⋇ **Avoid drill, repetition and rote memorization**. Use more conceptual approaches. Give them fewer, more difficult problems. For example, let them demonstrate mastery by answering the hardest questions in the unit, skipping the practice sets.

In school I noted that I did not excel a bit through repetition, which the others needed. Example: I was forced to learn Latin vocabulary for hours, yet it didn't help a bit.

Unlike other children, A needs no practice, drilling, or reinforcement of a concept. Given the definition and applicability of prime numbers, he needed no further practice (nor was he interested in any) to determine that the number eleven was prime.

⋇ **Avoid timed tests!** Give power tests, which will better reveal mastery. Students with severe processing lags can apply to take their college board examinations untimed if the disability is documented through IQ and achievement testing within three years of the exams, and if teachers have provided extended time for tests.

I hate to do anything where I feel pressured by time, especially timed tests.

When he was in third grade I was pulled in to discuss why he does not know his multiplication math facts. ...Later I learned all multiplication tests were timed. A downward spiral has since taken place.

⚬ **Do not require them to show their work.** Trust that they got the correct answer in their own way. Respect visual, intuitive methods of knowing.

He can't "show his work" or explain his intuitive leaps, and so his grades get lowered.

I took the college math test for upgrading. I answered almost all the questions correctly. I should have been able to proceed to the course I wanted, except for the fact that I didn't write the process for the questions, to show how I got the answers. ...I didn't know how I just knew the answer.

⚬ **Allow time for thought, images, and word retrieval.** Support well thought-out answers above fast ones. "Take a few moments to think about the question before you raise your hand. Write down your ideas if you are afraid you'll forget them."

⚬ **Allow them to construct, draw or otherwise visually represent what they have learned as a substitute for some written assignments.**

Anything that is made into an art project helps. Science experiments work well with her.

⚬ **Give more weight to content of papers than to format.** Allow them to use computer software, such as spell check and grammar check, to help them with the mechanics. These technological supports provide instant feedback, which is important for VSLs to learn skills. Don't penalize students in other subject areas when they haven't mastered these skills.

⚬ **Teach the mechanics of language** (spelling, punctuation, grammar, capitalization, word usage, and sentence structure) **as a separate subject.** Use punctuation manipulatives. Construct large punctuation marks on different colored sticky notes and have the students insert them in large-sized unpunctuated sentences.

❧ **Incorporate more technology into instruction.** Use the computer to introduce concepts. Have the students use computer programs in learning skills. Involve them in Internet research projects. Let some of the students teach others in the class how to program.

❧ **If their handwriting is poor, let them use a keyboard.** Teach keyboarding as soon as possible. If they cannot master a keyboard, allow them to use a voice-activated computer.

M cannot spell. His handwriting is almost unreadable.

Dreadful handwriting seems to be another common problem.

❧ **Make the learning significant to them.** Meaningful, relevant material will be remembered, while insignificant information will be quickly forgotten. How does this learning relate to their experience? In what way can they apply it to solving a problem they care about?

I've found that the things I remember best are things that aren't contrived and artificial, but natural things that I have experienced, seen, or witnessed. So, the closer one makes something to things like this, the more natural the learning will be.

❧ **Teach to their interests.** Find out what turns them on. What are their hobbies? What do they do after school? What do they want to be when they grow up? Have them do independent studies in areas of interest.

The way I taught him to read at three was to show him that symbols on a page had meaning. He likes cars, so I taught him to recognize all the common car logo symbols, Chevy, etc. Once he was clear on the concept that what one saw written could mean something, then I taught him the alphabet. This worked very well. I've also used it to teach reading to some of his little buddies who were having reading difficulties.

Plenty of room for exploration and self study on his favorite subjects.

❧ **Use hands-on experiences.** Employ construction, movement, action, and manipulatives, such as Cuisinaire rods, Tangrams, dice, card games, etc.

When she had to memorize the bones of the body, we bought a Halloween skeleton for her to practice on. When it was clouds...she replicated the types with cotton balls. Simple machines...made analogies to body parts...(teeth...wedges, etc...) For math, she always diagrams the problem.

Manipulatives...tangrams...computer games...all have helped.

- **Use color-coding as an aide to memorization.** Mnemonics also help (e.g., "Please Excuse My Dear Aunt Sally"—PEMDAS—for the order of operations: parentheses, exponents, multiply, divide, add, subtract).

  I colored things to help remember them in school. I could more easily recall the "stuff in red was all about George Washington," and then I could see that red paragraph in my mind, and read it to get the answers.

  I made visual codes with dots and lines that corresponded to memorized information, like an alphabet of my own. It made studying meaningless stuff more "meaningful" because I was memorizing a new code. I also found that I could remember a lot more of a lecture in class if I doodled during the lecture rather than take notes. And sometimes I would tape record the professor in college and play the tape in head-phones as I slept. That was a very effective "memorization" tool.

- **Teach organizational skills.** Pocket dividers in one large folder or notebook can be used for them to keep track of homework in each subject area. Provide a weekly written schedule of homework. Help them to visualize their schedule.

- **Teach them about their learning style.** Help them understand their strengths as well as giving them hints about improving their weaknesses.

- **Put it to music.** Let them sing it, dance it, chant it. Rhythm will be remembered.

  Singing my studies helped me remember mundane facts. I could remember things for a history test because of the tune of the sentence I memorized rather than the actual words.

- **Make it challenging.** Challenge integrates the two hemispheres.

- **Use humor whenever possible.** Humor and playfulness actually increase learning, getting the right hemisphere into the act. Use them liberally, but avoid sarcasm and teasing.

  Everything must be presented visually. Humor helps, as does tactile learning.

- **Get their attention.** Talk louder, talk faster, be more animated, use gestures, do something silly.

- **Group them together for instruction.** VSLs learn best with other VSLs.

- **Engage them in group projects.** Group or individual projects involve problem finding and problem clarification, as well as problem solving.

- **Make them winners.** Let them compete against themselves, not others (e.g., read one more book than last week; beat your record on times tables).

- **Let them observe others before attempting new tasks.** Show examples of the finished product requested.

  He was a Look/Do child.

- **Teach them to look up to retrieve material in their visual memory.** People naturally look up when they are thinking. Children who are embarrassed by mistakes or word retrieval difficulties often look down to avoid eye contact. Teach them to look up where the information is likely to be stored.

- **Allow them to display what they know in their own way.** For example, with flash cards, spread the cards out and allow them to pick out what they know, instead of drilling them on the cards one at a time to see if they are right or wrong.

- **If they struggle with easy, sequential tasks, give them more advanced, complex work.** These upside-down learners surprise us: hard is easy and easy is hard. Acceleration is more beneficial than remediation.

- **Show them you care about them.** Emotion works wonders. Use emotionally charged material. These learners are keenly aware of their teachers' reactions to them. Success is related to perceptions of teachers' empathy. Be emotionally supportive.

- **Assure them that they will get smarter as they get older.** Teach them about late bloomers. Be their cheering team. Believe in them and they will blossom.

  I was a very late bloomer (and not very popular in school).

⚬ **Expose them to role models of successful visual-spatial adults.**
Many of the most celebrated physicists, artists and statesmen
were visual-spatial learners. Biographical sketches of famous VSLs
can be found in *The Spatial Child* (Dixon, 1983), *In the Mind's Eye*
(West, 1991), and the spatial intelligence chapter in *Frames of
Mind* (Gardner, 1983).

Post script: A teacher who made a difference

Dana first came to my attention when he was in the second grade in a
small school in Vermont in which I held a position as enrichment coordinator. [He] demonstrated unusual curiosity and understanding.

By the time Dana reached the third grade, it was apparent that he had
severe learning difficulties in reading and writing and he had been diagnosed as dyslexic. A small, very active boy, he was in constant motion,
had difficulty sitting still in class, had difficulty concentrating, and was
frequently out of class meeting with reading and writing specialists. He
was diagnosed as having AD/HD and was put on Ritalin. In spite of
these difficulties, Dana's teacher suggested that he work with me explor-
ing a topic in which he was interested: rockets. ...He actually wanted to
build a rocket, but his mother was reluctant to encourage this because
of the possible danger involved. We decided instead to concentrate work
on aerodynamics and/or airplanes. ...I was most impressed with the high
level of deductive reasoning that he verbalized, when prompted by my
questions. I would ask him:

"What do you suppose is happening here, Dana?"

"What do you think is causing this to happen?"

"Can you draw a conclusion—or perhaps state a hypothesis—based on
what has just happened?

Dana very quickly grasped the steps and causes and effects of the
experiments and had a clear understanding of what it all meant.

One of the experiments was to make a steam-reaction motor illustrating
Newton's third law, which Dana understood immediately. When Dana
would muse, "I wonder what would happen if I changed this a little,"
I would suggest, "Try it."

The first time I suggested he try it, he looked at me incredulously and
said, "Really?"

And I replied, "Yes, try it."

He seemed amazed that he would be allowed to work outside the boundaries of the written page, to experiment, to explore, to be creative. In this
work, Dana was entirely focused, engaged, excited about learning, and
seemed so pleased.

Because a number of students had indicated an interest in computers,
including Dana, I arranged for these students to meet with computer
technicians at the medical school to learn how computers were being
used interactively by patients and doctors. This provided another
hands-on learning experience for Dana. In April of that same year,
I arranged for a NASA Space Ambassador to make presentations for all
students. Her presentation for Dana's class and other classes was on
"Future Space Explorations."

In September of the next school year, I asked all students in the school
to complete interest inventories. Dana, now a fourth grader, indicated
that his main interests were jet engines, robotics, rockets, and
computers. Because of his dyslexia, I knew that I had to provide Dana
with other means of acquiring knowledge about rockets and other topics
he so desperately craved. A student from another grade had attended
Space Camp during the summer and met with Dana to explain some of
the things he had learned there.

When reading my local newspaper one evening, I noticed an article about a
retired engineer who had helped design the second satellite that our
country put into orbit. I phoned this elderly gentleman and asked if he
would be willing to meet with a student of mine who was very interested
in rockets and space. He readily agreed to do so and I merely observed.
Dana was fascinated with the model of the satellite that this gentleman
brought along as he explained how it all worked, what it accomplished,
how it was launched, and many other aspects of its design. Dana was
most interested in what this engineer explained to him, asking him many
questions and discussing details about the satellite as they met for
more than an hour. During that time, Dana was entirely focused,
interested, quiet, and involved. The engineer also brought along a Global
Positioning Satellite device and showed Dana how that worked, too.

It was clear to me that Dana was highly intelligent and creative and that
he wanted so much to learn about specific topics. During the part of the
school year when I met weekly with him, Dana would sometimes greet me
with, "Mrs. Palmer, I've been thinking." I would then ask, of course, what he
had been thinking about, and he would tell me about ideas he had. One
day he sat quietly for a little while, staring out the window, then said, "I've
been wondering about electricity." When I asked him to tell me more, he
said he wondered why electricity needed wires in order to travel from one
place to another. If light and sound could "travel" without wires, why
couldn't electricity do the same, he wondered. Dana always had wonderful,
creative ideas, and I always took his ideas and interests seriously,
encouraging him to explore these ideas further.

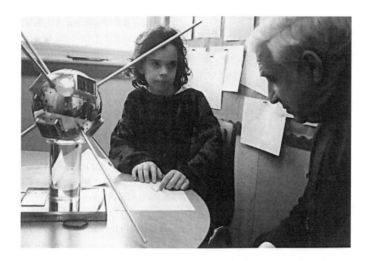

One day in the early spring of that year, he said, once again, "Mrs. Palmer, I've been thinking." When I asked him what he had been thinking about, he said that he thought that bridge supports were built wrong. He then explained that when he was watching the ice break apart on a nearby river, sending huge chunks of ice slamming against the bridge supports, he noticed that the bridge supports were rectangular concrete shapes. He thought that the repeated slamming of ice chunks on these flat surfaces would eventually wear out and/or weaken the bridge supports. He then thought that bridge supports were designed wrong. Instead of rectangular piers, the supports should be built like the bow of a ship, with a pointed surface headed upstream and that the point should be built of something stronger than concrete. Then when ice chunks churned down the river, they would simply break apart and be carried harmlessly along the flanks of the bridge support. Dana then asked if I thought this was a good idea. I replied that I thought it sounded good and suggested he draw a sketch of this design and bring it in the following week, hoping this interest of his would continue.

This was a student who frequently forgot his homework, but a week later, Dana appeared with his sketch. Again he asked if I thought this would work, and I replied that we would take the idea to someone who knew a great deal more about ice and its effects than I did.

The U.S. Army Corps of Engineers operated the Cold Regions Research and Engineering Laboratory (CRREL) in Hanover, New Hampshire, about a 30-minute drive from the school. I called the lab and asked if an ice engineer would meet with a student I had who had an idea about bridge supports. We readily received an appointment, and two weeks later, Dana and I drove to CRREL. He met with an ice engineer who was quite impressed with Dana's ideas, his inquisitiveness, his comprehension of the physics of stresses and strains caused by ice, and his interest.

The engineer then called a second engineer to go over with Dana some problems on which the lab was working. After showing us a video of the 1992 floor in Montpelier, Vermont, and on ice studies being conducted on the Connecticut River, the natural boundary between New Hampshire and Vermont, this engineer asked Dana if he would please think about a particular problem on which they were working. A week later, Dana did, in fact, draw a sketch of an idea he had to solve that problem and wrote a letter, dictated to me, to this engineer.

Dana is now a high school junior, and a few years ago when I happened to see his mother, she told me that in all of Dana's years of schooling, I was the only person who recognized his unusual intelligence. This made me realize once again how important it is to pay attention to the gifts that children like Dana have. We simply must focus on what these children can do, not only on what they cannot do. Certainly we need to help these children overcome their learning difficulties and learn strategies to compensate for those differences, but we must encourage and celebrate their gifts as well.

Celebrate the diversity of learning styles, celebrate the unique gifts of the right hemisphere, celebrate the delightful differences that visual-spatial learners bring to the classroom. Focus on their phenomenal strengths instead of their deficits—this is the message of this chapter. Indeed, the message of this entire book. It is fitting to end this chapter with a quotation from Annemarie Roeper advising us to adapt to the children instead of asking them to adapt to us:

> Once we find out something about them, we try to change them to make them fit the norm instead of listening to them and creating an open environment in which they can grow.

If we want these children to learn from us, either as teachers or parents, then we must accept who they are instead of trying to rearrange them to be like everyone else.

We have a Visual-Spatial Identifier!

For over a decade, the only way I had of identifying visual-spatial learners was through test score patterns and parent questionnaires. When these sources conflicted, I trusted the child's interests as revealed in the parent questionnaires, rather than the test scores. (See Child "D" in Chapter 1.) Both of these methods depended on clinical judgment, and were not easily taught to others. As word got around Colorado about these maverick learners, we realized that we needed some quick way to spot them at home and in school. So, Betty Maxwell and I decided to establish a multidisciplinary study group to help us create a systematic method of identifying VSLs.

On April 13th, 1992, we held our first meeting of the Visual-Spatial Learner Study Group. The participants were George Dorry, a psychologist who specializes in AD/HD; Lynn Hellerstein, a behavioral optometrist; Barb Ziek, a gifted education (G/T) coordinator; Jeff Freed, a great tutor (now author of *Right-Brained Children in a Left-Brained World*); three parents of VSLs—Jan Rahm, Judy Spolum and Melanie Eulberg; Betty and me. Steve Haas, a math teacher and mentor, joined the group shortly afterward, and eventually became the Project Director for the *Visual-Spatial Identifier.* The group was fluid, involving professionals from many disciplines. This allowed us to examine the idea from many different perspectives: psychiatry, neuropsychology, clinical psychology, social psychology, optometry, audiology, speech pathology, occupational therapy, educational therapy, kinesiology, dyslexia, gifted education, mathematics education, art, business, and parenting. The volunteers worked diligently for nearly 9 years constructing various versions of the *Identifier.* Some were involved for a few months, while others devoted several years to the project. Steve, George, Betty and I are still absorbed in this effort.

All of us had worked with or lived with visual-spatial learners, and felt that it was essential to have a way of locating these children so that they could be better understood. We wanted the *Identifier* to be useful throughout the range of intelligence. Countless meetings were spent teasing out the characteristics of VSLs from the symptoms of giftedness, dyslexia, AD/HD, sensory integration dysfunction, and central auditory processing disorder. As VSLs often had one or more of these other labels, it proved to be quite a challenge to isolate which indicators related primarily to their visual-spatial learning style. It felt like trying to unravel a finely woven tapestry so that we could examine each thread individually. This chapter gives you the flavor of that experience.

Squirrelly kids

The sorting problem surfaced at our very first meeting. Barb Ziek, the G/T coordinator, had been one of my students at the University of Denver (DU), so she was one of the first to learn about visual-spatial learners in the early 1980's. In the interim, Barb conducted a most interesting study in her school district. She asked the G/T teachers she worked with to select their eight top students and their eight most annoying students. She dubbed the groups "bluebirds" and "squirrels." I'll bet you can guess which ones were the "squirrels"! All the bluebirds were well-balanced and sequential. The squirrels were spatial, and they had all had child studies done. None had reading difficulties. (Dyslexic children probably didn't get into that G/T program.) Two were taking Ritalin, and a few wore glasses. They all had very uneven profiles: spikes in certain areas and slumps in others. They showed amazing originality and creativity. Here is a list of the commonalities Barb found in her "Squirrelly Kids."

Characteristics of "Squirrelly Kids"

- Show sensitivity to different types of clothing
- Are sensitive to light
- Tend to suffer from asthma
- Are holistic learners
- Think in images
- Learn by means of visualization
- Emotions are very important to them
- Have heightened imagination
- Are "delicate instruments"—react to many things
- Need imagery in order to learn
- Highly creative

- ⚘ Uneven in their abilities
- ⚘ Organizationally impaired
- ⚘ Spatial rather than sequential
- ⚘ Their learning process is the reverse of the normal one

Barb compared her "squirrels" to different lists of traits of the creatively gifted, fluid learners, right-hemispheric learners, children with AD/HD, and gifted children with learning disabilities, and found tremendous overlap. Nearly all of Barb's characteristics eventually proved to be classic indicators of a visual-spatial learning style. Only a few are questionable. Barb's description of squirrelly kids being sensitive to different types of clothing, as well as "delicate instruments," who react to many things, can signify sensual overexcitability, which relates to creativity, or sensory integration (S-I) dysfunction. Sensitivity to light is another sign of S-I dysfunction; it can also indicate vision issues. Asthma may be related to high intelligence, but couldn't auditory-sequential learners have asthma? However, it wouldn't surprise me if future research reveals a higher incidence of S-I dysfunction and asthma among visual-spatial learners.

At our second VSL Study Group meeting, Lynn Hellerstein's sister, Beth Fishman, who is an occupational therapist, described some of the symptoms of sensory integration dysfunction. "S-I kids," as Beth calls them, may have either gross motor (large muscle) or fine motor (eye-hand control) problems or both. Their bodies may not support them well; instead of sitting up straight in their chairs, they may resemble floppy, wet noodles. They may be anxious and fearful, particularly in new situations. S-I kids may also be extremely sensitive to touch, which is called "tactile defensiveness." Children with tactile defensiveness don't like being held as infants. They have to initiate contact with others. If someone brushes up against them, they push the person out of their space. They're often finicky eaters, not liking the textures of certain foods. They may need to have something in their mouth all the time, so they chew on their shirts. S-I symptoms also overlap with symptoms of AD/HD, like having to move in order to think.

Betty Maxwell and I have observed that children who had difficult births often have S-I symptoms, AD/HD symptoms, and trouble with sequential tasks. They appear more visual-spatial. Robert Ornstein explains how birth complications compromise the left hemisphere, making it more likely that the child will favor the right hemisphere.

> An important key to hemisphere differences is that the left *is far more vulnerable than the right...* The right hemisphere develops first... So if there is a shortage of oxygen, the left hemisphere suffers first.

...One of the things that can harm the left hemisphere is the male hormone testosterone. If too much is produced it can slow down development. Then during birth, because of the normal position of the baby's head, the blood supply to the left hemisphere is more likely to be temporarily cut off. Any damage of this sort to the left hemisphere can cause a switch to the right brain...such as cesaran, breech birth, forceps delivery, being born premature, etc. (Ornstein, 1997, p. 84)

(More on birthing issues can be found in Chapter 9.)

There is also an overlap between some S-I symptoms and Kazimierz Dabrowski's sensual overexcitability (OE). In Chapter 11, I described how the overexcitabilities were based on the study of creative children and adults. A study we did of creatively gifted adults revealed that most were high in Sensual OE. Creative children tend to be sensitive to clothing. Labels have to be removed, clothes have to be washed before they can be worn, socks may have to be worn inside-out, certain materials are "too scratchy," and the child will often dissolve into tears if his or her clothing doesn't feel just right.

> But the sensitivities. Oh, the sensitivities. When I was a child...I could hardly go outside without being blinded. ...I used to stick the tags out of my shirt so that they wouldn't scratch my neck. ...I started cutting out the rest... Many of these sensitivities died with childhood, some did not, still some others have taken a different form. Some cause me trouble. The winters up here are terrible, but yet I cannot wear a coat...I think these sensitivities, coupled with the frustration of trying to do linear things, makes me in some way "turn off."

It's difficult to determine whether we're looking at S-I dysfunction or Sensual OE. But Sensual OE also includes positive qualities, such as aesthetic appreciation and the capacity for pleasurable sensual experiences, like chocolate, shopping, music, chocolate, sex, dance, sunsets, chocolate, perfume, being the center of attention, and, of course, chocolate.

So far, Betty and I haven't observed a connection between visual-spatial learning and asthma. However, brain researcher Norman Geschwind suggested a link between left-handedness and immune disorders, such as asthma. Camilla Benbow and her associates, building on Norman Geschwind's research, found increased incidence of left-handedness, nearsightedness, and immune disorders (asthma and allergies) in extremely gifted youth. All of these factors correlated with enhanced right-hemispheric development. There definitely are VSLs who have S-I dysfunction or asthma, but until we have some funding to undertake research, we won't know for sure the nature and extent of the relationship.

Barb thought that about 20 to 25 percent of the school population fit the description of squirrelly kids. If you're an educator, you might be interested in duplicating Barb's study with your most and least successful students, to see if you get similar results. Squirrelly kids, the creatively gifted, fluid learners, and right-hemispheric learners may all be different terms for visual-spatial learners. But please bear in mind that while many children with S-I dysfunction, AD/HD, and learning disabilities may be visual-spatial, there are a vast number of visual-spatial learners who do not suffer from any of these problems. (See Chapters 4, 9, and 11, for more on VSLs with these issues.)

Will the real visual-spatial characteristics please stand up?

It was actually great fun to argue about whether a particular trait fit most VSLs, or was due to something else. Would you like to get a taste of what it was like to be part of our VSL Study Group? OK, below are the characteristics that emerged from our first few brainstorming sessions. Before you read the next paragraph, guess which ones eventually proved to be attributable to this learning style rather than to some other issue.

Suggested Characteristics of VSLs from the VSL Study Group

1. "Right-brained"   Yes_____ No_____
2. Do poorly on Coding and Digit Span on the Wechsler tests   Yes_____ No_____
3. May have acute hearing but poor auditory processing   Yes_____ No_____
4. Clothes have to be washed before they're worn; labels cut out   Yes_____ No_____
5. May have migraines, allergies, asthma   Yes_____ No_____
6. Left-handed   Yes_____ No_____
7. Red-haired   Yes_____ No_____
8. Extremely intuitive—some even seem psychic   Yes_____ No_____
9. Able to read patterns   Yes_____ No_____
10. Look for essence and meaning   Yes_____ No_____
11. Have problems with spelling   Yes_____ No_____
12. Are slow processors   Yes_____ No_____
13. Mini-panic sets in during phonics   Yes_____ No_____
14. Their first impression sticks in memory, and once it gets in there, it's difficult to get out   Yes_____ No_____

15.	Sensitive to light; can get depressed by fluorescent lighting	Yes_____	No_____
16.	May dress in black and avoid sunlight	Yes_____	No_____
17.	Easily overstimulated	Yes_____	No_____
18.	Natural born scanners	Yes_____	No_____
19.	Perfectionistic—all or nothing thinkers	Yes_____	No_____
20.	Non-sequential	Yes_____	No_____
21.	Intense moodiness	Yes_____	No_____
22.	Writing is often below average	Yes_____	No_____
23.	Dyslexic	Yes_____	No_____
24.	Read differently; can pick up an immense amount of information through silent reading, but are very poor at oral reading	Yes_____	No_____
25.	Difficulty dealing with change	Yes_____	No_____
26.	Distractible	Yes_____	No_____
27.	Go with their first impression and then react	Yes_____	No_____
28.	Get carsick	Yes_____	No_____
29.	Cannot remember a complex set of directions	Yes_____	No_____
30.	Can be incredibly competitive	Yes_____	No_____

While there are some VSLs who fit each of these descriptors, only 8 of the 30 qualities turned out to be generalizable to most VSLs: 1, 8-12, 20, and 22. Visual-spatial children have enhanced right-hemispheric development, and are non-sequential, slow processing, highly intuitive pattern-finders, who are always looking for meaning! They tend to have problems with spelling and handwriting. Many VSLs are also easily overstimulated (#17) as a function of their introversion, but I imagine that not all VSLs are introverts. Introverts avoid parties, freak out at the noise level at carnivals, concerts and theaters, and cannot deal with noisy classrooms. This can also be a symptom of S-I dysfunction or AD/HD. All of the other characteristics fit some VSLs, but not the majority. See why it took us so long to separate these variables?

Constructing the questionnaires

Our first groping attempts to create an *Identifier* were laughable, but they forced us to fine-hone our thinking. We tried out the questionnaires with teens and adults known to be visual-spatial, and learned which items they didn't relate to, and which were poorly worded. Our early versions were very long, wordy and unwieldy. Jan Rahm, a parent, happened to be a top-notch editor. She suggested that we try to chunk the questions into related groups. (Jan also created handouts that married our characteristics with some of Jeff Freed's teaching ideas: "Teaching Visual-Spatial Learners in Elementary School" and "Teaching Visual-Spatial Learners in Secondary School." Typical of the selflessness of this group of volunteers, she refused to take any credit for either handout.) Jan led us in looking for essential similarities among items.

Eight Clusters of VSL Traits

✧ **visual rather than auditory**
✧ **spatial rather than sequential**
✧ **holistic rather than detailed**
✧ **focused on ideas rather than format**
✧ **pattern-seeking**
✧ **divergent rather than convergent**
✧ **sensitive and intense**
✧ **asynchronous (exhibiting large disparities between strengths and weaknesses)**

These clusters guided the development of all of our subsequent questionnaires. We described visual-spatial learners in positive terms, then presented the types of potential school problems that could be associated with each characteristic. Betty Maxwell simplified the wording, creating "*The Visual-Spatial Learner in School*" (Appendix A) that is very useful for teachers. It consists of 32 positive characteristics of VSLs, clustered in 8 groups, with 71 related school problems that may (but do not always) accompany the strengths.

In 1994 and 1995, we were truly blessed when three top-notch researchers decided to do postdoctoral internships at the Gifted Development Center. First came Frank Falk and Nancy Miller, social psychologists from the University of Akron, and then, Karen Rogers, from the University of St. Thomas at St. Paul. Frank and Nancy had organized the Dabrowski Study Group with me in the '80s when we were all at DU. They were well-versed at creating instruments, and helped us turn our descriptors into clear questions that could be coded and analyzed. But wait! We didn't own a computer! Frank and Nancy solved that problem by donating our first computer: a 286 PC.

In addition, no one had time to enter the data. Fortune smiled on us again, and a gifted young woman, Amy Frisbee, happened to see our sign in the front yard, and came in out of curiosity. She asked if she could volunteer and we immediately put her to work entering data on the VSL study.

We were truly amazed when Karen Rogers, a leading researcher in gifted education, asked if she could do a post-doc with us. In addition to entering and analyzing data on 241 children above 160 IQ, using a system that Frank and Nancy had devised, Karen contributed significantly to the effort of simplifying the *VSL Identifier*. Frank, Nancy and Karen let us know (nicely, of course) that our *Identifier* was a lovely set of descriptors, but not a real tool of measurement. We had made it so complex that it took 3 researchers a year and a half to make it usable, and, even then, study participants thought the wording was at too high a level!

The *Identifier* was created mostly for teachers, but it contained many items that teachers could not observe directly, such as "Thinks primarily in images." (See Appendix A.) So we created a much simpler *Self-Report* consisting of 50 brief items to go with an *Observer Report* of 72 items and tried them out with several visual-spatial teens and adults. Frank and Nancy analyzed the results. Then we reworded the items, tossing out the most confusing ones. At this point, the streamlined *Self-Report* contained 36 items, and the *Observer Report*, 57 items. We tried out the two VSL questionnaires in 1995 and 1996 with 65 students thought to be highly visual-spatial by their parents or teachers. After each attempt, we labored for months to improve the questions.

Attempts at validation

(If you aren't fascinated by the perils of validating a questionnaire, feel free to skip to the chase. Don't miss the list of questions in the *Identifier* and last two pages of this chapter!) In April of 1997, Steve Haas procured a grant from the Morris S. Smith Foundation for us to validate the *Identifier*. That's when refinement of the questionnaires went into high gear. Several versions later, we now had a paired set— the *Observer Report* and the *Self-Report*—each with 36 items, covering all eight of our VSL clusters. We were ready to roll! Amy helped collect the data and Frank and Steve analyzed it.

Our first validation study was conducted with 56 of our clients at the Gifted Development Center. Their parents had signed authorization forms allowing us to involve their children in research. I thought the discrepancy between Block Design and Digit Span scores on the *Wechsler Intelligence Scale for Children (WISC-R and WISC-III)*, would be the best way to locate visual-spatial and auditory-sequential learners. Block Design (copying designs with red and white blocks) is the best measure of visual-spatial reasoning on the *WISC* and it seemed like Digit Span (repeating random sequences of numbers forward and back-ward) would be the best estimate of auditory-sequential ability.

Wading through 2,500 files, Amy pulled those of children between the ages of 6 and 16 who had taken a *WISC*. We had her look for children who had a 7-point discrepancy between these two subtests, in either direction. Finding visual-spatial learners by this method was fairly easy. There were lots of children who scored 7 points higher on Block Design than on Digit Span. But it was nearly impossible to find gifted auditory-sequential learners who scored 7 points higher on Digit Span than on Block Design. So we lowered the discrepancy. If Digit Span was 3 points (1 s.d.) higher than Block Design, the child was included in the study as an auditory-sequential learner.

Amy called all the families selected and most were excited to participate. She sent out the questionnaires and got an excellent rate of return. Unfortunately, the results of the study were dreadful. The groups didn't separate well at all. We were obviously doing something wrong. So we went back to the drawing board and tried to look at all the possible sources of error. Were the questions worded clearly? Did the title "*Visual-Spatial Identifier*" on the instrument affect the results? Frank and Karen had suggested that some of the questions should be phrased in reverse order. We hadn't done that. Was that the trouble? Was the discrepancy between Block Design and Digit Span not a good basis for dividing the groups? Was the fact that we used a gifted population the source of the problem? So I contacted Alan Kaufman, author of *Intelligent Testing with the WISC-R* and *Intelligent Testing with the WISC-III* for input.

Alan said that Block Design yielded higher scores for gifted groups since it's so heavily loaded on abstract reasoning. He also felt that Digits Forward was a better indicator of auditory sequencing than the entire Digit Span test. We knew that VSLs often did better on repeating Digits Backward, because they **saw** the numbers in their mind's eye. (For some reason, they generally don't do that with Digits Forward.) Amy had to dig out of the *WISC* protocols the number of Digits Forward items that each child answered correctly, because there is no score for just Digits Forward. Then Steve and Amy had to create a formula translating the Digits Forward portion of the subtest into a 19-point scale. Then they compared it with the 19-point scale for Block Design, as we had done with the first study. This meant recalculating all of the scores, and some of the participants changed categories. After all the recalculations, we had to invent a third category: "neither." Then we had to find some more participants in order to get sufficient numbers of VSLs and auditory-sequentials for a second pilot study. (Are you tired yet?)

Out of the blue, Michele Kane asked her gifted 5th graders in Antioch, Illinois, to turn the self-report measure into kid-friendly language. Their wording was fabulous—much better than ours! So we reworked the questions yet again, this time wording the *Observer Report* similar to the *Self-Report*. We put every third question in reverse order, so that it was positive for auditory-sequentials and negative for visual-spatials. And we changed the name of the questionnaire to the *Visual-Spatial/Auditory-Sequential Identifier* to guard against leading information in the title.

We had asked the first group of participants if we could use them to test out two different versions of the *Identifier* and they were agreeable. So we sent the second draft out to 62 individuals, most of whom had taken the first version. I am sad to say that the results were just as abysmal in the second study. Our *Identifier* failed to separate the two groups. Again, we went back to the drawing board. (We may be slow, but we're tenacious!) We realized that many of our problems were due to sample selection.

The files at the Gifted Development Center spanned 20 years, so the participants now ranged in age from 6 to 25. We had significantly more males than females in the sample. The group was predominantly middle and upper middle-class Caucasian, so there was not enough diversity. And the fact that these children were gifted, or gifted and learning disabled, confounded our results. Gifted VSLs can often excel in areas that other VSLs cannot—sometimes due to excellent abilities to compensate, and sometimes out of sheer determination and stubbornness. Gifted people don't like to fail.

Success at last!

In May of 1998, the Morris S. Smith Foundation was kind enough to award us a second grant to complete another validation study. We realized that we had to find a sample of students from the general population in order to create an instrument that would be usable with the whole range of school children. Our next study, conducted in April of 1999, involved an entire middle school of 447 fifth and sixth grade students at Baker Central School in Fort Morgan, Colorado. We chose Baker Central because it contained the full socio-economic spectrum; an ethnically diverse student body (44% of the students are Hispanic); it had a close gender balance (55% girls, 45% boys); it was rural; and it allowed us to control for age. Most of the students were 10, 11 and 12, with a few 13 year olds. But most of all, we chose it because Dennis Corash, the visual-spatial principal of Baker Central Middle School, had been one of my graduate students at DU, and he offered his school to us! Thanks, Dennis!

We constructed a Spanish version of the *Identifier* for the students and parents who preferred to respond in Spanish. The questionnaires were translated into Spanish and retranslated back into English from the Spanish version to assure that each translation was accurate. We hired bilingual personnel to assist us in the data entry and reading of comments on the forms. All the students and their parents were asked to complete the questionnaires, and teachers were asked to rate all of their students. After we collected the data, Steve and I provided a half-day in-service to the faculty at Baker Central School on the characteristics of visual-spatial learners and auditory-sequential learners. Then we asked the teachers to list the most visual-spatial and most auditory-sequential students in each class. (This method was actually quite similar to Barb Ziek's request that teachers nominate their top 8 students and their 8 most annoying students.) These ratings were also entered into our database. This constituted a multi-trait, multi-factor, multi-method study (Are you impressed?) incorporating:

- ⚬ self-ratings by students
- ⚬ observer reports by parents
- ⚬ observer reports by teachers
- ⚬ subjective assessment by teachers

The data were grouped in a number of different ways:

* By race and ethnicity: White, Hispanic, Black and American Indian
* By type of questionnaire: Completed by student, parent, or teacher
* By gender (sex)
* By age
* By learning style: visual-spatial vs. auditory-sequential, using subjective identification by teachers (For this analysis, we left out the large group of students the teachers did not select as strongly one or the other.)
* By scaled score (The total score for each questionnaire adding up all the responses to the most reliable 14 questions.)

We then ran correlations of each of these six kinds of information with each other and developed a 6 x 6 matrix. Of the 15 possible combinations, six were statistically significant (although only barely in some cases). The best correlation (0.517) was from the subjective teacher evaluations compared with the total score on the questionnaire. Group averages found for those who were identified by their teachers as visual-spatial, auditory-sequential, or neither, fit a neat linear model, with a correlation (r^2) of 0.95. (In case you don't know much about statistics, this is **great!**)

The bad news was that the majority of our questions turned out to be unusable. Nearly half (15) of the 36 questions were dumped for one of the following reasons:

* they had been left out by 50 or more respondents;
* they displayed an extreme mean (more than 3.5 or less than 2.5); or
* they lacked sufficient variability (standard deviations less than 1.2)

Twenty-one questions escaped the cutting board. But after further statistical analysis, Frank felt that only 14 of the questions could reliably separate the two groups, so we had to discard another 7 of them. (Hey, we worked for years to come up with those questions, and we thought they were really good.☹) This slimmed down our 36-item questionnaire to a trim 14. Here's what was left:

* I hate speaking in front of a group.
* I think mainly in pictures instead of words.
* I am good at spelling. **(not)**
* I often lose track of time.

 ⋇ I know more than others think I know.

 ⋇ I don't do well on tests with time limits.

 ⋇ I have neat handwriting. **(not)**

 ⋇ I have a wild imagination.

 ⋇ I like to take things apart and find out how they work.

 ⋇ I hate writing assignments.

 ⋇ I solve problems in unusual ways.

 ⋇ It's much easier for me to tell you about things than to write about them.

 ⋇ I have a hard time explaining how I come up with my answers.

 ⋇ I am well organized. **(not)**

The *VSL Identifier* was now a "robust instrument." But statistical significance is not an end in itself. The real question was, "Can the *Identifier* be used with any confidence in identifying an individual as visual-spatial or auditory-sequential?" To answer that question, we looked at the mean scores of the students who were identified by their teachers as visual-spatial or auditory-sequential. If the scores on the *Identifier* matched the teachers' ratings, then our questionnaires must be measuring what the teachers were observing.

It was a challenge to determine the cut-off point that would clearly indicate that a student was visual-spatial, because the distributions of the two populations overlapped. If we set the bar too high, we would miss a number of VSLs. If we cast too wide a net, we would label some students visual-spatial who weren't. Steve decided that instead of a clear-cut designation of visual-spatial above this line and auditory-sequential below this line, it made more sense to discuss the *degree* to which a student favored a visual-spatial (VSL) or auditory-sequential (ASL) learning style. Steve writes:

> Happily, the overlap in the two populations occurs mostly at the extremes of the two curves. At each point along the scaled score from 1 to 5, I checked to see what percentage of VSLs were correctly included and what percentage of ASLs were correctly excluded. Those two confidence levels were then averaged. Our "lowest average error" method takes both kinds of errors into account. The point between the two curves with the lowest average became the "cutoff" between the VSL and ASL populations.
>
> When we used that method, we got surprisingly good results. The overall reliability of the instrument, based on the information from the teachers' reports, was 89%. The students' reports yielded an overall reliability of 80% and parents' reports 77%. The cut-offs we

found were identical for both the teachers' and the students' reports at 2.90. For parents' reports, the cut-off was 2.68.

Once the cut-offs were determined with the "lowest average error" scoring protocol, those cut-offs were applied against the pool of all students to see how prevalent the visual-spatial learning style is in a general population. The teachers' data, based on familiarity with students exhibiting visual-spatial characteristics, gives the most reasonable results. Using the cut-off of 2.90 from the teachers' data, 37.6% (88 of the 234 students) would be identified as visual-spatial and 62.4% would be auditory-sequential.

Teacher rating of students after a brief in-service on the model proved the best predictor of the students' classification on the *Identifier*. The teachers identified 37.6% of their students as visual-spatial learners!

When we began our VSL Study Group, most of us (except Steve) thought only a small percentage of the school population were visual-spatial. Barb Ziek guessed 20-25%, which seemed at the time like an overestimate. A decade later, it looks like as many as 30-40% of the student body may be VSLs. And that percentage could be increasing throughout the planet. (Re-read page 1 of the Introduction.) We definitely need to be paying better attention to the needs of this segment of the school population.

Although the statistical properties of the 14-item questionnaire were sound, we still were not completely happy with the *Identifier*. It seemed to favor boys in both ethnic groups. So we added back 3 questions that favored girls:

(6) It was easy for me to memorize my math facts **(not)**;

(17) It's hard for me to learn if the teacher doesn't like me;

(28) I'm good at art.

In the summer of 2001, we repeated the study with the 17-item questionnaire at Lasley Elementary School in Jefferson County, Colorado, an urban school with an ethnic distribution similar to Baker Central Middle School. We extended the age range downward to include 4th graders. Again, we collected the data first, then provided an in-service workshop for teachers and had them select the students they felt certain were more auditory-sequential and the students they felt certain were more visual-spatial.

We were astounded by what we found! The results for 305 4th, 5th, and 6th graders matched the results for Baker Central so closely that we ended up being able to pool the data. This time, Steve divided the students into three groups: those who were mostly visual-spatial, those who were mostly auditory-sequential, and those who were in between.

Using all sources of information, *approximately 1/3 of the students in both schools appear to be strongly visual-spatial,* and about 23%, strongly auditory-sequential. The rest are a little of each. *Teacher judgment, after a brief in-service on the model, remains the best source of information.* Even more amazing, the principal at Lasley reported to us a couple months later that *the teachers had immediately put into practice the visual-spatial methods* with the students that Steve and I had recommended. When Steve heard this news, he had tears in his eyes.

As a result of this second validation study, we added back the item, "It was easy for me to memorize my math facts" **(not)**. Unfortunately, the other two questions still failed to discriminate between the two groups. Although the *Identifier* still doesn't pick up as many girls as boys, it is finding a considerable number of visual-spatial girls. We now have a fully validated 15-item questionnaire, in an *Observer Report* version and a *Self-Report* version, in English and Spanish, and an in-service model that really works to change educational practice. The model works because it's teacher-friendly.

We've established the validity of the *Identifier* for White and Hispanic males and females, ages 9-13, with 750 students in urban and rural geographic areas. The scoring protocol produced excellent results at Baker and Lasley. We're now able to report an individual student's raw score and profile compared to students of the same age, gender, and ethnicity. We can conclude whether a student is predominantly a VSL or an ASL, and the degree of confidence we have in that judgment. However, we still need to undertake studies of different age groups to expand the validity of the Identifier and determine the age and grade levels for which it is best suited. If you can obtain clearance from your school district to help us conduct further validation studies of the *Visual-Spatial Identifier,* please contact us at **www.gifteddevelopment.com.**

It looks like the visual-spatial learning style may well describe about **one-third** of the students in a regular classroom. How about that! At least when they ask how many we're talking about, we now have an educated estimate of the percentage of the population that is visual-spatial.

The *Identifier* is now available on our website. We hope that it will enable you to easily identify VSLs in your families and classrooms. One of the reasons that visual-spatial learners have not been well served prior to this point is that there hasn't been a simple, valid method of finding them. Now that we have the *Identifier,* we have no excuse. It's time to pay attention to the needs of this underserved group of children.

Visual-Spatial Adults and
the Future of Education

Wow!!! This is amazing!!! I am 39 years old. I am one of these Visual-Spatial Learners and I never knew this until I read your web page.

Hello, I randomly came across your website today and was quite surprised at how closely I matched the list of things describing a visual-spatial learner. I went down the list going, "Yup, yup, that's totally me!" I have known for a long time that I was a visual learner, but to read a list of things that fits me so well was pretty weird. After being in college for three years now, I have come to the conclusion that I reason and function quite differently from most of my peers. And after reading some of the stuff on your site, it's a lot easier to put words to the thoughts.

So here we are at the last chapter of this book, or maybe it's the introduction to the next book on this topic. I've been looking forward to writing this chapter for well over a year, gaining new insights about it all the time. It feels like the cake is fully baked—the story of how the VSL idea came about has been told. I've shared with you how to recognize, assess, parent and teach visual-spatial children. I've explored introversion, which often comes with the territory, the giftedness of VSLs, as well as learning disabilities and attention deficits that may accompany this learning style. This chapter is the icing on the cake. I used to decorate cakes when my kids were little, a hobby I adored, so I hope you'll indulge me as I embellish the VSL theme with fanciful rosebuds—whimsical musings of the wide-ranging inferences of the VSL concept.

This last chapter is dedicated to you, Dear Reader, the visual-spatial adult. Please join me on my first excursion into this fascinating territory. These are new thoughts, open to revision as the mysteries of the terrain reveal themselves. I also invite you to accompany me on my quest to understand the spiritual significance of our two hemispheres. The book ends with my vision of education in this new millennium.

The imposter syndrome

I now understand why I have heard myself saying countless times, "Can't you see it?" I would like someone to address the psychic pain we have experienced for trying to make ourselves "fit," and being largely misdiagnosed and misunderstood.

Visual-spatial adults are at a disadvantage in adult life, as well as in childhood. Individuals with this different way of knowing feel like imposters—interlopers—who can "pass for normal," but know they aren't as smart. VSLs believe that people who are *really* smart (instead of faking it) know where their ideas came from and can retrace their steps from beginning to end. Smart people can "show their work"; smart people can cite references to support each of their ideas; smart people are quick thinkers, can dominate discussions and be heard; smart people have long, impressive resumes. These beliefs generate feelings of inferiority in VSLs that remain throughout the life cycle.

The knowledge that visual-spatial adults gain is from direct, concrete experience, from intuition, and from imagery. These sources do not hold up in court, they make it hard to "prove" your point, and they fail to impress your dissertation committee. Because their way of knowing is less provable, visual-spatial adults feel like pretenders for much of their adult lives—a condition Pauline Clance has dubbed, "The Imposter Phenomenon." They are afraid that if they are challenged, they will be "found out" as frauds. They will not be able to explain how they know what they know. "I don't know how I know; I just know." This fear is magnified when a VSL attains a position that is usually held by someone with "better credentials" or supervises people with "better credentials."

Individuals with right-hemispheric strengths and left-hemispheric weaknesses believe that their knowledge is illegitimate—even if they have achieved wealth, fame or awards for their contributions. Legitimacy is attributed to knowledge that has been accumulated in traditional ways: coursework, degrees, credentials—all of which involve passing tests. Tests are ordeals to be endured in one's youth, like vaccinations, and to be avoided at all costs for the remainder of one's life. Rarely can VSLs demonstrate on a test all that they know about a subject. Here is why VSLs hate taking tests:

- **Tests are timed,** and VSLs can't think straight when they're being timed. They don't have sufficient time to translate their pictures into words.

- **There are no pictures in tests.** "No image, no understand." And trying to conjure up an image in one's mind under the pressure of testing is nearly impossible.

- Math **tests** that **require you to show your work** are deadly for VSLs who arrive at answers intuitively or by way of an image.

- Multiple-choice **tests involve reading** and deciphering written information. Some VSLs are dyslexic; some are highly gifted or divergent thinkers who see many more possibilities than the test constructor. It's difficult for VSLs to grasp exactly what the test constructor had in mind. They can see how most of the answers might be correct under different circumstances.

- Written, **essay-type tests** are even worse, because they **must be "well-organized"** (which means sequential), and if they have to be hand written, the physical act of writing may be daunting and painfully slow. In addition, they are terrified that they'll misspell words and look stupid.

- **Tests** often **require the regurgitation of memorized information**, and VSLs are poor at rote memorization.

- **Tests** usually **require cramming** a whole lot of possibly irrelevant **information into short-term memory**. VSLs don't have any short-term memory to cram things into, and only meaningful information stands half a chance of getting in.

Any time an adult VSL goes back to school to obtain a degree, it's an act of great courage, and needs to be appreciated as nothing short of heroic.

> I was always afraid of tests. I was very sick when I was a child and I only got as far as 8th grade in school. When my children were all grown up and away from home, I decided to go back to school. The first day the teacher said we would all have to be tested, and I started to leave. But she told me that the test was only to decide where we were, so they would know what to teach us. Each person in the class would be taught

individually. I was tested and discovered that I was at the 3rd grade level in arithmetic, and in the 3rd year of college in reading comprehension. I found a quiet room to study at the Y.W.C.A., and didn't tell any of my relatives or friends what I was doing. In 4½ months, I completed all the requirements for my high school diploma, but I left for Los Angeles before I took my G.E.D. exam. When I returned, I received a call from my teacher saying she felt so bad that I didn't stay for the G.E.D. because I was the highest in my class. With that I sat down and cried for joy that I hadn't failed the class.

Where do ideas come from?

"Legitimate" knowledge can be supported by citing facts and expert opinion (i.e., somebody else said it first, and you can rattle off the study, book or article, and the name of the author). Ideas can be traced to their sources if they were built sequentially on other people's ideas. But for VSLs, ideas come out of the blue. And the notion that ideas have "owners" (e.g., patents and copyrights) is something that only the left hemisphere can conceive. For the right hemisphere, ideas are as abundant as air. What would be the point of owning them? An idea only exists so that it can be shared; there are infinitely more where that one came from.

One of the qualities of the visual-spatial mind is originality. A second quality is intuition. A third is the ability to synthesize information from a variety of sources. Originality, intuition, and synthesis are essential ingredients for inventors and trail blazers, but they don't enable their hosts to analyze the sources of information that led to their conclusions. VSLs don't remember which authors gave them which elements of the picture in their minds. Like paints, other people's ideas are just the raw materials they use to create an entirely new canvas. Asking them, "How do you know that?" is like asking them to tell you where they bought the yellow paint they used to create this portion of the sunset. What difference does that make? How do you like the sunset?

Over and over in the history of science, two people in different parts of the world, who had had no contact with each other whatsoever, came up with the same idea at about the same time (prior to Internet!). In Western (left-hemispheric) philosophy, we don't have a logical explanation for this phenomenon. Even the basic Western concept that all effects have causes is sequential reasoning. It's not shared worldwide. The Eastern notion of events occurring synchronistically, by the law of attraction, is so non-sequential that the left hemisphere can't wrap itself around it at all. (Read *The Tao of Psychology* by Jean Shinoda Bolen if you want accessible information on synchronicity.)

So where do ideas come from? To an auditory-sequential learner, ideas come from previous knowledge, in a nice, linear fashion. To a visual-spatial learner, they come "out of nowhere," out of the All That Is.

Why gifted women and VSLs feel like imposters

If you're a female visual-spatial learner, you're in double trouble. Pauline Clance's research showed that well-educated, highly successful women—bursting with credentials and distinctions and recognition—often feel like imposters. Lee Ann Bell also found gifted women extremely vulnerable to the Imposter Phenomenon.

> Despite external evidence to the contrary, many bright and capable women continue to doubt their competence, downplay or dismiss their abilities, and subscribe to the disabling belief that they are impostors or fakes or frauds. This debilitating syndrome blocks women's ability to realize their full potential. (Bell, 1990, p. 55)

There is a good deal of research revealing that smart girls and women often attribute their successes to "luck" and their perceived failures to lack of ability. Feeling like an imposter erodes self-confidence and aspirations. It erects walls to keep others at a distance so one isn't "found out." It leads to intense discomfort in work and social situations when others disagree with your viewpoint. So what makes intelligent women and VSLs tend to feel that they are fooling everyone into thinking they're smarter than they really are?

For one thing, both groups rely heavily on intuition as a key source of information. Women's intuition is legendary and VSLs hang out a lot in their right hemispheres, the likely home of intuition. Jerre Levy said that the right hemisphere is superior to the left in "reaching accurate conclusions in the absence of logical justification" (1980, p. 253). I may be stretching scientific knowledge here, but this sounds to me like a definition of intuition. Another brain researcher, Sandra Witelson, reports that women have between 10 and 33 percent more neuronal fibers in the forward part of their corpus callosum than men. This enables the right hemisphere to communicate better with the left hemisphere.

> The higher the number of connecting neurons, the greater must be the integration between the two sides. Women and most men freely concede that women are more aware of and can better express their feelings than men. The extra connecting neurons seem to enhance the communication of emotions and increase global awareness, field perception, and understanding of the moods of offspring. Generally, women can perform multiple tasks simultaneously better than men. (Shlain, 1998, p. 23)

If certain intuitive information is more readily accessible to the right hemisphere, then perhaps it's easier for women to access intuitive information and translate it into words. But intuition often is not accepted as real knowledge.

A less obvious similarity is that a large percentage of VSLs and gifted women are introverts. The brighter the woman, the more likely she is to be introverted. Visual-spatial learners tend to be introverts, as well. (See Chapter 10.) Introverts are afraid of being exposed, of being publicly humiliated by their mistakes. They die a thousand deaths at the thought of standing up in front of a group, presenting, and being asked a question they can't answer. VSLs rely on imagery, and introverts rely on introspection. These are both internal sources of information, not easy to validate externally. While I haven't seen it mentioned in any of the literature I've read on this topic, I think introverts are much more likely to suffer from the Imposter Phenomenon than extraverts.

Last, and perhaps most important of all, VSLs and highly intelligent women both live outside the range of acceptability—on the fringes of society. Lee Ann Bell refers to this condition as being marginalized. Any group that *has to pretend to be like everyone else* in order to get through school, gain and keep employment, and succeed by societal standards feels marginalized. Gifted people, visual-spatial learners, women, and minority groups all feel the need to hide who they really are, and don the attire and mannerisms of the dominant group. The narrower the restrictions of this group, the harder it is for those who are not a part of it to feel that they can disclose who they really are. If the key to success is adopting a façade that makes one appear more like the mainstream, then all nonstandard groups who attempt to pass for the standard model are "imposters." The gifted visual-spatial woman of color must continuously struggle to believe in herself. The antidote is for society to develop greater appreciation of different perspectives and greater acceptance of diversity. Perhaps that will be one outcome of September 11th, 2001.

Visual-spatial women

This discussion leads us to the mystery broached in the Introduction about women's visual-spatial abilities. According to most research, males are superior to females in visual-spatial abilities, and females are superior to males in verbal abilities. So why do so many women consider themselves visual-spatial? I have some theories, but at this point I have more questions than answers. I've noticed that gifted women who identify themselves as VSLs are not particularly adept at making mental maps. Visual memory and sense of direction are not necessarily their strong suits. But they have superb intuition, and are emotionally tuned in to others. Is it possible that women and men use visual-spatial capacities for different purposes?

For 20 years, I've pondered how the brains of males and females might have developed for the survival of the species. Cave men, who were hunters, had to develop a good sense of direction so that they didn't get lost in the jungle. They would have needed well-developed depth perception, awareness of velocity, and a sense of their position in space, so that they could slay the saber-toothed tiger before the saber-toothed tiger devoured them. These are obvious right-hemispheric visual-spatial skills.

Cave women would have needed an entirely different set of skills in order to protect the young. They would have developed the ability to read facial expressions and body language, to interpret different types of cries, to have an intuitive/instinctive/psychic knowing when their children were in danger, to be aware of a great deal of sensory information all at once, and to have eyes that could see behind their heads (so that while they tended to their infants they could know what their toddlers were into). Without women's vital abilities to read the nonverbal cues and emotional environment of preverbal children, our species wouldn't have survived. Similarly, Leonard Shlain (1998) writes:

> A hunter must maintain a singularity of purpose when focused on prey; a mother must keep a field awareness of all that is going on around her. While scouting for edibles, she cradled her infant in the crook of her left arm and had to monitor constantly the activity of her other children, playing at the periphery of her vision and consciousness. She could rarely carry out a task without, at the same time, remaining vigilant. Failure to do so often meant the death of, or serious injury to, her offspring. (pp. 15-16)

These right-hemispheric abilities are less often regarded as "visual-spatial." Could equally visual-spatial males and females be wired to use right-hemispheric abilities in different ways? And could these differentiated functions have been culturally reinforced by thousands of years of rigid sex-role stereotyping?

My next hypothesis was based on Carl Jung's concept of the *contrasexual*, which means the masculine in women and the feminine in men. As Leonard Shlain says, "Every human is a blend of these two principles" (1998, p. 5). My friend, Sharon Conarton, a Jungian therapist, introduced me to the idea of the contrasexual.

> Men primarily exhibit masculine characteristics. Their feminine characteristics are recessive. Women's characteristics are primarily feminine; their masculine characteristics are recessive. Jung (1954) refers to men's feminine energies as the anima, and women's

masculine energies as the animus. The anima and animus are the contrasexual in an individual. (Conarton, 1999, pp. 99-100)

As I read Sharon's article, it struck me that perhaps visual-spatial adults had superior contrasexual development: that visual-spatial males had greater openness to their inner feminine and visual-spatial females had greater openness to their inner masculine.

I had observed that many (but not all) visual-spatial males were unusually sensitive, particularly dyslexic artists. Forty years ago, Donald MacKinnon found that creative architects "gave more expression to the feminine side of their nature" (1962, p. 488). Creative individuals in general appear to have greater emotional sensitivity and intensity—considered feminine traits. The creative adults in the study I mentioned in the last chapter also showed extremely high emotional overexcitability. These studies suggest that males who are in touch with their feminine side demonstrate higher levels of creativity. My guess is that creative individuals are probably VSLs.

As I received website responses from women, I noticed that many of them were in male-dominated fields, such as computer technology and robotics. The women seemed less gender-role stereotyped than other women. When I listened to Jerre Levy's tape, I was reminded that all abilities vary to a greater degree among men and among women than between men and women. Jerre said that 15 percent of females surpass the average male in visual-spatial abilities and 30 percent of males surpass the average female in verbal fluency. So visual-spatial females may simply be those who are in the top 15 percent of women. Does 15 percent of the female population have greater connection with their inner masculine? Would VSL men and women be more like each other than like others of their gender? These questions would certainly be worth studying.

In *The Alphabet Versus the Goddess,* Leonard Shlain suggests that the right hemisphere is the "feminine" side of both men and women, and that the feminine principle (the Goddess) is rising, after 5,000 years of subjugation. The right hemisphere is coming into its own.

> To perceive things such as trees or buildings through images delivered to the eye, the brain uses wholeness, simultaneity, and synthesis. To ferret out the meaning of alphabetic writing, the brain relies instead on sequence, analysis, and abstraction. Custom and language associate the former characteristics with the feminine, the latter with the masculine. As we examine the myths of different cultures, we...see that these linkages are consistent. (Shlain, 1998, p. 5)

> Since World War II, the technologies of information transfer have formed the foundations of world culture and, in the process, helped it balance feminine and masculine. Iconic information proliferating

through the use of television, computers, photocopiers, fax machines, and the Internet have enhanced, and will continue to enhance, the positions in society of images, women's rights, and the Goddess. (p. 428)

If Leonard is right, we should see an increase in right-hemispheric visual-spatial abilities in both genders, as imagery continues to become more and more of a staple in our lives. In addition, we would expect both men and women to have greater integration of their masculine and feminine aspects. Perhaps the Age of Literacy enhanced the verbal abilities of women, but did nothing for their spatial abilities. The Age of Imagery may be offering more opportunities for women to develop dormant visual-spatial skills. Will we see more visual-spatial women in the years to come?

So women and men may be using their visual-spatial abilities for different purposes. Or VSLs may have greater contrasexual development, which means that they would be less gender-role stereotyped and more androgynous (having characteristics of both males and females). Or visual-spatial ability may be buried in women, repressed during the Age of Literacy, when verbal abilities had more of an opportunity to flourish. Or none of the above! Regardless of which of these hypotheses (if any) seem plausible, it's clear that a large number of women identify themselves as visual-spatial learners.

The VSL way of processing isn't a guy thing. As imagery plays an increasing role in our daily lives, we may see greater transcendence of traditional gender-role limitations. The area is still open to discussion, and I would welcome any of your ideas on this subject. Please email me and I'll incorporate your thoughts in my next book. It's about unrecognized giftedness in women, and I'm calling it, *I'm Not Gifted, I'm Just Busy.*

Do we have two minds?

And now, please come with me on my spiritual journey. When the visual-spatial learner concept first came to me, I only thought of it as an explanation of a strange pattern of test scores that Craig (in Chapter 1) and other children demonstrated. VSL was simply a new learning style. That was all. But I have to confess that when I listened to Jerre Levy's tape in 1982 (see Chapter 2), I was struck with a rather shocking notion.

Jerre had worked with Roger Sperry and other brain researchers on the effects of split-brain surgery. In the 1970s, this procedure saved individuals with life-threatening forms of epilepsy that doctors could not control by other means. In split-brain surgery, the corpus callosum, which is the relay station between the two hemispheres, was surgically disconnected, preventing communication between the hemispheres. In everyday life, individuals who had undergone this surgery looked perfectly normal, because both hemispheres were receiving the same information, and each hemisphere handled the part for which it was best suited. In the laboratory, however, information could be given to one hemisphere without the other hemisphere's awareness; this made it possible to discover the differentiated functions of the two hemispheres.

From the experiments with split-brain patients, Joseph Bogen, Roger Sperry, and their colleagues and students, came to a remarkable conclusion: It became apparent to them that there were *two minds running along together in the same head!* Joseph Bogen called the duality of the hemispheres the yin and yang of human experience—the basis for dualities throughout history.

Let me give you an example. In one of the simplest experiments, the experimenter and the patient sat on two sides of a table with a curtain between them. The patient would put his or her hand through the curtain, and the experimenter would place a plastic shape in either the left or right hand that the patient could not see. If the experimenter placed the shape in the patient's right hand, where the information is fed into the left hemisphere, the patient could name the shape instantly. However, if the shape was placed in the patient's left hand, which sends information to the right hemisphere, he or she could not say what it was. If the examiner held up a set of pictures of a square, a rectangle and a circle, the patient was able to point to the correct picture with perfect accuracy. The right hemisphere recognized shapes, but the left hemisphere supplied the names. When the two hemispheres couldn't communicate with each other, the patient could recognize, but was unable to name, unseen objects placed in his or her left hand.

But there was one split-brain patient in Jerre's study who managed to do the impossible: a 15-year-old boy, "L.B." L.B. presented a project on split-brain research in his biology class, complete with detailed drawings, and explained how objects placed in his left hand, from behind a screen, could not be named by his right hemisphere, which has no speech. After L.B. gave Jerre a "freshman-level lecture on the split-brain syndrome," Jerre handed him discs, squares and rectangles in his hidden left hand. L.B. would pause for a long time after each presentation, and then correctly name the shape. He performed this feat ten times in a row. Jerre was stunned. "Something funny was going on" and it was messing up her dissertation! She said, "All right L.B., you just told me not ten minutes ago why you're not supposed to be able to name anything in your left hand. How were you doing it, then?" Amazed that he had gotten every one of them right, L.B. exclaimed, "I did??" He said he wasn't sure how he had done it, but he would tell her what had happened if she would take him to Baskin-Robbins and buy him a banana split! (Now, doesn't that sound like a gifted kid?)

L.B.'s description of what happened to him left an indelible impression on me. He said that he felt himself looking around the room, and then his eyes would fixate on something, like the doorknob, and he figured it must be a circle. Sometimes he would stare at a tile on the floor and he'd think, "I'll bet that it's a square." And sometimes his eyes would trace the outline of the door and he knew it was a rectangle. Jerre asked L.B. whether he thought his right hemisphere guided his eye movements. He responded:

"No! I did!"
"But how did you know what to look at?"
"The shape I was feeling."
"But how did you know what you were feeling?"
"Because I was looking at the shape!" (He couldn't see the shape.)

L.B.'s left hemisphere denied any role to the right hemisphere and went around in circles in trying to explain his success in naming the shapes. Jerre used this anecdote about L.B. to demonstrate that the right hemisphere is aware that it is not alone, and that it attempts to communicate with this other consciousness through clever strategies it invents.

The left hemisphere, on the other hand, does not appear to share this awareness. "I think the left hemisphere is totally egocentric. The left hemisphere only has an apprehension of itself." Jerre shared that there had been many occasions when experimenters had the distinct impression that the right hemisphere is aware that it is cohabitating the brain with another consciousness. But she could think of no instances in which the left hemisphere tried to communicate with the right. "The left hemisphere never gives any indication that it is aware of another being in there."

Jerre told me recently that the fact that there are two minds in split-brain patients does not mean that normal people have two minds. However, the thought that we might have two minds has fascinated me for two decades. We all are aware that we carry on mental arguments. Who is arguing with whom? Learning about L.B.'s experience was a catalyst for me to become aware of another consciousness that seems to have access to information that my logical left hemisphere doesn't have. Let me tell you a couple of stories about myself. See if you have ever had anything like this happen to you.

I have a large wrought iron key with four hooks that I hang my necklaces on. (It probably was made for keys!) One evening, when the hooks got too full, I had to find another place to put some of the necklaces. I decided to move the shorter ones, and I didn't want to put them in a jewelry box where they might get entangled. It occurred to me that they sell Lucite necklace racks in jewelry departments and I could buy one the next day. But suddenly I received a very strong impression that I had something in the house that would work perfectly. I can't explain whether it was a feeling, a sense, a message, or an intuitive knowing (or all of these), but it sure was insistent.

I found myself looking around the room, exactly the same way that L.B. had described. Nothing. I looked in my closets. Nothing. Then I walked into another room. Nothing. I was starting to get annoyed, and began arguing mentally with this entity (or whatever it was) that it was sending me on a wild goose chase. It was persistent. I couldn't shake the feeling. I went downstairs and began to look in each room. Nothing. I was getting more and more irritated and argumentative, but it was to no avail. The impression would not go away.

When I went into the living room, my eyes drifted until they fixated (just like L.B.'s) on this beautiful wooden eagle that our son, Damion, had given to me as a gift. "The eagle??" I asked, in disbelief. This made absolutely no sense to me. Remember, I have no spatial relations. So, with enormous skepticism, I took the eagle upstairs and hung the necklaces on the bird's wings. They fit perfectly, cleverly turning a statue that was just collecting dust into a most unusual necklace stand. I was flabbergasted. I had no logical way of knowing that the eagle would serve this purpose. And I could not figure out who or what was communicating this information to me. I decided it must be my

"Guardian Angel." Perhaps my Guardian Angel is actually my right hemisphere!

On another occasion, I was speaking in Vancouver, British Columbia, and I tore one of my fingernails. I needed some kind of nail wrap to keep the nail together. If I had just used glue, it would have broken off completely in no time. (This would not have been a major tragedy, but I'm vain about my nails.) I had a cold, the hotel I was staying in was not close to any stores, and it was freezing outside, so I wasn't inclined to go out. Another message came to me, like the first one, that there was something in the room that I could use to repair my nail. I looked around, couldn't find anything, and began to get irritated, like I had with the necklace episode. I argued in my head that I wasn't going to destroy a pillowcase. I was certain that there was nothing in that little room that would be useful. But, again, the impression was insistent.

I kept hunting, getting more and more agitated. (My irritation had absolutely no effect on the feeling either time.) Then my eyes fixated on the wet teabag in my cup. "The teabag?" Sure enough, cutting up a small piece of the used teabag and gluing it to the nail worked perfectly. Who would've thought... These two incidents convinced me that Jerre was right. The "me" I identify with is my logical, thinking, talking mind that lives in time and has limited experience. But there clearly was another part of me that "knew" things that "I" didn't know and could communicate with "me" through images. I would love to know if you've had similar experiences.

On the tape, Jerre said, "The...right hemisphere is encompassing the whole world." I shivered when I heard this. Is it possible that we all have two consciousnesses within us—one that is caught in time, projects the past onto the future, and feels alone and separate—and another that lives outside time, in the eternal now, and is aware of—and connected with—All That Is? If so, do these two consciousnesses inhabit different hemispheres?

> The right hemisphere is also the portal leading to the world of the invisible. It is the realm of altered states of consciousness where faith and mystery rule over logic. There is compelling evidence that dreaming occurs primarily in the right brain. (Shlain, 1998, pp. 19-20)

Living with two realities

If each hemisphere does represent a different reality, what would this mean? Here is the most recent picture that has come to me about how our two minds might function. Let's suppose that our right hemisphere allows us to absorb all that is happening in a given situation and our left hemisphere is the recording secretary—the archivist. The left hemisphere records snapshots of our experience and preserves them in memory so that we can use them to make future judgments. There is no possible way for our secretary to keep an accurate account of every single detail in our lives. In one instant, we take in much more information visually, auditorally, viscerally, emotionally, intuitively and cognitively than we can store in our memory banks. Our secretary must determine what is "important" to record and file in memory. It selects elements that fit with our belief systems, and filters out all the rest.

This filtered set of perceptions becomes our reality, our convictions, our truths, and influences everything else that we store in memory. Our accumulated judgments, based on selective memories, become the basis of our stories about ourselves and others, and color what we remember in any situation. This phenomenon can be seen in the fact that several witnesses to the same event often describe it entirely differently, depending on the meaning they make of the event.

The snapshots of life that the left hemisphere records give us a static perception of reality that we use to explain, predict and control our environment. By rapidly scanning its snapshots, the left hemisphere can create the illusion of movement through space, in much the way a movie looks to us like it is continuous action instead of a collection of individual frames. But the right hemisphere actually grasps movement in space and captures the dynamic flow of change. It not only sees more at a glance, it perceives it all in motion. So there is, in fact, much more information available in all situations than whatever our left hemisphere recollects and records. Our right hemisphere, which sees the whole, has access to this additional information.

> In computer language, the left brain is digital and the right brain is analog. Even if the left brain is recording information at very tiny intervals, between any two points on a line, no matter how closely spaced they are, there are an infinite number of other points, hence an infinite amount of information that the right brain has that the left brain loses.

When we believe that the information our left-hemispheric secretaries have stored in our memory banks is the whole truth and nothing but the truth, we become rigid and judgmental. We think there is only one reality and that our perceptions and recollections are perfectly accurate. Instead of thinking, "I remember this differently; I wonder if I'm missing something," we dogmatically assume, "I'm right and you're wrong. You're distorting The Truth." This leads to conflict among families, friends, colleagues, clans, and countries. When we realize that we probably don't have the whole picture because there is no way to retain it all in memory, we're more open to other viewpoints, and more willing to listen to people who see the situation differently.

Regularly tuning into the right hemisphere allows us greater flexibility, tolerance, and wisdom.

The cost of denigrating our other reality

We all have two hemispheres. We all have access to the two modes of awareness that they represent. More and more people are embarking on a spiritual quest, sometimes in midlife, sometimes earlier, that involves tuning into inner wisdom. Many cultures, religions, spiritual groups, and individuals engage in practices aimed at reducing inner chatter and allowing more access to "higher consciousness."

> Context, in our life, trumps text, not the other way around. "Higher consciousness" is another way of putting it. (Ornstein, 1997, p. 159)

> An emphasis on activities of the right hemisphere...is the way many of the esoteric Christian, Jewish, Sufi, and other mystical traditions operate. They listen to low tones in chants, view spatial diagrams, puzzle over phrases that have no rational meaning, and attempt exercises to produce a state of "no conceptualizing while remaining fully awake."

> That is why some of the techniques of the spiritual efforts are described as "not for your mind," or are held by others to be "anti-rational." The aim is the simulation of a new kind of mental configuration... Even the very different forms of meditation serve this purpose: They are nonverbal, or they use music, or they are movement oriented. The meditation method most often used consists of silently repeating or chanting a phrase over and over, or of concentrating on one object not only to become relaxed but also to turn off the normal internal talk, lessening the hold of the verbal mode. (pp. 164-165)

Still, there are many who dismiss the possibility that there may be another reality besides the one available to us through logic. This rejecting attitude has taken its toll on all who trust intuition, spiritual awareness, and their own inner knowing. But overly logical people also pay a heavy price for this stance. It's damaging to our psychological health and spiritual development when we give our left hemisphere the power to reject our right hemisphere.

We expend an inordinate amount of psychic energy defending ourselves from blame and ridicule, and the vast majority of time the judgments we're defending against are from *ourselves*! Can you imagine what it would be like to totally accept yourself, and not have to justify your thoughts, your actions, your reasoning? Not have to defend yourself? Not have to answer, "Why did you do that?" "Why didn't you...?" No, "you should haves"? We're so used to living in an internal court of law that we assume it's natural and appropriate to continually prosecute ourselves. But it's only our left hemispheres running amok.

Our left hemisphere demands reasons for our actions. Our right hemisphere could care less why we did what we did. Judgment is a left-hemispheric function. Lacking discernment, the right hemisphere simply accepts what is; it makes no judgment about what "should be." It has no concept of right and wrong, so it doesn't hold grudges. It has no attachment to being right, so it isn't intent on making others wrong. It never hollers at us for being late, because it has no concept of time. It doesn't blame or lay guilt trips. (To break my own defensive patterns, I've come up with a new house rule. If I'm there, "it's my fault"—regardless of what it is. If I'm not there, it's not my fault. It's amazing how freeing it is when you stop trying to defend yourself from blame.)

I'm **not** implying that your right hemisphere is the good guy and your left hemisphere is the bad guy. The right hemisphere is perceptive, receptive, and accepting, but it's not capable of action. It *is* rather than *does*. Is-ness is nice in the ethereal sense, but it doesn't feed your family. If you only exist and you don't do anything, what are you contributing? If you're totally work oriented, and never stop to smell the roses, where is the joy in living? *You need both **being** and **doing** to be whole.*

However, we've spent the last 5,000 years subordinating our right hemispheres to our left, and this is what I'm questioning. The left hemisphere explains, predicts, controls, compares, contrasts, rank orders (e.g., best to worst), and creates hierarchies. Hierarchies are pecking orders or chains of command, specifying power relations: who has the most power and who is subordinate to whom. The right hemisphere sees the whole—the vast network of inter-relationships—in a non-hierarchical manner. It has no mechanism for determining good, better or best. Everyone and everything is of equal value. There are no subordinates. We think hierarchies are the natural order of things because left-hemispheric values have dominated society for so long. But consensual decision-making for the good of all is a wise alternative.

When the left hemisphere is allowed to dominate without guidance from the right hemisphere, it isn't a pretty picture. The inner prosecution we subject ourselves to is a step away from persecution. Some of us bludgeon ourselves with unrelenting self-blame. When we pooh-pooh this other way of knowing in ourselves and in others, we engage in an unconscious, perfectly acceptable form of bigotry. If logic is better than emotion, then objective is better than subjective; facts are better than intuition; scientific proof is better than folk wisdom; right-handedness is better than left-handedness; civilized is better than tribal; boys are better than girls; and our people are better than your people. Pitting the left hemisphere against the right fosters domination and aggression. There are winners and losers. The result is war—internal and external.

The right hemisphere isn't territorial. There's no "we against them": there's only *us*. Our right hemisphere recognizes that all that exists is an indispensable part of the whole. Boundaries of any kind are all born in separateness, rather than in the Oneness. In the Oneness, no one owns anyone or anything, so there's nothing to fight over.

> The left brain cleaved the right brain's integrated sense of wholeness into a duality that resulted in humans creating a distinction between me-in-there and world-out-there. The ego requires duality to gain perspective. Dualism also enhanced the human penchant for objective thinking, which in turn increased our reasoning skills and eventually led to logic.

> Logic is not holistic, nor is it conceived as a gestalt. It click-clacks along the left brain's linear railway of sequence. If-then syllogisms, the basis of logic, have become the most reliable method of foretelling the future. They have all but replaced omens, visions, and intuition. The rules of logic form the foundation of science, education, business, and military strategy. (Shlain, 1998, p. 22)

I once went looking in every bookstore in Raleigh, North Carolina, for a history book that wasn't about war, and couldn't find one. That says something about what we consider important enough to document as "history." We record all our battles—who won, who lost, who controlled which territory for how long. History begins with the written word. "Prehistoric" conjures up dinosaurs, and "historical" sends our minds back to ancient Greece. But what happened in between? Archeologists are finding that prior to the chronicle of conquerors in history books were tens of thousands of years when people lived peaceably—when the right hemisphere appears to have guided civilization.

Am I recommending that we go back to those innocent times? No, that isn't possible. Our later developing left hemisphere is here for a reason. It's responsible for the advancements that have brought us to modern times. However, we can no longer afford to live in the shadow of its domination. It needs to be tempered by the values of the right hemisphere. Leonard Shlain describes these as follows:

> The values that typify the right brain include empathy with the plight of one's companions, generosity toward strangers, tolerance of dissent, love of nature, nurturance of children, laughter, playfulness, mysticism, forgiveness of enemies and nonviolence. These aspects, in both men and women, express the feminine gatherer/nurturer side of human nature. (Shlain, 1998, p. 338)

If you're a woman or a visual-spatial learner, please don't get the idea that you're above the fray. The values, attitudes, beliefs and imbalance that create war are in all of us—not just males or those who live in their left hemispheres. We're all members of the same species, so we're all in the same boat. Throughout time, the oppressed have had exactly the same value system as the oppressors, and have been the major enforcers of that value system with their peers and the young. Slaves believed in slavery. No matter what the rules of our society are, or how bizarre they may appear to future generations, the job of parents and teachers is to help children adapt to those rules so that they can survive. And we really show how much we buy into the system in the way we persecute ourselves with our own internal messages. So none of us is exempt from this predicament.

Our species has been war-like for so many centuries that it seems sometimes that there is no other way we can be. The 20th century hosted the holocaust, the atom bomb, ethnic cleansing, and children annihilating their classmates. During my lifetime, we've come dangerously close to wiping out the entire planet. But I believe we have a greater destiny. I'm convinced that we can move beyond our war-mongering history, and create a world in which both hemispheres work together for the good of all. We've demonstrated many times in the past that humankind is capable of cooperation, of partnership, of acceptance of individual differences, of peaceful co-existence. And, despite the terrorist attacks of late (and maybe even because of them), I'm convinced that we will move closer and closer to this ideal in the 21st century. To my way of thinking, the first step is accepting and integrating the two different realities that lie within us all.

Toward integration

A *holistic, simultaneous, synthetic,* and *concrete* view of the world are the essential characteristics of a feminine outlook; *linear, sequential, reductionist,* and *abstract* thinking defines the masculine. Although these represent opposite perceptual modes, every individual is generously endowed with all the features of both. They coexist...with no feature superior to its reciprocal. (Shlain, 1998, p.1)

Our left and right hemispheres are of equal value, and are most effective when they cooperate with each other. Problems occur when our hemispheres don't communicate and when the balance of power between them is out of whack. Remember the quotation in the last chapter from Robert Ornstein (1997, p. 84) about the right hemisphere developing first and the left hemisphere being "*far more vulnerable than the right*"? When I combined Leonard Shlain's and Robert Ornstein's ideas metaphorically, it conjured up an interesting fairy tale of the sibling relations of the two hemispheres. (The following parable was written for your right hemisphere. If you get literal on me, you'll miss the point. It's **not** about males and females; it's about the relationship between everyone's inner masculine and feminine.)

A Parable on Inner Harmony

Once upon a moonbeam, there lived a sister and brother. The older sister was mute, elusive, forgetful, and had no appreciation of time whatsoever, but she adored her younger brother, and was very protective of him. She understood that because he was younger, he was less aware, less experienced, and extremely vulnerable. She lived in darkness and only made her presence known to him in dreams and visions. The youth was completely unaware of his sister's existence because she did not appear during his waking hours. He was the prince. He had the power to determine good and bad, right and wrong, what will be and what will not be, by his own will. When he was very young, he became infatuated with his power and desired to see how vast his empire could become. He tried to conquer the whole world and bring it under his dominion. Still, his sister held him in her heart. For thousands of years he waged war. Though he became the mightiest warrior, it never fulfilled him. He was lonely. His sister waited. Sometimes, in the stillness of night, he sensed a mysterious entity beyond his control. Slowly his curiosity about her grew stronger. When she visited him in his dreams, he felt peaceful and whole. He wished he could have more connection with her. As he matured, he began to appreciate how much he needed his silent partner. She needed her brother as well, to give voice to her visions. His respect for her wisdom grew and grew. Finally, he grasped the depth of their connection and knew that his sister would be with him for all time. He was no longer alone. They formed an enduring partnership and beauty, peace and prosperity flourished throughout the land.

Regardless of how we write the tale, in the end, the younger brother and the older sister become equal partners, because they must. (Besides, I like happy endings!) After all, Homo sapiens are wise, intelligent creatures, even if in our youth, we show little wisdom. We're still very much in our youth as a species, but we're beginning to grow up.

Higher development—growing up spiritually—requires paying attention to the gentler part of ourselves. We need to make room for it in our lives. We can access our right hemispheres through meditation, music, art, movement, being close to nature, delighting in children—anything that brings us joy. All of these enable us, at least temporarily, to quiet our continuous stream of words and our constant torrent of judgments. Our judgments are so overpowering, and so much a part of our upbringing, that it's difficult to truly love and accept all parts of ourselves. Learning how to accept ourselves allows us to fully accept others—our mates, our children, our friends, our colleagues, our teachers, our students. Each time we judge ourselves, each time we judge another, we enter into separateness. Only that which is separate can stand in judgment as if it were outside the Oneness. In the Oneness all that we are is acceptable. This is the gift of higher consciousness— a gift well worth striving toward.

> When we move our minds beyond polarity thinking of Imagination versus Intellect, we no longer have to think about moving from one to the other or balancing them or questioning one or the other. When we move out of duality, the two work smoothly together as they were designed to do. (Stephanie Tolan, personal communication, August 4, 2002)

A vision of education in the 21st century

On January 1st, 2001, we planted our feet firmly in a new millennium. Its newness is fertile soil for fresh ideas. A new millennium permits us to question the traditional ways of doing things. It invites change. We're all pioneers in this brave new world. I'd like to share with you the inevitable changes that I see coming very soon in our schools. I'm excited about the future of education.

We heard a lot in the 20th century about educational "reform." "Reform" implies an outside force imposing its will on a reluctant party. Remember when kids were threatened that if they didn't behave they would be sent to "reform" school? There is a genuine inner transformation—a metamorphosis—in the wind. Momentous changes are coming, but they will come from within, rather than from reformers. They'll mirror the momentous changes that are occurring in our culture. They'll be a natural adaptation to the alterations in our way of life.

Through their inventions, visual-spatial learners are bringing about this cultural transformation, and VSLs of the future will find school a wondrous, happy place to grow. Before we go there, let's view the future within the context of the past.

Once upon a time, very few people were educated. Education was the privilege of an elite, wealthy class that held all the power and ruled the uneducated masses. Each book was handwritten and very expensive. Then the printing press was invented (probably by a VSL—they're the inventors). This revolutionized cultures worldwide, allowing more people access to knowledge. Knowledge is power. Someone came up with the brilliant idea of educating the masses so that everyone would be able to read the books and share the power of knowledge. Schools cropped up all over the world to accomplish the ambitious endeavor of teaching everyone to read and write and calculate (all left-hemispheric functions). School became the route to knowledge and, eventually, the portal to well-paying positions in adult life.

Educational institutions gradually became all powerful, determining what would be taught, who would be eligible to receive the information, and who was sufficiently "trained" (a military term) to be able to practice a field in adult life. In a very left-hemispheric, analytical way, the curriculum of life was dissected into courses, the courses were dissected into "hours" of instruction (time, another left-hemispheric concept), and knowledge was accumulated in units of "credit hours." Number of "hours one sat" through courses somehow equated with expertise. Instead of fellow travelers sharing knowledge, educators became gate-keepers, giving assignments and tests to preserve the standards of their fields, and evaluation (a left-hemispheric function) ran the entire production. This system seemed perfectly reasonable until quite recently, when another invention revolutionized access to information: the computer.

The computer is to the Age of Information what the printing press was to the Age of Literacy. The Age of Information means that we can gain access to whatever information we want or need if we know how to ask the computer the right questions. Encyclopedias are obsolete. Libraries are available at our fingertips. Instead of waiting forever in a line or on the phone, the answer to every question is, "Search the Net." Technology has already altered our lives, our culture, our role as educators, and the changes are going to be even more dramatic in the coming years.

Have you noticed that there are teenage millionaires who made their fortune outside of school inventing software? (They were on Oprah.) Have you noticed that the computer industry is hiring talented teens right out of high school, rendering college degrees less essential than they once were? Have you noticed that hundreds of the most advanced children are dropping out of elementary school and being home-schooled? Have you noticed that many brilliant young children are attending college? These are all harbingers of the shifts we can expect to see in the 21st century. Educational institutions are losing their control (a left-hemispheric need).

Life with computers requires reading and writing, but also some additional skills. The visual presentation of information, the keyboard, the mouse, icons, graphic displays, the de-emphasis on time, all bring the right hemisphere into the act. Internet has made information much more widely accessible than books. There's greater interaction with the learner. The computer doesn't decide in advance what it wants to tell you about. You have to ask it questions. You have to learn how to ask the right questions, where to look for the information, and how to quickly scan through irrelevant information to find what you're looking for. You have to be wise enough to discern the wheat from the chaff. You have to be able to synthesize the information you receive. These are some of the important life skills that children of the 21st century will need to learn in school.

The 20th century belonged to auditory-sequential learners. Literacy reigned supreme. "Literate" and "educated" were synonymous, and "illiterate" equated with "ignorant." (So says the computer thesaurus!) Reading, spelling and handwriting depend on auditory-sequential skills and develop linear sequential reasoning further. The emphasis on literacy in the schools since the end of the last century is a testament to the panic our society is experiencing as consciousness begins to shift from the word to the image.

> Although we cannot be sure that dyslexia was not always among us, it seems to have erupted at the very moment that an entire generation was devaluing the left-hemispheric mode of knowing. Perhaps television is the agent equilibrating the human brain's two differing modes of perception...
>
> Many dyslexics are talented artists, architects, musicians, composers, dancers, and surgeons.... As culture becomes more comfortable with its reliance on images, it may turn out that dyslexia will be reassessed as another of the many harbingers that announced the arrival of the Iconic Revolution. (Shlain, 1998, p. 413)

Reading ability is still necessary in this millennium, but it's not as central as it was in the 20th century. There are many more ways to gain information now, so that a non-reader can be highly educated: film, video, Books (on tape) for the Blind and Dyslexic. Computers are already beginning to talk to us and voice-activated computers are becoming common. And we've barely dipped our toe into this century.

On the other hand, "visual literacy," technological proficiency, and imagery, will become increasingly important as the century progresses. We'll need to learn how to think visually ourselves and to teach visual skills to the next generation of learners. It's very likely that in the near future another type of disability will gain our attention.

> We are all born with the ability to think visually, to what extent depends on each individual's genetic inheritance. A great deal of the human brain's wiring is devoted to vision. But whereas a lack of ability to think in terms of the one-directional sequential aspect of language, whether in words or figures, is regarded as a "disability" in our society, the disability of those who have difficulty in recognising or developing their visual (three-dimensional) cognitive capacity goes unnoticed. (Sue Parkinson, February 17, 2000).

The beneficial aspects of visual-spatial reasoning will become more prized in this century as technology continues to advance. The main advantages of this way of knowing, as Steve Haas has summarized them, are:

- Perceiving the whole quickly
- Finding patterns easily
- Thinking graphically
- Understanding dimensionality

We may find that we're devoting as much classroom instruction to the above skills as we do now to the auditory-sequential skills involved in literacy.

Testing will be commonplace to determine the type of learner our students are before we teach them. This is already starting to happen.

> I am a visual-spatial learner. I did not realize this until I was out of college. I arranged to take a battery of tests to see what type of job would suit me best. One of the tests involved 3 dimensional cubes with multiple choices on how the cube would look if laid out flat. I scored in the 99 percentile on this test. Even then, I did not realize what this meant....

> I am a 31-year-old female who has recently taken a test which stated that I was a visual-spatial learner... I was in a gifted class back in the 7th grade about 1984. Can you please help me find out more information about how I am different and others like me, and how I could maybe help myself finally achieve something in life instead of always struggling to survive...

Students are eager to find out how they learn best. This type of testing will be welcomed instead of feared—especially when there is no *right* way to learn.

I predict that soon the amount of time we spend teaching manuscript and handwriting is going to be drastically reduced. Each child will have his or her own computer, so keyboarding will replace handwriting as the most important life skill we can teach children—that is, of course, until voice-activated computers become so inexpensive that they replace keyboards in the classroom. Penmanship may come under the umbrella of art in future classrooms, with lots of time to develop one's own artistic hand.

Handwriting, once essential to recording information so that it could be preserved and handed on, is now a very inefficient method of note taking—rarely used for that purpose in adult life. Most of us prefer to type than to write. So handwriting is likely to follow the same path as sewing. Do you remember when sewing was a requirement rather than an elective? For girls, that is. When I was in 8th grade, I had to take sewing and home economics, while the boys took woodshop. For thousands of years, sewing was an indispensable part of the curriculum of girls. The sewing machine (another VSL invention) rendered it obsolete. Now, inexpensive, ready-made clothes are readily available, and sewing is considered an art form.

When each child has a computer, all education will be individualized. Computers individualize with ease. Bright children will not be sitting in class waiting for the others to catch up. And no child will be lagging behind the class. All children will progress at their own rate. Grades will disappear. So will grading. Computers will eliminate their necessity. They will decide when each child is ready to go on to the next step in learning. When computers become the dispensers of knowledge, teachers will be free to become facilitators of learning. More time will be spent on *class discussions, group projects, real-life experiences, community building, conflict resolution,* and *global awareness.* The fun stuff!

Students are going to play a much more active role in their learning in the 21st century than they did in the 20th. They won't be passive recipients taking up space, getting grades, and accumulating credits. I'd be willing to bet that students will begin to decide what they want to learn instead of our deciding that for them. School will become much more relevant, motivating and exciting. No more cries of "boring." Of course, we'll still need schools, but they'll be a more joyous, integrated part of our experience than they are today. You're going to love it!

As our emphasis shifts from memorization to *concept formation, problem finding, gathering of information, pattern recognition,* and *creative expression,* visual-spatial learners will no longer feel like dunces. They'll shine. And auditory-sequential learners won't be left in the dust either. They, too, are going to love school more, when there's more *visual stimulation, hands-on materials, discovery learning,* and *meaningful curriculum.* We don't have to wait for the distant future for this to happen. We're already in the 21st century. These changes can happen today. Please share this vision with me.

Notes:

Afterword

I wrote **Upside-Down Brilliance** to legitimize the VSL experience. I hope it's helped all of you to appreciate this other way of knowing. That it has reduced the fears of all of you parents and allowed you to celebrate the uniqueness of your child. That it has provided all of you teachers with simple ways of finding visual-spatial students and practical methods of reaching them from preschool to graduate school. As more and more VSLs appear in the world, we need to have greater awareness of their differences and knowledge of how to meet their needs. These are the children of this new millennium.

And I hope that this book will make all of you VSLs love and accept yourselves more. In the 20th century, visual-spatial learners were misfits.

> I had/have few friends. The ones I have are very close. I always felt like I didn't "fit in".

We need you. We need you to lead us into the 21st century, to help us understand how to parent and teach children who are like you. You're the forerunners of the shifting consciousness on the planet and we have much to learn from you. The 20th century is over. Let's leave the hurt behind and build a new world together.

> What matters to me right now is there is an explanation for the problems I experienced in school. There is an explanation, proof, support for the awkwardness, for not seeing things the way others see them. I finally have a place I fit in.

If you know individuals—young or old—who fit the characteristics of the visual-spatial learner, they'll be grateful to you for passing on this information. Until now, they've just felt weird or stupid. You're welcome to copy Appendix C and share it. I pray that this book will be healing to those wounded spirits who have spent most of their lives burdened by self-doubt because of their differences.

It's hard to say goodbye. Although I've been waiting for this book to be finished for years, now that it is, I'm going to miss it. **Upside-Down Brilliance** has been writing me, changing my awareness. Most of what I've written before this was largely guided by my left hemisphere. Each time I tried to import something I had written previously, the book rejected it and demanded that it be completely reconstructed, line by line, word by word. The message was, "wrong tone." Whenever my left hemisphere took over the writing, I got an insistent: "wrong voice." My right hemisphere may not have speech, but it stops me cold whenever something doesn't "sound right."

I've learned a lot in writing this book. Many of the best ideas in the book I didn't know until I wrote them! I'm grateful to my right hemisphere for all the guidance I received in the process. I learned that the right hemisphere simply will not be rushed. It refuses to spew out ideas on the left hemisphere's time schedule. I learned that I cannot force good writing by number of hours in which seat is planted on chair and eyes are glued to screen. If I don't take time out for fun, the writing isn't fun, and the book isn't fun to read (not to mention what it does to my back and my eyes).

My mother said I should write for two hours as soon as I get up in the morning and then take a break. You know, I found that if I listened to her, the writing came much easier. Realizations would come to me just before I fell asleep or woke up and my access to them was better first thing in the morning.

I wrote a sunny ending to this book in the spring of 2001. but September 11th, 2001 changed everything. It was a terrible wake-up call. We learned in the blink of an eye the extent of our planetary inter-dependence. People of all faiths, all colors, all ethnic groups, all nationalities, bonded in sorrow, and vowed to end terrorism on the planet. The bigotry and blind hatred of a few is fostering greater appreciation of diversity among the many.

We all pray for peace. But we've known for a long time that peace begins from within. I believe that in order to end terrorism in the world, we need to end our inner terrorism. If we invite the wisdom of our right hemisphere, context (what is good for all) will inform the text of our lives. It's time to end the war of the hemispheres and develop all of our inner resources. The fate of the world depends on it. If we have not grown enough to take on this developmental task, we will remain in an internal battle, which spills over into the world. Every single human being who is brave enough to embark on the journey toward integration brings the planet that much closer to peace.

Bibliography

References for Preface

Roeper, A. (1989). Empathy, ethics, and global education. *Understanding Our Gifted,* 1(6), 1, 7-10.

Shlain, L. (1998). *The alphabet versus the goddess*: The conflict between word and image. New York: Penguin/Arkana.

References for Introduction

Eliot, J., & Smith., I. R. (1983). *An international directory of spatial tests.* Windsor, Berks, England: NFER-NELSON.

Flynn, J. R. (1984). The mean IQ of Americans: Massive gains 1932 to 1978. *Psychological Bulletin, 95,* 29-51.

Flynn, J. R. (1999). Searching for justice: The discovery of IQ gains over time. *American Psychologist, 54,* 5-20.

Freed, J., & Parsons, L. (1997). *Right-brained children in a left-brained world: Unlocking the potential of your ADD child.* New York: Simon & Schuster.

Gohm, C. L., Humphreys, L. G., & Yao, G. (1998). Underachievement among spatially gifted students. *American Educational Research Journal, 35,* 515-531.

Grandin, T. (1995). *Thinking in pictures and other reports from my life with autism.* New York: Doubleday.

Humphreys., L. G., Lubinski., D., & Yao, G. (1993). Utility of predicting group membership and the role of spatial visualization in becoming an engineer, physical scientist, or artist. *Journal of Applied Psychology, 78,* 250-261.

Jacobson, L. (2000, August 14). A virtual class act; Technology aims to help hyperactive students. *Washington Post,* p. A07. [Discusses work of A. Rizzo]

Shlain, L. (1998). *The alphabet versus the goddess: The conflict between word and image.* New York: Penguin/Arkana.

West, T. G. (1991). *In the mind's eye: Visual thinkers, gifted people with learning difficulties, computer images, and the ironies of creativity.* Buffalo, NY: Prometheus Press.

References for Chapter One: How It All Began

Davis, R. D. (1994,1997). *The gift of dyslexia.* New York: Perigee, Penguin Putnam.

Dixon, J. P. (1983). *The spatial child.* Springfield, IL: Charles C. Thomas.

Gardner, H. G. (1983). *Frames of mind: The theory of multiple intelligences.* New York: Basic.

Lohman, D. F. (1994). Spatially gifted, verbally inconvenienced. In N. Colangelo, S. G. Assouline, & D. L. Ambroson (Eds.). Talent development: *Proceedings from the 1993 Henry B. and Jocelyn Wallace National Research Symposium on Talent Development* (pp. 251-264). Dayton, OH: Ohio Psychology Press.

Ringle, J., Miller, S., & Anderson, R. (2000). *Reading achievement results integrating Davis Learning Strategies in the special education and special reading classroom.* Year 1 — 1999-2000. Report for Sherrard Elementary School. Sherrard, IL: Authors.

Silverman, L. K. (1989c). The visual-spatial learner. *Preventing School Failure, 34*(1), 15-20.

Springer, S. P., & Deutsch, G. (1998). *Left brain/Right brain: Perspectives from cognitive neuroscience* (5ᵗʰ ed.). New York: W. H. Freeman.

References for Chapter Two: The Power of the Right Hemisphere

Hein, R. (in preparation). *It takes one to teach one.*

Levy, J. (1980). Cerebral asymmetry and the psychology of man. In M. C. Wittrock (Ed.), *The brain and psychology* (pp. 245-321). New York: Academic Press.

Levy, J. (1982, November 1). *Brain research: Myths and realities for the gifted male and female.* Paper presented at the Illinois Gifted Education Conference, Chicago, IL. (private cassette recording)

Levy, J. (2000). Hemispheric function. In A. E. Kazdin (Editor-in-Chief), *Encyclopedia of psychology* (Vol. 4, pp. 113-115). Oxford University Press, Oxford, England: American Psychological Association Books.

Lohman, D. F. (1994). Spatially gifted, verbally inconvenienced. In N. Colangelo, S. G. Assouline, & D. L. Ambroson (Eds.). *Talent development: Proceedings from the 1993 Henry B. and Jocelyn Wallace National Research Symposium on Talent Development* (pp. 251-264). Dayton, OH: Ohio Psychology Press.

Ornstein, R. (1997). *The right mind: Making sense of the hemispheres.* New York: Harcourt Brace.

Shlain, L. (1998). *The alphabet versus the goddess: The conflict between word and image.* New York: Penguin/Arkana.

Silverman, L. K. (1998a). Personality and learning styles of gifted children. In. J. VanTassel-Baska (Ed.), *Excellence in educating gifted & talented learners* (3ʳᵈ ed., pp. 29-65). Denver: Love.

Springer, S. P., & Deutsch, G. (1998). *Left brain/Right brain: Perspectives from cognitive neuroscience* (5ᵗʰ ed.). New York: W. H. Freeman.

West, T. G. (1991). *In the mind's eye: Visual thinkers, gifted people with learning difficulties, computer images, and the ironies of creativity.* Buffalo, NY: Prometheus Press.

References for Chapter Three: The Hidden Culprit in Underachievement

Downs, M. P. (1985). Effects of mild hearing loss on auditory processing. *Otolaryngologic Clinics of North America, 18*, 337-343.

Feagans, L. (1986). Otitis media: A model for long term effects with implications for intervention. In J. Kavanaugh (Ed.). *Otitis media and child development.* Parkton, MD: York Press.

Grandin, T. (1995). *Thinking in pictures and other reports from my life with autism.* New York: Doubleday.

Kimura, D. (1993). *Neuromotor mechanisms in human communication.* New York: Oxford University Press.

Levy, J. (2000). Hemispheric function. In A. E. Kazdin (Editor-in-Chief), *Encyclopedia of psychology* (Vol. 8). Oxford University Press, Oxford, England: American Psychological Association Books.

Ornstein, R. (1997). *The right mind: Making sense of the hemispheres.* New York: Harcourt Brace.

Peterson, K. (1985a, May 7). Madonna maniacs! *USA Today*, pp. 1D-2D.

Peterson, K. (1985b, May 17). Undervalued siblings of the gifted. *USA Today*, p. 1D.

Shlain, L. (1998). *The alphabet versus the goddess: The conflict between word and image*. New York: Penguin/Arkana.

Silverman, L. K. (1986). An interview with Elizabeth Hagen: Giftedness, intelligence and the new Stanford-Binet. *Roeper Review, 8,* 168-171.

Silverman, L. K. (1989a). Invisible gifts, invisible handicaps. *Roeper Review, 12,* 37-42.

Silverman, L. K. (1996). Lost IQ points: The brighter the child, the greater the loss. In D.J. Lim, C.D. Bluestone, M. Casselbrant, J.O. Klein, & P.L. Ogra (Eds.), *Proceedings of the Sixth International Symposium on Recent Advances in Otitis Media* (pp. 342-346). Hamilton, Ontario: B.C. Decker.

Silverman, L. K. (2001). Diagnosing and treating visual perceptual issues in gifted children. *Journal of Optometric Vision Development, 32*(3), 153-176.

Springer, S. P., & Deutsch, G. (1998). *Left brain/Right brain: Perspectives from cognitive neuroscience* (5th ed.). New York: W. H. Freeman.

Teele, D. W., Klein, J. O., Rosner, B. A., & The Greater Boston Otitis Media Study Group. (1984). Otitis media with effusion during the first three years of life and development of speech and language. *Pediatrics, 74*(2), 282-287.

Yoshinaga-Itano, C., Sedey, A. L., Coulter, D. K., & Mehl, A. L. (1998). Language of early- and later-identified children with hearing loss. *Pediatrics, 102,* 1161-1171.

References for Chapter Four: Are All Visual-Spatial Learners Brilliant?

Davis, R. D. (1994,1997). *The gift of dyslexia.* New York: Perigee, Penguin Putnam.

Dixon, J. P. (1983). *The spatial child.* Springfield, IL: Charles C. Thomas.

Freed, J., & Parsons, L. (1997). *Right-brained children in a left-brained world: Unlocking the potential of your ADD child.* New York: Simon & Schuster.

Ringle, J., Miller, S., & Anderson, R. (2000). *Reading achievement results integrating Davis Learning Strategies in the special education and special reading classroom. Year 1 — 1999-2000.* Report for Sherrard Elementary School. Sherrard, IL: Authors.

Silverman, L. K. (1989a). Invisible gifts, invisible handicaps. *Roeper Review, 12,* 37-42.

Silverman, L. K. (1989b). Spatial learners. *Understanding Our Gifted, 1*(4), 1, 7-8, 16.

Silverman, L. K. (1989c). The visual-spatial learner. *Preventing School Failure, 34*(1), 15-20.

Silverman, L. K. (1992, January 16). *The visual-spatial learner.* Closed-circuit television broadcast sponsored by the Missouri Department of Education. [Available from the Gifted Development Center, 1452 Marion Street, Denver, CO 80218]

Silverman, L. K., & Freed, J. N. (1991). *Strategies for gifted visual-spatial learners.* Unpublished manuscript. [Available on-line at **www.gifteddevelopment.com** or write to the Gifted Development Center, 1452 Marion Street, Denver, CO 80218]

References for Chapter Five: Different Strokes for Different Folks

Davis, R. D. (1994,1997). *The gift of dyslexia.* New York: Perigee, Penguin Putnam.

Dunn, R., & Dunn, K. (1975). *Learning style inventory.* Lawrence, KS: Price Systems. (Revised edition, with G. Price, 1979).

Gardner, H. G. (1983). *Frames of mind: The theory of multiple intelligences.* New York: Basic.

Guilford, J. P. (1967). *The nature of human intelligence.* New York: McGraw-Hill.

Lovecky, D. V. (1992). The exceptionally gifted child (Part II). *Understanding Our Gifted, 4*(5), 3.

Lovecky, D. V. (1994a). Exceptionally gifted children: Different minds. *Roeper Review, 17*, 116-120.

Myers, I. B. (1962). *Manual: The Myers-Briggs Type Indicator.* Palo Alto, CA: Consulting Psychologists Press.

Ornstein, R. (1997). *The right mind: Making sense of the hemispheres.* New York: Harcourt Brace.

Shlain, L. (1998). *The alphabet versus the goddess: The conflict between word and image.* New York: Penguin/Arkana.

Silverman, L. K. (1998a). Personality and learning styles of gifted children. In J. VanTassel-Baska (Ed.), *Excellence in educating gifted &talented learners* (3rd ed., pp. 29-65). Denver: Love.

Silverman, L. K. (2000). The two-edged sword of compensation: How the gifted cope with learning disabilities. In Kay, K. (Ed.). *Uniquely gifted: Identifying and meeting the needs of the twice exceptional student* (pp. 153-165). Gilsum, NH: Avocus.

Silverman, L. K. (2001). Diagnosing and treating visual perceptual issues in gifted children. *Journal of Optometric Vision Development, 32*(3), 153-176.

West, T. G. (1991). *In the mind's eye: Visual thinkers, gifted people with learning difficulties, computer images, and the ironies of creativity.* Buffalo, NY: Prometheus Press.

References for Chapter Six: Two Different Food Groups: Which one are YOU?

Asimov, I. (1990). Worlds in order. *Fantasy & Science Fiction, 78*(4), 139-149.

Baum, S. (1984). Meeting the needs of learning disabled gifted students. *Roeper Review, 7*(1), 16-19.

Bloom, B. S. (Ed.) (1956). *Taxonomy of educational objectives: The classification of educational goals. Handbook I: The cognitive domain.* New York: David McKay.

Boring, E. G. (1950). *A history of experimental psychology* (2nd ed.). Englewood Cliffs, NJ: Prentice-Hall.

Dixon, J. P. (1983). *The spatial child.* Springfield, IL: Charles C. Thomas.

Dweck, C. S. (1986). Motivational processes affecting learning. *American Psychologist, 41*, 1040-1048.

Goldberg, E., & Costa, L. D. (1981). Hemispheric differences in the acquisition and use of descriptive systems. *Brain and Language, 14*, 144-173.

Goldberg, E., Vaughan, H., Jr., & Gerstman, L. J. (1978). Nonverbal descriptive systems and hemispheric asymmetry: Shape versus texture discrimination. *Brain and Language, 5*, 249-257.

Grandin, T. (1995). *Thinking in pictures and other reports from my life with autism.* New York: Doubleday.

Levy, J. (1982, November 1). *Brain research: Myths and realities for the gifted male and female.* Paper presented at the Illinois Gifted Education Conference, Chicago, IL. (private cassette recording)

Rimm, S. B., & Lovance, K. J. (1992). How acceleration may prevent underachievement syndrome. *Gifted Child Quarterly, 36*(2), 100-105.

Ringle, J., Miller, S., & Anderson, R. (2000). *Reading achievement results integrating*

Davis Learning Strategies in the special education and special reading classroom. Year 1 — 1999-2000. Report for Sherrard Elementary School. Sherrard, IL: Authors.

Shlain, L. (1998). *The alphabet versus the goddess: The conflict between word and image.* New York: Penguin/Arkana.

Silverman, L. K. (1997). The construct of asynchronous development. *Peabody Journal of Education, 72* (3&4), 36-58.

Sowell, T. (1997). *Late-talking children.* New York: Basic.

Springer, S. P., & Deutsch, G. (1998). Left brain/Right brain: Perspectives from cognitive neuroscience (5th ed.). New York: W. H. Freeman.

West, T. G. (1991). *In the mind's eye: Visual thinkers, gifted people with learning difficulties, computer images, and the ironies of creativity.* Buffalo, NY: Prometheus Press.

West, T. G. (1996). Upside down: Visual-spatial talents and technological change. *Understanding Our Gifted, 8*(3), 1, 6-8.

Wirszup, I. (1986, March). Education and national survival: Confronting the mathematics and science crisis in our society. Inservice presentation in Glenview District #34, Glenview, IL.

References for Chapter Seven: How Early Can We Tell if Our Child is Visual-Spatial?

Clyde, A. (1994, March/April). There's a genius in the house. *Family Life,* pp. 72-74.

Rogers, M. T. (1986). *A comparative study of developmental traits of gifted and average children.* Unpublished doctoral dissertation, University of Denver, Denver.

Rogers, M. T., & Silverman, L. K. (1988). Recognizing giftedness in young children. *Understanding Our Gifted, 1*(2), 5, 16, 17, 20.

Selfe, L. (1977). *Nadia: A case of extraordinary drawing ability in an autistic child.* New York: Academic Press.

Silverman, L. K. (2000). The two-edged sword of compensation: How the gifted cope with learning disabilities. In Kay, K. (Ed.). *Uniquely gifted: Identifying and meeting the needs of the twice exceptional student* (pp. 153-165). Gilsum, NH: Avocus.

Sowell, T. (1997). *Late-talking children.* New York: Basic.

Tolan, S. (1992, May). *Is it a cheetah?* Keynote address for the Hollingworth Center Conference on Highly Gifted Children, Massachusetts Institute of Technology, Boston, MA. [Available on-line at **www.gifteddevelopment.com.** (See Links: Other Important Gifted Links: Stef's Cheetah article.)]

References for Chapter Eight: How Do You Assess Visual-Spatial Abilities?

Benbow, C. P. (1986). Physiological correlates of extreme intellectual precocity. *Neuropsychologia, 24,* 719-725.

Geschwind, N. (1982). Why Orton was right. *Annals of Dyslexia, 32.* Orton Dyslexia Society reprint no. 98.

Gallagher, S. A., & Johnson, E. S. (1992). The effect of time limits on performance of mental rotations by gifted adolescents. *Gifted Child Quarterly, 36,* 19-22.

Kaufman, A. S. (1992). Evaluation of the *WISC-III* and *WPPSI-R* for gifted children. *Roeper Review, 14,* 154-158.

Lezak, M. D. (1983). *Neuropsychological assessment* (2nd ed.). New York: Oxford University Press.

Linn, M. C., & Petersen, A. C. (1985). Emergence and characterization of sex differences in spatial ability: A meta-analysis. *Child Development, 56*, 1479-1498.

Matarazzo, J. D. (1981). David Wechsler (1896-1981). *American Psychologist, 36*, 1542-1543.

O'Boyle, M. W., & Benbow, C. P. (1990). Enhanced right hemisphere involvement during cognitive processing may relate to intellectual precocity. *Neuropsychologia, 28*(2), 211-216.

Olson, M. B. (1977). Right or left hemispheric information processing in gifted students. *The Gifted Child Quarterly, 21*, 116-121 .

Silverman, L. K. (1989a). Invisible gifts, invisible handicaps. *Roeper Review, 12*, 37-42.

Silverman, L. K. (2001). Diagnosing and treating visual perceptual issues in gifted children. *Journal of Optometric Vision Development, 32*(3), 153-176.

Silverman, L. K., & Freed, J. N. (1991). *Strategies for gifted visual-spatial learners.* Unpublished manuscript. [Available on-line at **www.gifteddevelopment.com** or write to the Gifted Development Center, 1452 Marion Street, Denver, CO 80218]

Silverman, L. K., & Kearney, K. (1992). The case for the Stanford-Binet L-M as a supplemental test. *Roeper Review, 15*, 34-37.

Thorndike, R. M., & Lohman, D. F. (1990). *A century of ability testing.* Chicago: Riverside Press.

Voyer, D., & Bryden, M. P. (1990). Gender, level of spatial ability, and lateralization of mental rotation. *Brain and Cognition, 13*, 18-29.

Wechsler, D. (1941). *The measurement of adult intelligence* (2nd ed.). Baltimore: Williams & Wilkins.

References for Chapter Nine: Visual-Spatial, Learning-Disabled, or Both?

Cowley, G. (2000, July 24). Understanding autism. *Newsweek.* [Eric Hollander's research]

Davis, R. D. (1994,1997). *The gift of dyslexia.* New York: Perigee, Penguin Putnam.

Dixon, J. P. (1983). *The spatial child.* Springfield, IL: Charles C. Thomas.

Eden, G. F., VanMeter, J. W., Rumsey, J. M., Maisog, J., Woods, R. P., & Zeffiro, T. A. (1996). Abnormal processing of visual motion in dyslexia revealed by functional brain imaging. *Nature, 382*, 66-69.

Krevisky, J. (1985). *The bad speller's dictionary.* New York: Random House.

Levy, J. (1982, November 1). *Brain research: Myths and realities for the gifted male and female.* Paper presented at the Illinois Gifted Education Conference, Chicago, IL. (private cassette recording)

Rogers, K. B., & Silverman, L. K. (1997, November 7). *Personal, medical, social and psychological factors in 160+ IQ children.* National Association for Gifted Children 44th Annual Convention, Little Rock, AK. [Summary of data available on-line at **www.gifteddevelopment.com.**]

Sattler, J.M. (1992). *Assessment of children* (3rd ed., Revised). San Diego, CA: Author.

Silverman, L. K. (1989a). Invisible gifts, invisible handicaps. *Roeper Review, 12*, 27-42.

Silverman, L. K. (1998b). Through the lens of giftedness. *Roeper Review, 20*, 204-210.

Silverman, L. K. (2000). The two-edged sword of compensation: How the gifted cope with learning disabilities. In K. Kay (Ed.). *Uniquely gifted: Identifying and meeting the needs of the twice exceptional student* (pp. 153-165). Gilsum, NH: Avocus.

Silverman, L. K. (2001). Diagnosing and treating visual perceptual issues in gifted children. *Journal of Optometric Vision Development, 32*(3), 153-176.

Sowell, T. (1997). *Late-talking children.* New York: Basic.

Springer, S. P., & Deutsch, G. (1998). *Left brain/Right brain: Perspectives from cognitive neuroscience* (5th ed.). New York: W. H. Freeman.

Tallal, P., Miller, S. L., Bedi, G., Byma, G., Wang, S., Nagarajan, S. S., Schreiner, C., Jenkins, W. M., & Merzenich, M. M. (1996). Language comprehension in language-learning impaired children improved with acoustically modified speech. *Science, 271,* 81-84.

West, T. G. (1991). *In the mind's eye: Visual thinkers, gifted people with learning difficulties, computer images, and the ironies of creativity.* Buffalo, NY: Prometheus Press.

Whitmore, J. R., & Maker, C. J. (1985). *Intellectual giftedness in disabled persons.* Austin, TX: Pro-Ed.

Yoshinaga-Itano, C., Sedey, A. L., Coulter, D. K., & Mehl, A. L. (1998). Language of early- and later-identified children with hearing loss. *Pediatrics, 102,* 1161-1171.

References for Chapter Ten: The Inner World of Introverts

Boring, E. G. (1950). *A history of experimental psychology* (2nd ed.). Englewood Cliffs, NJ: Prentice-Hall.

Bradway, K. (1964). Jung's psychological types. *Journal of Analytical Psychology, 9,* 129-135.

Card, C. N. W. (1994). *Discover the power of introversion: What most introverts are never told and extraverts learn the hard way.* Gladwyne, PA: C. O. Type and Temperament Press.

Dabrowski, K., & Piechowski, M. M. (1977). *Theory of levels of emotional development* (Vols. 1 & 2). Oceanside, NY: Dabor Science.

Dixon, J. P. (1983). *The spatial child.* Springfield, IL: Charles C. Thomas.

Jung, C. G. (1938). *Psychological types or the psychology of individuation.* (H. G. Baynes, Trans.). London: Kegan Paul, Trench, Trubner, & Co., Ltd. (Original work published 1923)

Keirsey, D., & Bates, M. (1978). *Please understand me: Character and temperament types.* Del Mar, CA: Prometheus Nemesis Books.

Levy, J. (1982, November 1). *Brain research: Myths and realities for the gifted male and female.* Paper presented at the Illinois Gifted Education Conference, Chicago, IL. (private cassette recording)

Lohman, D. F. (1994). Spatially gifted, verbally inconvenienced. In N. Colangelo, S. G. Assouline, & D. L. Ambroson (Eds.). *Talent development: Proceedings from the 1993 Henry B. and Jocelyn Wallace National Research Symposium on Talent Development* (pp. 251-264). Dayton, OH: Ohio Psychology Press.

Mill, J. S. (1869). *The subjection of women.* Bungay, Suffolk, Great Britain: Richard Clay.

Myers, I. B., & McCaulley, M. H. (1985). *Manual: A guide to the development and use of the Myers-Briggs Type Indicator.* Palo Alto, CA: Consulting Psychologists Press.

Rowe, M. B. (1974). Relation of wait-time and rewards to the development of language, logic, fate control: Part II rewards. *Journal of Research in Science Teaching, 11,* 291-308.

Silverman, L. K. (1999). Perfectionism. *Gifted Education International, 13,* 216-225.

References for Chapter Eleven: Double Jeopardy: AD/HD and Visual-Spatial

American Psychiatric Association. (1994). *Diagnostic and statistical manual of mental disorders* (4th ed.). Washington, DC: Author.

Benbow, C. P. (1986). Physiological correlates of extreme intellectual precocity. *Neuropsychologia, 24,* 719-725.

Dabrowski, K. (1972). *Psychoneurosis is not an illness.* London: Gryf.

Dabrowski, K., & Piechowski, M. M. (1977). *Theory of levels of emotional development* (Vols. 1 & 2). Oceanside, NY: Dabor Science.

Hallowell, E. M., & Ratey, J. J. (1994a). *Answers to distraction.* New York: Pantheon.

Hallowell, E. M., & Ratey, J. J. (1994b). *Driven to distraction.* New York: Pantheon.

Kutner, D. R. (1999). Blurred brilliance: What AD/HD looks like in gifted adults. *Advanced Development, 8,* 87-96.

Lovecky, D. V. (1994b). Gifted children with attention deficit disorder. *Understanding Our Gifted, 6*(5), 1, 7-10.

Lovecky, D. V. (2004). *Different minds: Gifted Children with AD/HD, Asperger Syndrome and Other Learning Deficits.* London: Jessica Kingsley.

Piechowski, M. M. (1979). Developmental potential. In N. Colangelo & R. T. Zaffrann (Eds.), *New voices in counseling the gifted* (pp. 25-57). Dubuque, IA: Kendall/Hunt.

Rapp, D. (1993). *Recognize and manage your allergies.* Lincolnwood, IL: NTC Contemporary.

Ratey, J. J., & Johnson, C. (1997). *Shadow syndromes.* New York: Random House.

Rogers, K. B., & Silverman, L. K. (1998, May). The physical, social, emotional, and environmental differences of profoundly gifted children: A comparative study. *Talent development IV: Proceedings from The 1998 Henry B. & Jocelyn Wallace National Research Symposium on Talent Development,* Iowa City, IA. [Available from first author, University of St. Thomas, St. Paul, MN]

Silverman, L. K. (1989a). Invisible gifts, invisible handicaps. *Roeper Review, 12,* 27-42.

Solden, S. (1995). *Women with attention deficit disorder.* Grass Valley, CA: Underwood.

Young, J., & Johnson, D. (1991). Up by our own bootstraps. *Understanding Our Gifted, 4*(1), 1, 13-15.

References for Chapter Twelve: The Challenge of Parenting Visual-Spatial Learners

Crowe, J. (2001, Winter). The odd-isy. *Global Connections, 7*(2), 3.

Dreyer, S. S. (1993). *The bookfinder 5: A guide to children's literature.* Circle Pines, MN: American Guidance Service.

Emerick, L. J. (1992). Academic underachievement among the gifted: Students' perceptions of factors that reverse the pattern. *Gifted Child Quarterly, 36,* 140-146.

Feldman, D. H., with L. T. Goldsmith (1991). *Nature's gambit: Child prodigies and the development of human potential.* New York: Teachers College Press.

Gaunt, R. I. (1989). *A comparison of the perceptions of parents of highly and moderately gifted children.* Unpublished doctoral dissertation, Kent State University, Kent, OH.

Goldman, W. (1973). *The Princess Bride.* New York: Ballantine.

Grandin, T. (1995). *Thinking in pictures and other reports from my life with autism.* New York: Doubleday.

Lester, H. (1988). *Tacky the penguin.* Boston: Houghton Mifflin.

Lester, H. (1994). *Three cheers for Tacky.* Boston: Houghton Mifflin.

Lester, H. (1998). *Tacky in trouble*. Boston: Houghton Mifflin.

Lewis, B. A. (1991, 1998). *The kids' guide to social action: How to solve the social problems you choose—and turn creative thinking into positive action.* Minneapolis: Free Spirit.

Lewis, B. A. (1992). *Kids with courage*. Minneapolis: Free Spirit.

Lewis, B. A. (1993). *Young lions. Ordinary kids with extraordinary courage.* Salt Lake City: Deseret.

Lewis, B. A. (1995). *The kid's guide to service projects: Over 500 service ideas for young people who want to make a difference.* Minneapolis: Free Spirit.

Lewis, B. A. (1998). *What do you stand for? A kid's guide to building character.* Minneapolis: Free Spirit.

Lewis, B. A. (2000). *Being your best: Character building for kids 7-10.* Minneapolis: Free Spirit.

Maxwell, E. (1998). "I can do it myself!" Reflections on early self-efficacy. *Roeper Review, 20,* 183-187.

Roeper, A. (1995). *Annemarie Roeper: Selected writings and speeches.* Minneapolis, MN: Free Spirit Press.

Sendak, M. (1962). *Chicken soup with rice.* New York: Harper & Row.

Shlain, L. (1998). *The alphabet versus the goddess: The conflict between word and image.* New York: Penguin/Arkana.

Silverman, L. K. (1994b). The moral sensitivity of gifted children and the evolution of society. *Roeper Review, 17,* 110-116.

Silverman, L. K., & Kearney, K. (1989). Parents of the extraordinarily gifted. *Advanced Development, 1,* 41-56.

Tolan, S. S. (1994). Psychomotor overexcitability in the gifted: An expanded perspective. *Advanced Development, 6,* 77-86.

Walberg, H. (1984). The effects of homework on learning: A quantitative analysis. *Journal of Educational Research, 78,* 97-104.

References for Chapter Thirteen: Teaching Techniques that Work

Ashton-Warner, S. (1963). *Teacher.* New York: Simon & Schuster.

Davis, R. B. (1964). *Discovery in mathematics.* Palo Alto: Addison-Wesley.

Davis, R. B. (1967). Mathematics teaching—with special reference to epistemological problems. *Journal of Research and Development in Education* (Whole No. 1).

Davis, R. D. (1994,1997). *The gift of dyslexia.* New York: Perigee, Penguin Putnam.

Dixon, J. P. (1983). *The spatial child.* Springfield, IL: Charles C. Thomas.

Farris, D. (2000). *Type tales* (rev. ed.). Gainesville, FL: Consulting Psychologists Press.

Gardner, H. G. (1983). *Frames of mind: The theory of multiple intelligences.* New York: Basic.

Goertz, J. (1991). Drawing: A visual approach to learning. *Understanding Our Gifted, 3*(5), 1, 11-13.

Grandin, T. (1995). *Thinking in pictures and other reports from my life with autism.* New York: Doubleday.

Grow, G. (1990). *The writing problems of visual thinkers.* [Available from the author at Florida A & M University, Talahassee, FL]

Levy, J. (1982, November 1). *Brain research: Myths and realities for the gifted male and female.* Paper presented at the Illinois Gifted Education Conference, Chicago, IL. (private cassette recording)

Ornstein, R. (1997). *The right mind: Making sense of the hemispheres*. New York: Harcourt Brace.

Ringle, J., Miller, S., & Anderson, R. (2000). *Reading achievement results integrating Davis Learning Strategies in the special education and special reading classroom. Year 1 — 1999-2000*. Report for Sherrard Elementary School. Sherrard, IL: Authors.

Roeper, A. (1995). *Annemarie Roeper: Selected writings and speeches*. Minneapolis, MN: Free Spirit Press.

Silverman, L. K. (1991). Help for the hidden handicapped. *Highly Gifted Children*, (Spring) 7(2), 10-11.

Steiner, R. (1982). *Balance in teaching*. Spring Valley, NY: Mercury Press.

West, T. G. (1991). *In the mind's eye: Visual thinkers, gifted people with learning difficulties, computer images, and the ironies of creativity*. Buffalo, NY: Prometheus Press.

References for Chapter Fourteen: We Have a Visual-Spatial Identifier!

Ayres, A. J. (1981). *Sensory integration and the child*. Los Angeles: Western Psychological Services.

Benbow, C. P. (1986). Physiological correlates of extreme intellectual precocity. *Neuropsychologia, 24*, 719-725.

Dabrowski, K., & Piechowski, M. M. (1977). *Theory of levels of emotional development* (Vols. 1 & 2). Oceanside, NY: Dabor Science.

Gallagher, S. A., & Johnson, E. S. (1992). The effect of time limits on performance of mental rotations by gifted adolescents. *Gifted Child Quarterly, 36*, 19-22.

Gechwind, N., & Behan, P. (1982). Left-handedness: Association with immune disease, migraine, and developmental learning disorders. *Proceedings of the National Academy of Science, USA, 79*, 5097-5100.

Hellerstein, L. F., & Fishman, B. (1990). Vision therapy and occupational therapy: An integrated approach. *Journal of Behavioral Optometry, 1*(5), 122-126.

Kaufman, A. S. (1979). *Intelligent testing with the WISC-R*. New York: John Wiley.

Kaufman, A. S. (1994). *Intelligent testing with the WISC-III*. New York: John Wiley.

Lezak, M. D. (1983). *Neuropsychological assessment* (2nd ed.). New York: Oxford University Press.

O'Boyle, M. W., & Benbow, C. P. (1990). Enhanced right hemisphere involvement during cognitive processing may relate to intellectual precocity. *Neuropsychologia*, 28(2), 211-216.

O'Boyle, M.W., Benbow, C. P., & Alexander, J. E. (1995). Sex differences, hemispheric laterality, and associated brain activity in the intellectually gifted. *Developmental Neuropsychology, 11*, 415-443.

Ornstein, R. (1997). *The right mind: Making sense of the hemispheres*. New York: Harcourt Brace.

Piechowski, M. M., Silverman, L. K., & Falk, R. F. (1985). Comparison of intellectually and artistically gifted on five dimensions of mental functioning. *Perceptual and Motor Skills, 60*, 539-549.

Rogers, K. B., & Silverman, L. K. (1997, November 7). *Personal, medical, social and psychological factors in 160+IQ children*. National Association for Gifted Children 44th Annual Convention, Little Rock, AK. [Summary of data available on-line at **www.gifteddevelopment.com**.]

Silverman, L. K. (in press). Identifying visual-spatial and auditory-sequential learners: A validation study. In N. Colangelo & S. G. Assouline (Eds.), *Talent development V: Proceedings from the 2000 Henry B. and Jocelyn Wallace National Research Symposium on Talent Development*. Scottsdale, AZ: Great Potential Press.

Silverman, L. K., & Freed, J. (1993). *Helping visual-spatial learners with school problems to succeed in elementary school.* Denver: Gifted Development Center. [Available on-line at **www.gifteddevelopment.com** or write to the Gifted Development Center, 1452 Marion Street, Denver 80218]

Silverman, L. K., & Freed, J. (1994). *Helping visual-spatial learners with school problems to succeed in secondary school.* Denver: Gifted Development Center. [Available on-line at **www.gifteddevelopment.com** or write to the Gifted Development Center, 1452 Marion Street, Denver 80218]

Wechsler, D. (1941). *The measurement of adult intelligence* (2nd ed.). Baltimore: Williams & Wilkins.

References for Chapter Fifteen: Visual-Spatial Adults and the Future of Education

Bell, L. A. (1990). The gifted woman as impostor. *Advanced Development, 2,* 55-64.

Bogen, J. E. (1969). The other side of the brain. II: An appositional mind. *Bulletin of the Los Angeles Neurological Society, 34,* 135-162.

Bolen, J. S. (1979). *The Tao of psychology: Synchronicity and the self.* New York: Harper San Francisco.

Clance, P. (1985). *The imposter phenomenon.* Atlanta: Peachtree.

Conarton, S. (1999). After the hero. *Advanced Development, 8,* 97-112.

Eisler, R. (1988). *The chalice and the blade.* New York: Harper San Francisco.

Jung, C. G. (1954). Marriage as a psychological relationship. The development of personality. *The collected works of C.G. Jung, Vol. 17.* (R.F.C. Hull, trans.). New York: Bollingen Foundation.

Levy, J. (1980). Cerebral asymmetry and the psychology of man. In M. C. Wittrock (Ed.), *The brain and psychology* (pp. 245-321). New York: Academic Press.

Levy, J. (1982, November 1). *Brain research: Myths and realities for the gifted male and female.* Paper presented at the meeting of the Illinois Gifted Education Conference, Chicago, IL. (private cassette recording)

MacKinnon, D. (1962). The nature and nurture of creative talent. *American Psychologist, 17,* 484-495.

Ornstein, R. (1997). *The right mind: Making sense of the hemispheres.* New York: Harcourt Brace.

Parkinson, S. (2000, February 17). Visual literacy. [Letter to the editor]. *Times Educational Supplement.* [Available from the Arts Dyslexia Trust, Lodge Cottage, Brabourne Lees, Ashford Kent.TN25 6QZ England]

Piechowski, M. M., & Cunningham, K. (1985). Patterns of overexcitability in a group of artists. *Journal of Creative Behavior, 19*(3), 153-174.

Piechowski, M. M., Silverman, L. K., & Falk, R. F. (1985). Comparison of intellectually and artistically gifted on five dimensions of mental functioning. *Perceptual and Motor Skills, 60,* 539-549.

Shlain, L. (1998). *The alphabet versus the goddess: The conflict between word and image.* New York: Penguin/Arkana.

Silverman, L. K., & Conarton, S. (1988). Feminine development through the life cycle. In M. A. Douglas & L. E. Walker (Eds.), *Feminist psychotherapies* (pp. 37-67). Norwood, NJ: Ablex.

Witelson, S. F. (1989). Hand and sex differences in the isthmus and anterior commissure of the human corpus callosum. *Brain, 112,* 799-835.

Notes

Appendix A

The Visual-Spatial Learner in School

Betty Maxwell

There are two main ways of organizing the world. These are *spatial* (using space) and *sequential* (using time). Spatial people tend to use space as a whole. They get a sudden "aha" recognition of patterns or significant relationships that they see in their mind. Sequential people organize information by following a logical sequence of steps to a conclusion. Even when they are organizing space, they do it in a linear, orderly way, such as writing from left to right, or building an outline from the top down. There are also two basic learning styles: *visual-spatial* and *auditory-sequential.*

Auditory-sequential learners are good listeners. They do well with a step-by-step presentation of information. They process what they hear quickly and are usually able to express themselves well when they speak. Most schools teach in this auditory-sequential style. They break down complex information into small bits and present the easier steps first. Then they gradually move into the more complex and difficult parts.

In contrast, visual-spatial learners (VSLs) are fine observers. They think in images and usually see things as a whole. It may take a while for them to express themselves verbally, because they have to translate their images and thoughts into words. Sometimes it is hard for them to find the right words. Their thinking and emotions are very entwined. Their different learning style often makes them feel out-of-step in traditional school settings. Visual-spatial learners are not all the same. They are a varied group that includes persons talented in art, science, mechanics, technology, computers, math concepts, and understanding of human relationships—anything that uses strong visualization skills.

Recognition of the visual-spatial learning style is new in our society and it is not as well understood as the more established auditory-sequential style. This instrument is designed to help identify and understand visual-spatial learners. A cluster of VSL traits is needed for identification. The more traits, the more strongly spatial a learner will be. Some of the characteristics might also belong to sequential learners, because there is no dividing line between these two natural ways of organizing the world.

We have identified 8 basic categories, 32 *positive traits* (bold, coded with plus signs) clustered under these 8 categories, and 71 *potential school problems* (coded with minus signs.) Many VSLs are successful in school because they have good sequential abilities to complement their strong spatial abilities. They exhibit the 32 positive characteristics without many of the related school problems. Those VSLs who have problems in school usually have sequential weaknesses. When the degree of sequential weakness is severe, the student may suffer from a learning disability. However, "school problems" as used here does not necessarily mean a learning disability. It is necessary to refer a child to a qualified examiner to determine if a learning disability exists.

Identifying Characteristics
of Visual-Spatial Learners

Are Visual, Not Auditory

+ Have a strong visual learning style.
  - May find it hard to follow spoken directions, explanations or instructions, unless pictures, charts or other visual aids are also used.
  - Some can pay attention only to a teacher who uses lots of visual aids and has a dramatic presentation style. Speaking in a monotone is especially hard for them to follow.

+ Are excellent visualizers and learn best through visual imagery.
  - Need to visualize in order to follow and remember, but may not be aware they can do this. Some may need help and practice in visualizing.

+ Think primarily in images instead of words.
  - May need extra time to translate their images and ideas into words.
  - May know the answer but not be able to get it out quickly when asked a quick response question. (Need a longer response time.)
  - If their eyes are looking upward, they may be searching for an image. If they are interrupted, the image can easily be lost.

+ Learn from seeing better than from listening.
  - May have trouble learning from listening alone.
  - May need to look away from a speaker in order to focus their listening attention, because looking and listening at the same time is too much.
  - May have had many ear infections when young. This can result in problems of processing what they hear. Sometimes this kind of inattention may be mistaken for attention deficit disorder.

+ Remember lectures best through their own kind of note taking, which may be pictures, doodles or webs showing relationships.
  - They may try to capture complex ideas with "chicken scratch" notations.
  - They may be restricted from "doodling" by teachers who do not understand what they are doing.
  - Note taking may be a real problem, especially in middle and high school. They often cannot listen and write.

Are Spatial, Not Sequential

+ **Are more space oriented and less time oriented.**
(For example, when very young, may know how to get to a favorite place even when the route is complicated. Or may know exactly what rooms are above or below them in a large building. But they won't be dressed on time or ready to go.)
  - Have little sense of time. Scheduling is not a strength.
  - May have a terrible time meeting deadlines and need help with organizational strategies.

+ **Reach correct conclusions without taking any visible steps.**
  - May not be able to show their work.
  - Because they don't know the steps they took (if any) to get their answer, they may not be confident about being able to do it again.
  - May be accused of cheating by teachers because they cannot show their steps.
  - May blurt out an answer because they are afraid they will lose their idea and not be able to reconstruct it.

+ **Are natural non-linear processors. They are global thinkers.**
  - May not learn readily when material is presented in the usual sequential order.
  - May have a lot of difficulty following someone else's line of thinking.
  - May not become automatic in left-to-right reading. They may have difficulty remembering right from left.
  - May reverse words or letters or numbers and this problem may persist throughout school years.
  - May not learn to read directly from phonics instruction. May need to apply analytic phonics after learning many whole words by sight.
  - May solve problems by starting at the end and working backward or at the middle and working toward both ends. This may not be acceptable in a class situation.

Are Holistic, Not Detail Oriented

+ **Are whole-to-part learners who need to see the big picture first. They grasp concepts and systems all at once and only later learn the details.**
  - Need a frame of reference to help them in their learning process.
  - Putting information in a larger context is essential for them to absorb new material.

- May fail to remember details unless they are helped to see the big picture first or are given a framework to fit details into so that it all makes sense to them.

- May score poorly on tests because they fail to focus on small details.

- Have much difficulty learning and remembering isolated bits of information.

+ Often grasp a concept or process with only one or two examples—the "aha" phenomenon.

- Many examples of the same kind don't make a concept any clearer to them and may turn off their thinking processes. If they don't get the idea with the first few examples, they need a different approach, a new angle.

+ Grasp ideas as a complete whole, with all the parts connected.

- May be upset when their ideas are analyzed, revised, or "improved" because it feels as if the whole idea has been destroyed.

- May need to visualize something as complete before beginning a project.

- May not turn in a school assignment because it feels incomplete—only a part of what they see as a bigger whole.

- May find it hard to take tests until they feel they have an understanding of the whole.

+ See the interrelationships between ideas. This is very important to them.

- Have difficulty separating out main and supporting ideas or summarizing.

- May have difficulty with multiple choice tests because they can see ways in which many answers could be right. If asked, they can support these answers.

- May find the expected answers in true/false tests too simplistic. They see the situations as more complex.

Are Focused On Ideas, Not Format

+ Continually build permanent frameworks of ideas instead of memorizing rote information that is easily forgotten.

- Do not learn through drill, practice or repetition.

- Learn best when information is meaningful to them. May need to ask a series of questions to understand fully.

- Rote memorization is a weakness.

+ Are much more interested in ideas than in the particulars of their presentation.

- Are likely to make errors in computation, grammar, spelling and punctuation.

+ **Are oriented to the process, not the product.**
  - What is important to them is their own understanding of an idea. They may be less interested in demonstrating their mastery to someone else in the form of a product.
  - They may know much more than they show.

Seek Patterns

+ **Look for patterns and connections. Often they will find patterns no one has noticed before. Sometimes they will notice connections between things that other people see as quite different.**
  - May have difficulty learning unless they see a pattern or can make connections with something they already know.
  - May find these patterns, connections, and explorations more interesting than what is being taught. May find it hard to hold their focus on narrowly focused topics.

Are Divergent, Not Convergent

+ **Are divergent thinkers, preferring solutions that are more creative.**
  - May be actually unaware of the more usual methods of problem-solving or classification—or they may be unable to use these because they have things framed in a different way.

+ **Are highly imaginative and creative.**
  - May have their own creative approach which conflicts with a teacher's conventional approach.

+ **May be artistic.**
  - May be a persistent doodler or sketcher, even during teacher presentations.

+ **Tend to be rhythmic and musical.**
  - May be a finger drummer. May need rhythm and music to enhance learning. May actually do homework better with the radio or TV on.

+ **May be inventive and have mechanical aptitude.**
  - May daydream, visualizing machines or inventions rather than the subject at hand.
  - May require a hands-on approach to learning.

+ May be used to setting their own agenda for learning because they learn in their own way.

  - May find it hard to leave a project and move on to the next scheduled thing.

Are Sensitive and Intense

+ May have acutely developed senses.

  - Can be distracted easily by a variety of sounds, movements, etc.

  - It may be difficult for them to ignore things in the environment that probably wouldn't bother others, such as bright lights, noises of motors, fans, etc.

+ Respond very readily to many things in their environment.

  - Are easily irritated by many conditions, such as wool or nubby socks, clothing tags, certain foods, changes in air pressure, environmental chemicals, even the presence of others around them.

+ May exhibit a great deal of energy.

  - May need to move their bodies or their hands to learn, think, or talk fluently.

+ Are highly sensitive emotionally. Learn best when emotionally involved.

  - May need emotional involvement in order to learn.

  - Do not respond well to criticism, even when it is intended to be constructive.

  - May need what they learn to be personally significant to them.

+ May be highly aware of other people's feelings.

  - May be aware of unspoken disapproval by a teacher or other students.

+ Are able to focus extremely intently on a topic.

  - May have trouble moving from one task to another.

Display Variable "Asynchronous" Development

+ Think faster than their hands can capture, because mental development is often ahead of fine motor skills.

  - May have illegible handwriting with poorly formed letters. Sometimes this is a jumble of cursive and manuscript letters without spacing between words.

- May never feel comfortable with cursive writing and choose to print, even as adults.
- May be frustrated with writing assignments and unwilling to write down their thoughts. May be unable to capture thoughts in writing.

+ May be spatially gifted and "verbally inconvenienced."*

- May be afraid of public speaking and other situations where quick responses are needed.
- May have trouble finding the right words to express their ideas.
- May not be able to retrieve words quickly enough to explain themselves when asked to justify their ideas. This can be very embarrassing.

+ Often succeed at more complex tasks yet continue to have difficulties with simple tasks.

- May have found it difficult to memorize math facts, yet can do well with more complex mathematical concepts.
- May write at a much lower level than they speak because they are afraid of misspelling words.
- *May be frustrated and even turned off from learning by being held to mastery of simple material when they are capable of excelling at complex work. (This is important.)*

+ May have wide discrepancies on different portions of IQ tests. Scores may be much higher on spatial relations (e.g., Block Design) and measures of verbal abstract reasoning (e.g., Vocabulary, Similarities, Comprehension, Information) than on measures of attention and sequential memory (e.g., Arithmetic, Digit Span, Coding).

- If discrepancies exceed 9 points, learning disabilities may be indicated.

*Lohman, D. F. (1994). Spatially gifted, verbally inconvenienced. In N. Colangelo, S. G. Assouline, & D. L. Ambroson (Eds.). *Talent development: Proceedings from the 1993 Henry B. and Jocelyn Wallace National Research Symposium on Talent Development* (pp. 251-264). Dayton, OH: Ohio Psychology Press.

Notes:

ABC's of the Writing Process, Specific Graphic Organizer Links www.angelfire.com/wi/writingprocess/specificgos.html	Complex graphic organizers, including diagrams, webs, etc.
Concept Mapping www.uwp.edu.academic/stec/MBASC/Concept_Mapping/concept.mapping.faq.html	Instructions on how to present material in a more visual manner
Creative Publications/Wright Group www.wrightgroup.com 1-800-523-2371	Attribute Blocks, Balances, Base Ten Blocks, Marilyn Burns' Math Books, Fraction manipulatives, Geoboards, Hundreds Boards, Pattern Blocks, Tangrams (Lots of great stuff plus work/idea books)
Critical & Creative Thinking for the Gifted www.criticalthinking.com 1-800-458-4849	Critical thinking books and software across all subject areas and grade levels
Cuisenaire-Dale Seymour www.etacuisenaire.com 1-800-445-5985	Cuisenaire Rods™; Excellent math manipulatives and creative visual-spatial materials that extend through Grade 12
Delta Education www.delta-education.com 1-800-258-1302	Math and science products
fLearn www.fLearn.com 303-499-4386 1-800-499-4386	Advice regarding software for math, science, language arts, social studies, etc.; Wipe-off Hundreds Boards; Fractiles™; Zometool®; Triangular Flash Cards (multiplication & division); great science equipment
Graphic Organizers www.graphic.org/goindex.html	Venn diagrams, webs, and more
Hands-On Equations www.borenson.com 1-800-993-6284	A visual and kinesthetic teaching system for introducing algebraic concepts to students in grades 3 to 8
Inspiration Software www.inspiration.com 1-800-877-4292	Inspiration (software for mind maps, Grades 5-12); Kidspiration for younger children (Grades K-4)

Math-U-See www.mathusee.com 1-888-854-MATH 1-800-225-6654 in Canada	K-12 math program that uses visual-spatial methods to teach mathematics; instructional videos; manipulative; student and teacher textbooks
Mindware www.mindwareonline.com 1-800-999-0398	Collection of spatial games: mazes, puzzles, Tower of Hanoi™, Rubik's™ Cubes, Fractiles™, building equipment, math, science and geography materials
Multiplication www.multiplication.com	Multiplication made easy through the use of silly stories and cartoons
Prufrock Press www.prufrock.com 1-800-240-0333	Mind Benders® (Anita Harnadek) Math Mind Benders®, Grades 3-12 Science experiment books, Grades 2-9
Science, Math & Gifted SMG Products Catalog www.smgproducts.com (715) 235-1840	Science toys and resource books, critical thinking; math activities; gifted resources; puzzles; strategy games; Continuo™; Rhombo Continuo™; mysteries; lateral thinking; logic; problem solving
Teach with Movies www.teachwithmovies.org	Resource for using movies to teach in a variety of subject areas
Teacher Ideas Press www.lu.com/tips/ 1-800-225-5800	Creating Success in the Classroom: Visual Organizers And How to Use Them (Tarquin & Walker, 1996)
Teaching Company www.teachco.com	College courses on videotape and audiotape for advanced learners
Zephyr Press www.zephyrpress.com 1-800-232-2187	Mapping Inner Space (webs) Smart-Rope Jingles; Rappin' and Rhymin'
Zometool, Inc. www.zometool.com 303-733-2880 1-800-966-3386	Lesson plans for using the Zome System® in the classroom

BOOKS

Burchers, S., Burchers, M., & Burchers, B. (1998). *Vocabulary cartoons: Building an educated vocabulary with visual mnemonics.* Punta Gorda, FL: New Monic Books. [314-C Tamiani Trail, Punta Gorda, FL 33950 (941) 575-6669]

Buzan, T. (1983). *Use Both Sides of Your Brain* (revised). New York: E. P. Dutton.

Clark, F., & Clark, C. (with M. Vogel). (1989). *Hassle-Free Homework: A Six-Week Plan for Parents and Children to Take the Pain out of Homework.* New York: Doubleday.

Dixon, J. P. (1983). *The Spatial Child.* Springfield, IL: Charles C. Thomas.

Freed, J., & Parsons, L. (1998). *Right-Brained Children in a Left-Brained World: Unlocking the Potential of your ADD Child.* New York: Simon & Schuster.

Levitt, P. M., Burger, D. A., & Guralnick, E. S. (1985). *The Weighty Word Book.* Longmont, CO: Boomaker's Guild.

Parks, S., & Black, H. (1998). *Building Thinking Skills: Book 2* (2nd ed.). Pacific Grove, CA: Critical Thinking Books and Software.

Parks, S., & Black, H. (2000). *Building Thinking Skills: Beginning Figural.* Pacific Grove, CA: Critical Thinking Books and Software.

Pearson, J. (1995). *Drawing on the Inventive Mind: Exercises in Thinking, Language and Self-Esteem.* Los Angeles, CA: Creative Thinking Programs.

Pearson, J. (1999). *Drawing Out the Best in Your Students.* Los Angeles, CA: Creative Thinking Programs.

Vitale, B. (1982). *Unicorns Are Real.* Rolling Hills Estates, CA: Jalmar Press.

Williams, L. V. (1983). *Teaching for the Two-Sided Mind.* Englewood Cliffs, NJ: Prentice-Hall.

West, T. G. (1997). *In the mind's eye: Visual thinkers, gifted people with dyslexia and other learning difficulties, computer images, and the ironies of creativity.* (Updated ed.). Amherst, NY: Prometheus.

CONSTRUCTION MATERIALS

Chaos Tower
Construx
K'nex
Legos
Technics
Zometool

GAMES

Battleship
Chess
Go
Hexed
Mastermind
Othello
Rhombo Continuo
Rush Hour
Rubik's Cube
Set
Tangoes
Tetris
Tower of Hanoi

MATHEMATICAL MANIPULATIVES

Base Ten Blocks
Cuisenaire Rods
Chip Trading
Dienes Blocks
Geoboards
Mira Math
Number-Blox
Unifix Cubes

SPATIAL ACTIVITIES

Attribute Blocks
Escher Drawings
Fractiles
Line Designs
Paper and Scissors Polygons
Pattern Blocks
Pentominoes
Perceptual Puzzle Blocks
Polyominoes
Tangrams
Tesselations

Appendix C
Visual-Spatial Learner

Characteristics Comparison

The Auditory-Sequential Learner	The Visual-Spatial Learner
Thinks primarily in words	Thinks primarily in images
Has auditory strengths	Has visual strengths
Relates well to time	Relates well to space
Is a step-by-step learner	Is a whole-part learner
Learns by trial and error	Learns concepts all at once
Progresses sequentially from easy to difficult material	Learns complex concepts easily: Struggles with easy skills
Is an analytical thinker	Is a good synthesizer
Attends well to details	Sees the big picture; may miss details
Follows oral directions well	Reads maps well
Does well at arithmetic	Is better at math reasoning than computation
Learns phonics easily	Learns whole words easily
Can sound out spelling words	Must visualize words to spell them
Can write quickly and neatly	Much better at keyboarding than handwriting
Is well organized	Creates unique methods of organization
Can show steps of work easily	Arrives at correct solutions intuitively
Excels at rote memorization	Learns best by seeing relationships
Has good auditory short-term memory	Has good long-term visual memory
May need some repetition to reinforce learning	Learns concepts permanently; does not learn by drill and repetition
Learns well from instructions	Develops own methods of problem solving
Learns in spite of emotional reactions	Is very sensitive to teachers' attitudes
Is comfortable with one right answer	Generates unusual solutions to problems
Develops fairly evenly	Develops quite asynchronously (unevenly)
Usually maintains high grades	May have very uneven grades
Enjoys algebra and chemistry	Enjoys geometry and physics
Masters other languages in classes	Masters other languages through immersion
Is academically talented	Is creatively, technologically, mechanically, emotionally or spiritually gifted
Is an early bloomer	Is a late bloomer

Notes:

Index

Auditorization, 57
Auditory
distractibility, 95, 97
timing, 168, 292
Auditory processing. *See also*
Central Auditory Processing
Disorder (CAPD)
activities, 41–43
difficulties, 37
dyslexia, 168
enhancing, 40–43
infections, 32
memory, 95–96
reader story, 29
weakness, 66, 167
Auditory-sequential
learners (ASLs), xvi–xvii, 23, 58–61
skills and learning disabilities, 172
Autism, 174
Awareness, 346, 348, 351–353

B
Bagels, 212–213
Barkley, Russell, 231
Barr, Steven, 46
Baska, Lee, 15
Bates, Marilyn, 209
Bear hunt activity, 42
Bed wetting, 227
Bell, Lee Anne, 338, 339
Benbow, Camilla, 148, 226, 321
Big picture, 18, 82, 307
Birthing issues, 66, 320–321, 352
Block Counting test item, 152
Block Design subtest, 139,
140–141, 146, 148, 155, 326
Body language, 19
Bogen, Joseph, 343
Bolen, Jean Shinoda, 337
Borderline, 178
Born *vs.* made, VSLs, 37
Boston Otitis Media Group, 35
Brain research
complementarity, 26–28
different realities, 17–18
eye movement patterns, 23-26
hemispheres, 14-16, 38, 102-103
verbal *vs.* spatial, 18-23
Briggs Myers, Isabel, 56

Brilliance, xv, 45, 53
Burleigh, Joan, 40–41
Buscaglia, Leo, 30

C
Caffeine, 226, 227
Calculation
auditory-sequential learners, xvii
vs. math reasoning, 85–86
VSL weakness, x
written, 11
California Achievement Test (CAT),
141
CAPD. *See* Central Auditory
Processing Disorder (CAPD)
Card, Cheryl, 209
Case studies
Adam, 182–184
Bill, 185
"Child A," 176–177
"Child B," 178–179
"Child C," 180–181
"Niles," 146–148
"Rebecca," 150–154
Tripper, 154–160
Casein, 226
Central auditory processing
battery, 40–41, 141, 167,
180, 225
Central Auditory Processing
Disorder (CAPD). *See also*
Ear infections
accommodations for, 43
and AD/HD, 224–225
signs of, 39–40, 167
Challenging
gifted children, 225–226
VSLs, 64–65, 311
Cheating, 93–94
Chemistry, 106–107
Chocolate, 226, 227
Choices, 265
Clance, Pauline, 335, 338
Classroom climate, 210, 276–277
Clay, 292
Cleaning, 247–249, 253
Clip art, 278

About the author

Linda Kreger Silverman, Ph.D., is a licensed psychologist, noted author, editor, researcher and international lecturer on all aspects of high ability. She founded and directs the Institute for the Study of Advanced Development and its subsidiary, the Gifted Development Center, in Denver, Colorado, where over 4,500 children have been assessed in the last 25 years. For nine years, she served on the faculty of the University of Denver in gifted education and counseling psychology. Linda coined the term "visual-spatial learner" in 1981 and has been developing methods of finding and serving this population ever since. A prolific writer, she has written 300 articles and chapters that are research-based, informed by clinical practice and insights and yet warm and accessible to non-scholars. *Counseling the Gifted and Talented* has been adopted at more than 50 colleges and universities. She founded the only journal on adult giftedness: *Advanced Development.* A passionate advocate for the gifted, visual-spatial learners and twice exceptional children, Linda affirms the positive aspects of thinking and feeling differently. Her award-winning website is **www.gifteddevelopment.com**.

For more information on the visual-spatial learner, including the Visual-Spatial Resource Access Team, please visit **www.visualspatial.org**.

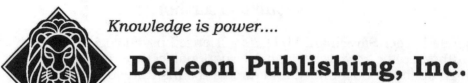

Knowledge is power....

DeLeon Publishing, Inc.

Empowering the world one book at a time.

P.O. Box 461027, Denver, CO 80246   *www.deleonpub.com*

Full-Sized Forms Available for download online!

To download full-sized 8.5 x 11 inch reproducible forms used in this book, please visit http://www.deleonpub.com/authors.html or http://www.visualspatial.org.

They are in PDF format. You will need to have Adobe® Acrobat Reader installed on your computer in order to view the forms. Please visit Adobe's website at www.adobe.com to download this program.